Multinational Enterprises, Economic Structure and International Competitiveness

WILEY/IRM SERIES ON MULTINATIONALS

IRM

Appropriate or Underdeveloped Technology?
Arghiri Emmanuel

The Threat of Japanese Multinationals:
How the West can Respond
Lawrence G. Franko

The New Multinationals:
The Spread of Third World Enterprises
Sanjaya Lall, in collaboration with Edward Chen, Jorge Katz,
Bernardo Kosacoff and Annibal Villela

Information Disclosure and the
Multinational Corporation
S. J. Gray, with L. B. McSweeney
and J. C. Shaw

Multinational Enterprises, Economic
Structure and International Competitiveness
John H. Dunning

Multinational Enterprises, Economic Structure and International Competitiveness

Edited by

JOHN H. DUNNING
*Professor of International Investment
and Business Studies,
University of Reading*

JOHN WILEY & SONS
Chichester · New York · Brisbane · Toronto · Singapore

Library of Congress Cataloging in Publication Data:
Main entry under title:

Multinational enterprises, economic structure and
    international competitiveness.

   (Wiley/IRM series on multinationals)
   Includes index.
   1. International business enterprises—Case studies—Addresses,
essay, lectures. I. Dunning, John H.
I. Series.
HD2755.5.M8343   1985   338.8'8   84-27149
ISBN 0 471 90700 6

British Library Cataloguing in Publication Data:

Multinational enterprises, economic structure and
    international competitiveness.—(Wiley/IRM
    series on multinationals)
    1. International business enterprises
    I. Dunning, John H.
    338.8'8   HD2755.5

ISBN 0 471 90700 6

Printed and bound in Great Britain.

Contents

List of Contributors

Professor John H. Dunning, University of Reading.

Professor Thomas A. Pugel, New York University, New York.

Professor Charles-Albert Michalet, Université de Paris X, Nanterre.

Professor Paulgeorg Juhl, Gengenbach, Germany.

Professor Terutomo Ozawa, Colorado State University, U.S.A.

Professor Steven Globerman, Simon Fraser University, Canada.

Dr Birgitta Swedenborg, Stockholm, Sweden.

Professor Daniel Van Den Bulcke, Universities of Limburg and Antwerp, Belgium.

Dr Bohn-Young Koo, Korean Development Institute, Seoul, Korea.

Dr Sanjaya Lall, Institute of Economics and Statistics, Oxford.

Dr Vitor Corado Simões, Sub-Director, Instituto do Investimentae Estrangeiro, Portugal.

Professor Donald Lecraw, University of Western Ontario, London, Canada.

Foreword

The world economy is in one of the fastest phases of restructuring. The process of transformation is felt acutely in industrialized countries who have to close down ailing industries, and in developing countries suffering from low commodity prices and high indebtedness. Oil producing countries adapted their potential in the seventies to their expanding income in expectation of a further oil price rise. In the eighties they had to reappraise the situation completely and adapt to a lower oil demand at falling prices.

The rapid change in demand for commodities and for new manufactured products and services asks for a high capacity to adapt to changing situations. Not all the participants in the world economy are able to follow the pace. The rapid change is not only felt in the extracting industries and in traditional branches like steel or textiles. The change in the high technology industries and in the service sector is sometimes even faster. The R&D effort for a new series of computers or video sets can be obsolete even before it reaps its first income, if a competitor has been quicker or better on the same line.

ACTIVE AGENTS IN RESTRUCTURING

Multinational enterprises (MNEs) play an important role in the process of economic restructuring of the world economy. Though they are originating in one specific home country they are operating in many host countries, making use of the particular opportunities which each of these countries is offering to their activities. Is the role of the multinational as active agents in the process of permanent and accelerated restructuring a positive one?

This question ought to be answered on world-wide scale as the process of restructuring is not limited by national borders and as the larger multinationals consider the world as their potential operating ground. But it is easier to pose than to answer the problem on the world scale. Economic and social statistical data is still assembled on national or regional levels and the nation state is still alive in reasoning about economic advantages and disadvantages.

This study tries to give an answer by raising the question on the positive and negative contributions of MNEs for a limited but representative number of countries of the world economy.

Twelve economists have studied the impact of the MNE on the restructuring of twelve significant home and host countries of multinationals in developed and developing economies.

The questions put to the authors were the same, the working methods of the team were similar, but each author did his work individually, taking account of the specific national situation.

The group met several times to compare and discuss the findings, once for a week at the Rockefeller Centre in Bellagio, Northern Italy, with representatives of the European Trades Union Confederation (ETUC) and the International Confederation of Free Trade Unions (ICFTU), and with journalists specialized in the field of international direct investment and multinational corporations.

DISTRIBUTING A SMALLER CAKE

There has been no time in the post-war period in which the contribution of MNEs for world-wide economic development has been so universally recognized as today.

In the sixties, the discussion was dominated by fears on the part of Europeans of losing the control over their industry to universally expanding US MNEs. In the seventies, less developed countries and the oil exporting countries united in the demand for a new economic world order. The drafting of a UN Code of Conduct for Transnational Corporations was started, but the project is still on the conference table. The emphasis has meanwhile changed. If a code is finally adopted it will regulate not only the behaviour of multinationals but also that of nation states *vis-à-vis* transnationals. Under these conditions the less developed nations are hesitating to subscribe to rules which can also limit their sovereignty.

The industrialized world has shown foresight. In 1976 it proclaimed non-mandatory but morally-binding guidelines of behaviour for MNEs, completed by rules on non-discriminatory treatment of international investment and on incentives and disincentives for foreign investment. These rules are addressed to governments and not only to MNEs.

The change in emphasis is due to the changes in the world economy since the end of the seventies and the beginning of the eighties. In a period of world-wide slow down of trade and investment, multinationals are not so much considered primarily as invaders who might limit a nation's economic sovereignty. No longer is the control of foreign investment the main political issue as it was in the period of fast growth of the sixties and early seventies. In many countries new investment is more likely to come from foreign multinationals than from domestic companies. Therefore the main issue of the eighties seems to be the struggle of nation states for an adequate share in the investment cake which multinational corporations are still distributing.

But the cake which multinationals can distribute (or in some cases only redistribute) has become smaller. Therefore the MNE problem is dominated today by the fears of nation states and of trade unions to become the victims of the restructuring of multinational investments. Transnationals are the most mobile factor in a stagnant or only moderately growing world economy. They are still prone to bring new investment of their own, and new incentives for investment of others, to a country offering the adequate conditions. But transnationals may also be the first to leave a country whose investment conditions are no longer considered as satisfactory. This may mean less expense on infrastructure by local governments and less employment for the local manpower which is not as mobile as the transnational investor. The monographies of this study are full of examples of such painful but often inevitable restructuring.

FOUR GROUPS OF COUNTRIES

The study had to be limited to not more than a dozen countries, mainly in the industrialized world. Nine studies cover industrialized countries and three studies developing countries.

Inside the industrialized countries three main groups can be distinguished. A first group of countries in which outward foreign direct investment (FDI) dominates: United States, Japan and Sweden. In this group the main question asked about FDI is whether the capital outflow does not result in a loss of export, employment and knowledge insufficiently equilibrated by the reflux of earnings out of foreign investment. In a second group of countries, Canada, Portugal and Belgium, a net inflow of FDI is registered. In this group two contradictory questions are raised: Is the economic, cultural and political independence not menaced by new foreign capital investment? And is a slowing down, a lack of new FDI, or an outflow of existing FDI not even more menacing for the country's economy due to its dependence on FDI? In a period of recession and of rapid restructuring the second question has been asked much more frequently and has become more important than the first question.

The third group of countries: United Kingdom, West Germany, and France, has a broadly balanced FDI position. Therefore, in these countries the value of both outward and inward FDI is discussed and the accent on one or other problem is changing.

In the fourth group, the three developing nations considered are all in the stage of becoming newly industrialized countries. They have already developed industries of their own and they host FDI. But the attitude to FDI differs widely. In India, the government's policy to FDI is highly restrictive; in Korea it is moderately restrictive, while Singapore's policy to FDI is very open.

This difference in attitude may invite certain comparisons between the effects of a more open and a more restrictive policy towards FDI in newly industrialized countries (NICs). But it would be risky to go too far in drawing conclusions, because the difference in structure between the three NICs analysed is too important: India is a subcontinent of its own, Singapore is a freeport and city state, whilst Korea is following closely, though critically, the Japanese example of development.

THE NET OUTWARD INVESTOR COUNTRIES

In the first group of the industrialized countries with net outward FDI, the United States has long been recognized as the pre-eminent home country of MNEs, creating wealth or problems in countries with net inward FDI. Today the situation has partially changed, as the United States has also become a major host to affiliates of foreign MNEs. For the first time, in the seventies, the US itself had to ask whether a restrictive policy towards foreign investment and takeovers was desirable. This question was answered negatively, but the fact that it was raised made American policy-makers more aware of the problems with which foreign-host countries of FDI are confronted.

The US policies towards inward and outward FDI are largely non-existent or neutral. According to Thomas A. Pugel this probably serves the national interest well, given the complexities of the activities of MNEs and of the US economy. This neutrality does not prevent the US government from favouring liberal policies of foreign governments towards FDI: a policy beneficial to US companies' investments abroad.

Inside the US the substitution of FDI for exports is the main argument about foreign investment. Trade unions fear that the jobs of their members are expatriated to countries with lower wage costs or that American know-how is used outside the US. But existing studies provide evidence that US outward FDI tends to act as net complement, rather than as net substitute, to US exports in industry. Many of the 'lost' exports might have been sales lost anyway to foreign firms, and outward FDI may enhance certain US exports.

Foreign trade barriers have played an important role in the orientation of US outward foreign FDI. According to Pugel, MNEs are responsive to location factors, comparative cost differences and barriers to trade in much the way that trade theory suggests business would be. As MNEs can hardly be blamed for responding to trade barriers, it is understandable that the US government is advocating a world-wide policy of trade liberalization combined with a liberalization of services and of foreign direct investments. In a more liberal world order for trade, services, and FDI, the neutral US home policy towards FDI would find its international justification.

The US has become quite unconsciously, due to the power of its economy and the importance of its companies, the largest foreign investor in the world. US companies are influencing the structure and development of host countries and are playing an important role in restructuring the economies of a great number of industrialized and newly industrialized countries.

But the US is no longer alone in the limelight as an agent in the restructuring process. Japan, an industrial power which is very new on the scene as a foreign investor, is nevertheless confronted already with numerous problems of outward FDI. Japanese MNEs are in the centre of the debate about the restructuring process in the car, the electronics and the engineering sectors of several European countries.

The Japanese official policy towards foreign investment is, and was always, clearly different from the American neutrality and liberalism. The visible hand of government has been at least as important as the invisible hand of the market place in Japan's structural transformation and growth. According to Terutomo Ozawa, Japan was more conscious than other nations of the vital link between FDI and industrial restructuring. This is certainly an important fact explaining the permanent and consequent linkage between Japanese policies in trade, technology and FDI. In the first decades after the war, this overall course of action implied a very restrictive policy toward inward FDI motivated by the fear of foreign domination of domestic industries. The policy intended the development of an industrial structure avoiding the dependence on direct investments of Western corporations. As soon as this aim was realized in one sector then that sector was opened to foreign direct investment.

The restrictive policy towards outward FDI has not prevented Japan from acquiring foreign technology, because foreign MNEs do not between themselves coordinate their policies in a planned system as do the Japanese authorities. Instead each acts individually on its own account. So for Japan, licensing has become a far more important vehicle of acquiring knowledge than direct investment.

The gradual opening of Japan to inward FDI, mainly by joint ventures, occurred under the increasing foreign pressure for reciprocity in liberalization of trade and FDI. It allowed Japan to acquire the latest foreign technologies, which could no longer be purchased under licensing agreements.

Japan's policy toward outward FDI was designed to help its own export activities in sectors in which the increasing wage cost structure or foreign trade barriers made exports more difficult or impossible. Its second and not less important aim was to secure vital supplies to an economy poor in its own natural resources. A further aim was to transfer overseas those segments of manufacturing activities that were no longer suitable to be home-based for such reasons as competition or environment.

Japan has managed to implement its main strategic aims with the help of a planned and coordinated policy between state authorities and business. This success was certainly facilitated by the structure of the Japanese society and the direct government influence on business, without exclusion of the market forces. So Terutomo Ozawa can conclude that foreign ownership advantages have been translated into home-based ownership advantages, which now constitute the basis of new comparative advantages for the Japanese economy. Japan has solved its problems of inward FDI to its own advantage, but Japanese MNEs are increasingly becoming involved in problems of restructuring of the foreign host countries in which they are operating.

Sweden is a substantial net foreign investing country in that investment abroad by Swedish firms is several times larger than investment in Sweden by foreign firms. But Swedish authorities are rather suspicious about the effects of outward investment and are scrutinizing capital exports for FDI very closely. Initially the main concern was the influence of investment outflow on the balance of payments. Later the emphasis changed and Swedish trade unions complained about export substitution of outward foreign investment which influence the level and structure of employment negatively. Birgitta Swedenborg's empirical findings do not confirm these complaints. According to her, the product mix and production technology of outward investing firms undergo constant change. The technology and skill-intensive part of output, in which the home-based parent has a competitive advantage, remains in the home country, while complementary output is moved abroad. The change results in increased specialization, higher efficiency and a net increase in exports. Only artificial trade barriers cause a less efficient allocation of resources. Swedish exports are even somewhat larger than they would have been in the absence of foreign production.

The indirect and long term effect of Swedish companies going foreign is that they became larger and financially stronger by FDI, and that they can invest more in research, advertising, sales promotion and the distribution network, as their costs spread over a larger sales volume than the restricted Swedish market would have permitted. The special merit of this study is that it has to some extent quantified the positive effect of increased R&D investment by MNEs on Swedish exports. The study shows that there are important efficiency gains from inter-firm specialization through MNE production just as there are from inter-country specialization through trade. So it establishes in the case of Sweden—but certainly also for countries in comparable conditions (as for instance the Netherlands and Switzerland)—a strong argument for a non-interventionist policy towards outward MNE investment. The three studies on outward investor countries can find no empirical proof for the charge that being a net outward foreign investor has a negative impact on the home economy.

THE NET INWARD INVESTOR COUNTRIES

While Sweden is a country which scrutinizes outward FDI very closely, Canada, the most important in the group of net inward investor countries, is one of the industrialized nations which up to recently has scrutinized inward FDI most intensely. This is not astonishing, as Canada is unique among all industrialized countries with its substantial percentage of private sector assets owned and controlled by foreigners. It is also unique in that the southern neighbour, the United States, is clearly the dominant source of inward FDI as well as the primary destination of outward FDI. The relation of inward to outward FDI declined significantly from 1955 to 1978 (from 5:1 to 3:1), as did the relative importance of the US as the destination for Canadian outward FDI. Nevertheless the US clearly remains the dominant source of inward FDI as well as the primary destination of outward FDI.

The Canadian fear is that due to foreign investment in the long run, Canadians are deprived of the opportunity to develop their skills at innovation and that American subsidiaries are perpetuating Canada's technological dependence, thereby preventing the creation of dynamic comparative advantages in the growth industries of the future.

Steven Globerman's study concludes that the benefit of foreign investment for Canada would increase, if foreign subsidiaries would engage more intensively in indigenous R&D activities and in exporting, even if it led to reduced inward FDI and reduced efficiency for the firms. The very special Canadian situation and sensibility might result in the seeking of solutions which are not entirely justifiable by mere economic reasoning.

This does not mean that Globerman advocates restrictions on inward FDI and judges policies designed to reduce existing levels of foreign ownership as necessarily being in the national interest. He rather advocates a more comprehensive and liberal trade policy, because inward FDI has been promoted by government-imposed trade barriers. Canada's trade and investment policies were never as closely coordinated as the Japanese ones. In accordance with Birgitta Swedenborg, Globerman advocates policies designed to promote efficient behaviour of all economic units, foreign or domestically-owned. Such policies favour a competitive domestic industry better than policies which encourage or discourage inward or outward FDI.

Belgium is a country whose inward direct investment is twice as high as the stock of outward investment. From 1967 to 1978 the increase of inward FDI was more rapid than in the market economies of Western Europe and the world. Nevertheless Belgium never resented inward FDI and never expressed fears of foreign domination. This is certainly attributable to the fact that multinationalization in the fields of trade and investment is a main structural characteristic of the Belgian economy. Another reason for the openness with which foreign investors are received in Belgium is the fact that no single nation is dominating the investment scene, with no more than half of the investment originating from EEC countries and no more than one third from the US.

The main problem of inward FDI for Belgium is how to remain or become attractive again for foreign investors. Daniel Van Den Bulcke points out that the Belgian economy, accustomed to a steady inflow of foreign investment in the sixties and early seventies, was hit hard by the changed general economic conditions and by the ensuing slowdown in economic growth in the second half of the seventies.

Again, as in the case of Sweden and Canada, it proved that general economic conditions which discourage domestic investment even more discourage mobile foreign capital. The increasingly expensive social security system and the increase in labour costs, compared with international standards, were factors working against inward FDI. Not only did foreign investors no longer choose Belgium as a location, but Belgium had to combat an increasing trend of foreign disinvestment. The fact that the government insisted on the enforcement of the OECD guidelines for foreign investment in order to safeguard workers' rights of bankrupt subsidiaries of foreign MNEs did not make Belgium more attractive for new foreign investment.

The Belgian authorities supported ailing companies in order to protect employment, a policy which did not help to make Belgium more attractive for foreign investors. Recently more emphasis has been put on aiding restructuring by special employment zones and coordination centres aimed at technologically innovative firms. The Belgian study makes clear that countries with a traditionally open policy for inward FDI, and countries who need the inflow of FDI should not rely primarily on special incentives for investors. If the general economic situation and the wage cost structure is considered discouraging for investment, foreign investors do not react upon special incentives and they are even more mobile than domestic firms in leaving a country. In such a situation a large dependence on inward FDI may be dangerous, if it is not understood as a need to act quickly and to restore the competitivity of the national economy.

For Portugal, at the eve of its entrance into the European Community, Vitor Simões advocates a policy which creates the right climate for domestic and foreign investment. Foreign investment is considered necessary for Portugal. It should play a dynamic role *vis-à-vis* domestic investment. The internal market of Portugal is much too small to permit large scale production without exports. MNEs are in a position to use their marketing structure for sales abroad. Foreign investments mainly in the forms of joint ventures and licensing, are considered desirable according to Simões, because the high trade protection and the maintenance of monopolistic and oligopolistic situations preserved low efficiency for a long time. They also permitted inward FDI to reap extra rent and to make foreign investors inclined to repatriate a relatively high share of their profits by direct means or by means of transfer pricing. MNEs also preferred to use domestic credit facilities in order to avoid the risks of investing foreign capital. All this contributed to tarnish the picture of foreign MNEs' contribution to the Portuguese economy though there was, according to the findings of Simões, a positive contribution to the restructuring of Portugal's industrial system to a higher technical level and to higher productivity.

Portugal has no choice but to open its markets for trade and investment to the EEC in the next decade. For Portugal this opening will above all mean a common market with its neighbour Spain, as well as open and fierce competition with Spain for the location of foreign direct investment. Investors who choose Portugal to serve the domestic market could just as well choose Spain or another location within the EEC.

The three studies on net inward investor countries show that it depends mainly on the general economic policy, whether inward FDI is profitable for a country or whether it tends to weaken its own creative and dynamic capacities.

THREE COUNTRIES IN A BROADLY–BALANCED SITUATION

The three most important EEC member states, the United Kingdom, France and Germany are countries with a long tradition of outward and inward FDI. The United Kingdom has a broadly-balanced position between inward and outward FDI. But as MNEs became more footloose in their production, this may mean only, according to John H. Dunning, that British interests may be hurt both ways if the economic conditions inside the country are judged unfavourable to MNEs. In fact the United Kingdom has become one of the main battlefields in the restructuring process of mobile and aggressive Japanese MNEs.

The study makes a clear distinction between the social interest of the British society and the private interest of MNEs. Because of the possible divergence of these interests, government has, according to Dunning, a responsibility of positive intervention whenever there are costs and benefits which individual firms cannot reasonably be expected to bear. The main problem raised by British trade unions is the expatriation of employment by outward FDI of British MNEs. Empirical studies permit Dunning to conclude that the involvment in international production has made a positive net contribution to domestic allocative efficiency in the United Kingdom.

In order to increase the welfare which inward FDI can give to the British society, Dunning advocates positive and negative interventions. The first should assist the adjustment process and gain a fair share of investment. The latter should protect against distortions between social and private interests due mainly to market imperfections. This is no easy task as national monopolistic legislation is no adequate countervailing power against transnationally operating MNEs.

France is the country from which the theory of the 'économie dominante' (François Perroux) and the 'défi américain' (Jean-Jacques Servan-Schreiber) originated. Though the phenomenon of American investment in Europe was discussed so widely in France, US foreign investment never played a really dominant position either in the French economy or inside the inward FDI in France. Between 1962 and 1980 the US contribution to inward FDI accounted for only 13% against 50% from EEC countries. Neither did France suffer from the role of unilaterally hosting foreign investment. French MNEs were always participating actively on outward foreign investment in industrialized and developing countries. After 1973 the emphasis in French outward FDI in less developed countries (LDCs) turned away from the former dependent African countries to a larger spectrum of LDCs and oil exporting countries.

Public opinion follows very closely all moves of American foreign investors in France. But the authorities rarely opposed themselves to US new investment projects in France. With or without success, French industrial policy aimed at strengthening French companies, for example in electronics and data processing. Many of the apprehensions of the past did not concern new investments but rather takeovers in traditional and prestigious sectors like agricultural machinery, the perfume and footwear industries.

Since the beginning of the seventies, foreign MNEs have lessened their involvement in industries of low technology and profitability. They have shown a greater capacity for adaption than their indigenous counterparts. Charles-Albert Michalet and Thérèse Chevallier point out that this may be due partially to the fact that foreign investors are allowed even greater freedom of action by the government than domestic companies. The authorities have more control over French firms in trying to prevent the adverse social consequences of the shutdown of factories.

On outward FDI the study comes to the conclusion that the successful modernization of the French economy is partly dependent on the recognition that international production is as important as trade in goods. French outward FDI was certainly motivated in many cases rather by financial reasons and it seems to have had a negative impact on the French trade balance. But French MNEs have sharpened their competitive advantages by investing abroad. Government policies have encouraged the multinational growth in French firms in order to strengthen those firms. But in the present accelerating pace of restructuring, France may be caught in a difficult situation between the redeployment of French firms abroad and a slow down—in some cases even a retreat—of foreign productive activities in France. This situation cannot be mastered by French industrial policy with regard to MNEs alone, a policy which was always hesitating between different and sometimes contradictory objectives. A general economic policy prone to facilitate the restructuring process is necessary and this necessity has been recognized by government.

The situation in Germany is perhaps not very different from the one in France. The ratio between inward and outward FDI which was 1,5 : 1 in 1971, has turned to 1 : 2,5 in the eighties. Germany became a net FDI exporting country, after having been in the post-war decades one of the preferred net recipient countries, mainly of American MNEs. This does not exclude the fact that Germany may also one day find itself in a broadly-balanced situation. Paulgeorg Juhl insists that Germany needs to create a climate favourable to the creation and application of firm-specific skills, complemented by a stable regulatory framework which encourages successful future industrial activities.

His study points out that in Germany inward and outward FDI is concentrated in a few branches of industry: chemicals, machinery, electrical engineering and transport equipment. This points to the assumption that the sources of corporate advantages upon which foreign investors have to rely, are comprised in those skills which have been acquired at firm-level management. The rising outward investment dynamics result from major changes in Germany's politico-economic environment.

The reversibility of this process is, in the absence of a specific FDI policy, largely dependent on Germany's competitive position and its domestic economic environment.

In a country where industrial policy is part of the overall planning, a specific policy versus FDI is hardly conceivable. The impetus must come from the continuation of a policy of capital import and export neutrality, the readiness not to retard the relocation of outdated industrial activities abroad and the search to make Germany remain an attractive location for high level new investment, including FDI. So the objectives in the three countries with a   ore or less balanced FDI situation are very similar.

THE NEWLY INDUSTRIALIZED COUNTRIES

In the Third World, no market economy with a substantial industrial sector has constricted MNE entry anywhere near to the extent of India. This tight exercise of control is not restricted to MNE entry, it is a part of a system of almost total protection against imports, of restrictions on licensing and of widespread price controls. India's overall industrial policy as a NIC is differing from the one Japan adopted when it was at a comparable stage of development. India is attempting an industrialization with the lowest possible reliance on the technology of the industrialized world. The result is an export performance markedly poorer than other NICs, though India excels as the largest NIC exporter of turnkey projects and as one of the leading exporters of industrial technology specifically designed for the Third World. Sanjaya Lall shows that the combination of restrictive policies pursued towards imports, inward foreign investment and licensing, is partially responsible for India's poor export performance and for the low average growth in per capita income, which between 1960 and 1980 was only 1.4% compared to 7% for Singapore.

By its policies India has obtained a greater technological autonomy as compared to other NICs. But this independence has been paid for with slower growth. According to Lall the technological prowess of Indian MNEs investing abroad could be economically beneficial for the home economy and could create an export drive, if the conditions of India's economy were not so restricted and distorted. Liberalization of FDI alone would not be enough to change the situation. Greater freedom in a less restrictive economic system is considered necessary for domestic and foreign investors.

Korea is an intermediate case between the highly restrictive Indian and the very liberal Singapore economic policy. Korea followed a restrictive foreign investment policy until recently: a policy inspired to a certain extent by the successful example given by Japan two decades ago. Korea permitted majority foreign ownership only in special cases, such as for export-oriented or highly technology-intensive projects. Basically inward FDI was permitted only where the entry of foreign firms was considered compatible with the government's development strategies, which were planned as accurately as in Japan.

Only two types of direct FDI were permitted: the substitution for imports of raw materials and the export-oriented investments. According to Bohn-Young-Koo's findings the strategy to admit FDI in order to substitute for imports was less effective than the export-oriented strategy.

Korea is a NIC which has determined its foreign investment policy itself and which has tried always to adjust its trade and licensing policy harmoniously with the FDI policy in order to acquire the necessary know-how for domestic MNEs. In the process of the maturation of the Korean economy and of gradually increasing wage changes, Korean outward FDI increased, first by construction firms and later in the plywood and in the textile industry. Up to now Korean authorities dominated the phenomenon of FDI and the influence of FDI on changes in Korea's economic structure remained marginal.

Of the three NICs considered, the example of Singapore is the most striking. Its strategy is completely different from India's restrictive policy. Singapore adopted an open strategy towards inward FDI, a strategy which nevertheless differs also from the neutral non-interventionist policies of certain industrialized nations such as Germany. Singapore's government planned its policy as precisely as Japan or Korea with the objective of taking advantage of foreign FDI for the necessary restructuring of the economy of a small open state. While Japan tried to rely mainly on licensing, Singapore relied mostly and much more than Korea on inward FDI, in order to create the conditions for its own future outward FDI. In 1982 the gross fixed investment by MNEs in Singapore was almost equal to one third of the GDP: the highest percentage of any country in the world. Foreign capital financed one third of total investment in the period 1960 to 1980.

The result of the Singapore FDI policy was highly positive but this result cannot be compared without the necessary precaution and reserves with the disappointing results of the Indian restrictive FDI policy.

Singapore is a small island state with a traditional dependence on international trade and shipping while India is an almost self-dependent subcontinent.

Nevertheless the example of Singapore is worth being studied closely by other NICs. As Donald J. Lecraw points out, the Singapore authorities took advantage of foreign investment in restructuring Singapore's manufacturing sector and overall development from a low wage and low productivity economy to a relatively high wage and high added value economy. The authorities did not hesitate to abandon whole low wage sectors of the economy to outward FDI of their own, in order to allow for higher added value productions at home. Thereby the government made use of a certain political authoritarianism and of wage controls. But it did not regulate specifically inward or outward FDI, but rather the macroeconomic environment. This is a rather unique precedent in the less developed world.

The twelve studies all imply one common conclusion to a question which was not formally asked to the authors. It is not primarily the policy towards FDI which decides on the more positive or negative results of FDI for a national economy. The benefits which a country can draw from the extra wealth originated by MNEs are dependent on its general investment climate and are determined by its economic and social environment. This environment is partially determined by its historical, geographical, and social data, but also to a large part by its economic and social policies.

Industrialized countries with a favourable economic environment have a fair chance of being on the winning side when applying rather open policies to FDI. MNEs have a stimulating influence on their economy. Countries with an unfavourable economic environment are at risk with an open as well as with a restrictive FDI policy. Countries with degrading economic conditions cannot count on foreign investment for a change. The rules are hardly different for countries with net inward or outward FDI. Those with a more balanced position risk being badly affected by decreasing inward and increasing outward FDI when their economic environment is unsatisfactory.

Developing countries face the same underlying rules. If their economic environment is satisfactory, they have a chance to make a maximum use of the potential of MNEs by applying a specific FDI policy designed to channel MNE efforts in the directions desired or planned for their economic development. Such a specific foreign investment policy can only be pertinent and successful if it is closely coordinated with the trade and licensing policy. Japan has given the example of an originally restrictive

FDI policy closely coordinated with its trade and licensing policy. Korea is following this path today, while Singapore has experienced the benefits of liberal but nevertheless coordinated policies.

The studies on NICs confirm the findings of the tenth economic summit of industrialized nations of June 9, 1984, in London, when considering methods of relief in the debt crisis of the Third World, the seven leaders for the first time invited the developing countries to help themselves by encouraging investment from the industrialized nations. They pointed out that MNE investment may be an important element in substituting more stable long term finance for short term bank lending.

The Institute for Research and Information on Multinationals greatly appreciates the importance of the work undertaken by all the authors concerned in this project. It will certainly make a valuable contribution to the study of multinational companies and to the debate on their role and impact on society.

I should personally like to thank the distinguished researchers who have made this study possible, especially Professor John Dunning who coordinated and edited the project and whose talent and tenacity have been indispensable in achieving this end product.

Eneko Landaburu,
Director,
Institute for Research and Information
on Multinationals (IRM), Geneva

The Institute for Research and Information on Multinationals (IRM) promotes and finances independent academic research on multinational companies and their impact on society. This research is undertaken by academics of various disciplines from all over the world. The findings are made available to the widest possible audience through the publication of books, reports and bulletins, through the media, and through the organization of conferences, seminars and other activities.

Introduction

0.1 ECONOMIC STRUCTURE, RESTRUCTURING, AND GOVERNMENTS

This volume addresses itself to the question: 'To what extent and in what ways have the operations of multinational enterprises (MNEs) affected economic structure or changes in economic structure in a selection of countries in the 1970s?' It incorporates twelve case-studies of the impact of both foreign-based MNEs, via their affiliates, and home-based MNEs, via their foreign activities, on the allocation of indigenous resources between industrial sectors and the utilization of resources within industrial sectors. Most studies also consider the role of MNEs as actors in influencing the restructuring of economic activity, consequential upon changes from both market- and supply-oriented forces over the past decade or more.

The subject of economic restructuring is topical and commanding increasing attention by scholars. Since the early 1970s, the world economy has been subject to a number of shocks which have dramatically affected the level and distribution of international economic activity. In varying degrees, the oil price hikes, anti-inflation government policies, institutional rigidities, and deficiencies in the international financial system have been held responsible; though it is perhaps fairer to describe these rather as catalysts to change, or determinants of the way in which change is dealt with (including its distributive effects) than as underlying reasons for it. Of these latter, the emergence of new industrial societies, of a new generation of far-reaching technological advances and shifts in consumer demand, have made the greatest impact.

There is, in a sense, nothing new in structural change in modern industrial society. The first industrial revolution saw fundamental changes in the nature and structure of economic activity; no less far-reaching were the effects of the new technologies (including organizational technologies) in the last quarter of the nineteenth century, although these were not felt in older industrialized economies like Britain until the inter-war years. During both world wars, considerable economic restructuring took place, but because it was accompanied by an increase in employment, and geared to a commonly acceptable and easily identifiable goal, it was smoothly accomplished.

The first two decades of the post-Second World War period saw a recovery which lulled western industrial societies into a false impression of economic security. Nowhere was this more clearly seen than in the UK shipbuilding industry where Britain's share of the world tonnage launched fell from 55% in the mid 1950s to 8% in the later 1970s. But this could not, and did not, last. Europe regained its pre-war economic stature, while Japan emerged as an even more potent industrial competitor. In the 1970s, newly industrializing developing economies with plentiful, cheap, and well-motivated labour, which they combined with technology and capital imported from the developed economies, began to offer a new challenge; this, coupled with the introduction of new technologies and a world recession in the 1970s, caused a decline in the demand for labour from traditional sectors in the older, high-wage, industrial nations. Quite apart from the policies pursued by governments towards these developments, they were bound to result in challenges to the existing patterns of resource allocation.

The response of most industrial nations to these changes has been schizophrenic. Where the costs of adjustment were relatively low or could be adequately absorbed, and the benefits of restructuring were seen to be substantial, then they have been positively embraced. But in most western economies, as in the past,[1] structural and institutional rigidities have seriously inhibited the movement of resources from declining to expanding industries. Improved labour utilization within declining industries has further exacerbated the problem of structural unemployment in these economies.

At the very least, structural adjustment requires governments to minimize the obstacles in the reallocation of resources from declining to expanding sectors; some of the Asian economies, now facing their own adjustment problems, led the way in the 1960s by positive interventionism to promote (what they perceived to be) their comparative dynamic advantage in a world of economic interdependence—but, at the same time, countering what they considered to be protectionism or unfair competition by other countries. Sometimes, this led (and still leads) to import-substitution policies which are justified by a kind of infant industry argument, but, in this case, the protection is likely to be directed revitalization of the older sectors rather than the cosseting of the young.

At the other extreme, governments have responded to changes in the international division of labour by reducing their participation in world commerce and pursuing a policy of self-sufficiency. In this case, economic restructuring is minimized by import controls and allowed only where it can be accommodated without causing unacceptable unemployment and other adjustment costs. Implicit in such a policy is that certain efficiency goals such as those based upon technical or scale economies and/or dependent on import of technology may have to be sacrificed to promote (or protect) other objectives. To be fair, such a move towards economic autarchy or isolationism is often taken for political reasons and/or in the belief that the type of international division of labour promoted by economic interdependence and often dominated by powerful industrial nations and/or MNEs does not work in the best interests of the particular country in question.

In practice, most governments in their industrial and technological policies—where they have any at all—adopt an intermediate and fluctuating stance, between positive and negative adjustment. But what is clear from the essays presented in this volume, and especially those dealing with India, Korea, and Singapore among developing countries, and Japan, France, and Canada among developed countries, is that the role of government is a vital ingredient of the determinants of the structure of resource allocation and the way in which such resources adjust to changes in supply and demand conditions for them; and that, to a very large measure, the impact of MNEs on economic structure will depend on the policies pursued.[2]

0.2 THE CONCEPT OF AN OPTIMUM ECONOMIC STRUCTURE

The previous paragraphs suggest that in a situation of economic change the concept of an ideal structure of resource allocation may be a difficult one to identify. Even at a particular point in time, the economist can only suggest which is the best pattern of resource allocation to meet certain efficiency goals. Alter or reorder the priority of goals, or incorporate others, for example to do with the distribution of income, economic sovereignty and so on, then the 'best' economic structure is changed accordingly. In a dynamic situation, where there are adjustment costs to change, then the most the economist can be expected to do is to evaluate the consequences of alternative adjustment programmes—again, primarily, from the viewpoint of output or other efficiency goals.

It follows that, if there is no consensus of an ideal economic structure because the goals, and/or trade-offs between goals, of various societies are different, there can be no general answer to the way in which MNEs may affect economic structure. This conclusion is further underlined by the fact that government economic policies to which MNEs react also vary widely between countries. Whether MNEs operate for the good of the Japanese, Portuguese or French economies, will thus depend as much on the respective government goals and policies as on anything which MNEs themselves may or may not do.

At the same time, the economist can identify the main components and determinants of economic structure and suggest reasons why foreign- or domestic-based MNEs may impinge on this economic structure differently from uninational firms. While each chapter in this book pursues its own particular approach to the subject, there is a common methodological thread running throughout the volume. This thread is explored in some depth both in this chapter and in the UK case-study which follows. Later chapters then take these analytical issues as read.

At its simplest, economic structure may be defined as the way in which resources are distributed among alternative uses. The question 'what goods or services should a nation produce' is essentially one of economic structure. Optimum allocative efficiency is defined as being reached when the distribution of resources between competing uses cannot be bettered by transferring a unit of any one resource from one activity to another, at any given moment of time. Economic welfare is commonly equated with the maximization of consumer surplus, though the value of output as measured by market prices may not always be a good measure of this surplus, partly because an individual's welfare embraces goods and services which are not normally bought and sold in the market, such as leisure, and partly because the price of some goods may not be an adequate reflection of their real worth.

However, the question of 'what to produce' cannot be separated from that of 'how to produce'. Most micro-textbooks on allocative efficiency assume that *all* resources can be or are utilized, i.e. that is there is full employment: the question they then ask is 'in what way?' But allocative efficiency is also dependent on the manner in which resources are used in any given activity, and this is essentially a 'how to produce' question. Again economists often limit their answers to this question by assuming that, in any given use, factor inputs are being used in the optimum way. In fact this may not be the case; firms may not be producing on their most efficient production functions; they may not be combining their factor inputs in the least cost way; and they may not be producing at the right scale of output. X inefficiency may exist within sectors. Output could be raised by improving sectoral productivity. Sometimes economists distinguish between the ability of firms to produce efficiently in a particular sector by referring to 'sectoral' efficiency; in other cases 'technical' efficiency.[3] We prefer the use of the term technical efficiency, and argue that, in practice, a country's economic structure and restructuring may be determined by the motivation and ability of its firms to optimize this efficiency, in allocating their resources among different activities.

For optimum technical efficiency to be achieved three conditions must exist:

(1) that all firms produce on their best production function;

(2) that they utilize their factor inputs in such a way as to minimize the costs of producing any given output; and

(3) that they produce at the right scale of output.

Neither allocative nor technical efficiency can be isolated from the market structure in which firms produce. In conditions of perfect competition, neo-classical economics asserts that the optimum social and private structures of resource allocation are the same. Where there is market failure, be it due to the presence of uncertainty, product differentiation, fewness of producers, or barriers to entry, then certainly condition (3) above may not apply and hence optimum allocative efficiency may not be attained. In conditions of market failure, due to imperfections in knowledge or uncertainty, then conditions (1) or (2) may not appertain. Where firms are not solely motivated by profits, the possibility of X inefficiency leading to sub-optimal technical efficiency may arise for a different reason. In conditions of technological change there may be a trade-off between investing in research and development with its uncertain (but possibly high) returns tomorrow and cost minimization today. Where the size of a market is small, then it may be only a few firms who are able to produce at optimum technical efficiency; but a structure could both create obstacles to entry and reduce technical and possibly allocative efficiency. By contrast, excessive product differentiation by firms may create surplus capacity and lead to each firm producing at below optimum level of output.

The scenario portrayed is even more complicated in the case of multi-activity firms; here the firm in addition to its production goals attempts to reach its objectives by organizing separate but interrelated activities in the best way possible. The idea of minimizing such organization or transaction costs presupposes that the use of markets does not allow the firm to capture the economies of independent activities, or to exploit its optimum strategy of organizing transactions. While the markets concerned in this instance are primarily those of intermediate products (including technology), the organizational options may equally apply to the final stages of service activities (e.g. as in retailing[4]).

Received theory suggests that where market failure exists firms will tend to internalize the transaction costs of such markets. This has implications for economic structure, by affecting both technical efficiency (due for example on the one hand to reduction of uncertainty but, on the other, to increasing monopoly power and thus the possibility of X inefficiency) and allocative efficiency, as resource allocation by administrative hierarchy may affect which kind of activity is pursued in which location. While in some cases the common ownership of separate activities may promote efficiency, in others it could be used as a form of monopoly power, and/or to negate or inhibit other non-market forces (e.g. governments) in their attempts to regulate or influence any one activity.

In view of all these forms of market impurities, it is not surprising that economists no longer talk about perfect competition (or the optimum economic structure based on it) but rather the concept of workable competition, which is defined as that which can be practically accomplished in the technological and environmental situation in which firms find themselves. Moreover, rather than identifying and determining an optimum (or equilibrium) situation, contemporary economists prefer to study ways in which resource allocation may be improved, that is disequilibrium lessened, and/or the extent to which and ways in which economic structure is sub-optimal.

0.3   THE MULTINATIONAL ENTERPRISE AND ECONOMIC STRUCTURE

How then might the MNE *qua* MNE impinge on economic structure and changes in economic structure? Clearly in so far as there is such an impact it implies that firms which undertake production (i.e. value-adding) activities in more than one country either have different objectives or respond to economic stimuli differently from uninational firms. In assessing these differences, one might draw upon the literature on the determinants of both MNE and industrial activity. A propos the former, it is now generally accepted that the extent and pattern of international production is determined by three interrelated factors:

(1) The extent to which firms of one nationality possess advantages relative to those of another nationality, in sourcing a market or groups of markets. The greater these ownership-specific (O) advantages, then, *ceteris paribus*, the more likely it is that international production will take place.

(2) The extent to which enterprises find it profitable to use these advantages (I) themselves (internalize them) rather than lease them to firms in foreign countries; this will be determined by the comparative transaction costs of hierarchies vis à vis those of the market, but the greater the latter then, *ceteris paribus*, the more likely it is that international production will take place.

(3) The extent to which it is profitable to combine the use of internalized O advantages (which are generally, but not exclusively mobile between countries) with immobile resources in a foreign country rather

than in the country which generates the O advantages (the home country). The more the location-specific (L) advantages favour a foreign country, then, *ceteris paribus*, the more likely it is that international production will take place.

In so far as these OLI advantages are not evenly distributed between countries, the activities of MNEs will affect the disposition of resources in both the home and host country and between them. Like international trade, international production may transform economic structure, but its potential impact is likely to be greater than that of trade. First, neo-classical theories of trade assume that the main function of trade is an increase in allocative efficiency obtained through making possible specialization based on comparative production advantage; but in each country it is assumed that every firm is operating on its most efficient production frontier. Later theories of trade, for example neo-technology theories, dropped this latter assumption by accepting the possibility that firms of different size or nationality possessed certain advantages unique to themselves, but it assumed that these, like other endowments, were immobile across national boundaries. We have suggested that it is an essential condition for international production that *some* allocative or technical inefficiency should exist, and hence by the transfer of assets, and their use in a foreign country, economic structure is affected. The greater the ownership advantages of foreign forms which can best be exploited by production outside their home countries, the greater the impact of MNEs on economic structure. This is a major proposition to be explored in this volume.

The literature suggests, however, that there are two distinct types of O advantage which firms may possess. The first is the exclusive or privileged possession of intangible or tangible assets which gives the owner some proprietary advantage in the value-adding process of a particular product.[5]

This may include a new product or production technology, marketing, purchasing, or organizational skills. But whatever it is, the net effect is the creation of new or improved products, and/or an increase in technical and scale efficiency. Some authors have called this kind of O advantage a *production* or an *asset* advantage.[6]

The second kind of O advantage is that which arises due to the ability of a firm to coordinate, by administrative fiat, separate but interrelated (productive) activities better[7] than (a) other firms (i.e. of different ownership) and (b) other organizational forms (e.g. the market). Were markets perfect, in the sense that the exchange values for a particular transaction fully captured the externalities associated with that activity, and there were no other failings, then multi-activity forms would not exist. In so far as an MNE is a multi-activity firm since it internalizes intermediate product markets across national boundaries, this type of advantage is an inherent feature of the MNE. Indeed some writers argue that this transaction cost-minimizing advantage is both a necessary and a sufficient condition to explain the existence of MNEs. This kind of O advantage may also affect economic structure, but *unlike* the first type of advantage for which there is often an imperfect external market, it is inherently internal to the MNE and thus unique to international production.

Economic structure may thus be affected by MNE activity in three ways. First, MNEs may transfer assets across national boundaries which otherwise might not have been transferred; second, they may internalize these assets; third, by assigning a common ownership to separate but interrelated activities, which would not otherwise have been coordinated, they might affect the disposition of these resources. These O advantages are different from those of non-MNEs; that is, they are specific to MNEs, therefore they impinge on economic structure.

The industrial organization literature is built around the structure, conduct, and performance (SCP) paradigm. While primarily addressed to examining the composition of *market* structure it can be readily adapted to examining *economic* structure. The determinants of the way in which resources are used relate to the *conduct* of firms, including their motivation and strategy, and their *performance*. Both conduct and performance affect and are affected by the structure of the market; this includes number and size of firms, ease of entry or exit, nature of products produced, and degree of vertical or other forms of integration. The presence or absence of these attributes affects the distribution of activity *between* firms, and in consequence may affect the technical and scale efficiency of individual firms. In so far as MNEs behave or perform differently from uninational firms, they may impinge on market structure and, through market structure, on the allocation of economic activity.

There is one other aspect of economic structure which deserves some mention. Structure may refer to the way in which resources are allocated both *within* a country and between countries. We have seen how trade affects the economic structure of the participating countries, and have argued that the activities of MNEs are likely to have even more pronounced effects. Some MNEs also have much wider implications as they promote the internationalization of economic structure by treating the world—or at least the major regions of the world—as a single market. In this sense, structure is not only about what the end products are, but the form and character of the firm's international economic involvement. This in turn will be related to its socio-political goals: to what extent, for example, does it wish to maintain a viable degree of self-sufficiency? For example, the common ownership of production by MNEs may lead to the concentration of high value-added activities in some countries and that of low value-added activities in others. From the viewpoint of the firm this might be the most sensible strategy. But it may also freeze a host country into an existing and unacceptable international division of labour. On the other hand, the MNE may be a vehicle for upgrading skills and thus make for a more desirable economic structure.

The way in which MNEs may affect or be affected by changes in economic structure is thus an essential part of this volume. Do they aid or retard restructuring in the light of changing world needs? As we shall see, the Singapore and Japanese experience suggests they may well do so. At the same time the Indian and Korean case studies argue that the answer depends as much on government policy as on anything else.

0.4 SOME METHODOLOGICAL POINTS

Several authors, notably Dunning, Swedenborg, and Globerman, touch upon some methodological issues common to each of the chapters. The first and most important of these is to assess the impact of MNEs on economic structure compared with that of uninational firms. The second is to identify how any differences so found may be attributed to the multinationality of such firms rather than to some of their other characteristics. For example it may be found that MNEs do have a different impact from uninational firms but that this is due to differences in their size or product structure or other variables rather than to their multinationality *per se*. All impact studies are faced with these problems and resolve them in different ways. These are described in the next chapter within a UK context, but essentially they all try to do what Swedenborg articulates in her chapter, that is to assess the difference between *the actual impact* of MNEs on structure *and that which would have occurred in their absence*. This, of course, poses enormous conceptual problems as, by definition, any counterfactual situation must be hypothetical. Would, for example, government policy towards indigenous firms be the same in the absence of inward or outward foreign direct investment? What would its policies be towards import controls? What would be the effects of reduced competition if, in the absence of inward investment, the gap in output left by foreign firms was supplied by the remaining firms? Would their competitive position be strengthened or weakened? If outward investment were curbed, what would be the effect on any attempts to redirect the capital outflow to domestic investment?

According to the answers to these questions, the impact of MNEs will vary. It follows from this that it is inappropriate to use micro-economic techniques to evaluate macro-economic propositions. Impact studies

made without assuming some alternative position can give highly misleading, if not erroneous, results.

At the same time, policies towards MNEs *do* require formulation, while
research (including that demonstrated in this volume) clearly reveals that
MNEs *do* have a distinctive impact on economic structure. It is therefore
incumbent upon economists to give some guidance on the effects, based
either on the *most* likely alternative position or on a range of likely alternative positions. The assumption that, in the absence of the operation of
MNEs, unilateral firms would have filled the output/investment gap and
that therefore the multinational effect is the difference between the impact
of the two groups of firms is one of these alternatives and is the one used
by Dunning and others in this volume. The separation of their multinationality from other attributes of MNEs, such as size and so on, is in one
sense easier and in the other more difficult. It is easier in that we should be
able to normalize for the non-multinational differences. It is more difficult
in that these attributes are often inextricably linked with each other; for
example MNEs may be big because the advantages of their being multinational help them to become larger vis à vis unilateral firms.

0.5   PLAN OF THE BOOK

The following chapters tackle some of the questions raised in this introduction. In doing so, they make use of the latest empirical data available,
and in some cases new data previously unpublished have been collated for
this volume. In some cases the data are good, in others they leave much to
be desired. It will be seen that the chapters vary somewhat in approach
and content; this is inevitable given the different role of MNEs, and the
part played by governments in the countries reviewed. But all the authors
have attempted to answer the basic questions posed at the beginning of
this chapter.

There are twelve case-studies, seven from developed and five from
developing countries. We have also chosen to include both large and small
economies in our sample, and countries with very different policies
towards MNEs. In all they embrace countries which between them generate about 90% of outward direct investment and account for 80% of
inward direct investment.

A final chapter draws together the main conclusions of the individual
case-studies and attempts to derive some policy implications for governments of both home and host contries to MNEs.

NOTES

1. For example the UK in the inter-war years.
2. This point is further taken up in Chapter 13.
3. As we are primarily interested in comparing the performance of firms rather than of sectors.
4. Compare for example the economics of chain stores with those of specialist shops.
5. We use this generic expression to cover any activity of a firm from primary production or the design of a new product through to the retailing of the end product.
6. In the works of D. J. Teece and J. H. Dunning cited elsewhere in this volume.
7. Better, that is, from the firm's viewpoint!

1

The United Kingdom

John H. Dunning

1.1 INTRODUCTION

The United Kingdom is, *par excellence,* a two-way international direct investor. Furthermore, the contribution of foreign and domestic multinational enterprises (MNEs) to gross national product, capital expenditure, employment, exports and profits, is considerably greater in the case of the UK than in that of any other major industrialized economy. To give just two examples: in 1981, the combined employment of the leading UK industrial MNEs at home and abroad and foreign-owned MNEs in the UK was 4.5 million[1] or nearly 70% of the labour force in UK manufacturing industry. Second, in that same year, the profits earned by the foreign affiliates of UK firms, and by UK affiliates of foreign firms, were 72% of all profits identified in the national income accounts.

The United Kingdom also has the longest experience as an international direct investor, and although this chapter is concerned with assessing the contemporary impact of MNEs, it may be helpful to set this within an historical context. Indeed, the UK is an excellent case-study of the developmental approach to our understanding of the impact of foreign direct investment.[2] Following this historical excursion, in which we shall draw mainly on qualitative and rather fragmented statistical evidence, the main part of the chapter will focus on the interaction between international production and UK economic structure in the 1970s. As with the other contributions to this volume, we shall seek to identify and evaluate the ways in which MNEs have influenced the disposition of resources within a particular economy, and how this has changed over time. To do this, we shall consider two types of impact: the first on technical and scale efficiency (or changes in that efficiency)—that is on the way in which resources are used by firms in a given sector; the second on allocative efficiency—that is the way in which resources are distributed (or redistributed) between sectors. We shall also examine the role of MNEs in the adjustment or restructuring process *per se.*

1.2   AN HISTORICAL OVERVIEW

For the first three-quarters of the nineteenth century, the international economic involvement of the UK followed a predictable pattern of a country which was not only the world's premier industrial nation, but also its largest overseas landlord, with vast overseas territories, mainly in developing or newly settled primary producing areas. From the start of the industrial revolution, British factories needed to import raw materials and intermediate products, and to export finished manufactured goods. Trade was the handmaiden of domestic prosperity. But such trade was often complemented by an outward flow of intangible assets—technology and management as well as capital—which helped extract the minerals and provide the raw materials for the factories at home, and the foodstuffs for an increasingly urbanized population with higher real incomes. Such asset transference was organized partly by the market, for example there was a highly sophisticated international capital market, and partly by firms engaging in foreign direct investment. Sometimes, as with the early mining companies, there were no comparable domestic activities, but the more usual pattern was for UK manufacturers to extend their territorial interests outside the UK, and establish or buy out foreign plantations, farms, and mines.[3]

Such direct investment, like its porfolio counterpart, was financed from a balance of payments surplus, built up from Britain's industrial exports. But to minimize the risks of supply disruptions and price increases, and to ensure product quality, ownership of foreign outlets was often preferred to spot-market transactions or long-term contracts. In other words, the international markets both for the assets required to supply the intermediate products and for the products themselves were highly imperfect. Had they not been so, foreign direct investment would have been unnecessary and trade would have been conducted between independent parties. This is an important point; the impact of MNE activity on economic structure will depend not only on the nature and extent of the mobile resources transferred across national boundaries, but also on the way in which control is exercised over the use of these resources, and other resources commanded by the investing company, once transferred. Indeed, it is the control aspect which leads to the distinctive impact of MNE activity, compared with other vehicles of resource transference.

In the nineteenth century, UK vertical foreign direct investment followed a pattern not dissimilar to that of vertical trade, and was explainable by neo-classical type, Heckscher–Ohlin (H–O), theories. It was complementary with, rather than competitive to, the domestic activities of UK MNEs. From a national economic viewpoint, although this has not been rigorously researched, the added transaction costs of concluding contractual arrangements with foreign suppliers were presumed to more than counteract any marginal gains from the reallocation of capital to domestic use. In any event, relative to other kinds of capital movements, foreign direct investment was very small for most of the nineteenth century.

But there was another type of outward direct investment emerging in these years. This was to finance production, mainly in developed countries, to service markets which could not be supplied, or supplied as cheaply, by exports. In some cases, the initial decision to go abroad rested on more favourable production costs in the foreign location and/or saving of transport costs between the place of production and the final market, but, more often than not, import restrictions imposed by the host governments made exporting an impracticable proposition.[4] Several options then became open to the exporting firm; the first was to abandon that particular foreign market altogether; a second was to license foreign firms; and a third was to set up a production subsidiary in the importing country. In the event, all of these routes were chosen by different companies, but it was the last which saw the emergence of some of the giant MNEs of today (Stopford, 1974). Why they chose foreign direct investment rather than licensing as a mode of entry rested mainly on the perception that the former would enable them to capture a fuller economic rent or better protect their proprietary rights, and/or that the control exerted over the resources transferred could recoup the gains to the parent company external to those accruing to the foreign subsidiary.

It is this kind of activity by MNEs which some commentators (Kojima, 1978) have criticized as being against the long-term economic interests of home countries—mainly on the basis that it helps to erode their comparative advantage. In turn, it is predicated that it is undertaken either to overcome barriers to trade imposed by host governments or as part of a defensive oligopolistic strategy of firms. In other words, it is assumed that the market for the sale of assets or rights transferred by foreign direct investment is imperfect and that the private price received for these assets or rights is below the social price. The social price might include any loss of competitive advantage, and the costs of structural alignment in the home country resulting from that investment. Contemporary writers (Baranson, 1979) suggest that the divergence between social and private interests is likely to be greatest in sunrise industries in which the market structure is monopolistic or oligopolistic. Two types of welfare losses are usually identified; one arising from private market imperfections, and the strategy of firms arising from such imperfection, and the other from adjustment costs external to the firm but borne by society.

Even in the heyday of Britain's technological hegemony, these conditions did not generally appertain. But it is true that, in the first part of the nineteenth century, and long before corporations began to invest overseas, the British government tried to stem—for the most part unsuccessfully—the outflow of knowledge and technology. By the last quarter of that century, the UK had already surrendered much of its earlier lead, and it was the US that was the source of the new generation of discoveries and inventions.[5] By 1914 only a small proportion of the UK's outward direct investment was made by firms in the (then) high-technology or growth industries; in 1919 over 70% of the largest two hundred UK manufacturing firms were in the older or mainly consumer goods industries (Chandler, 1981).

While it is frequently argued that the UK was exporting too much capital in the years prior to the First World War,[6] it would be difficult to extend this criticism to the activities of UK MNEs.[7] For not only were they active in sectors in which the home country's long-term comparative advantage was declining, but, in some of the newer industries such as manmade fibres, foreign direct investment enabled UK firms to break into foreign markets (e.g. the US), which otherwise might have been closed to them, or to steal a march on their foreign competitors.

It was not until the 1880s that there was any systematic activity by foreign MNEs in the United Kingdom. But in the following quarter of a century, US MNEs established bridgeheads in most of the newer industrial sectors including those in which the UK later built up a strong comparative advantage.[8] This investment was partly prompted by import controls and the oligopolistic strategy of US firms, but mostly because the kind of ownership advantages which foreign MNEs possessed could be more profitably exploited from a UK than a home-country base. More than this, some of the American organizational and managerial advances of the time (Chandler, 1977), which were exported along with the new technologies, raised both the allocative and technical efficiency of UK industry (Saul, 1960). Although there are no official estimates, our best 'guesstimate' is that in 1914 the value of the UK accumulated outward direct capital stake was thirty times greater than its inward counterpart.

The trend and direction of outward and inward direct investment since 1914, and its impact on UK economic structure, has strongly reflected the innovatory capacity and production efficiency of UK firms relative to that of their overseas competitors (i.e. their ownership-specific advantages), the comparative attraction of the UK as a production base (its location-specific advantage), the role of the UK government in effecting each of these, and the general economic climate. For example, in the inter-war years, as US technological and commercial viability strengthened, so its outward/inward direct capital stake rose from 1 : 8 in 1914 to 4 : 1 in 1938; by contrast that of the UK fell from 33 : 1 to 15 : 1. By 1971, the corresponding US ratio had risen to 6 : 1 while that of the UK had fallen to

8 : 1; by 1980 the respective ratios were 3.2 : 1 and 1.7 : 1 (Dunning, 1983b). The fall in the US ratio reflected the decline in that country's industrial hegemony. By contrast several European countries, for example Sweden and Germany, and Japan have become important net outward investors while in others, for example Canada, Australia, and India, the rate of new outward investment has outpaced that of inward investment.

The spread of industrialization over the past century, which has greatly accelerated since 1945, has had two effects; the first is, in so far as firm specific knowledge and technology have become more widely disseminated, the pattern of international production, like that of trade, has reflected this. The second is the convergence of the structure of production and taste patterns among the advanced industrial nations, which, coupled with the cross-penetration of national markets by MNEs and the growing importance of the economies of large-scale production, has made for more geographical plant specialization, and intra-industry trade and production (Dunning and Norman, 1985).

Up to around 1960, the main effect of these changes was for the UK's economic structure to be tilted more towards high-technology and growth manufacturing sectors as a result of inward investment, and for the foreign activities of UK MNEs to be directed to the primary and more traditional secondary sectors. In 1964, for example, some 71% of the net foreign assets owned by the leading UK manufacturing MNEs were in the less technology-intensive sectors of food, drink and tobacco, household products, paper, metal products, building materials, and textiles, and 29% in the more technology-intensive sectors of chemicals, engineering, electronics, and vehicles (Reddaway, Potter and Taylor, 1968). By contrast, in 1965, 67% of the net assets of foreign—mainly US—firms in UK manufacturing were in the more technology-intensive sectors and only 33% in the former industries in less technology-intensive sectors. The data set out in Table 1.1 clearly show that while the foreign activities of UK MNEs in the 1960s were more oriented towards the traditional sectors than those of UK industry in general, the activities of foreign subsidiaries in the UK were more oriented to the high-technology sectors.

To some extent, the pattern of activity by MNEs in the 1960s reflected their geographical destination or origin. Britain's past imperialistic ties steered investment towards those sectors in which it had a trading advantage. In 1960, 61% of the net foreign assets owned by UK MNEs outside oil, banking, and insurance was invested in Commonwealth countries. Over the last twenty years, the growing importance of the involvement by UK MNEs in Europe has shifted the sectoral distribution towards more high-technology sectors. At the same time, these investments, like those of foreign MNEs in the UK, reflect changing locational attractions of countries. Some foreign governments, for example, by nationalization or

TABLE 1.1   The industrial structure of UK inward and outward direct investment in the 1960s

	Inward (capital stake end 1965)		All UK firms (net output 1963)		Outward (capital stake end 1964)	
	£m	%	£m	%	£m	%
Food, drink and tobacco	207.9	12.7	1292.0	12.5	537.6	39.3
Chemicals and allied industries	211.9	13.0	949.9	9.2	194.5	14.2
Metal manufacturing	134.4	8.2	1500.2	14.5	132.2	9.7
Mechanical engineering	336.7	20.7	1435.8	13.9	19.9	1.5
Electrical engineering	185.1	11.4	954.0	9.2	67.5	4.9
Motor vehicles	303.5	18.6	1184.4	11.5	51.8	3.8
Textiles, clothing, and footwear	34.9	2.1	1234.1	12.0	94.1	6.9
Paper and allied products	46.2	2.8	845.6	8.2	118.8	8.6
Rubber products	58.4	3.6	167.7	1.6	74.3	5.4
Other manufacturing industries	110.4	6.8	755.3	7.3	76.2	5.6
All manufacturing including household products	1629.4	100.0	10,319.0	100.0	1366.7	100.0

Source: Inward capital stake, *Board of Trade Journal*, 26-1-1968; all UK firms net output, *Census of Production*, 1963; Outward capital stake, Reddaway, Potter and Taylor (1968).

other deterrents, have virtually outlawed some kinds of MNE activity; much of the fall in vertical direct investment by UK firms since the war is explainable in these terms. Changing locational advantages also explained a lot of import-substituting investment in the inter-war years (Dunning, 1983b). Tariff barriers and other import controls induced US firms to set up factories in the UK, as did the shortage of US dollars after the Second World War. In the 1980s, European and US protectionism against Japanese imports is prompting Japanese MNEs to follow a similar strategy. Natural or artificially induced shifts in the locational pull of countries both affect, and may be affected by, the extent and balance of international direct investment; in other words, the structure of foreign direct investment—and hence its impact on the economy—is influenced by the disposition of immobile resource endowments, including government policy, as well as that of more mobile resource endowments.

Finally, the organizational mode of exploiting the ownership-specific advantages of firms must be considered. It is, at least, possible that differences in the structure of outward and inward direct investment might reflect the differences in the relative costs of (international) intermediate product markets and those of hierarchies in the sectors, or between the investing and recipient countries in question. In the case of mature and codifiable technologies, where proprietary rights can be protected, and there are substantial risks attached to direct investment, licensing may be the best route to capture economic rent; by contrast, in the case of new idiosyncratic technologies, international markets, particularly between developed and developing countries, are so imperfect that only by internalizing the transfer of assets within the owning firm can such a surplus be appropriated.[9] Alternatively, the economies of size and organizational synergy may be more important in some sectors and in some firms than in others.

Over the past century, the interplay of foreign direct investment and the UK's international competitive position seems to have evolved in the following way. First, the UK, as a dominant industrialized power and high-wage economy, engaged in international trade and production to protect or advance the markets for its manufacturers and to safeguard its supplies of raw materials and foodstuffs.[10] In the manufacturing sector, UK firms first exploited their proprietary advantages through exports, but with the industrialization of the European and US economies there was some restriction of imports from the UK; as a consequence, local production by UK firms replaced trade. While the transfer of UK technology and human capital aided this process of industrialization, host countries were quick to assimilate and adapt these assets to their own requirements, while most of the finance capital for their development was transmitted through the international capital market. For a whole set of reasons, it was the US and Europe—and particularly the US—rather than the UK which pioneered the second generation of industrial discoveries in the 1870s. These were different from those they replaced, in that first they were more capital-intensive and required larger firms to exploit them; second they needed to be protected against immediate pirating—hence the introduction of the patent system; and third they needed more hierarchical organizational forms to operate successfully.[11] The UK now became the recipient of these product and process innovations, initially by imports, but later, where there were locational advantages of producing in the UK, by inward direct investment. Investment was preferred to licensing because of the higher transaction costs associated with the latter. These innovations were then disseminated through most industrial countries; they were copied, adapted and improved upon by indigenous firms. As a result, the UK economic structure underwent profound changes. In some cases, the presence of foreign firms induced new market structures (Dunning, 1958); in the inter-war years, for example, a good deal of rationalization occurred in those sectors, such as motor vehicles, in which foreign firms were especially well represented.

The Second World War was the next main watershed in the history of international production. The US emerged as the leading industrial nation with its firms having a decisive lead in the production of a whole range of technologically-intensive producer goods and high-income consumer goods. But to sell these goods at a time of dollar shortage meant that US firms had to penetrate foreign markets through licensing or foreign direct investment. The UK was a natural first choice for siting the European subsidiaries of US firms; moreover, it was an excellent springboard for serving the Commonwealth markets (Canada apart). Concurrently, US MNEs penetrated the Canadian and Latin American markets and ventured as far afield as Australia. By the time the UK had recovered from the war, many of these markets had been captured by US firms.[12]

Until the mid 1960s, the US remained the dominant source of new innovations and most of the newer and/or growth sectors of the UK economy were strongly influenced by US investment (Dunning, 1958; Steuer, 1973). At the same time, the failure of the UK to join the EEC at its inception certainly deflected a good deal of US investment away from the UK to the other European locations. In the late 1960s and 1970s, two things happened. First, there was a decline in the Pax Americana as there had been a century earlier in Pax Britannica. The technology gap eased between Europe and the US. A revitalized Germany and a prosperous and determined France led the recovery, and some sectors of UK industry were not far behind. The result was that although investment from the US continued to increase, European industry began to overtake US industry in the 1960s (Dunning and Cantwell, 1983); at the same time, to make headway and cover increasingly high R&D overheads, the new European leaders had themselves to expand outside their boundaries. This thrust was intensified as many sectors became *internationally* oligopolistic and there was more inter-market penetration by foreign direct investment (Knickerbocker, 1973; Graham, 1978, 1985; Flowers, 1976). In turn, this led to a growth in *intra*-industry international production, and the allocation of economic activity being based less on differential factor endowments and more on the economics of plant specialization and the exploitation of joint ownership advantages (Dunning and Norman, 1985). An additional difference between this specialization and that of the nineteenth century was that there was a greater propensity for the latter to take place *within* the MNE hierarchies. The common ownership of internationally mobile resources has distinctive allocative and distributive affects (Caves, 1980). This is because the transaction costs of MNEs differ from those of the market while, because of endogenous (mainly government-induced) imperfections, MNEs may respond via internalized (transfer) pricing *et al.* procedures by assigning inputs or distributing outputs differently (Katrak, 1981).

It is this latter aspect of MNE operations which has increasingly shaped market structure in developed countries in the last two decades and has been aided by liberalization of trade between OECD countries. Such intra-industry involvement is also playing a growing role in Latin America and the Asia/Pacific region. The effects on the international competitive position of countries resulting from the ownership of assets passing to foreign firms, or of own-country MNEs exploiting their assets outside their national territories, are basically twofold. First, some assets or rights are internationally traded that would not otherwise have been. Second, and partly related to the first, asset usage may be different. These effects relate the two main functions of an MNE: as a producer of goods using resources internally transferred across national boundaries, and as a transactor of resources replacing the market (Teece, 1983). Where there is a common ownership of resources and these are geared to meet a single rather than several goals, then there may be distinctive resource allocative and efficiency effects arising from that ownership.

Unfortunately, the separation of these effects is an extremely difficult task. But, analytically, the distinction is an important one. For it is this which distinguishes direct investment from non-equity, arms-length resource transfers. Foreign direct investment will be preferred where market failure prompts firms to internalize assets or rights which might otherwise be traded externally and/or where the ownership advantages of MNEs are of a kind which stem from transaction cost-minimizing activities and for which there is no external market. So in the one case, MNEs act differently because of their ownership and the fact that imperfections may lead to different decision-taking. In the other, it is the common governance ingredient based on economies of complementary activities and on other strategic considerations, for example to do with oligopolistic behaviour, that will bring about a different resource allocative patern.

1.3　THE STRUCTURAL IMPACT OF MNEs IN THE 1960s AND 1970s: SOME THEORETICAL CONSIDERATIONS

This volume is essentially interested in identifying and evaluating the extent and way in which MNEs *qua* MNEs affect international and domestic resource usage and efficiency over a period of time. This they may do both by directly affecting the strategy, performance, and conduct of their affiliates vis-à-vis their UK competitors, and indirectly by their impact on other firms, for example by linkages and competitive stimulus. By their choice of activity they may affect the way resources are allocated. By their internalization of product and factor markets they may impinge on both domestic and international market structures. Over time, the way they respond to changes in supply or demand conditions may influence the adaptive efficiency of the economies in which they operate. Finally by their mode of entry (takeover or green-field investment) and their global strategies, they may modify both market form and the ownership of output between firms. This chapter will be primarily concerned with some static and comparative static aspects of the impact of MNE activity.

Static aspects: (a) Allocative impact

Under the assumptions of neo-classical trade theory, a country's economic welfare will be optimal when it allocates its resources in a way which best exploits its comparative advantage; that is where its international competitiveness—as revealed, for example, by its share of world exports or export-import balance—is the most favourable. In exchange for the exports so generated, the resources of other countries are used to provide the importing country with the goods it is relatively least suited to produce. In this case, it should be noted that it is solely the distribution of location-specific (i.e. spatially immobile) factor endowments which determines both international and domestic economic structure.

International production theory is concerned partly with the location of immobile resources, and partly with that of mobile resources or intermediate products, which are traded *within* the MNE. In the present context, we wish to explain why foreign firms possess certain types of advantages, relative to UK firms, and perceive they can best capture the economic rent on these advantages by producing in the UK; and why UK firms possess advantages relative to foreign firms and find it profitable to exploit these outside their home country. We have already argued that ownership matters because it affects both the nature and form of assets or rights traded and the way in which they are used. But how, more specifically, does it impinge on economic structure or changes in economic structure?

From the viewpoint of MNEs (or potential MNEs) foreign production is likely to be favoured (i) the greater the ownership advantages such firms perceive they possess over their competitors, (ii) the greater the incentive to use these advantages with immobile resources located in a foreign country, and (iii) the more imperfect the markets for channelling intermediate products generated or used by MNEs across national boundaries.

The balance of the OLI advantages is determined by the geographical disposition of immobile resource endowments, the extent to which MNEs believe they can take advantage of the international division of labour by product or process specialization, the competitive strategy of MNEs, and the role played by governments in influencing trade and/or international production. Broadly speaking, most resource-based foreign direct investment (FDI) is prompted by the location of natural resources and the desire of companies to minimize the risk of relying on external markets for the supply of their products, while investment in manufacturing and service activities is usually undertaken either as a defensive response to government restrictions on trade, or in order to protect the ownership rights of property (e.g. technology) transferred and/or to exploit the economies of multinational integration and specialization. In any event, MNEs strive primarily to exploit absolute rather than comparative cost and/or marketing advantages, but once established, in considering the siting of multiple activities, they may take account of comparative as well as absolute costs.

These different rationales for foreign direct investment suggest there is no *a priori* reason to suppose MNEs will affect resource allocation in any particular way; international production may be complementary to or substitutable for trade in final products. On the one hand, if domestic producers are faced with barriers to entry, then by overcoming these foreign firms may improve economic structure; on the other hand import controls imposed by governments may promote inefficient resource allocation. Since too, *in practice,* obstacles to domestic firms may arise from technical inefficiency, it is possible that foreign firms might invest in domestically profitable sectors but not those which are the most internationally competitive.

From the perspective of countries wishing to maximize the benefits of international economic involvement, the above analysis would suggest that, in a no-growth situation, inward direct investment should be directed to those sectors which use the kind of mobile specific advantages with which non-resident firms are favoured, but which need to be used in conjunction with immobile resources with which the recipient country, is comparatively well endowed; while outward investment should occur where the home-country firms have comparative ownership advantages which are best combined with immobile resources located in a foreign country. This kind of hypothesis is a simple extension of the H–O paradigm to include mobile factor endowments and the possibility that firms rather than markets may be more efficient transaction modalities. Consider for example, three countries—the UK, the US, and Portugal. Suppose that the US has a comparative advantage in capital and in generating new technology; the UK has an asset advantage in medium-skill and marketing-intensive activities; and Portugal has an advantage in low-skill activities and land to supply most food products. In such a scenario, it might be in the UK's interest to import direct investment from the US to use in medium-skill industries, and export marketing skills to Portugal to upgrade its low-skill and primary product industries. As a result of the improved resource allocation, the gross national product of each country would be raised.

Such a view on international production is well suited as a policy guideline in respect of those MNE activities prompted by international differences in the structure of factor endowments. Moreover it is possible to justify the imposition of import controls to speed up a process of relocation. It is worth observing that, assuming a two-country world and each firm producing a single product, foreign production will take place where the home country has a comparative advantage in the production of mobile resources (which then becomes locked into its own firms) while the host country has a comparative advantage in the availability of immobile resources. But considering a multi-country, multi-product world, it is quite possible that the home country may still be able to retain its comparative advantage in certain types of immobile resources relative to a *third* country and/or that it develops new products sufficient to retain its comparative advantage vis-à-vis the host country. The timing of the investment may also be relevant with locational factors becoming relatively more important to ownership in the case of mature products (Vernon, 1974).

But this kind of model is less satisfactory in explaining the third kind of international production, which is rationalized production. This is for two reasons. The first is where there is specialization within the MNE, based either on the exploitation of plant economies of scale or the capturing of economies external to the plant but internal to the firm. In the past twenty or so years, the activities of MNEs involving the cross-hauling of international production in similar goods has become an important feature of economic transactions between developed countries: in this respect it has followed the pattern of intra-industry trade (Dunning and Norman, 1985). In such cases US tyre companies might invest in the UK while the UK tyre companies invest in the US; there might be a similar cross-hauling of Portuguese and UK MNE activity in the food-processing industry. How can one explain this phenomenon and what are the normative implications? The basic point is while the ideas set out in previous paragraphs are valid, the ownership and locational advantages and the motivation for internalization are different. In this case, investment flows are based more on ownership advantages specific to firms (synergy and product strategy) than on those which are specific to countries (e.g. a technology most suited to a country's resource endowments or market size); and the strategy of firms becomes as important an influence of inter-market penetration as any locational variable.

Such international production not only has different structural implications, for example it will have less to do with steering resources between sectors and more with the international or regional specialization of ownership within sectors and/or the fragmentation of sectors: it also usually involves the transfer of the type of proprietary advantages for which there is no external market.

In such cases, locational advantages are less easy to identify; indeed it is characteristic of such investment that it is two-way within MNEs producing in broadly similar territories. Where we see the development of genuine global industries and extend the concept of intra-industry trade to embrace intra-industry production, then some types of MNE activity arise simply because there are some industries which require firms to produce in several countries to survive, and their locational policies are to be explained differently from those which are influenced by the disposition of resource endowments and barriers to trade. Cars, computers, cigarettes, and pharmaceuticals fall into this group. Nevertheless, it is possible for locational forces to affect efficiency in (say) the UK vehicles industry, while changes in the balance between inward and outward direct investment may reflect changes in the relative efficiency of different production sites.

The neo-classical trade approach is inappropriate as an explanation or predictor of the impact of MNEs on economic structure for a second reason, and this is unique to intra-industry production (or trade). That is the internalization of the asset transfer and the type of assets possessed by MNEs bring about distinct effects. As we have said, these are not easy to operationalize. Hierarchical control or influence intended to raise the efficiency of the local affiliate, pursuing an 'every tub on its own bottom' policy, is one thing; control exerted to integrate production and marketing operations to promote a global strategy is quite another. In other words, it is possible for there to be an impact on economic and/or market structure which has nothing to do with asset transference *per se* but is simply a rearrangement of the international disposition of assets to reduce the transactions costs of the MNE *in toto*. Here the MNE, by affecting the allocation of resources between countries, may also affect the allocation of resources *within* countries. The assumption is that this will be different from the case if these resources were independently owned because of extra-plant or subsidiary economies which cannot be captured through the market.

Such a desire to control the use of resources for transaction cost-minimizing reasons will not affect all MNEs but only those which are both (i) product, process, or geographically diversified, and (ii) which are able to take advantage of externalities and exploit government imperfections. It is also assumed there is reasonable freedom of transactions within the MNE network. From a structural viewpoint, this should further encourage plant and market specialization—vertically as well as horizontally. At the same time, a regional or global strategy might lead to greater instability of economic activity in a particular country as the opportunities for resiting activity across borders *within* MNEs are widened. One example is the frequent change in the location of regional offices of MNEs in western Europe (*Business International,* 1981). Operations may be more or less truncated, and involve more or less highly skilled personnel. However, one might hypothesize that both inward and outward direct investment will be directed to sectors with an above average ratio of non-operative workers, but that foreign-owned affiliates will have a lower non-operative to operative ratio than domestic MNEs in similar sectors. MNE activity is also likely to be concentrated in sectors in which the market structure is oligopolistic and firms are trade-intensive in respect of either imports or exports (or both).

There is one final aspect of evaluating and/or predicting the impact of MNEs on economic structure. This results from market failure in the product market which may be government- or market-induced. MNEs respond both to government signals and to market structures, and influence resource allocation accordingly. These may not always operate as neo-classical theory would suggest. It is possible that import controls may lead to investment being inefficiently directed, while MNEs operating in an oligopolistic market framework may operate less than optimal strategies.

Static aspects: (b) Technical impact

The second way in which MNEs may impinge upon economic structure is by affecting the efficiency of sectors in which they participate. Here the OLI paradigm would suggest that non-resident firms should be attracted to sectors in which their (net) proprietary advantages over indigenous firms are most pronounced, and/or where there is X inefficiency among host country firms. In so far as any increases in productivity may affect a sector's comparative advantage, they will have allocative consequences as well. At the same time, one might reasonably hypothesize that UK firms which engage in outward direct investment possess advantages over and above those of their foreign competitors. Therefore, one would suppose an outward and inward direct investment would occur in different sectors, and reflect the international distribution of the *origin* of ownership-specific (but mobile) advantages. On the other hand, in the case of horizontal, rationalized foreign direct investment or where there is cross-hauling of production within a sector, as for example in the case of international industries or where domestic and foreign MNEs serve different markets, it is possible that, at least in economies with similar industrial structures, outward and inward investment will occur in the same sectors.

However, although higher productivity may be a *necessary* condition of inward direct investment, it is not a *sufficient* condition. If, for example, US firms can more profitably supply the UK market by exporting from the US, or by licensing UK firms, then, even if local production could be more efficiently undertaken than by their competitors, no inward investment may take place.[13] We would therefore expect, for the production of any particular good or service, inward direct investment to be negatively correlated with the local production of foreign firms/import ratio.

Similarly, as regards outward direct investment, it may be reasonable to suppose that UK firms which are domestically strong and technically efficient will be better able to engage in overseas production, and indeed, that overseas production might itself aid their overall performance vis-à-vis their non-MNE competitors. Again, however, it is necessary to show that locational forces favour foreign rather than domestic production, and that UK firms prefer to internalize their ownership advantages rather than lease them to foreign producers.

One aspect of technical efficiency worthy of special attention is that concerned with the capital (including human capital)—labour ratio. To what extent for example, are the affiliates of foreign MNEs more capital-intensive than their domestic counterparts? Or do UK firms prefer to invest abroad in those sectors which are human capital-intensive? Or how far is the allocation of high-value activities such as research and development affected by the internationalization of production?

Dynamic aspects: Structural adjustment

Finally, MNEs may impinge on economic structure (and changes in economic structure) according to whether they assist or inhibit the reallocation of resources in response to changes in demand or supply conditions. Inward foreign direct investment, for example, might aid UK structural adjustment if it was directed to those sectors producing goods for which the domestic and international demand was growing the fastest, even though these industries were not presently those in which the UK had a comparative trading advantage. Similarly, outward direct investment may be prompted where the prospects for sectors, in which foreign production had an advantage over domestic production, were growing.

In recent years, structural adjustment—other than that in response to short-term shocks—in most developed industrial economies has taken the form of a reallocation of resources towards technology- and/or human capital- and information-intensive sectors, that is, higher value-added activities; such a reallocation has occurred both within manufacturing and service sectors and between these sectors. In the case of the UK, one might pinpoint four contributing factors to such changes—three on the supply and one on the demand side. The first is the emergence of the new industrializing nations (NICs). Here, the theory would suggest the UK should realign its resource allocation away from labour-intensive and low-skill sectors into technology-intensive and high-skill sectors, and/or to promote labour-saving innovations in the former sectors. MNEs could assist this process: UK firms, for example, could invest in the rising prosperity of industrializing nations, in (relatively) labour-intensive sectors but which need the assets and skills and experience which UK firms are able to supply, while foreign MNEs might help to set up plants in the UK in technology- or skill-intensive sectors, but where the ownership advantages favour these, relative to domestic firms. The second change is technological advance, particularly in the area of information technology and changing factor cost ratios which is prompting a similar pattern of resource re-allocation. Again, foreign firms may help (or inhibit) this process in so far as they assist in the transfer of assets and upgrade UK resources in the desired way. The third change, allied to the former two, has been the pressure to reduce X inefficiency and to encourage the rationalization of sectors. Here it may be asked in what way and to what extent do UK firms need to become MNEs to compete in international markets? How far is UK market structure conducive to innovation and growth. Do foreign-based MNEs impede or encourage such adjustment? The fourth factor has been the shifts in consumer demand towards higher income goods. In so far as the direction of MNE investment is often from higher to lower income countries, they may be expected to be in the fore of such shifts. These are some of the questions to which we shall address ourselves.

1.4 EMPIRICAL EVIDENCE: METHODOLOGY

Before considering the empirical evidence for some of the propositions set out in the previous paragraphs, let us briefly summarize the methodology followed. There have been two main approaches to evaluating the impact of MNEs on national economies. The first is the 'alternative position' or 'counterfactual' approach which tries to measure the effect of FDI or foreign production as the difference between the actual impact and that which it is assumed would have occurred in its absence. Such an approach was used by Reddaway in the 1960s to evaluate the effects of outward direct investment on the gross national product of the UK (Reddaway, Potter, and Taylor, 1968). The second, which in some ways involves similar reasoning to the first, is the comparative factual approach: this seeks to compare the activities of MNEs with those of their non-MNE competitors, arguing that the difference between the two may be attributable to the multinationality of the former. This methodology was used by Cohen (1975) in a study of the export performance of US and indigenous firms in South Asia. Its advantages are obvious; actual data are available, and a comparison of, or changes in, performance can be made. But its pitfalls are many, not least that of isolating the 'multinational' effect from other differences between the two groups of firms. Moreover, to draw any policy conclusions, for example with respect to encouraging or discouraging inward or outward investment, implicitly assumes that the marginal and average impact is the same, and that the real opportunity cost lies in the ownership of activity rather than in its direction. Finally it assumes just one 'alternative position'.

Nevertheless, we shall adopt this approach. First, we shall review the main structural characteristics of inward and outward production in 1971 and 1979, compared with other UK companies, and (where data permit) changes in these between these two years. Second, we shall examine the statistical relationship between a number of structural variables and the sectoral distribution within manufacturing industry of three types of production:[14] (a) production of foreign-owned firms in the UK; (b) the foreign production of UK MNEs; and (c) the production of UK firms (including the UK-based MNEs) in the UK. Ideally we would have liked to have separated the UK production of UK MNEs from that of UK uninational firms, but the data do not allow us to do this. The purpose of this exercise is to compare the significance of the three groups of firms on economic structure. By itself, of course, any statistical association does not tell us anything about the direction of causation; we also accept that the level of significance of each variable may be influenced by other variables not included in the equation, and that there may be some multicollinearity between the independent variables.

We tackle the causation problem in the following way. First it could be argued that if, for example, foreign MNEs *respond* to a change in revealed comparative advantage (RCA) in a more positive and significant way than domestic firms, this will impact on future RCA. It is possible to test the impact of whether the activities of the MNEs lead or lag structural change by examining the relationship between the relative change in production between 1971 and 1979 and the value of structural parameters at the beginning and the end of the period. This a later section seeks to do.

The sources of the statistics used are set out in the Appendix to this chapter. Suffice it at this point to say that they embrace all firms in (a) and (b) engaged in manufacturing production from official statistics, and a selection of 188 of the largest UK MNEs covering an estimated 95% of overseas manufacturing of (c). Data specially provided by the Department of Trade and compiled from company accounts enables us to classify (a) and (b) firms by 44 minimum list headings; from an examination of the company accounts of UK MNEs, we have classified (c) firms by 29 headings.

The structural characteristics

Table 1.2 sets out some of the structural characteristics of the three groups of firms being considered. For each characteristic we wished to establish the proportion of the total output of the three groups which was in sectors with below or above the average value of the characteristic. For example, while 43.0% of the sales of UK indigenous firms was in sectors in which the RCA was below average, the corresponding proportion for foreign affiliates and the foreign activities of UK MNEs were 37.9% and 26.9% respectively. The conclusions of the Table are self-evident and suggest, *a priori*, that there are important differences between the groups and hence that there is likely to be a distinctive impact on these elements of economic structure arising from the nationality of ownership of UK based companies and/or geographical involvement of UK owned firms.

The statistical testing

Let us now list some specific propositions about the interaction between MNEs and economic structure.

Table 1.2 Comparison between industrial distribution of UK and MNE related sales and selected structural characteristics: 1979 and 1971–9[a]

		% of total output[b]		change in share of output[b]			
		UK_i	$FMNE_{UK}$	$UKMNE_f$	ΔUK_i	$\Delta FMNE_{UK}$	$\Delta UKMNE_f$
Allocative Efficiency							
(1) RCA	BA	44.2	37.9	26.0			
	AA	49.2	58.1	61.7			
(2) LP	BA	54.0	37.7	25.5			
	AA	45.5	62.2	73.9			
(2*) πs	BA	43.6	31.4	19.7			
	AA	49.9	68.5	78.8			
(3) K/L	BA	69.1	61.1	38.7			
	AA	30.4	38.8	61.7			
(4) NO/OWB	BA	72.8	79.7	75.8			
	AA	26.7	20.2	24.4			
(5) A/S	BA	81.3	81.0	87.0			
	AA	16.1	14.2	12.8			
(6) C	BA	48.0	31.4	19.4			
	AA	51.5	68.5	80.9			
(7) Sp	BA	72.5	76.4	64.2			
	AA	27.0	23.5	36.1			
Technical Efficiency							
(8) RLP	BA	58.8	48.7	37.0			
	AA	34.1	49.1	57.3			
(9) RTP	BA	55.1	47.0	37.4			
	AA	37.5	48.9	48.0			

TABLE 1.2 (continued)

| | | %·of total output change in share of output[b] | | | ΔUK_i | $\Delta FMNE_{UK}$ | $\Delta UKMNE_f$ |
		UK_i	$FMNE_{UK}$	$UKMNE_f$			
Adaptive Efficiency							
(10) GUK	BA	62.4	51.4	42.9			
	AA	37.1	48.5	57.4			
(11) GUKX	BA	58.1	27.1	26.0			
	AA	31.9	67.4	52.9			
(12) GUK	BA				0.87	0.91	0.93
	AA				1.60	1.31	1.34
(13) GUKE	BA				1.15	1.00	0.96
	AA				1.21	1.13	1.34
(14) ΔRCA	BA	50.5	50.0	30.9			
	AA	45.4	46.0	57.6			
(15) ΔLP	BA	89.7	58.1	67.4			
	AA	9.8	41.8	32.9			
(16) ΔNO/OWB	BA	40.8	60.1	66.6			
	AA	58.7	39.8	33.7			
(17) ΔRLP	BA	58.7	43.3	40.9			
	AA	30.5	50.2	43.7			
(18) ΔRCA	BA				0.80	0.95	0.98
	AA				1.70	1.25	1.31
(19) ΔLP	BA				1.13	1.04	1.08
	AA				1.32	1.20	1.23

(20) ΔNO/OWB	BA	1.01	1.13	1.43
	AA	1.33	1.02	0.79
(21) ΔRLP	BA	1.05	1.12	0.94
	AA	1.34	1.01	1.21
(22) VAR	BA	53.7	64.4	n.a.
	AA	45.6	33.4	n.a.
(23) ΔVAR	BA	65.5	59.6	n.a.
	AA	34.0	40.3	n.a.
(24) IIT	BA	23.8	19.0	10.8
	AA	35.1	51.8	48.8
(25) IFT	BA	49.5	20.3	37.3
	AA	26.1	56.4	48.2

[a]For interpretation of headings and structural variables (1)–(25) see text

[b]Change in share of output = share of growth of total output 1971–9 ÷ share of total output in 1971. The BA and AA figures represent the unweighted average of the change of the share of output in the sectors in which the value of the dependent variable is below or above average.

n.a. = not applicable

Source: See Appendix.1.

Totals may not add up to 100.00 where data on the variables are not available for all sectors, or where the shares of the sector are exactly equal to the average for all sectors.

(a) Allocative impact

We have suggested this may vary according to the type of MNE activity, the existing technical and allocative efficiency of UK-owned firms and the extent to which extra or imperfect market forces affect resource allocation. But first let us take a neo-classical type proposition.[15]

Proposition 1. Relative to UK-owned firms producing in the UK, foreign-owned MNEs will produce in those UK sectors which are the most internationally competitive; while the production of UK firms abroad will favour those sectors in which the UK is the least internationally competitive.

This proposition is intended to test the extent to which inward and outward direct investment, relative to the UK production of indigenous firms, is concentrated in sectors in which the UK economy is comparatively advantaged.

The relationship set out in equations (1) and (1a)[16] lends some support to this proposition. In 1979, compared with a negative, though insignificant association, between the ability of manufacturing sectors to compete

$$RCA = 1.03 - 0.0305\,UK_i + 0.0221\,FMNE_{UK} - 0.116\,UKMNE_f$$
$$\qquad\quad (1.46) \qquad\quad (1.18) \qquad\qquad\quad (0.77) \quad (1) \quad (n = 28)$$

$$RCA' = 0.951 - 0.0245\,UK_i + 0.161\,(FMNE_{UK}) \qquad (1a) \quad (n = 44)$$
$$\qquad\quad (1.06) \qquad\quad (1.14)$$

in foreign markets[17] and the distribution of domestically produced output of UK-owned firms (UK_i), there was a positive, though insignificant, association between RCA and the sectoral distribution of foreign affiliates ($FMNE_{UK}$). Indeed, in that year, 63% of the output of such affiliates was in sectors in which the RCA was greater than 1, compared with 44% of UK firms. In other words, relative to their indigenous competitors, foreign MNEs *are* more inclined to invest in sectors in which UK international competitiveness is above average.

The absence of any significant positive relationship between RCA and $FMNE_{UK}$, in either of the two variants of the equation[18] set out is explained by some major exceptions. In the office machinery and computer sectors, for example, the RCA ratio was 0.92, while the foreign participation ratio was 3.1; by contrast, the corresponding figures for bricks, pottery, and glass were 1.21 and 0.33. While, in some cases, such discrepancies reflect the level of disaggregation,[19] in others, even in narrowly delineated sectors, they occur for more substantive reasons. Two of these deserve especial mention. The first is that the RCA ratio is based on sales rather than value-added data and does not distinguish between cases in which imports and exports are competitive to each other and those in which they are complementary with each other. In resource-based sectors such as non-ferrous metals, timber, and food-processing, the latter is the more likely as imported semi-processed goods[20] are necessary ingredients of the final output of a product. While RCA measures based on gross exports overcome this difficulty, they tend to overstate competitiveness in so far as they take no account of imports of similar products. The second is that in some sectors—noticeably those in which there is international oligopolistic rivalry—the prevalence of inward FDI cannot be separated from that of outward FDI. In such cases, firm-specific ownership characteristics rather than locational forces dominate the cross-hauling of international production which is as likely to be complementary as substitutable between countries.

Equation (1) also shows that as far as outward direct investment is concerned, there is no suggestion that this is more concentrated (relative to the domestic activities of UK firms) in sectors in which the UK is comparatively *disadvantaged.* However, omitting oil refining and timber and furniture, the rank correlation coefficient between RCA and the industrial distribution of UKMNE$_f$ is -0.37 and significant at a 10% level. Other research (Dunning and Walker, 1982) has demonstrated that outward direct investment is significantly correlated with *domestic* competitiveness, that is it tends to be concentrated in those sectors which record above average productivity and profitability. That the relationship between the foreign activities of UK MNEs and lack of international competitiveness is not closer may again reflect the fact that, in some sectors, exports and outward direct investment complement, rather than substitute for, each other. Some MNEs find it profitable to exploit their O advantages to some countries via exports and others via foreign production; while, *ceteris paribus,* products at later stages of the product cycle are more likely to be produced abroad than those at earlier stages of the cycle. This is particularly likely to be so in the case of vertical *inter-* or horizontal *intra*-industry trade. We shall return to this point later.

The second proposition relates to the extent to which MNEs are, in some sense, better allocators of resources between sectors than uninational firms. Here, much depends on in which sectors the MNEs perceive they have an ownership advantage over their foreign competitors and whether the productivity advantages originate from the possession or use of mobile or immobile resource endowments. If the former, then both outward and inward investment may be concentrated in similar sectors; if the latter, for example in resource-based sectors, the structure of the two may be different. The proposition set out seeks to test the latter view. We take two measures of allocative efficiency: productivity and profitability.

Proposition 2. Relative to UK-owned firms producing in the UK, foreign-owned MNEs will produce in those UK sectors which are of above average productivity or profitability; while the production of UK firms abroad will favour sectors which are of below average productivity or profitability in the UK.

The only index of productivity which is readily available is the gross value added per head ratio, though ideally one would like to have used a total productivity index.[21] Equations (2) and (2a) suggest that this proposition

$$LP = 8253 - 3195\,UK_i + 1158\,FMNE_{UK} + 3159\,UKMNE_f$$
$$ (424)^{**} \quad\;\; (1.8) \qquad\qquad (6.4)^{**} \qquad (2) \quad (n = 29)$$

$$LP' = 8773 - 2946\,UK_i + 4229\,FMNE_{UK} \qquad\qquad (2a) \quad (n = 44)$$
$$ (3.32)^{**} + (7.78)^{**}$$

is upheld for inward direct investment but not for the foreign activities of UK MNEs. Indeed $UKMNE_f$ is significantly more concentrated in above average productivity sectors than is $FMNE_{UK}$; by contrast, domestic investment by UK firms is significantly concentrated in below average productivity sectors. Both regressions suggest that MNEs prefer to invest in high-productivity sectors; this may also reflect the fact that, in the case of the UK, there is a lot of investment cross-hauling leading to intra-industry production. Finally, it would appear that exports and FDI are most likely to be complementary to each other in above average labour productivity sectors.

The equations on the relationship between profitability and resource allocation portray a similar picture. Defining π as the profit/gross sales ratio, both $FMNE_{UK}$ and $UKMNE_f$ are seen to be positively, though not significantly, associated with profitability, while UK_i is negatively associated with π.

$$\pi = 18.4 - 0.796\,UK_i + 0.280\,FMNE_{UK} + 0.054\,UKMNE_f$$
$$ (1.64) \qquad (0.68) \qquad\quad (0.17) \qquad\quad (2^*) \quad (n = 29)$$

$$\pi' = 16.9 - 0.637 + 0.388 \qquad\qquad\qquad\qquad\qquad (2a^*) \quad (n = 44)$$
$$ (1.60) \quad\; (1.59)$$

Allied to the second proposition are two others to do with the direction of MNE activity towards capital- or technology-intensive sectors or those in which product quality, consistency and reliability is important. These latter industries, mainly supplying branded consumer goods (or inputs to same) may be expected to generate above average by advertising to sales expenditure. In this case, one is identifying O-type advantages which apply irrespective of whether they are being exploited by trade or production. One might then expect one and/or other of the advantages to be positively related to both $FMNE_{UK}$ and $UKMNE_f$.

Proposition 3. Relative to UK-owned firms producing in the UK, foreign-owned MNEs will produce in UK sectors which record an above average (a) net capital expenditure per employee (K/L), (b) non-operative/operative wage bill NO/OWB, and/or (c) advertising/sales ratio (A/S); UK firms abroad will also produce in these sectors, although the sub-sectors of their particular strengths will probably differ.

Equations (3) and (3a) show that, unlike UK firms producing in the UK, both foreign affiliates of foreign MNEs and UK MNEs abroad concentrate in capital-intensive sectors and that in both cases significantly so. There is a positive but insignificant association between inward MNE activity and the skill-intensity ratio, (see equations (4) and (4a)); but the reverse relationship applies to UK firms producing both in the UK and abroad. There was a very weak negative association between A/S and inward and outward MNE activity, (see equations (5) and (5a)); but relative to the domestic production of UK firms, such activity is geared more to sectors supplying branded consumer goods in which quality control is perceived to be especially important.

$$K/L = 852 - 242\,UK_i + 121\,FMNE_{UK} + 269\,UKMNE_f \quad (3) \quad (n = 29)$$
$$(3.59)^{**} \quad (2.1)^{*} \qquad (6.05)$$

$$K/L' = 829 - 207\,UK_i + 383\,FMNE_{UK} \qquad\qquad (3a) \quad (n = 44)$$
$$(2.67)^{**} \quad (8.05)^{**}$$

$$NO/OWB = 77.3 - 5.09\,UK_i + 1.97\,FMNE_{UK} - 1.24\,UKMNE_f$$
$$(1.64) \qquad (0.74) \qquad\qquad (0.6) \quad (4) \quad (n = 29)$$

$$NO/OWB' = 68.3 - 3.87\,UK_i + 0.97\,FMNE_{UK} \qquad\qquad (4a) \quad (n = 44)$$
$$(1.44) \qquad (0.59)$$

$$A/S = 3.27 - 0.364\,UK_i - 0.003\,FMNE_{UK} - 0.024\,UKMNE_f$$
$$(1.44) \qquad (0.01) \qquad\qquad (0.14) \quad (5) \quad (n = 29)$$

$$A/S' = 3.03 - 0.339\,UK_i - 0.011\,FMNE_{UK} \qquad\qquad (5a) \quad (n = 39)$$
$$(1.53) \qquad (0.08)$$

The final proposition in this section concerns the impact of *market* structure. Here the suggestion is that one of the main advantages of MNEs *qua* MNEs is the ability to exploit the advantages of international division of labour and the economies of synergy of multiple operations; that is, to capture economies internal to the MNE, but external to the individual affiliates of MNEs. If this is so, MNEs are likely to be directed to sectors which have economies of firm size or those in which the concentration ratio is above average.

Proposition 4. Relative to UK-owned firms producing in the UK, both foreign affiliates in the UK and UK MNEs abroad will concentrate in sectors in which the competition is oligopolistic, as reflected by an above average concentration ratio (C) and/or where size of enterprise confers some productivity advantage (Sp).

Equations (6) and (6a) show that the first part of this proposition is generally supported, but that the association between $FMNE_{UK}$ and $UKMNE_f$ and C is statistically insignificant. Equations (7) and (7a) reveal that while UK firms at home and abroad tend to concentrate in sectors in which the largest firms record above average labour productivity, this is not so with $FMNE_{UK}$; indeed, if anything the reverse seems to be the case. Excluding the oil-refining sector, the positive association between Sp and $UKMNE_f$ becomes significant at a 1% level, but the association between Sp and UK_i becomes negative, at near 5% level.

$$C = 56.4 - 1.93\,UK_i + 0.15\,FMNE_{UK} + 1.00\,UKMNE_f \quad (6) \quad (n = 29)$$
$$(1.14)(0.1)\phantom{\,FMNE_{UK} +}(0.9)$$

$$C' = 50.0 - 1.14\,UK_i + 1.52\,FMNE_{UK} \quad\quad\quad (6a) \quad (n = 44)$$
$$(0.78)(1.69)$$

$$Sp + 1.13 + 0.0130\,UK_i - 0.0362\,FMNE_{UK} + 0.0246 \quad (7) \quad (n = 29)$$
$$(0.38)(1.23)\phantom{\,FMNE_{UK} +}(1.09)$$

$$Sp' = 1.15 + 0.081\,UK_i - 0.0095\,FMNE_{UK} \quad\quad\quad (7a) \quad (n = 44)$$
$$(0.30)(0.57)$$

The conclusion of the above statistical exercises is that the interaction between a number of indices of UK economic structure and the distribution of UK manufacturing activity by the affiliates of foreign MNEs and that of UK MNEs abroad is generally different from that of UK-owned firms in the UK, and that the direction of the difference is such as to suggest that the UK's involvement in international production has made a positive contribution to domestic allocative efficiency.

(b) Technical impact

We now turn to examine some propositions concerning the extent to which activities of MNEs are related to the technical or sectoral efficiency of UK production. The literature strongly suggests that, locational considerations apart, MNEs will invest in those sectors in which they perceive they have the most technological and other advantages over their indigenous competitors. It may therefore be reasonable to hypothesize that these advantages may result in higher productivity ratios—particularly labour productivity ratios—as many of the advantages are capital- or technology-intensive and labour-saving.

Proposition 5. Relative to that of UK firms in the UK, production by foreign MNEs in the UK is likely to be concentrated in industries in which the productivity of the foreign affiliate is highest relative to the domestic firms; while the foreign production of UK firms is likely to be concentrated in sectors where domestic firms have a productivity advantage over their foreign competitors.

Acknowledging the usual caveats of any measure of the performance of firms—and particularly that between MNEs, or parts of MNEs,[22] and the total activities of uninational firms—we take two. The first is the relative net output per man year in the UK (RLP) of foreign affiliates;[23] and the other an index of relative total factor productivity of foreign affiliates (RTP).[24] Equations (8) and (9) show that there is some evidence to support both propositions, but that the association is more pronounced using the RLP than the RTP measure.[25]

$$RLP = 1.30 - 0.0396 \, UK_i + 0.0081 \, FMNE_{UK} + 0.0476 \, UKMNE_f$$
$$(1.65) \qquad (0.39) \qquad\qquad (2.99)^{**} \quad (8) \quad (n = 27)$$

$$RLP' = 1.34 - 0.491 + 0.0571 \qquad\qquad (8a) \quad (n = 41)$$
$$(1.55) \quad (2.93)^{**}$$

$$RTP = 1.07 + 0.0019 \, UK_i - 0.0071 \, FMNE_{UK} + 0.0235 \, UKMNE_f$$
$$(0.11) \qquad (0.45) \qquad\qquad (1.85) \quad (9) \quad (n = 27)$$

$$RTP' = 1.09 - 0.0001 \, UK_i + 0.0139 \, FMNE_{UK} \qquad (9a) \quad (n = 42)$$
$$(0.00) \qquad (1.27)$$

The detailed statistics reveal that in 34 of 41 sectors, foreign affiliates record a higher labour productivity than UK-owned firms, and in 30 of 41 sectors a higher total productivity. Moreover, equation (8a) clearly shows that relative to UK_i, $FMNE_{UK}$ favour sectors in which their ownership advantages are the most pronounced.[26] However, of greater interest, and contrary to expectations, is the highly significant *positive* association between outward investment and RLP. One possible explanation is that—as suggested by earlier equations—there is some complementarity between different forms of foreign involvement, and that *firm-* rather than *country-*specific O advantages explain the presence of MNEs in certain sectors. It would also seem that UK firms are relatively more profitable overseas in industries in which the UK is most internationally competitive.[27] For example, in 1979, 62% of the foreign sales of UK companies were in sectors in which the normalized RCA (net export) ratio was above average for manufacturing industry. Data on other structural variables for each of the three categories are not available to make other comparisons of technical efficiency. However, information on the comparative export propensity between all UK firms and US subsidiaries in 1973/74 (Dunning, 1976) suggests that, while in 22 of the 36 manufacturing sectors for which data are available, the export/sales of US subsidiaries exceeds that of all UK firms, there is significant correlation between the normalized share of the sales of US subsidiaries and differences in export propensity.

(c) Adjustment impact

There are various ways in which the efficiency at which resources are reallocated might be evaluated. We deal first with changes in market growth.

(i) *Adaptation to market needs*

To what extent do foreign MNEs invest in growth sectors or in those in which the UK is becoming more internationally competitive? How do the affiliates of UK MNEs adjust to market changes relative to UK firms in the UK? The hypothesis to be tested is that the O advantages of MNEs enable them to be better choosers of growth sectors or to create growth, and/or allow them to redirect their attention to those sectors which are becoming more productive and/or internationally competitive.

Proposition 6. Relative to UK firms, foreign MNEs are more concentrated in growth sectors, while they adjust to changes in market demand better than UK firms. Depending on their position in the product cycle and the relative significance of O and L advantages, UK firms overseas will invest in sectors in which the UK's international competitive position is deteriorating.

We present four pairs of equations. The first pair—(10) and (11)—relate the sectoral shares of gross sales of the three groups of firms in 1979 to two measures of market growth, *viz* growth of UK *output* (GUK) and growth of UK *demand* plus exports (GUKX); the second pair—(12) and (13)—the share of the *change* (Δ) in production between 1971 and 1979 of UK-based firms divided by the share of the production in 1971 of these sectors (UK_i and $FMNE_{UK}$)[28] to these same measures.

$$GUK = 319 - 12.1\,UK_i + 913\,FMNE_{UK} + 7.53\,UKMNE_f$$
$$(1.6)(1.41)(1.5)(10)\quad(n = 29)$$

$$GUK' = 327 - 12.0\,UK_i + 16.0\,FMNE_{UK}(10a)\quad(n = 44)$$
$$(2.02)*(4.4)**$$

$$GUKX = 349 - 11.7\,UK_i + 7.90\,FMNE_{UK} + 8.13\,UKMNE_f$$
$$(1.80)(1.28)(1.64)(11)\quad(n = 27)$$

$$GUKX' = 354 - 13.3\,UK_i + 16.1\,FMNE_{UK}(11a)\quad(n = 42)$$
$$(2.62)*(5.33)**$$

$$GUK = 95 + 112\,\Delta\,UK_i + 107\,\Delta\,FMNE_{UK} + 23.7\,\Delta\,UKMNE_f$$
$$(349)**(0.87)(0.72)(12)\quad(n = 17)$$

$$GUK' = 109 + 23.8\,\Delta\,UK_i + 195\,\Delta\,FMNE_{UK}(12a)\quad(n = 37)$$
$$(1.79)(4.28)$$

$$GUKX = 233 + 89.5\,\Delta\,UK_i + 26\,\Delta\,FMNE_{UK} + 27.1\,\Delta\,UKMNE_f$$
$$(2.32)*(0.17)(0.70)(13)\quad(n = 17)$$

$$GUKX' = 219 + 16.1\,\Delta\,UK_i + 122\,\Delta\,FMNE_{UK}(13a)\quad(n = 36)$$
$$(1.18)(2.59)*$$

The equations suggest that foreign firms in the UK and UK firms abroad are distinctly more inclined to invest in growth sectors than UK firms in the UK, and that this is particularly noticeable when growth includes exports from the UK (GUKX). In equations (10a) and (11a) the $FMNE_{UK}$ coefficient seems to be positively significant at the 1% level, but foreign production by UK MNEs is positively but not significantly related to growth. However, the bivariate correlation coefficients between the $FMNE_{UK}$ and $UKMNE_{UK}$ and the growth of the UK market plus exports work out at $+0.567$ and $+0.653$, and both are significant at a 1% level. While 67% of UK production by foreign affiliates in 1979 was in sectors which recorded above average rates of growth between 1971 and 1979, the corresponding proportion for indigenous firms was 32%.

Between 1971 and 1979, foreign affiliates in the UK increased the value of their output at more than twice the rate of indigenous firms in the

UK.[29] Moreover, as equations (12) and (13) show, there was also a tendency for foreign affiliates (relative to the UK competitors) to increase their market share in sectors which were growing the fastest; indeed, the correlation coefficient between GUK' and $FMNE_{UK}$ in equation (12a) was $+0.631$ and significant at a 1% level.

Over a slightly shorter period (1972/3–1979) the output of UK firms abroad grew relative to that of the domestic production by UK firms in 14 of 17 sectors. There was some tendency for domestic and foreign growth by UK MNEs to be complementary to each other:[30] two major exceptions were the drink and tobacco industries.[31]

(ii) *Adaptation to structural change*

The next set of propositions examines the extent to which MNEs and other firms adapt their output to changes in economic structure. We shall take indices of such change for the period 1971–9:

   (i) Changes in RCA;
  (ii) Changes in labour productivity;
 (iii) Changes in non-operative/operative wage bill;
 (iv) Changes in the labour productivity gap between foreign affiliates and indigenous firms;

and follow the methodology adopted in testing Proposition 7.

Proposition 7. Relative to UK firms producing in the UK, foreign affiliates of MNEs will produce in sectors in which (i) the RCA ratio has most improved, (ii) productivity has most increased, (iii) the human capital content has most increased, (iv) the productivity gap between affiliates and indigenous firms has (relatively) increased.

In the case of the foreign production of UK MNEs one might predict a positive relationship between its sectoral distribution and (ii) and (iii) and a negative relationship between that distribution and (i) and (iv).

And a dynamic version of Proposition 7:

Proposition 8. Relative to UK firms producing in the UK, foreign affiliates of MNEs may be expected to increase their share of productiom in sectors in which (i) the RCA ratio has most improved, (ii) productivity has most increased, (iii) the human capital content has most increased, (iv) the productivity gap between affiliates and indigenous firms has (relatively) increased.

The predictions for the activities of UK MNEs abroad follow those set out in Proposition 8.

The set of equations (14)–(16) and (17)–(21)[32] set out below suggest a mixed interaction between MNE involvement and structural change.

$$\Delta RCA = -\,0119 + 0.060\,UK_i - 0.438\,FMNE_{UK} + 0.0398\,UKMNE_f$$
$$(14) \quad (n = 28)$$
$$(0.37) \qquad\quad (3.02)** \qquad\qquad (3.41)**$$

$$\Delta LP = 3.76 - 0.273\,UK_i + 0.150\,FMNE_{UK} + 0.183\,UKMNE_f$$
$$(15) \quad (n = 29)$$
$$(3.04)** \qquad (1.96)* \qquad\qquad (3.1)**$$

$$\Delta LP' = 3.88 - 0.282\,UK_i + 0.330\,FMNE_{UK} \qquad\qquad (15a) \quad (n = 44)$$
$$(3.37)** \qquad (6.45)**$$

$$\Delta NO/OWB = 1.11 - 0.006\,UK_i + 0.012\,FMNE_{UK} - 0.013\,UKMNE_f$$
$$(16) \quad (n = 29)$$
$$(0.58) \qquad\quad (1.3) \qquad\qquad (1.84)$$

$$\Delta RLP = 1.13 - 0.0300\,UK_k + 0.0759\,FMNE_{UK} - 0.0505\,UKMNE_f$$
$$(17) \quad (n = 26)$$
$$(0.86) \qquad\qquad (2.39)* \qquad\quad (2.0)*$$

$$\Delta RCA = -0.396 + 0.186\,\Delta UK_i + 0.117\,\Delta FMNE_{UK} - 0.004\,\Delta UKMNE_f$$
$$(18) \quad (n = 13)$$
$$(2.85)* \qquad\quad (0.64) \qquad\qquad (0.08)$$

$$\Delta RCA' = -0.553 + 0.0439\,\Delta UK_i + 0.363\,\Delta FMNE_{UK} \quad (18a) \quad (n = 36)$$
$$(1.25) \qquad\qquad (3.0)**$$

$$\Delta LP = 2.41 + 2.73\,\Delta UK_i - 1.49\,\Delta FMNE_{UK} + 0.297\,\Delta UKMNE_f$$
$$(19) \quad (n = 13)$$
$$(3.6)** \qquad\quad (0.51) \qquad\qquad (0.38)$$

$$\Delta NO/OWB = 1.24 - 0.048\,\Delta UK_i - 0.26\,\Delta FMNE_{UK} + 0.071\,\Delta UKMNE_f$$
$$(20) \quad (n = 13)$$
$$(0.86) \qquad\qquad (0.12) \qquad\qquad (1.23)$$

$$\Delta RLP = 1.21 + 0.068\,\Delta UK_i - 0.291\,\Delta FMNE_{UK} + 0.12\,\Delta UKMNE_f$$
$$(21) \quad (n = 13)$$
$$(0.66) \qquad\qquad (0.74) \qquad\qquad (0.12)$$

$$\Delta RLP = 1.21 + 0.068\,\Delta UK_i - 0.291\,\Delta FMNE_{UK} + 0.12\,\Delta UKMNE_f$$
$$(21) \quad (n = 13)$$
$$(0.66) \qquad\qquad (0.74) \qquad\qquad (0.12)$$

$$\Delta RLP' = 1.61 + 0.123\,\Delta UK_i - 0.700\,\Delta FMNE_{UK} \qquad (21a) \quad (n = 37)$$
$$(1.98)* \qquad\qquad (3.27)**$$

For example, UK MNEs appear to be increasing their foreign activities in areas where the UK's RCA is increasing, while the reverse is the case for foreign affiliates in the UK, see equation (14). On the other hand, both UK firms and foreign affiliates in the UK seem to be redirecting their output to sectors in which RCA is improving, see equations (18) and (18a). Whereas UK MNEs tend to favour sectors in which labour productivity has risen the most, the opposite is the case for UK firms in the UK, see equations (15) and (15a). However, this latter group of firms appears to be redirecting its output towards sectors with rising productivity (see equation (19)). No relations of any significance emerge between changes in the skill-intensity ratio and the distribution of output of MNEs vis à vis UK firms in the UK. Changes in the productivity gap (favouring $FMNE_{UK}$) seem to be positively and significantly associated with the distribution of output of foreign affiliates, but negatively associated with that of UK firms abroad, see equation (17). On the other hand, UK firms producing in the UK have adjusted their output towards industries in which RLP is rising, while the opposite has occurred in the case of foreign affiliates in the UK, see equations (21) and (21a).[33]

MNEs, domestic and international market structure

There is one other structural aspect of MNEs which requires consideration. This concerns the role of MNEs as coordinators of separate economic activities across national boundaries, and the effect this has on domestic, that is UK, economic structure. While it is an inherent feature of MNEs that they internalize international intermediate product markets, they may also impinge on such markets *within* a country and on final goods traded between countries. This market-replacing effect is inadequately captured in the statistics but may have far-reaching implications both on the type of economic activity carried out and on its determinants. Received theory would suggest that relative to non-MNEs, MNEs will tend to concentrate in sectors in which there are the most opportunities for minimizing transaction costs. Data on such market-replacing activities are extremely limited. However, it might be reasonably argued that the greater the degree of product or process diversification within MNEs, and the more they practise product or process specialization between countries, the more likely the structural impact of MNEs will be of concern to those countries that do not wish to identify themselves with the resulting international division of labour. We illustrate from just two aspects of internalization: (i) vertical integration in the UK, and (ii) international product or process specialization between different parts of the same MNE in different countries.

Proposition 9. To minimize transaction costs or capitalize on market failure, UK affiliates of foreign MNEs, and/or UK MNEs abroad relative to UK firms producing in the UK will tend to concentrate in sectors which are vertically integrated (VAR), or are increasing their integrating (ΔVAR), and/or, within an international context, offer opportunities for intra-industry (IIT), intra-firm trade (IFT).

$$\text{VAR} = 37.8 - 0.203\,\text{UK}_i - 0.391\,\text{FMNE}_{\text{UK}} \qquad (22) \quad (n = 44)$$
$$\phantom{\text{VAR} = 37.8 - }(0.29) \qquad\quad (0.9)$$

$$\Delta\text{VAR} = 1.95 - 0.542\,\text{UK}_i + 0.403\text{FMNE}_{\text{UK}} \qquad (23) \quad (n = 44)$$
$$\phantom{\Delta\text{VAR} = 1.95 - }(5.03)^{**} \qquad\quad (6.1)$$

$$\text{ITT} = 0.838 - 0.0279\,\text{UK}_i + 0.0126\,\text{FMNE}_{\text{UK}} - 0.0016\,\text{UKMNE}_f$$
$$\phantom{\text{ITT} = 0.838 - }(1.4) \qquad\qquad (0.96) \qquad\qquad (0.15) \quad (24) \quad (n = 22)$$

$$\text{IFT} = 39.2 - 2.51\,\text{UK}_i + 5.20\,\text{FMNE}_{\text{UK}} - 2.74\,\text{UKMNE}_f$$
$$\phantom{\text{IFT} = 39.2 - }(3.45)^{**} \qquad\quad (2.34)^{**} \qquad\quad (25) \quad (n = 22)$$

These propositions are tested in equations (14) and (18).[34] We consider the results of each form of internalization separately.

(a) Vertical integration

There is no evidence that the affiliates of foreign-based MNEs are more vertically integrated in their UK activities than are indigenous firms (see equation (22)). In 1979, foreign affiliates in the UK recorded a higher net/gross output ratio than their UK competitors in 17 of 40 sectors and a lower ratio in 22 sectors. Neither is there any suggestion that the foreign participation ratio is highest in sectors with the highest value-added ratios. However, within industries, broadly interpreted, it would appear that foreign affiliates do concentrate in sectors with above average ratios (the main exception is oil). The degree of vertical integration in both foreign and domestic firms has changed little in the 1970s, but equation (23) suggests quite strongly that, in sectors in which foreign affiliates are most markedly represented, vertical integration has *fallen* either absolutely or relatively to indigenous firms. One reason for this may be that there is increasing specialization within sectors of products supplied by MNEs across national boundaries. The intra-industry trade equation (22), suggests there is a positive but insignificant association between ITT and the foreign participation ratio; excluding the UKMNE_f variable increases the observations to 37, and the significance of the $FMNE_{UK}$ variable to 1.68. On the other hand, equation (25) shows there is a significant positive association between the propensity of foreign affiliates to engage in intra-firm trade and the sectoral distribution of their output. The association goes in the opposite direction for UK MNEs, but all the data suggest that UK-related MNE activity is likely to have had as much, if not a greater, effect on market-replacing activities between the UK and the rest of the world, than within the UK.

(b) International product specialization

Regrettably, intra-industry data are rarely presented in sufficient detail to allow us to separate *vertical* from *horizontal* transactions. But again casual empiricism suggests that both UK and foreign-based MNEs are increasingly viewing Europe as a single market, and engaging in intra-plant product specialization. *Inter alia,* this is confirmed by the propensity of MNEs to concentrate in sectors in which the trade intensity of the UK is increasing. Between 1971 and 1979 the value of imports plus exports to total manufactured goods produced in the UK of all firms rose from 36% to 50%. However, in sectors in which foreign-based MNEs had a participation ratio of 1 or more, the average rise was from 44% to 74%. A rank correlation between the $FMNE_{UK}$ ratio in 1979 and change in trade intensity between 1971 and 1979 was +0.424. Data on changes in intra-industry trade ratios and the distribution of MNE activity tell the same story. Both foreign affiliates and UK MNEs abroad are strongly concentrated in sectors in which the intra-industry trade ratio rose the sharpest between 1971 and 1979; this is not the case with domestic production of UK firms. That these latter sectors happen to be those in which MNEs are more likely to adopt a global strategy and maintain a 100% equity interest, suggests growing internalization of economic activity across national boundaries vis à vis that within national boundaries. This is an important conclusion which has far reaching policy implications; these are taken up in the final chapter of this volume.

(c) Product diversification

Data on industrial diversification are extremely limited but what there are[35] do not support the proposition that MNEs, either absolutely or relative to non-MNEs, tend to concentrate in sectors which themselves diversify into other sectors; indeed, compared with an average diversification index[36] for the leading MNEs in 1981 of 24.3, petroleum, automobiles, and office equipment—three of the most international of sectors—recorded ratios of 12.6, 16.9, and 20.5 respectively. And while it might be expected that enterprises, in a particular industry, which are the most multinational will be more diversified than non-MNEs, partly because they are larger and partly because they operate in different economic environments; in any one country, the range of output of their affiliates may well be less than that of indigenous firms. But the very fact that an affiliate is linked with an enterprise which is more diversified than its indigenous competitors may give it a competitive edge. Certainly there are several examples leading the diversification of many sectors, such as drink, tobacco, and chemicals in the last five years; unfortunately as far as the UK is concerned, there are no recent data on diversification trends to enable us to go beyond the casual empiricism.[37]

1.5 CONCLUSIONS AND POLICY IMPLICATIONS

The previous sections have demonstrated that, in a variety of ways, MNEs have had an impact on UK economic structure different from that of UK indigenous firms producing in the UK (including the UK output of UK MNEs). This is a reflection both of the differences in the configuration of the OLI advantages facing MNEs and the way in which they have translated these into conduct and performance. Despite the imperfections of data, there are strong suggestions that the O advantages of MNEs have assisted the UK's economic restructuring in the 1970s towards higher allocative and technical efficiency; and that MNEs have adjusted to changing L advantages of UK resource endowments rather more positively than uninational indigenous firms. However, one cost of the greater internationalization of the UK economy may have been the loss of some structural autonomy on the part of the UK, as MNEs may encourage more corporate internalization between different parts of their operations and less sectoral or cross-sectoral integration within the UK. This may have the effect of reshaping both market and economic structure and, in so far as the common ownership of separate production affiliates matters, is relevant to the pattern of resource allocation. There is insufficient evidence to suggest whether or not this kind of impact on structure has worked to the long-term advantage of the UK economy; much depends on the international market structure in which MNEs compete and the signals given to them by various governments. There can, however, be little doubt that, by promoting structural interdependence between national markets,

MNEs have made the UK economy more vulnerable to changes in international demand and supply conditions.

What should UK government policy be to MNE activity? What modifications of existing policies are needed? Clearly much depends on how far it is considered that foreign ownership and/or control of domestic resource allocation matters, and on one's judgement of the possible risk of being dependent on external economic and political forces. In practice, too, much will rest on the domestic macro-economic policies pursued and particularly those relevant to structural change. What also seems to be increasingly likely is that, at least as far as investment within the OECD is concerned, internationalization of some industries by some form of cross-border affiliation[38] will continue. The important question is to ensure that, where it is thought appropriate, one's own firms can survive and compete with foreign firms. This inevitably requires governments to re-examine their role in producing the right economic environment and to promote that goal. As MNEs become more footloose in their choice of markets to exploit and/or sites from which to produce, inevitably locational factors will enter into the calculation, factors which governments can affect by their policies. These range from import controls to encourage import-substituting investment, to providing the right educational, technological, and communications infrastructure to aid firms in newer sectors in the restructuring process.

The fact that the kind of impact we have attributed to MNEs has been associated with their increasing involvement in the UK economy suggests that the market itself may be the main adjustment mechanism. Why then should any government intervention be required, other than to ensure the market works properly? The answer lies in the divergence between private and social economic welfare and the very specific impact which MNEs have on this divergence. It is well accepted that in conditions where governments seek only economic goals, and in the absence of no externalities or structural market imperfections, then a laissez faire policy might be appropriate. But in a modern industrialized economy, particularly one subject to rapid technological change and faced with all kinds of institutional rigidities and structural disequilibria, this is an extremely unlikely situation, as indeed is the belief that the only role of governments is a negative interventionist one. Indeed, in the long run, this could be worsened by foreign firms which might be equipped to overcome the market failure gaining a monopoly position and creating an even more unacceptable market position. Governments have the responsibility of positive interventionism whenever there are costs and benefits which it is not reasonable to expect individual firms to bear. In the past this included the provision of roads and public utilities. Today the modern equivalents include airports and telecommunications facilities.

Since the early 1970s, successive UK governments have adopted liberal policies towards both inward and outward investment. And yet, as demonstrated in the negotiations over the Nissan involvement in the UK, the influence which the government can exert *de facto* is very considerable indeed.[39] In general, our findings would support a continuation of such policies, with one caveat which we shall now discuss.

The question is why government interventionism should be different as a result of MNE activity? This question is tackled in more detail in the final chapter, but in the UK context, two policies—as they are applied to all firms—may need to be modified as a result. For example, monopoly and restrictive practices legislation presupposes that competition is being suppressed by the behaviour of firms. If MNEs, because of their multi-nationality, introduce additional imperfections, then such legislation may become the more pressing or reviewed. The fact too that MNEs may need to be more flexible in their locational policies may require governments to pay more attention to various areas of adjustment assistance than they would in their absence.

The second is that there may need to be additional policies to be specifically directed to MNEs. These almost exclusively result from the ability of MNEs to gain or improve market positions, or to circumvent government policy as a result of their geographical flexibility. In a competitive situation these can work for good; in a dynamic or monopolistic situation they may work against social well-being. Unfortunately for a particular country, it is not the affiliate but the MNE which is the decision-taking centre and hence its range of action may be limited.

One example is international transfer pricing which is specific to MNEs. Transfer pricing can clearly distort the productivity and profitability figures of affiliates; the ability to benefit from it may also affect the allocation of investment between countries. The case of Hoffman La Roche is a well known one; the Inland Revenue now operates a separate unit to monitor transfer prices which can be a problem arising from the operation of UK as well as foreign MNEs.

Transfer pricing is an example of the benefit of corporate integration which may not necessarily benefit the host country. In other words, though justified as a means of overcoming market failure, it may worsen the resource allocative effects between countries, if structural market failure is increased via the power of MNEs and/or the distributive benefits of such internalization are recouped by the home country.[40]

This kind of structural impact is extremely difficult to deal with as it is to do with the extent to which the corporate international division of labour of MNEs is consistent with that perceived by host countries to be in their best interests. Moreover, the power of MNEs gained as a result of geographical and product diversification may not be easily identifiable or dealt with by national monopolies legislation. From a structural developmental aspect this is especially seen in developing countries with respect to high value-added activities, but it is no less important in the UK in sensitive and high-technology industries, where there is an important foreign presence. It would seem the best the government can do is to attempt, at a negotiating stage with MNEs, to ensure that their intentions are consistent with national goals and any major modification to these intentions is discussed. And while, in some cases, legislation may be taken at a supranational level, for example by the EEC to ensure that abuses arising from monopoly power are minimized, in some cases—and this is best seen by the debate over supplies by affiliates of US MNEs to the Siberian pipeline—the conflict is not so much between the MNE and the host government as between home and host governments.

Another area of concern may be the pace of adjustment. A recent OECD study has shown that MNEs have adjusted to recession and technological changes more speedily than indigenous firms. In one sense this is to be applauded; in another it creates short-term employment problems, particularly in those regions most hard hit. The case for governments being informed about such changes is a persuasive one, although the balance between social responsibility and protecting one's competitive position is a difficult one.

The dilemma between seeking the benefits of economic interdependence and national sovereignty is being increasingly brought into sharp focus as a result of the activities of MNEs. In the UK, as in most developed countries, it is witnessed by the role of MNEs in technological innovation, and the industrialization of newly industrializing countries. There can be little doubt that MNEs are at the forefront of such changes which have far-reaching implications for both positive and negative interventionism by governments. Negative interventionism may be necessary to protect against distortion between social and private interests due to structural market imperfections and the actions of other governments. Positive interventionism may be required to assist the adjustment processes by firms (including MNEs), and to promote the economic and technological infrastructure needed for countries if they are to optimize their share of inward and outward investment, and fully benefit from it.

Together with closer monitoring and appreciation of plans of MNEs, these moves could accomplish much. But there is still a residual of concern to do with distributional questions between countries, and the growth of international transactional economic power which does not fit comfortably under the umbrella of domestic economic policy. These issues may well prove to be one of the main challenges posed by the MNEs in the later 1980s.

NOTES

1. Of which foreign-owned MNEs in the UK accounted for 1 million and UK MNEs 3.5 million; of the latter figure employment outside the UK was 1.4 million.
2. As set out in Dunning (1981), Chapter 5. See also the introductory chapter of this volume.
3. The best known examples include Cadbury (cocoa), Lever (palm oil), Dunlop (rubber) and Tate & Lyle (sugar). For further details see Stopford (1974) and Dunning (1983b).
4. The history of UK direct investment is particularly instructive on this point. See Coram (1967) and Buckley and Roberts (1982).
5. According to Streit (1949) of the 327 important inventions discovered between 1750 and 1850, Britain was responsible for 38%, France for 24%, Germany for 12%, and the US for 16%. In the following half-century the corresponding figures were 16%, 19%. 21% and 32%.
6. For example, Keynes (1920), Cairncross (1953), and Brinley Thomas (1967).
7. Except presumably in cases where these were unsuccessful. For example, see Coram (1967) and Svedberg (1981).
8. In some cases, such as pharmaceuticals, this is still retained, but in others, such as motor vehicles, it has been eroded since around 1960.
9. The literature on this subject is extensive. See for example Teece (1981), Casson (1979), Contractor (1980), and Dunning (1983).
10. That is, by internalizing supplies it avoided some of the transaction costs associated with an uncertain market (Vernon, 1983).
11. These developments are summarized in Dunning (1983b). For a more extensive treatment see Chandler (1977).
12. The development of the motor car industry in Australia is particularly instructive (see e.g. Penrose, 1956).
13. In other words inward investment will occur only when (a) foreign firms are more productive than local firms, and (b) direct investment is the most profitable way of exploiting the market it is intended to serve.
14. We would be the first to accept that changes in the distribution of activity *between* manufacturing and the service sector in the UK have been at least as significant as those *within* manufacturing industry. Unfortunately, data on MNE activity in the service sector are extremely limited.
15. We refer to the neo-classical *type* proposition, as, taking a literal interpretation of the H–O assumptions, there would be no foreign direct investment by or in an economy.
16. In this, and in later relationships, we test the association of inward MNE activity together with outward MNE activity and separately from it. This is because we have 44 observations for the former and only 29 for the latter.
17. As measured by revealed comparative advantage (RCA) RCA is defined as $1 + (Xi - Mi)/(Xi + Mi) \div 1 + (Xt - Mt)/(Xt + Mt)$ where X = exports, M = imports, i a particular sector, t = all sectors.
18. Defined as the proportion of the total sales of foreign affiliates accounted for by a particular sector divided by the corresponding share of all UK enterprises of that sector.
19. As the extent of foreign participation may not be evenly distributed *within* the sectors.
20. NB: Not raw materials which would be classified to the non-manufacturing sector.
21. Similar to the one used in testing Proposition 7. See also Appendix 1.
22. As set out, for example, in Dunning and Pearce (1981).
23. = net output per head of foreign affiliates − net output per head of indigenous firms.
24. See Appendix for definition.
25. This suggests that the relatively higher labour productivity of $FMNE_{UK}$ is at least partially offset by a lower capital productivity.
26. One major exception being other clothing where RTP of foreign affiliates in the UK was 188 while their participation ratio was 0.10.
27. For example, in terms of price cost margins, the rank correlation between the industrial distribution of the outward capital stake (a) and (b) net output per head and (c) profit-

ability, outward capital stake in 1971, 1974, and 1978 varied from $+0.60$ to $+0.94$ and in every case it was significant at a 5% level (Dunning and Walker, 1982).

28. For example, taking a sector j

$$UK_{ij} = \frac{UK_{ij}\,1979 - UK_{ij}\,1971}{UK_{it}\,1979 - UK_{it}\,1979} \div \frac{UK_{ij}\,1971}{UK_{it}\,1971}$$

29. The growth of output of foreign affiliates was 446.5% compared to that of indigenous firms (in the UK) of 195.0%. Between 1972/3 and 1979, the output of UK firms abroad rose by an estimated 275.1%.
30. The rank correlation between the relative rate of growth of UK firms abroad and the growth of UK output being $+0.29$.
31. Excluding these sectors, the rank correlation increased to $+0.45$.
32. We have set out the two (independent) variable equations only when the statistical significance of one or more of the variables is improved.
33. This is further evidence of narrowing of the spillover effect of inward investment in the UK and the productivity gap between foreign affiliates and UK firms. See also the Globerman contribution to this volume (Chapter 6).
34. A dynamic version of proposition 10 was also tested. This supported the findings of proposition 10 but revealed no new relationships.
35. As reviewed in Stopford and Dunning (1983)
36. The percentage of sales in other than the industry to which firms are classified.
37. For a more thorough examination of the interaction between the geographical and industrial diversification of MNEs see Pearce (1983).
38. That is, not just via MNEs, but through licensing, sub-contracting, and other non-equity routes.
39. A review of UK government policy towards inward investment is set out in Hood and Young (1982).
40. The point that unlike within a country there are no means of compensating for an uneven distribution of income at an international level is explored in Chapter 1 of Dunning (1974). See also the chapter by Vaitsos in the same volume.

APPENDIX 1. SOURCES OF DATA

(a) The independent variables

Data on the sectoral distribution of output (= gross sales) of indigenous firms in the UK (UK$_i$) were obtained from the *Censuses of Production 1971 and 1979 return.*The gross sales of indigenous firms are equal to gross sales of UK enterprises less those of the subsidiaries of foreign-owned firms. Data on the sales of foreign affiliates (FMNE$_{UK}$) were obtained from the same censuses, supplemented by additional data provided by the Business Statistics Office. Data on UK firms abroad (UKMNE$_f$) for 1979 were calculated by the author directly from the accounts of 188 of the largest UK MNEs accounting for between 90% and 95% of all UK foreign direct investment. The data were then checked for consistency with those on UK assets owned abroad published triennially by the Department of Trade (in *Business Monitor* M4). Data for UK MNEs for 1972/3 were derived from Houston and Dunning (1976).

(b) The dependent variables

Much of the data on production-related variables was obtained from the *Censuses of Production 1971 and 1979*. This includes: (i) labour productivity (LP) (net output ÷ total employment); (ii) profitability (π) (gross output − gross value added ÷ gross output); (iii) skill ratio (NO/OWB) (non-operative wage bill ÷ operative wage bill; (iv) concentration ratio (C) (% of gross output accounted for by 5 largest enterprises); (v) size effect (Sp) (average productivity of largest two groups of enterprises in any sector ÷ by average productivity of rest of sector); (vi) output growth (GUK) (growth of gross output in UK 1971/1979); (vii) the value added ratio (VAR) (gross value added ÷ gross output). The advertising ratio (AS) (advertising/sales) was obtained from data published in the *Census of Production, 1968*. The relative total productivity index (RTP) which attempts to measure the efficiency of $FMNE_{UK}$ relative to that of UK_i is obtained by calculating (for 1979) the formula:

$$\frac{WL + \pi S}{W*L + \pi*S} \text{ for } FMNE_{UK}$$

where W = wage bill L numbers employed, π the profit/sales margin S = sales of $FMNE_{UK}$ and W* + π* the wage bill and profit/sales margin for UK_i. Separate calculations were made for non-operative and operative wages. The formula essentially relates to the actual value added of $FMNE_{UK}$ to the opportunity cost of the resources used; as a proxy this opportunity cost the payments to the same quantity of comparable factor services by indigenous firms is used. For further details, see Dunning (1971).

For the main trade-related variable (RCA) as defined on p. 51, data were provided by the Department of Trade Statistics Division and are similar to those used to produce import and export ratios published by *Economic Trends*. The variable GUKX estimates the total demand for goods (= UK-produced goods and imports) plus exports and is derived from the same source, as were data for the ratio intra-industry trade (IIT). The intra-firm trade ratio (IFT) was derived from data published by the US Department of Commerce (1981). As a proxy for this latter variable we took the imports from a proportion of total US imports in 1977 accounted for related parties (e.g. US affiliates abroad) as published in Helleiner (1981).

REFERENCES

Baranson, J. (1979). *Technology Transfer to Developing Countries*, New York: Praeger

Buckley, P. J. and Roberts, B. R. (1982). *European Direct Investment in the U.S.A. before World War I*, London: Macmillan

Business International (1981). *Locating a West European Office*, Geneva: Business International

Cairncross, A. K. (1953). *Home and Foreign Investment 1870–1913*, Cambridge: Cambridge University Press

Casson, M. C. (1979). *Alternatives to the Multinational Enterprise*, London: Macmillan

Casson, M. C. (1984). General Theories of the Multinational Enterprise: A Critical Examination, University of Reading Discussion Papers in International Investment and Business Studies, No. 82, April

Caves, R. E. (1974). Causes of direct investment: foreign firms' shares in Canadian and United Kingdom manufacturing industries, *Review of Economics and Statistics*, **56**, August

Caves, R. E. (1980). Investment and location policies of multinational companies, *Zeitschrift für Volkswirtschaft und Statistik*, **3**, 321–327

Caves, R. E. (1982). *The Multinational Enterprise and Economic Analysis*, Cambridge: Cambridge University Press

Chandler, A. D. Jr (1977). *The Visible Hand: The Managerial Revolution in American Business*, Cambridge, Mass.: Harvard University Press

Chandler, A. D. Jr (1981). *Global Enterprise, Economic and National Characteristics: an Historical Overview*, Harvard University (mimeo)

Cohen, R. B. (1975). *Multinational Firms and Asian Exports*, New Haven: Yale University Press

Contractor, F. J. (1980). The composition of licensing fees and arrangements as a function of economic development of technology recipient nations, *Journal of International Business*, **XI**, Winter

Coram, T. C. (1967). The Role of British Capital in the Development of the United States, M.Sc. thesis, University of Southampton

Dunning, J. H. (1958). *American Investment in British Manufacturing Industry*, London: Allen & Unwin

Dunning, J. H. (1971). *Studies in International Investment*, London: Allen & Unwin

Dunning, J. H. (1976). *US Industry in Britain*, London: Wilton House Publications

Dunning, J. H. (1981). *International Production and the Multinational Enterprise*, London: Allen & Unwin

Dunning, J. H. (1982). International business in a changing world environment, *Banco Nazionale del Lavoro*, December

Dunning, J. H. (1983a). Market power of the firm and international transfer of technology, *International Journal of Industrial Organization*, **1**, 333–351

Dunning, J. H. (1983b). Changes in the pattern of international production: The last 100 years, in Casson, M. C. (ed.), *The Growth of International Business*, London: Allen & Unwin, 1983

Dunning, J. H. and Cantwell, J. A. (1983). American direct investment and European technological competitiveness, *L'Actualité Economique*, July–September

Dunning, J. H. and Norman, G. (1985). *Intra-industry Production as a Form of International Economic Involvement*, in Erdilek, A. (ed.), *Multinationals as Mutual Invaders*, London: Croom Helm

Dunning, J. H. and Pearce, R. D. (1981). *The World's Largest Industrial Enterprise*, Farnborough: Gower

Dunning, J. H. and Walker, P. (1982). *The Competitiveness and Allocative Efficiency of UK Manufacturing Industry and Foreign Direct Investment* (mimeo)

Dunning, J. H. (ed.) (1974). *Economic Analysis and the Multinational Enterprise*, London: Allen & Unwin

Flowers, E. B. (1976). Oligopolistic reactions on European and Canadian direct investment in the US, *Journal of International Business*, **7**, No. 2, Fall–Winter

Graham, E. M. (1978). Transnational investment by multinational firms: a rivalistic phenomenon, *Journal of Post-Keynesian economics*, **1**, 82–99

Graham, E. M. (1985). *Intra-Industry Direct Foreign Investment, Market Structure, Firm Rivalry and Technological Performance*, in Erdilek, A., op. cit.

Helleiner, G. K. (1981). *Intra-firm Trade and Developing Countries*, London: Macmillan

Hood, N. and Young, S. (1982). British policy and inward direct investment, *Journal of World Trade Law*, **15**, No. 3, May–June

Houston, T. and Dunning, J. H. (1976). *U.K. Industry Abroad*, London: Financial Times

Katrak, H. (1981). Multinational firms' exports and host country commercial policy, *Economic Journal*, **91**, 454–465

Keynes, J. M. (1920). *The Economic Consequences of the Peace*, London: Macmillan

Knickerbocker, F. T. (1973). *Oligopolistic Reaction and Multinational Enterprise*, Boston, Mass.: Graduate School of Business Administration, Harvard University

Kojima, K. (1978). *Direct Foreign Investment*, London: Croom Helm

Krugman, P. (1981). Intra-industry specialisation and the gains from trade, *Journal of Political Economy*, **89**, 959–973

Lake, A. W. (1979). Technology creation and technology transfer by multinational firms, in R. G. Hawkins (ed.), *The Economic Effects of Multinational Corporations*, Greenwich, Conn.: JAI Press

Pearce, R. D. (1983). Industrial diversification amongst the world's leading multinational enterprises, in Casson, M. C. (ed.), *The Growth of International Business*, London: Allen & Unwin, 1983

Penrose, E. T. (1956). Foreign investment and the growth of the firm, *Economic Journal*, **66**, 220–235

Quirin, G. D. (1980). *Changes in the Parameters of Comparative Advantage: the Multinational Corporation*, Toronto, Working Paper 80–04

Reddaway, W. C., Potter, S. J., and Taylor, C. T. (1968). *The Effects of UK Direct Investment Overseas: Final Report*, Cambridge: Cambridge University Press

Saul, S. B. (1960). The American impact on British industry 1895–1914, *Business History Review*, **3**, No. 1, December

Steuer, M. D. *et al.* (1973). *The Impact of Foreign Investment in the United Kingdom*, London: HMSO

Stopford, J. M. (1974). The origins of British-based multinational manufacturing enterprises, *Business History Review*, **48**, 303–335

Stopford, J. M. and Dunning, J. H. (1983). *Multinationals: Company Performance and Global Trends*, London: Macmillan

Streit, C. (1949). *Union Now: A Proposal for an Atlantic Federal Union of the Free,* New York: Harper

Svedberg, P. (1981). Colonial enforcement of foreign direct investment, *Manchester School of Economic and Social Studies,* **50,** 21–38

Teece, D. J. (1981). The multinational enterprise: market failure and market power considerations, *Sloan Management Review,* **22,** 3–17

Teece, D. J. (1983). Technological and organisational factors in the theory of the multinational enterprises, in M. C. Casson (ed.), *The Growth of International Business,* London: Allen & Unwin, 1983

Thomas, B. (1976). The historical record of international capital movements, in J. H. Dunning (ed.), *International Investment,* Harmondsworth: Penguin

US Department of Commerce (1981). US Direct Investment Abroad 1977, Washington DC: US Government Printing Office

Utton, M. A. (1979). *Diversification and Competition,* Cambridge: Cambridge University Press

Vernon, R. (1974). The location of economic activity, in J. H. Dunning (ed.), *Economic Analysis and the Multinational Enterprise,* London: Allen & Unwin

Vernon, R. (1983). Organisational and institutional responses to international risk, in R. Herring (ed.), *Managing International Risk* Cambridge: Cambridge University Press

2

The United States

THOMAS A. PUGEL*

2.1 INTRODUCTION: RECENT HISTORICAL TRENDS

The United States, long considered the most important home country to multinational enterprises (MNEs), in the latter half of the 1970s also became the largest host to inflows of foreign direct investment (FDI). The US share of total outflows of FDI from 13 large developed countries was 61% during 1961–7, falling to 29% during 1974–9, but still the largest single source. The US share of the stock of outward FDI by these countries has fallen more slowly, from 54% in 1967 to 48% in 1976. The US share of total inflows of FDI into these 13 countries was less than 3% during 1961–7, but rose to almost 27% during 1974–9.[1]

The activities of US-based MNEs are of major importance to the US economy, and the activities of US affiliates of foreign MNEs are rather quickly developing some importance. There are a variety of ways of quantifying this importance. For instance, profits earned by foreign affiliates of US firms ($31.8 billion) plus the profits earned by US affiliates of foreign firms ($8.9 billion) equalled 25.5% of all after-tax corporate profits identified in the US national income accounts in 1981.[2] More spectacularly, home employment in US manufacturing MNEs (12.5 million) plus employment in foreign manufacturing affiliates of US MNEs (4.9 million) plus employment in US manufacturing affiliates of foreign MNEs (0.6 million) equalled 96.9% of total domestic employment in US manufacturing industries in 1977.[3]

Inward and outward FDI have generated ongoing debates about the proper posture of US government policies towards each. To date, US policies towards inward and outward FDI have been liberal, and thus consistent with the general policy approach towards the economy. This

*The author is grateful for the support and inspiration of the Jules Backman Faculty Fellowship in Business Economics in pursuing this research. He also gratefully acknowledges the provision of certain data by Keith Maskus from the study by Stern and Maskus (1981), and the research assistance of Jang Ro Lee.

approach is based on a belief in the ability of market forces to 'guide' the economy through the interplay of decentralized private decision-making. The ideology of this approach is grounded not only in the history of the United States but also in a pragmatic realization of the difficulties of designing systematic activist government policies towards a large, complex and dynamic economy. The government then intervenes on an *ad hoc* basis in specific areas of the economy in response to particular economic problems or political pressures. This general approach is evident, for instance, in policies towards international trade, where relatively free trade is taken as the norm, but departures occur as particular industries acquire substantial protection from imports, and as exports are controlled in a small number of industries, usually for reasons of national security and defence.

US government policy towards inward and outward FDI is noticeably more liberal than its policy towards trade. Policy towards FDI attempts to be essentially neutral, thus permitting free play to market forces in FDI decisions, with exceptions largely limited to a few industries where considerations of national sercurity and defence lead to policy restrictions on FDI. Another exception of sorts exists in that many state and local governments actively compete to attract inward FDI (and domestic investment) by offering various packages of incentives.

US outward and inward FDI have both grown substantially over the last several decades, but the rates of growth have varied within this period. The stock of US outward FDI, as measured by the 'direct investment position', totalled $11.8 billion in 1950 and had nearly tripled by 1960. The stock of US inward FDI was $3.4 billion in 1950 and had slightly more than doubled by 1960. The growth of outward and inward FDI continued in the 1960s and 1970s, as shown in Table 2.1. The growth rate of outward FDI continued to be higher during the 1960s, but inward FDI then grew more quickly during the 1970s and into the 1980s.

The growth of outward FDI was especially rapid in the manufacturing sector during the 1960s, as shown in Table 2.1, while the share of petroleum in outward FDI fell during the 1960s and 1970s. By 1970 manufacturing was the single most important sector in both outward and inward FDI, accounting for more than 40% of the stock of each. Since 1970 the share of manufacturing in outward FDI has remained roughly constant. The share of manufacturing in inward FDI has fallen off rather sharply since 1970, to about one-third in 1982, but it is still the single largest sector. The share of trade in inward FDI rose dramatically during the 1970s.

Several factors appear to be influencing the recent growth of inward FDI. In general, the United States is an attractive market within which to locate, given its large size and high per capita income, although its growth

TABLE 2.1 Stock of US inward and outward FDI, total and selected sectors, 1962–82, US$ million (and percentages of totals)

Sector	1962 Inward	1962 Outward	1970 Inward	1970 Outward	1979 Inward	1979 Outward	1982 Inward	1982 Outward
Total	7612 (100)	37226 (100)	13270 (100)	75480 (100)	52260 (100)	192648 (100)	101844 (100)	226359 (100)
Manufacturing	2885 (37.9)	13250 (35.6)	6140 (46.3)	31049 (41.1)	20029 (38.3)	83564 (43.4)	32186 (31.6)	92386 (40.8)
Petroleum	1419 (18.6)	12725 (34.2)	2992 (22.5)	19754 (26.2)	9903 (22.3)	41553 (21.6)	20488 (20.1)	51223 (22.6)
Trade	750 (9.9)	NA	994 (7.5)	6201 (8.2)	11167 (21.4)	20709 (10.7)	20630 (20.3)	28332 (12.5)
Insurance and finance	1943 (25.5)	NA	2256 (17.0)	7190 (9.5)	7155 (13.7)	27459 (14.3)	14844 (14.6)	35083 (15.5)

Stock of FDI defined as 'direct investment position', net claims of parents on affiliates' assets. FDI is defined as ownership or control of 10% or more of an affiliate's voting equity by one foreign person or company.
NA: Not available.
Sources: OECD (1981), and *Survey of Current Business*, August 1983.

rate is only moderate. Several influences specific to the 1970s can be identified. First, many foreign firms had strengthened their technological, marketing, and management capabilities, providing them with stronger ownership-specific advantages that could be exploited through FDI. Second, there were several shifts in relative economic environments (i.e. in locational factors). Comparative production costs became more favourable to the United States, largely due to the decline in the international value of the dollar, although this factor has more than reversed itself since 1979. Actual or threatened US protectionism has drawn in FDI in some industries, such as consumer electronics. The depressed US stock market made entry by acquisition more attractive and more prevalent in the 1970s. Furthermore, the United States became relatively more attractive due to shifts in the economic and political environments in other countries, especially European countries. The United States maintains rather few regulations on layoffs and plant relocations, providing an edge to that country in business perceptions of the flexibility of operations. More general concerns about political stability and political trends also favour the United States, so that US operations are viewed as a way of diversifying against political (and economic) risks. The confluence of these factors has resulted in rapid growth of the stock of inward FDI since 1970, as inward FDI was only 17.6% as large as outward FDI in 1970, but had risen to 45.0% by 1982.

This study endeavours to examine some of the important relationships between US inward and outward FDI and the economic structure of the manufacturing sector of the US economy. In the first section the patterns of inward and outward FDI are documented and compared, both to each other and to the US pattern of commodity trade in manufactures. In the second section the relationships between inward and outward FDI and technology creation and transfer are explored, especially as FDI affects research and development (R&D) activities. In the final section implications of these various relationships for the structure and international competitiveness of the US economy and for US and global economic welfare are discussed, with special attention to propositions by Kojima (1978, 1982) that US outward FDI is generally trade-destroying and thus often harmful to US economic welfare.

2.2   FDI AND COMMODITY TRADE

The extent of multinational activity varies across industries. This variation has been used to develop an understanding of the causes or determinants of multinational operations, and also to develop some understanding of the effects of inward and outward FDI on the national and global economy.

This research methodology is used here. The section begins by presenting and examining measures of US inward and outward FDI intensities for a sample of 56 manufacturing industries. The determinants of the inter-industry pattern of outward and inward FDI intensities are then presented by outlining the eclectic paradigm of ownership-specific advantages, internalization advantages, and locational factors and by summarizing the relevant empirical evidence. Next, relations between the patterns of FDI and the patterns of US commodity trade are explored, through correlation analysis and by summarizing research on the extent to which US outward FDI acts as a substitute for or complement to US exports.

The inter-industry pattern of inward and outward FDI intensities

A formal analysis of the patterns of inward and outward US FDI requires an appropriate set of matched data on these patterns. No such data are readily available, and apparently no previous researcher has amassed such data. Such a data set nonetheless can be constructed from publicly available information.

The FDI intensity of an industry is often defined as the ratio of some measure of the size of FDI activity in the industry to the total size of the industry. Size can be measured by value added, assets, employment, or sales, although more exotic measures such as profits are sometimes used when the former measures are not available (Bergsten, Horst, and Moran, 1978; Pugel, 1978, 1981). In general, data availability dictates the choice of size measure.

The source of data on outward US FDI used here is the benchmark survey of 1977 (US Department of Commerce, 1981). This source includes data on assets, employment, and sales of the foreign affiliates of US-based multinationals. The data on employment and sales can be readily, if not perfectly, concorded with data on domestic employment and shipments in each industry, creating two alternative measures of outward US FDI intensity. All variable definitions and data sources are discussed further in Appendix 2.1.

Data on inward US FDI are available in the 1974 benchmark survey (US Department of Commerce, 1976) and the 1980 benchmark survey (US Department of Commerce, 1983). Data from each benchmark survey can be used to generate two measures of inward FDI intensity, one based on employment and the other on sales. These are thus closely comparable

TABLE 2.2 Inward and outward FDI employment ratios

Industry (BEA)	Outward FDI employment as a percentage of domestic employment 1977	Inward FDI employment as a percentage of domestic employment 1980	Inward FDI employment as a percentage of domestic employment 1974
Meat products (201)	6.40	4.87	2.68
Dairy products (202)	27.44	2.53	NA
Canned and preserved fruits and vegetables (203)	25.02	2.59	4.72
Grain mill products (204)	49.78	6.37	NA
Bakery products (205)	15.29	10.17	4.89
Beverages (208)	28.81	7.13	6.82
Other food products (209)	57.82	9.47	6.65
Tobacco manufactures (210)	85.40	NA	NA
Textile mill products (220)	7.44	2.48	2.37
Apparel (230)	6.11	0.80	1.12
Lumber and wood products (240)	5.84	1.86	0.70
Furniture and fixtures (250)	3.83	1.36	0.46
Pulp, paper, and board mills (262)	38.80	6.73	2.92
Miscellaneous converted paper products (264)	24.21	5.23	1.21
Paperboard containers and boxes (265)	13.18	3.72	2.03
Printing, publishing (270)	3.11	3.27	2.47
Industrial chemicals, plastics materials, and synthetics (281)	53.31	16.96	14.99
Drugs (283)	113.98	24.92	16.02
Soaps, cleaners, and toilet goods (284)	105.41	14.14	10.46
Paints (285)	23.75	1.23	1.00
Agriculture chemicals (287)	51.57	27.19	25.51
Chemical products, n.e.c. (289)	67.51	16.28	5.53
Petroleum and coal products (291 + 292 + 299)	126.53	38.77	49.75
Rubber products (305)	68.41	6.41	3.25
Miscellaneous plastics products (307)	8.61	4.72	1.59
Leather and leather products (310)	6.01	NA	NA

Industry			
Glass products (321)	38.95	3.59	NA
Stone, clay, cement, and concrete products (329)	19.05	6.61	0.69
Primary ferrous (331)	8.61	3.19	2.66
Primary non-ferrous (335)	31.26	10.88	9.77
Metal cans, metal plumbing fixtures, and fabricated metal products, n.e.c. (341 + 343 + 349)	21.06	3.56	2.86
Cutlery, handtools, and hardware (342)	16.07	1.13	0.98
Fabricated structural metal products (344)	6.72	2.81	2.11
Screw machine products (345)	12.81	0.96	0.28
Metal stampings and forgings (346)	12.33	4.21	0.13
Engines and turbines (351)	14.19	4.36	NA
Farm and garden machinery (352)	39.53	5.80	NA
Construction, mining, and materials handling machinery (353)	45.64	6.74	2.35
Metalworking machinery (354)	13.11	2.59	0.50
Special industry machinery (355)	17.67	12.31	3.72
General industry machinery (356)	21.44	4.03	3.31
Office, computing, and accounting machines (357)	79.63	4.70	2.60
Refrigeration and service industry machinery (358)	16.20	1.22	0.36
Machinery, except electrical, n.e.c. (359)	9.39	1.45	0.36
Household electrical applicances and electric lighting and wiring equipment (363 + 364)	46.97	NA	2.15
Radio, television, and communication equipment (366)	44.92	5.63	2.75
Electronic components and accessories (367)	58.64	14.40	3.90
Electrical machinery, n.e.c. (369)	28.68	NA	3.82
Motor vehicles and equipment (371)	95.63	8.24	0.45
Other transport equipment (379)	8.05	2.06	0.15
Scientific instruments and measuring and controlling devices (381)	24.69	5.45	2.61
Optical and ophthalmic goods (383)	13.05	4.83	NA
Surgical, medical, and dental instruments and supplies (384)	35.30	16.59	1.96
Photographic equipment (386)	48.78	2.96	0.86
Watches and clocks (387)	45.96	33.51	NA
Miscellaneous manufactured products (390)	22.21	5.90	3.65

Note: NA: Not available.

to the measures of outward FDI intensity, but refer to 1974 and 1980 rather than 1977. It is believed that the 1974 survey was incomplete, which would lead to an understatement of the inward FDI intensity, but the extent of the downward bias is not known. The 1980 survey apparently is more accurate.

Data on the three employment-based measures are shown in Table 2.2, for a breakdown of the US manufacturing sector into 56 industries at the 2-digit and 3-digit level. Several observations are immediately apparent. First, in every industry the extent of outward FDI is larger than that of inward FDI, with the exception of printing and publishing for the 1977–80 comparison. Second, the extent of inward FDI in 1980 is proportionately greater than the extent in 1974, for all but three industries for which comparisons can be made. Of these three, only petroleum and coal products shows a substantial decline. Third, two industries, petroleum and coal products and watches and clocks, exhibit inward FDI intensities of over 30%. Of these two, watches and clocks, one of the smallest industries in the sample, appears to be atypical, and thus may create 'outlier' problems in any statistical analysis. Although the 1974 inward FDI measure is not available because data on employment and sales were suppressed for disclosure reasons, data reported on 1974 assets is consistent with the large presence of inward FDI in this industry.

Casual inspection of Table 2.2 suggests that the patterns of inward and outward FDI intensities are positively correlated. This can be explored more formally using correlation coefficients among the various measures of inward and outward FDI intensities, as reported in Table 2.3. The sample size varies from correlation to correlation because of variations in missing data. The correlations between the two measures of 1977 outward FDI and between the two measures of 1974 or 1980 inward FDI are all very high. Essentially the same information is contained in the measures based on employment and sales. Most of the subsequent analysis will report results using only the employment-based measures, as results using sales-based measures are very similar.

The correlations between the 1974 inward FDI measures and the 1980 measures are also very high. It is not surprising that the correlations are not perfect, given changes that probably occurred over this time period, in which inward FDI grew appreciably.

Of major interest are the positive correlations between the patterns of inward and outward FDI intensities. The inward measures based on employment are positively correlated with the outward measures at the 0.001 level of significance or better. The measure of inward FDI based on 1974 affiliate sales is also highly correlated with the measures of outward FDI, but the inward measure based on 1980 affiliate sales shows somewhat lower, though still highly significant, correlations. If the

	Outward FDI sales as a percentage of domestic shipments 1977	Inward FDI employment as a percentage of domestic employment 1974	Inward FDI sales as a percentage of domestic shipments 1974	Inward FDI employment as a percentage of domestic employment 1980	Inward FDI sales as a percentage of domestic shipments 1980
Outward FDI employment as a percentage of domestic employment 1977	0.87 (56) 0.001	0.62 (47) 0.001	0.62 (47) 0.001	0.67 (52) 0.001	0.43 (55) 0.001
Outward FDI sales as a percentage of domestic shipments 1977		0.66 (47) 0.001	0.60 (47) 0.001	0.61 (52) 0.001	0.37 (55) 0.001
Inward FDI employment as a percentage of domestic employment 1974			0.95 (47) 0.001	0.88 (45) 0.001	0.65 (47) 0.001
Inward FDI sales as a percentage of domestic shipments 1974				0.90 (45) 0.001	0.76 (47) 0.001
Inward FDI employment as a percentage of domestic employment 1980					0.90 (52) 0.001

Note: The number in parentheses below the correlation coefficient is the number of observations, and the number below this is the significance level using the one-tailed test.

watches and clocks industry is omitted from the sample, these latter cor-relations rise to 0.51 and 0.48 with the employment- and sales-based measures of outward FDI, respectively.

Determinants of the patterns of inward and outward FDI intensities

The previous section demonstrates that the extent of both inward and outward FDI varies across industries. Some agreement has been reached that the variation can be explained by a Dunning's eclectic theory or OLI paradigm, perhaps augmented by the influences of the dynamics of oli-gopolistic competition.

The eclectic theory can be summarized with reference to a company based in one country that is considering selling one of its products in a foreign country. The essential choices facing the company are to export the product to the foreign country, to license a foreign firm to produce and sell the product in the foreign market, or to establish a foreign affiliate to produce and sell the product in the foreign market under the administra-tive control of the parent. The latter is termed 'horizontal FDI'. Of course, variations such as joint ventures and exporting under long-term contract can also be included, but they are not necessary to the basic thrust of the theory.

The choice between exporting and foreign production in some form is largely dependent on locational factors, including production cost differ-ences, transport costs, tariffs or non-tariff barriers, and differences in taxa-tion or regulation. In addition, the choice may be influenced by the need to adapt the product to the foreign market, which may be done more effec-tively if production is located within the market, or by the desirability of establishing the image of a local supplier.

If production in the foreign market is potentially attractive, the decision between licensing and foreign direct investment is largely dependent on the ownership-specific advantages that the firm uses in its production and marketing of the product, and on any advantages to internalizing the use of these ownership-specific assets in the foreign market.

Other things equal, the firm is expected to be at a disadvantage in com-peting with foreign firms in their local market, because the firm initially lacks knowledge of the local situation. Thus, the firm requires some offset-ting ownership-specific advantages to be successful in local production through FDI. The advantages that the firm is likely to exploit through FDI are proprietary intangible assets, because of internalization advan-tages. Such intangible assets include product and process technology, capabilities in marketing (promotion, distribution, customer servicing), and organizational and managerial capabilities or methods. Licensing of such assets requires arm's-length transactions that are often beset by a variety of infirmities, including impacted information, the danger of opportunism, and attendant high negotiating and enforcement costs. Thus, use of these ownership-specific advantages in foreign production is often effected through FDI to establish administrative control of affiliate production and sales.

The dynamics of oligopolistic competition may also influence the extent of FDI. An oligopolist may often react to a competitive move by one of its rivals through imitation, in order to prevent the rival from gaining any competitive move by one of its rivals through imitation, in order to prevent the rival from gaining any competitive advantages. Thus, when one oligopolistic firm moves to establish a foreign affiliate in an area, several of its rivals may follow closely.

Aspects of these theories can be extended to forms of FDI other than horizontal. For instance, a firm may integrate forward internationally, to form a foreign sales and service affiliate, in order to control administratively the marketing of its products and avoid the infirmities of arm's-length transactions with independent local distributors.

The implications of these theories have been tested empirically against the pattern of outward US FDI in numerous studies (see Pugel, 1981, for a recent study that includes references to many previous studies). A number of these studies examine the inter-industry variation in outward FDI intensity, either in total or in terms of penetration into particular host countries. Most studies find that FDI intensity is positively and significantly related to measures of R&D intensity and advertising intensity, variables proxying the importance of technology and marketing capabilities as proprietary intangible assets to the industry. The study by Pugel (1981) also finds positive relations between FDI intensity and a measure of the importance of managerial capabilities, and between FDI intensity and capital cost advantages based on capital requirements for the establishment of a plant of minimum efficient scale. Thus the importance of ownership-specific and internalization advantages is generally supported by these studies.

Some locational factors can also be studied in this framework. The importance of tariffs in drawing in FDI is often found in studies of penetration of host markets. High transport costs are not found to be as closely related to FDI as might be expected. High transport costs should favour FDI, but firms in such industries, which tend to be regional or local, may simply fail to consider any form of foreign operations. Scale economies should favour centralization of production, and (Pugel) 1981 finds that the importance of scale economies was negatively and significantly related to outward FDI intensity.

Studies of individual firms have reinforced some of these findings, especially the role of R&D and advertising in explaining the extent of multinationality. In addition, Bergsten, Horst, and Moran (1978) and Caves and Pugel (1982) show that, within an industry, the larger firms tend to be more multinational. The meaning of this latter result is not obvious, but it is at least consistent with the proposition that ownership-specific advantages might explain both the competitive success of a firm in the domestic market, leading to its large size, and its ability to engage in FDI successfully.

The influence of oligopolistic reaction was studied directly by Knicker-bocker (1973), who examined the dates of establishment of foreign affiliates in various countries by US firms in a number of industries. He found that bunching of entry dates became more pronounced across the industries studied as the concentration level increased, although bunching was less evident in industries with very high concentration. This is consistent with the importance of imitative oligopolistic reaction in loose-knit oligopolies, those with medium levels of concentration.

The importance of oligopolistic behaviour as an influence on FDI is also suggested by the positive and significant relationship between outward FDI intensity and concentration often found in inter-industry studies, after controlling for other influences such as R&D and advertising intensity. This could reflect the higher levels of FDI resulting from imitative oligopolistic reaction. It could also result from the difficulties facing large forms in more concentrated industries that attempt to grow through an increase in domestic market share. Rivals can be expected to react strongly against any losses in their own shares, and any increase accomplished could lead to an anti-trust action. These firms may then turn to growth through FDI.

In contrast to outward US FDI, there are relatively few studies of FDI into the United States. Arpan, Flowers, and Ricks (1981) survey research on inward FDI. They cite a variety of studies that explore the motivations of individual foreign firms investing in the United States. The motivations elicited largely comprise locational factors, such as the size of the US market, US political stability, access to skilled labour or natural resources, access to US technology, rising US protectionism, and the devaluation of the dollar in the 1970s and the attendant improvement in relative labour costs. This naturally follows because the individual firm is responding to the question, 'why did we invest in the US rather than elsewhere?' The firm would be much less able to answer a question such as, 'why did we invest in the US while a firm in another industry (or even one of our rivals) did not?' Yet answers to the latter sort of question are necessary to examine the importance of ownership-specific and internalization advantages.

There is apparently no solid study of the inter-industry variation in inward FDI intensities. The study by Lall and Siddharthan (1982) is perhaps the best in terms of its research design, but it results appear to be undermined by a failure to apply the correct concordance between the BEA industry definitions and SIC industries.[4] For instance, Lall and Siddharthan find insignificant simple and partial correlations between inward FDI intensity in 1974 and R&D intensity. Yet in the data assembled for this study, the correlations between each of the measures of 1974 inward FDI intensity and a measure of R&D intensity (scientists and engineers as a fraction of the industry's labour force) are both positive and significant at the 0.03 level using a one-tailed test.

A variant of the oligopolistic reaction hypothesis has been studied using data on FDI by European firms into the United States. Both Flowers (1976) and Graham (1978) found a bunching of the establishment of the US affiliates of European firms soon after US firms in each of a number of industries established European affiliates, during the 1950s and 1960s. This is consistent with oligopolistic reaction on an international level, in which oligopoly firms cross-penetrate each others' home markets in order to establish hostages in the pursuit of a stable oligopolistic equilibrium.

As shown in the previous section, the pattern of inward FDI intensity is similar to that of outward FDI. It is likely that some of the influences determining outward FDI also affect the inward FDI pattern. This is confirmed for the bunching of entry predicted by oligopolistic reaction.

To date there is no study that confirms the importance to inward FDI of variables like R&D and advertising intensity, as the results of Lall and Siddharthan (1982) are largely negative. A pattern of inward FDI intensity that is similar to that of outward FDI is at least consistent with the eclectic theory. According to this approach, foreign firms require ownership-specific advantages, largely proprietary intangible assets, in order to invest successfully in the United States. Given the potential for differentiation in the development of new technologies, and perhaps also in marketing and managerial capabilities, foreign firms are able to amass ownership-specific advantages in many of the same industries that US firms also develop them. There is evidence that the pattern of R&D intensity across industries is similar among the major home countries to MNEs, the United States, Japan, the United Kingdom, France, and West Germany. Pugel (1982) shows that US and Japanese R&D intensities are closely correlated across manufacturing industries, and Lall and Siddharthan (1982) report a similarly close correlation for US and UK R&D intensities. An examination of Table A5 in Walker (1979) suggests that this is also true for comparisons among US, West German, and French R&D intensities.

At the same time, the pattern of inward FDI is not likely to be exactly the same as that of outward FDI. As Lall and Siddharthan (1982) point out, in some industries the ownership-specific advantages that enable US firms to invest abroad successfully may be so extensive or relatively so dominant that foreign firms generally cannot compete successfully in the US market. This may be the case in the computer industry. In other industries, foreign firms may have built up proprietary intangible assets that enable investment in the United States on a scale far larger than expected in relation to the extent of outward US investment in that industry. This may be the case in the watches and clocks industry, and thus could explain why it is an 'outlier' in the sample used here.

The relations between patterns of FDI and patterns of trade in goods

Several important issues arise in considering relations between the patterns of inward and outward FDI intensities and the commodity pattern of trade. First, to what extent do patterns of FDI resemble patterns of commodity trade? Second, to what extent does FDI substitute for, or complement, commodity trade? Third, does intra-industry commodity trade have any relation to two-way or intra-industry FDI? And finally, do these various relationships have specific implications for national or global economic welfare? The first three of these issues are taken up in the following sub-sections. The final issue, the relations to economic welfare, is considered in the concluding section.

(c) The pattern of commodity trade

A variety of studies have explored the determinants of the commodity pattern of US trade in manufactures, in order to shed light on the bases of US comparative advantage. Some agreement has arisen that three basic factors of production must be considered: non-human capital, raw labour, and human capital (or labour skills). A more dynamic influence usually included is the importance of new technology developed in the United States in determining the commodity pattern. New technology is often developed through the efforts of skilled labour, especially scientists and engineers, so that the importance of this influence may largely represent a specific manifestation of a more basic aspect of comparative advantage.

A comprehensive recent study by Stern and Maskus (1981) reaches conclusions in agreement with a variety of other studies. Net exports across industries are positively related to the employment of human capital and negatively related to raw or unskilled labour. Net exports are often found to be negatively related to the use of non-human capital, although this relation is usually not as significant as the former two. The latter result is consistent with the Leontief paradox, and interpretation of it is difficult. Furthermore, when these influences are controlled, net exports are positively related to one or another measure of the importance of new technology in the industry, such as the R&D intensity or numbers of scientists and engineers employed as a fraction of the labour force.

On the basis of at least one common determinant, the importance of new technology in the industry, it might be expected that the pattern of outward FDI is positively correlated with the commodity pattern of US (net) exports. These correlations are examined in Table 2.4. The 1977 pattern of outward FDI intensity is positively related to the pattern of US exporting, as measured by either of the revealed comparative advantage (RCA) indexes, one based on the US share of OECD exports, and the other defined as net exports in relation to total trade. Only the correlation with the former RCA index is statistically significant. The pattern of inward FDI intensity appears to be essentially unrelated to the commodity pattern of trade, although a rather weak positive correlation with the RCA index based on the US share of OECD exports is found if industry 387, i.e. watches and clocks, is removed from the sample.

The patterns of outward FDI intensity and inward FDI intensity are each more closely correlated with the underlying determinants of US comparative advantage than with the trade pattern itself. Consistent with the studies previously cited, the commodity pattern of US trade, as measured by either RCA index, is positively and significantly correlated with measures of R&D intensity and with the average skill level or human capital of workers (either all workers or production workers only). As shown in Table 2.4, the pattern of outward FDI and the pattern of inward FDI (especially if watches and clocks is omitted) are both positively and significantly correlated with the measure of R&D intensity, scientists and engineers as a fraction of the labour force, and with the skill index for all workers. But the patterns of FDI are essentially uncorrelated with the skill index for production workers only, even though the two skill indexes themselves have a correlation of 0.87, highly significant.

In short, although the patterns of FDI and commodity trade share certain underlying determinants, there are presumably also influences that cause divergences between the patterns. Locational factors would be expected to explain much of the divergence in some cases favouring exports and in others FDI. For instance some foreign firms may be attracted to locate in the United States in order to tap the large pool of skilled production workers. But others may be attracted in order to locate inside US tariffs and non-tariff barriers, that tend to offer greater protection to less skill-intensive production. The net of these two motivations produces no significant correlation between inward FDI and production worker skill levels.

TABLE 2.4   Correlations between measures of outward and inward FDI intensity and industry trade and employment charactersics

	Outward FDI employment as a percentage of domestic employment 1977	Inward FDI employment as a percentage of domestic employment 1980	Inward FDI employment as a percentage of domestic employment 1980 (excluding 387)
RCA index–Relative export shares, 1978	0.29 (56) 0.016	0.01 (52) 0.488	0.10 (51) 0.243
RCA index–Net trade ratio, 1978	0.11 (56) 0.212	−0.12 (52) 0.190	−0.03 (51) 0.407
Scientists and Engineers fraction, 1970	0.41 (56) 0.001	0.29 (52) 0.017	0.37 (51) 0.004
Skill index–All workers, 1970	0.30 (56) 0.012	0.19 (52) 0.083	0.34 (51) 0.008
Skill index–Production workers, 1970	0.03 (56) 0.420	−0.01 (52) 0.482	0.10 (51) 0.242

Note: The number in parentheses below the correlation coefficient is the number of observations, and the number below this is the significance level using the one-tailed test.

(b) FDI as a substitute for or complement to commodity trade

The summary of the eclectic approach to FDI discussed earlier suggests that (horizontal) FDI should be considered a substitute for trade, in that the firm faces a choice between exporting and FDI in reaching decisions about servicing a foreign market for a particular product. Yet the simple correlation between outward FDI from the United States and either RCA index is positive. This positive correlation suggests a closer examination of the ways in which FDI may substitute for, or complement, commodity trade. The discussion, although general, is couched in terms of US outward FDI and US trade, for convenience of exposition.

Most simply, the underlying substitution may be masked in the correlation by certain common underlying determinants, such as the importance of new technology in the industry. In this view, and notwithstanding the positive correlation between outward FDI and exporting, US (net) exports would be even higher if FDI were lower. This is the basic substitution involved in the eclectic approach to horizontal FDI. Research has isolated one specific aspect of this apparent substitution. Pugel (1978), Lall (1980), and Bergsten, Horst, and Moran (1978) report that FDI exports are negatively related to advertising intensity, other things equal, while as noted previously, advertising intensity is positively related to outward FDI. US firms selling highly advertised products in foreign markets often prefer to manufacture these abroad as well. This may reflect the advantages of locating production within the market, in order to monitor and respond to consumer preferences more effectively, if product, packaging, and promotion must be adapted to local situations.

Yet, even if this conceptual basis for viewing horizontal FDI and exporting as alternatives is accepted, this is not sufficient to conclude that US exports would be higher if outward FDI were lower. Could markets now served by FDI production alternatively be served by US exports? Or would local or third-country firms capture these sales if US firms ceased foreign production? Several of the locational factors, including the importance of transport costs, foreign government barriers to imports and relative production cost (or factor availability) differences, suggest that US exports might be little higher even if US outward FDI were lower. Thus, although FDI and exporting are viewed as substitutes in terms of a firm's planning, they need not be substitutes in terms of the ultimate economic equilibrium.

Once vertical relationships are considered, the notion that FDI and commodity trade are substitutes may be challenged in another way. Backward vertical FDI to secure sources of supply could result in higher levels of international trade in raw materials and intermediate inputs. FDI based on international vertical integration of a series of stages in the firm's manufacturing process could increase trade in components and finished products. And forward vertical integration into sales and service affiliates could enhance parent exports by improving the effectiveness of local marketing efforts. If the extra sales represent a broadening of the market or are gained at the expense of local producers, the global level of trade is increased. If the extra sales are at the expense of exporters in third countries, global trade does not increase but its country pattern is affected.

Thus vertical FDI can increase trade. Of major importance is the fact that much FDI usually termed horizontal is actually a mixture of horizontal and vertical linkages with the parent, so that it too has the potential to complement trade. For instance, some local production may be sufficient to establish credibility as a local supplier that is dependable and responsive to local needs. Marketing of other imported products, perhaps used to fill out the firm's line of product offerings, is then enhanced.

Most empirical research on the substitutability or complementarity of trade and FDI has focused on US outward FDI and US exports. This is clearly part of the debate concerning an emotional political and economic issue, the extent to which US outward FDI affects jobs and unemployment (in the short run) and real incomes and income distribution (in the long run). As Bergsten, Horst, and Moran (1978) note, this is not a new issue, but was discussed and researched as early as the 1920s and 1930s. Discussion then died out, but was resurrected in the 1960s as organized labour came to oppose US outward FDI.

Two carefully done studies of the relationship between US outward FDI and US exports exist. Bergsten, Horst, and Moran (1978) examine the determinants of the 1966 US export-shipments ratio across 23 US manufacturing industries and 8 destination countries or regions. They find, while controlling for other industry and destination characteristics, that their measure of outward FDI, the net foreign affiliate sales-US shipments ratio, is positively related (and significant), while its square is negatively related (and significant). They conclude that modest levels of outward FDI complement US exports, while higher levels become less related and may even begin to substitute, at the margin, for FDI exports.

Lipsey and Weiss (1981) explore the determinants of 1970 US exports to 44 destinations, for each of up to 14 industries. After controlling for country characteristics including size, distance from the United States, and destination membership in the EEC, they find that US exports were positively related to the level of activity (output) or local affiliates of US firms in 12 of 14 industries (ten significantly) with respect to developed country destinations, and in 11 of 11 industries (nine significantly) with respect to developing country destinations. Furthermore, they also find the exports of thirteen other developed countries to the destinations generally were negatively related to local US affiliate activity, with statistically significant negative relationships for most of the industries with respect to developing country destinations. They conclude that the foreign affiliate activity of US firms appears largely to complement US exports, and that the local sales of US firms often come at the expense of exports from third countries.

Thus, there is evidence that US outward FDI tends to act as net complement, rather than a net substitute, to US exports in the industry. Other aspects of the links between US outward FDI and trade, including the effects on US imports in the industry and on trade in other commodities (e.g. raw materials or components not classified into the same industry) have not been studied so carefully.

Little is known about the relationships between US commodity trade patterns and inward FDI. In an attempt to shed some light on this issue, data on US export-sales ratios for US MNE parents and the US affiliates of foreign MNEs were assembled from the benchmark surveys for a sample of 2-digit and 3-digit industries, as shown in Table 2.5. For US MNE parents, as expected, the export-sales ratios are highest for the chemicals industries, the non-electrical and electrical machinery industries, the transport equipment industries, and the instruments industries.[5] The export-sales ratios for US affiliates of foreign MNEs are generally similar to those of US MNE parents, including high ratios in most of the industries just cited. But there are also some noticeable differences. For instance, the export propensity of foreign-owned affiliates in the lumber, wood products, and furniture industry is relatively large, perhaps reflecting inward FDI in this area to exploit US timber resources for export back to foreign parents. Export propensities lower than expected are found in the stone, clay, and glass products, electronic components and accessories, and instruments industries. In these industries foreign-controlled affiliates are more oriented to domestic sales than are US MNE parents.

(c) Intra-industry FDI and intra-industry trade

Intra-industry trade involves two-way trade, simultaneous exports and imports in the same commodity category. It is now recognized as a major part of trade in manufactured products, especially trade between developed countries. It arises mainly because many manufactured products that are closely substitutable, and thus are placed in the same commodity category, are still differentiated in terms of physical characteristics, brand name, image, or on some other basis. Thus, some consumers

TABLE 2.5   Export-sales ratios for US MNE parents and US affiliates of Foreign
MNEs, in percentages

Industry (BEA)	Export-sales ratio, US MNE parents 1977	Export-sales ratio, US affiliates of foreign MNEs 1980
Food (20)	3.3	5.2
Tobacco manufactures (210)	NA	NA
Textiles and apparel (22 + 23)	2.6	3.8
Lumber, wood, furniture (24 + 25)	5.8	19.0
Paper products (26)	6.4	10.2
Printing and publishing (27)	2.1	2.8
Chemicals (28)	9.5	7.6
Industrial, etc. (281)	11.3	9.7
Drugs (283)	8.7	8.5
Other	6.5	4.6
Petroleum and coal products (29)	NA	NA
Rubber and plastics products (30)	5.6	3.6
Leather and leather products (31)	NA	NA
Stone, clay, and glass products (32)	4.5	1.5
Ferrous metals (331)	2.6	6.5
Non-ferrous metals (335)	7.8	9.2
Fabricated metal products (34)	5.3	7.3
Machinery, except electrical (35)	15.5	16.8
Construction and related machinery (353)	23.8	19.5
Office, computing, and accounting machines (357)	13.8	23.5
Other	12.5	13.8
Electrical machinery (36)	12.4	12.0
Electronic components and accessories (367)	23.1	14.3
Other	11.2	9.7
Motor vehicles and equipment (371)	11.5	18.8
Other transport equipment (379)	15.5	17.9
Instruments (38)	16.4	9.3
Miscellaneous manufacturing (39)	NA	NA

in a country prefer one product configuration, others another. In the presence of scale economies, producers in the country do not produce all possible configurations. Some consumers in this country will prefer, and purchase, imported configurations, while simultaneously firms in the country can export to consumers in other countries that prefer their configurations. Intra-industry trade arises.

Dunning (1981) has hypothesized that the intra-industry FDI, i.e. simultaneous outflows and inflows of FDI in the same industry, is likely to become more important, especially in the industries where intra-industry trade is already important. Industries where product differentiation is important are likely candidates for FDI, since the pursuit of product differentiation often gives rise to intangible proprietary assets in technology and marketing that serve as ownership-specific advantages in the FDI process. Furthermore, the importance of product differentiation in these industries makes it likely that firms in different countries can develop differentiated approaches to technology and marketing, leaving no one home country predominant. However, to the extent that scale economies provide more than a minor threshold effect in limiting product differentiation, they may limit FDI, at least that based purely on horizontal replication of production of the same product configuration in different countries. Thus the coexistence of high levels of intra-industry trade and intra-industry FDI may also depend upon the placement of production of different configurations in different countries under the ownership of one firm, perhaps in order to exploit firm-level economies in R&D or marketing (Dunning and Norman, 1985).

The relation between intra-industry trade and intra-industry FDI can be explored using the data developed for this study, although the dynamic hypothesis that intra-industry FDI is increasing in industries where intra-industry trade is already important cannot be tested. Intra-industry trade and intra-industry FDI are each measured using the standard index, $1 - |X - M|/(X + M)$, where X is US exports (or outward FDI), and M is US imports (or inward FDI). Two measures of intra-industry FDI are developed, one using absolute levels of outward and inward FDI, and the other using levels corrected for the fact that outward FDI in manufacturing in total is much larger than this total for inward FDI. Using 1977 employment to measure outward FDI and 1980 employment to measure inward FDI, the correlation across 52 industries between the 'absolute' intra-industry FDI index and the 1978 intra-industry trade index is -0.04, and that for the 'corrected' measure -0.23. If industry 387 is omitted, the correlations are almost the same. Thus no support is found for the proposition that high levels of intra-industry FDI tend to exist in industries with high levels of intra-industry trade.

2.3 RESEARCH AND DEVELOPMENT

Multinational activity tends to be more important in industries that are relatively intensive in R&D. This appears to result from advantages to internalization of the international use of new technical knowledge, the output of R&D, in order more fully to appropriate the rents on such use and to slow the imitation of such intangible proprietary assets by competitors, a process that speeds the erosion of these rents.

This section examines two important issues in the understanding of R&D activities of MNEs. First, how important are foreign markets in achieving returns to R&D? And by how much would firms reduce their R&D spending if certain channels of technology transfer to generate rents from foreign markets were closed off? Second, to what extent do MNEs disperse their R&D efforts outside their home countries? What influences this dispersion?

These issues are of importance because contributions of MNEs to technological change and technology transfer are arguably their most important influences on national and global welfare. These welfare effects are discussed further in the concluding section.

The impact of FDI on R&D spending

The level of R&D spending by a firm depends upon the expected profitability of the outputs (new technologies) of the R&D efforts. The earning of rents from the exploitation of the outputs in foreign markets increases the profitability of R&D over what it would be if used only in the home market of the firm, and thus should tend to expand the R&D spending of the firm, other things equal. FDI is a major method to earn such rents. Thus, FDI, viewed as partly the consequence of a firm's internalization of the use of new technologies generated from R&D, may then raise the level of R&D spending by increasing its profitability. FDI and R&D reinforce each other.

A study by Mansfield *et al.* (1982, Ch. 3) addresses a number of these relationships by obtaining data from two small samples of US firms, most of whom are presumably MNEs. They first establish that foreign sales and utilization are important in generating returns to R&D, accounting for an average of 34% of total returns in a sample of 20 large firms in 7 industries, and for an average of 29% for 53 specific projects of 10 large chemical firms. The percentage of foreign returns tends to be higher for product technologies than for process technologies.

They proceed to explore the extent to which transfer to foreign affiliates is the preferred mode of international transfer of technology. In the first five years of use of the new technology, transfer to a foreign affiliate is the principal channel for 85% of the firms in the first sample and 62% of the projects in the second sample. Exporting is used somewhat more often than international licensing in both samples. Licensing becomes somewhat more important than exporting in the second five years of use, but transfer to affiliates remains the major channel. Use of affiliates (and licensing) is higher for product than for process technologies, while use of exporting is higher for process technologies. Firms indicated that they were less willing to send new process technologies to their affiliates, in part because it is more difficult to limit subsequent diffusion to foreign competitors once the process technology is transferred. The general predominance of transfer to affiliates is affirmed in a study by Vernon and Davidson (1979), who also found that US MNEs became quicker to transfer new technology into production abroad as they gained experience with multinational operations.

Mansfield *et al.* then asked firms to estimate the decline in their total R&D spending that would occur if certain channels of international transfer were closed off. If firms were not permitted to utilize new technologies in foreign affiliates, R&D spending would fall by an average of 15 and 12%, according to firms in the two samples. If no foreign rents could be earned at all, R&D spending would be cut by an average 26 and 16%.[6] Larger cuts would tend to occur in product rather than process R&D. The percentage size of the R&D reduction, across firms, is positively related to the share of affiliate sales in total firm sales, and to the firm's R&D-sales ratio.

Another issue, one related to the use of FDI to earn foreign rents on new technologies but also having broader implications, is the extent to which transfer to affiliates speeds imitation by foreign rivals. US MNEs transfer process technologies less frequently, in part to slow imitation, as noted previously. Mansfield *et al.* (1982, Ch. 5) asked a number of US firms about their beliefs on the effects of transfer to affiliates, for a sample of 25 technologies actually transferred. In 12 cases the US firms felt that transfer to affiliates had no effect on how quickly foreign competitors imitated, but in 9 cases the transfers were thought to have speeded up imitation by two and a half years or more. Transfer of process technology was more likely to lead to faster imitation. The quickening was thought to be due to increased awareness by foreign firms of the existence or profitability of the new technology. Once aware, foreign firms, not necessarily based in the same country as the affiliate, could then use standard techniques, for instance reverse engineering of hiring away employees, to speed the imitation.

Thus, Mansfield *et al.* provide empirical support for several important relationships between FDI and R&D. First, transfer to affiliates is often the preferred mode to earn foreign rents on new technologies. Second, R&D spending would be reduced significantly if this mode were somehow eliminated. And finally, transfer to affiliates often does not speed imitation by foreign rivals. Furthermore, firms are aware of the possibility of quickened imitation and, among other responses, tend to transfer new processes abroad less frequently. In terms of a broader issue, some observers suggest that transfer to affiliates may narrow the technological lead of the United States in some industries by speeding diffusion of the transferred technologies to foreign competitors. The results cited here suggest that this may not be that serious a problem, that US firms are aware of the possibilities, and that the positive effects on R&D spending of foreign rents earned through transfers to affiliates are likely to be more important in affecting the status of international technological competition.

International dispersion of R&D within MNEs

US MNEs in manufacturing (excluding petroleum) performed almost 11% of their total R&D in foreign affiliates in 1977, according to benchmark survey data. This percentage has been rising over the last several decades. Several studies exist of the determinants of the international dispersion of R&D spending by US MNEs and these are summarized in this sub-section. Less is known about the international dispersion of R&D by foreign MNEs but some insights are gained by examining R&D spending by US affiliates of foreign firms.

Studies of the international dispersion of R&D by US MNEs usually begin with the supposition that the level and location of R&D spending are part of the decisions necessary to maximize global profits. Three influences on the location of R&D can be identified. First, some factors favour centralization of R&D efforts, probably (but not necessarily) in the firm's home country. These include economies of scale in R&D, the avoidance of duplication, and the importance of interchange with top management who determine company strategy. On the other hand, the importance of close contacts among R&D, marketing, and production personnel favours decentralization of R&D, especially for development and adaptation efforts. Finally, more common locational factors, including the cost and availability of R&D inputs, and government policies, may also influence the location of R&D.

Mansfield *et al.* (1982, Ch. 5) and Hirschey and Caves (1981) recently completed studies of the determinants of the international dispersion of R&D by US MNEs. Mansfield *et al.* found in interviews that the major reason for foreign R&D work, as expected, is the value of close contacts with markets and manufacturing facilities in enhancing the effectiveness of R&D efforts to adapt product and process technologies to the economic conditions in foreign markets. Thus, development work tends to be a larger part of foreign R&D than is true for the company as a whole, and applied and basic research a smaller part (see also Creamer, 1976). They affirm the importance of these decentralizing influences statistically, using two small samples of companies. Specifically, they find that the extent of dispersion of R&D is positively related to the share of foreign affiliate sales in total company sales and negatively related to the share of US

TABLE 2.6　R&D-sales ratios of foreign affiliates of US MNEs, US affiliates of foreign MNEs, US firms performing R&D (in percentages)

Industry (BEA)	R&D-sales ratio		
	Foreign affiliates of US MNEs 1977	US affiliates of foreign MNEs 1980	US firms performing R&D 1977
Food (20)	0.3	0.2	0.4
Tobacco manufactures (210)	0.7	NA	NA
Textiles and apparel (22 + 23)	0.3	0.3	0.4
Lumber, wood, furniture (24 + 25)	0.1	0.1	0.8
Paper products (26)	0.3	0.2	0.9
Printing and publishing (27)	0.4	NA	NA
Chemicals (28)	1.1	3.0	3.6
Industrial, etc., (281)	0.6	3.1	3.6
Drugs (283)	2.6	9.5	6.2
Other	0.7	1.3	2.1
Petroleum and coal products (29)	0.1	NA	0.7
Rubber and plastics products (30)	0.9	0.8	2.4
Leather and leather products (31)	NA	NA	NA
Stone, clay, and glass products (32)	0.5	0.2	1.2
Ferrous metals (331)	0.3	0.1	0.6
Non-ferrous metals (335)	0.1	0.3	1.1
Fabricated metal products (34)	0.4	0.8	1.2
Machinery, except electrical (35)	0.6	2.1	5.0
Construction and related machinery (353)	0.8	0.9	NA
Office, computing, and accounting machines (357)	0.4	6.7	11.8
Other	0.7	1.2	NA
Electrical machinery (36)	1.6	2.7	6.3
Electronic components and accessories (367)	1.3	3.2	7.0
Other	2.3	2.1	6.2
Transport equipment (37)	1.3	1.6	6.2
Motor vehicles and equipment (371)	NA	1.7	3.1
Other transport equipment (379)	NA	1.3	11.7
Instruments (38)	1.5	2.0	6.1
Miscellaneous manufacturing (39)	NA	NA	NA

exports. They also find that the dispersion of R&D by US drug companies is larger than would otherwise be expected, a result that they attribute to the effect of strict US regulations on the US production and sales of new drugs.

Hirschey and Caves (1981) use a sample of 24 industries in 1966, and affirm the positive influence of the share of foreign affiliate sales and the negative influence of US exports on the extent of international dispersion of R&D.[7] They also find some support for propositions, among others, that scale economies in R&D limit dispersion and that imitative reaction in the process of oligopolistic competition may result in higher levels of foreign R&D in industries with moderate to high levels of concentration.

Less is known about the international dispersion of R&D by foreign MNEs. Some insight can be gained by examining data on the 1980 R&D–sales ratios of US affiliates, as shown in Table 2.6. Ratios for foreign affiliates of US firms and for all US firms performing R&D, for 1977, are also presented there.[8] Several observations can be made on comparisons of these data. First, the level of R&D spending in relation to the sales of US affiliates of foreign firms is approximately equal to or larger than that of foreign affiliates of US firms in the industries for which comparison can be made. This general tendency presumably reflects locational factors, especially the availability of skilled personnel, that favour R&D in the United States, but do not favour R&D in some locations where affiliates of US firms operate. Second, the industry pattern of R&D spending by US affiliates is similar to that of all US firms performing R&D, although the former is a smaller percentage of sales for all industries except drugs. The tendency for somewhat lesser proportionate spending in most of the higher R&D industries may reflect the ability of US affiliates to draw upon new technologies developed through the R&D of their parents. The one industry in which US affiliates are *much* less R&D-intensive, other transport equipment, reflects a difference in product focus. US firms perform substantial R&D on aircraft, much of it funded by the federal government, while US affiliates of foreign MNEs are less important in this part of the 'other transport equipment' industry.

One issue that has received some attention in this area is the proposition that foreign firms often invest in the United States in order to 'drain off' proprietary US technology and strengthen their own competitive positions internationally. One way that this might be accomplished is through the purchase of US firms with the requisite technological capabilities, although the market for corporate control presumably should assure that foreign firms find few economic bargains here. Another way would be to use US affiliates as 'listening posts' to monitor and, where desirable, to obtain the technological knowledge, through licence or otherwise, for transfer back to the parents. Several careful studies of this issue done in the late 1970s are cited by Arpan, Flowers, and Ricks (1981). The conclusions of these studies are that net inflows of technology are far more prevalent in the operations of US affiliates of foreign MNEs and that cases of significant technology outflows apparently are rare. Inward FDI does not generally occur to gain access to US technology. Rather, internalized exploitation of technologies proprietary to the foreign MNE within the large, politically stable US market is the more general motivation.

2.4 CONCLUSIONS AND POLICY IMPLICATIONS

The United States has long been recognized as the pre-eminent home of MNEs and has now become a major host to the affiliates of foreign MNEs as well. This study has provided new evidence on and summarized existing studies of the relationship of US outward and inward FDI to aspects of US economic structure and international competitiveness, focusing on the manufacturing sector, the single largest sector in terms of both outward and inward FDI. An appreciation of the eclectic approach to understanding FDI indicates that the efficiency and welfare implications of FDI are *complex*, so that conclusions about these effects must necessarily be tentative.

In considering the relationship of FDI to economic structure, trade in goods, and welfare, there is a danger of oversimplification. Kojima (1978, 1982), for instance, observes that US outward FDI is concentrated in industries in which the US has a comparative advantage. He claims that this FDI is therefore 'anti-trade', reducing US exports and creating unemployment and structural problems as well as balance of payments difficulties.

The evidence presented here has confirmed the positive correlation between outward FDI and trade-based measures of revealed comparative advantage, across manufacturing industries. The positive correlation itself suggests that the substitution of FDI for exports that concerns Kojima is not gross and overwhelming, but it still could be more subtle—US exports in these industries could be even higher if there were less outward FDI. But many of the 'lost' exports might have been sales lost anyway (to foreign firms). Furthermore, outward FDI may enhance certain US exports, including exports of capital goods, material inputs and components, and finished goods (the latter if local marketing of the MNEs full product line is improved, with only part of the line produced locally, and the rest imported). These complementary exports offset to some extent any direct substitution, and the net effect becomes an empirical question. Two carefully done studies conclude that, on net, US outward FDI generally is a net complement to US exports, even within the same industry (and thus ignoring any effects on other US exports such as capital goods).

More generally, MNEs are responsive to location factors such as comparative cost differences and barriers to trade in much the way that trade theory suggests businesses would be. Among other implications, this indicates that MNEs should not be 'blamed' for responding to governmentally imposed barriers to trade (or other governmental policies). The trade restrictions themselves, and not the MNE responses, create the distortions, unless the MNEs somehow persuade the governments to impose or maintain the restrictions.

US inward FDI shows a cross-industry pattern similar to that of outward FDI, and thus appears to share a number of common determinants. But inward FDI is not significantly correlated with measures of US revealed comparative advantage or a measure of average production worker skill levels. The locational factors influencing inward FDI again appear to be complex. For instance, some MNEs are drawn by the availability of skilled labour in the United States, while others may respond to US protection of industries intensive in less-skilled labour. From the US point of view, both may be desirable. The former enhances the exploitation of US comparative advantage, while the latter generates employment for the less-skilled workers whose relatively high unemployment rates can be viewed as an ongoing structural problem. The exploitation of US comparative advantage is seen in the finding that the cross-industry pattern of exports by US affiliates of foreign MNEs is similar to that of other large US companies.

The areas of activity that generate the most important implications for national and global welfare are the creation and international transfer of technology by MNEs. In relation to national welfare and international competitiveness, outward FDI raises the expected profitability of R&D. The extra incentive raises the amount of R&D undertaken by US firms, by about one-seventh according to the study by Mansfield *et al.* (1982). In many of the industries in which MNE activity is prominent, ongoing success in creating technological advances is the key to continued international competitiveness, based on the need continually to augment older advantages that naturally dissipate. FDI currently (or soon to be) in place generates expected returns that justify extra R&D, assisting US-based companies in their international technology competition. A number of studies demonstrate that this benefits the US economy through the links of R&D spending to more rapid real industry growth and more rapid productivity growth (see Pugel, 1982, and references cited therein).

Outward FDI at times also speeds the diffusion or dissipation of newer

US technologies to foreign rivals. US MNEs are aware of this problem, and make decisions to optimize the trade off between better short-run profitability if technology is transferred to affiliates, and the erosion of longer-run profitability. The net impact on profitability is positive. The national interest is presumably served reasonably well, with the major effect being the ongoing enhancement of R&D efforts that speed the pace of technology creation.

Fears have been expressed that inward FDI harms US welfare in that foreign firms use their US affiliates to acquire US technology (at too low a price) and build their own technological capabilities. Several studies found no general support for these effects; rather, the affiliates mainly were the recipients of inward technology transfer from the foreign MNEs. Inward technology transfer generally creates gains to US welfare through the US applications of foreign technology obtained at a reasonable price. In addition, foreign MNEs may enhance welfare by increasing the vigour of competition in oligopolistic high-technology industries.

These latter observations lead to several on the contributions of MNEs to global welfare. The economic activities of technology creation and transfer are beset by a variety of market imperfections, both static and dynamic. MNEs often internalize technology creation and transfer, thus circumventing the market imperfections. This leads to a higher level of R&D and technology creation, a likely second-best welfare improvement if there would otherwise be underinvestment in R&D. Furthermore, MNEs transfer technology as a 'public' good within the company, a likely second-best welfare improvement in moving toward the static first-best outcome of technology (and knowledge in general) as a public good available to anyone willing to incur the marginal cost of transfer.

The second-best nature of these arguments renders implications for global welfare tentative. Other aspects of MNE activities also point to ambiguous implications for welfare. Internalization in the face of exogenously given market imperfections is likely to improve welfare. But MNEs may also create or enhance market imperfections, for instance by altering the focus of competition and raising barriers to the entry of new competitors into the industry. Enhancement of imperfections is likely to be privately profitable but welfare-reducing from the broader social perspective. Kojima focuses on the latter set of effects, thus finding another reason to suggest that US MNEs, based largely in oligopolistic industries, are welfare-reducing. Kojima fails to recognize the extent and importance of the former welfare-enhancing effects—by ignoring the complexity of the activities of US MNEs he is able to draw strong but probably misleading conclusions.

US government policies towards inward and outward FDI are largely non-existent or neutral. This seems to be sensible given the complexities of the activities of MNEs and of the US economy. The framing of any general interventionist policies that would create clear national welfare benefits would be very difficult in terms of the economics involved and of the political pressures that would be brought to bear by special interest groups. The economics suggest that a case-by-case approach to government intervention in the activities of MNEs could increase the net national benefits of outward and inward FDI. But such an ideal approach is hampered not only by a lack of full understanding of the economic effects on national welfare, but also by the likely intrusion of special interest politics into the governmental decisions. Given these shortcomings in economic capabilities and the governmental process, the current largely neutral government policies probably serve the national interest well.

APPENDIX 2.1

Variable definitions and data sources

Several sources were used to form a data set for ratios and statistical results reported in this study. Definitions of variables and data sources are described here, along with some difficulties encountered in amassing the data set.

Tables 2.2, 2.3, and 2.4

Data reported or used in these tables are organized according to the system of detailed BEA industries used in reporting data on US outward and inward FDI, yielding a sample of 56 industries. Data were also obtained from other sources, requiring the use of concordances among several systems of industry classification. The concordance between BEA industries and the SIC is extremely good. The concordance between BEA industries and Census of Population industries is also good, although a number of Census of Population industries had to be allocated to more than one BEA industry. The concordance between BEA industries and the SITC should be regarded as approximate. There is simply no way to conform US trade data to 3-digit BEA (or SIC) industries. This limits the direct comparability of trade variables with other variables. A table showing the concordances used is available from the author on request.

Data on US outward FDI are obtained from the 1977 benchmark survey. FDI is defined as ownership of 10% or more of the voting stock of a foreign affiliate by one US entity, such as a corporation or person. The data are reported by industry of affiliate. Total income, almost the same as net sales, and employment are taken from Table C, and matched with shipments and employment from the 1977 *Census of Manufactures* to form the FDI intensity ratios.

Data on US inward FDI are obtained from the two benchmark surveys available. Net sales and employment are taken from Table 2 of volume 2 of the 1974 benchmark survey, and matched with shipments and employment data from the 1974–5 *Annual Survey of Manufactures* to form two inward FDI intensity ratios. FDI is defined as 10% ownership, and data are reported by industry of affiliate. There is a belief that this survey actually missed a significant amount of inward FDI, but the extent of under-counting is not known.

Sales and employment are taken from Table 6 of the 1980 benchmark survey, and matched with shipments and employment data from the 1980 *Annual Survey of Manufactures* to form two more inward FDI-intensity ratios. FDI is again defined as 10% ownership, and data are reported by industry of sales (essentially, industry of establishment). This survey is believed to be substantially more thorough in its coverage.

Trade data used in the correlations reported in Table 2.4 are taken from OECD *Statistics of Foreign Trade, Series B*. The ratio of US exports to total OECD exports is the basis for the RCA index-relative export shares. The RCA index-net trade ratio is defined as industry exports minus imports, divided by industry exports plus imports.

The scientists and engineers fraction (of total US industry employment) is taken from the 1970 *Census of Population,* Subject Report 7C. The skill indexes are defined as the weighted average of economy-wide mean annual occupation earnings of workers employed for 50–52 weeks, where the weights are the shares of each occupation in total industry employment. Differences in skill across occupations are assumed to be reflected in differences in earnings. Economy-wide mean annual earnings for each occupation are used to reduce the influence of industry-specific factors, such as unionization, on the earnings-based measure of skill. Thus, the skill indexes can be thought of as 'expected' average annual earnings for the industry, if all workers were paid the economy-wide mean earnings for their occupations. Data to calculate these skill indexes are taken from the 1970 *Census of Population,* Subject Reports 7A and 7C. For the variables obtained from the *Census of Population,* allocations, where necessary, were done based on 1970 employment as reported in the 1970 *Annual Survey of Manufactures.*

Tables 2.5 and 2.6

Data reported in Tables 2.5 and 2.6 have somewhat less industry detail because of the more limited industry breakdown reported in the benchmark surveys for these variables. For Table 2.5 US parent exports are from Table II. T. 1 of the 1977 benchmark survey, and US parent sales from Table II. R. 1. Exports of US affiliates of foreign firms are from Table G-3 of the 1980 benchmark survey, and sales from Table 5.

For Table 2.6 data on the R&D and sales of foreign affiliates of US MNEs are taken from Tables III. F. 6 and III. J. 8 of the 1977 benchmark survey, and refer only to majority-owned affiliates. Data on the R&D-sales ratios for all US firms performing R&D are taken from the NSF *Research and Development in Industry*, 1977, Tables B-3 and B-35.

NOTES

1. Data as reported in OECD (1981).
2. *Survey of Current Business*, July 1982, p. 93. The percentage for 1979, a year in which business activity and profits were not depressed, was 26.3%.
3. These data are not fully comaparable. Those on employment in US manufacturing affiliates is for March 1978, and probably is an underestimate (US Department of Commerce, 1980).
4. Specifically, they appear to fail to note that in a number of cases a single BEA 3-digit industry includes several SIC 3-digit industries. In private correspondence Lall and Siddharthan have reported to the author that their conclusions are essentially unchanged if the concordance is corrected.
5. The value for the automobile industry is positively affected by the special agreement on trade in motor vehicles between the United States and Canada.
6. Generalizing these estimates to an impact on the entire US economy is not straightforward for two reasons. First, they are based on small samples of firms that may not be representative of the whole population. Second, the estimates represent impact effects or partial equilibrium outcomes. The ultimate effect on R&D spending in the US economy as a whole would be the outcome of these impact effects and the subsequent indirect and feedback effects as the economy moves to a new general equilibrium. Nonetheless, the estimates are suggestive of significant short-run effects, even though the long-run effects are more difficult to ascertain.
7. Somewhat more detailed data of a similar nature are available in the 1977 benchmark survey, and could be used to update and expand these results.
8. Comparison of 1980 R&D-sales ratios for US affiliates and 1977 R&D-sales ratios for the other two groups should pose few problems, as these ratios are generally very stable over time. Thus, comparison with the 1980 ratios for all US firms performing R&D would result in the same conclusions.

REFERENCES

Arpan, J. S., Flowers, E. B., and Ricks, D. A. (1981). Foreign direct investment in the United States: the state of knowledge of research, *Journal of International Business Studies*, **12**, No. 1, Spring/Summer, 137–154

Bergsten, C. F., Horst, T., and Moran, T. H. (1978). *American Multinationals and American Interests*, Washington, DC: Brookings Institution

Caves, R. E. and Pugel, T. A. (1982). *Intra-industry Differences in Conduct and Performance: Viable Strategies in U.S. Manufacturing Industries*, New York University, Graduate School of Business Administration, Monograph Series in Finance and Economics

Creamer, D. B. (1976). *Overseas Research and Development by United States Multinationals, 1966–1975*, New York: Conference Board

Dunning, J. H. (1981). A note on intra-industry foreign direct investment, *Banca Nazionale del Lavoro Quarterly Review*, No. 139, December, 427–437

Dunning, J. H. and Norman, G. (1985). Intra-industry Production as a form of International Economic Involvement: in Erdilek, A. (ed.) *Multinationals as Mutual Invaders*, London: Croom Helm.

Flowers, E. B. (1976). Oligopolistic reactions in European and Canadian direct investment in the United States, *Journal of International Business Studies*, **7**, No. 2, Fall/Winter, 43–55

Graham, E. M. (1978). Transatlantic investment by multinational firms: a rivalistic phenomenon?, *Journal of Post-Keynesian Economics*, **1**, No. 1, Fall, 82–99

Hirschey, R. C. and Caves, R. E. (1981). Research and transfer of technology by multinational enterprises, *Oxford Bulletin of Economics and Statistics*, **43**, No. 2, May, 115–130

Knickerbocker, F. T. (1973). *Oligopolistic Reaction and Multinational Enterprise*, Boston: Division of Research, Graduate School of Business Administration, Harvard University

Kojima, K. (1978). *Direct Foreign Investment: A Japanese Model of Multinational Business Operations*, New York: Praeger

Kojima, K. (1982). Macroeconomic versus international business approach to direct foreign investment, *Hitotsubashi Journal of Economics*, **23**, No. 1, June, 1–19

Lall, S. (1980). Monopolistic advantages and foreign involvement by U.S. manufacturing industry, *Oxford Economic Papers*, **32**, No. 1, March, 102–12

Lall, S. and Siddharthan, N. S. (1982). Monopolistic advantages of multinationals: lessons from foreign investment in the U.S., *Economic Journal*, **92**, No. 367, September, 668–683

Lipsey, R. E. and Weiss, M. Y. (1981). Foreign production and exports in manufacturing industries, *Review of Economics and Statistics*, **63**, No. 4, November, 488–494

Mansfield, E. *et al.* (1982). *Technology Transfer, Productivity and Economic Policy*, New York: W. W. Norton

OECD (1981). *International Investment and Multinational Enterprises: Recent International Direct Investment Trends*, Paris: OECD

Pugel, T. A. (1978). *International Market Linkages and U.S. Manufacturing*, Cambridge, MA: Ballinger Publishing

Pugel, T. A. (1981). Determinants of foreign direct investment: an analysis of U.S. manufacturing industries, *Managerial and Decision Economics,* **2**, No. 4, 220–228

Pugel, T. A. (1982). Comparative industry growth rates in the U.S. and Japan: the role of technological change and technology transfer, unpublished, August

Stern, R. M. and Maskus, K. E. (1981). Determinants of the structure of U.S. foreign trade, *Journal of International Economics,* **11**, No. 2, May, 207–224.

US Department of Commerce (1976). *Foreign Direct Investment in the United States,* Vol. 2, Washington, DC: US Government Printing Office

US Department of Commerce (1980). *Selected Characteristics of Foreign-Owned Firms, 1978,* Washington, DC: US Government Printing Office

US Department of Commerce, Bureau of Economic Analysis (1981). *U.S. Direct Investment Abroad, 1977,* Washington, DC: US Government Printing Office

US Department of Commerce, Bureau of Economic Analysis (1983). *Foreign Direct Investment in the United States, 1980,* Washington, DC: US Government Printing Office

Vernon, R. and Davidson, W. H. (1979). Foreign Production of Technology-Intensive Products by U.S.-based Multinational Enterprises, Working Paper No. 79–5, Division of Research, Graduate School of Business Administration, Harvard University

Walker, W. B. (1979). *Industrial Innovation and International Trading Performance,* Greenwich, CT: JAI Press

3

France

CHARLES ALBERT MICHALET and
THÉRÈSE CHEVALLIER

3.1 INTRODUCTION

The internationalization of large French firms must be placed in the context of the continuous formation of large industrial groups (Bertrand, Mansuy, and Norotte, 1981). This process developed over the period 1965–74. The first phase was characterized by industrial concentration, the principal aim of which was to establish French companies on a 'foothold on the international ladder' and counter foreign competition. This first phase was followed by a period of financial and industrial diversification, and this, in turn, by territorial diversification. This last phase emerged in the early 1970s, and became an important part of the international strategy of French industrial groups, right up to the world economic recession of the late 1970s, and early 1980s.

Of course, the first French multinationals appeared long before 1970. Even in the last century, they played an important role both as an instrument of colonization, and in helping to create a viable domestic industrial infrastructure.[1]

For most of the post-war period, foreign direct investment has not been at the forefront of the international strategy of French firms. During the 1960s, their main preoccupation was to expand their exports. By the use of financial aid and legislative measures, the French government supported the process of concentration to enable those enterprises in sectors exposed to international competition to protect their market position. Even when French firms did venture abroad, the activities of their subsidiaries were rarely integrated into their domestic structures and business strategies.

The presence of foreign firms in France was comparatively unimportant and largely ignored. This situation did not radically change until the 1960s; and the establishment of foreign plants in the Republic has only been systematically recorded since the early 1970s.

This polarization in commercial activity and lack of interest in international production probably explain the lack of statistical data about the activities of foreign MNEs in France and French companies abroad. Even today data on the latter are only known through the 'Notes Bleues' published by the Ministry of Finance and derived from balance of payments figures. Investment flows are roughly broken down into sectors or into regions and their interpretation suffers from frequent changes, making the formulation of any time series of data extremely difficult. There are official data on stocks of foreign direct investment; and the only official data published on investment flows are those contained in the external accounts of the French economy. In this chapter, most of the information set out has been obtained from firms through official enquiries or private research investigation (eg. Michalet and Delapierre, 1975, 1976; Michalet and Chevallier, 1983; Savary, 1982).

This study is divided into two parts. First we set out the general picture of the internationalization of the French economy by activities of the foreign multinational enterprises (MNEs), and of foreign investment carried out by French MNEs. Next, an attempt will be made to analyse French international competitiveness, by relating the balance of inward and outward flows to (a) the specific ownership advantages of French MNEs, and (b) the locational advantages of the French economy. These results are obviously important to French industrial policy, which is the subject of the final section of this chapter.

3.2   THE INTERNATIONALIZATION OF THE FRENCH INDUSTRIAL STRUCTURES (1962–1980)

The internationalization of industrial structure will be taken to embrace both French foreign direct investment (I_o) and foreign direct investment in France (I_i). Our discussion will draw on two sets of data:

(i) direct investment flows registered by balance of payments statistics;
(ii) sales and other data obtained directly from firms.

The analysis will cover the period 1962–80 and will emphasize the distribution of I_o and I_i in different regions and different sectors.

French foreign investment

(a) Development and structure of direct investment flows

Table 3.1 shows that the flows of foreign direct investment (I_o) are characterized by a marked growth, multiplying twenty-one times between 1962 and 1980, while the level of domestic gross fixed capital formation (GFCF) increased only six and a half times over the same period. The trend of I_0 remained the same throughout the 1960s and 1970s, and seemed unaffected by the oil crisis of the 1970s. However, data on the level of flows reveals very marked variations from one year to another, changing by as much as $\pm 30\%$. Until 1974, the levels of I_0 and gross fixed capital formation (GFCF) in France moved in the same direction, but from 1976–7 they moved in opposite directions. This reflected different reactions to the oil crises, recovery being much quicker in the case of foreign than domestic investment.

(i) Geographical distribution

In 1980, 68% of I_0 was directed towards the industrial OECD countries, and the rest was divided between the newly industrialized countries (NIC), less developed countries, oil-exporting countries, and eastern countries. This distribution is very similar to that in the early 1960s. The redirection of flows towards the industrialized countries, a notable characteristic of the most recent period, must be compared with the years 1967–71, during which the share of these latter countries fell substantially. A more detailed analysis shows a series of developments over three subperiods:

—From 1962 to 1968: French I_0 is directed mainly towards the industrial countries; with an increasing share going towards Europe and other OECD countries excluding the United States. Investment in the developing countries is mainly directed to the Overseas Territories (OT).
—From 1968 to 1972: investments are redirected towards the third world, the OTs losing some of their earlier importance.
—From 1972 to 1980: investments are directed both towards industrialized countries and towards OPEC and Latin American countries. The share of French investment going to the United States rose from 14% in 1974 to 22% in 1980. By contrast, French interest in the rest of the OECD fell back during the second half of the 1970s.

The changing pattern of French investments in the developing countries is characterized by a drastic reduction in the share of former colonies. In the case of the OTs for example, the share fell from 29% of I_0 in 1968 to less than 5% in 1980. The NICs and OPEC have both increased their share of investment going to developing countries.

(ii) Allocation according to sector

We will consider three sectors: *viz* manufacturing industry, services, and

TABLE 3.1   Growth of French inward and outward investment and related economic variables, 1962–80

	I_oT MF	Δ%	I_iT MF	Δ%	GFCF MF	Δ%	I_oT/I_iT	%I_oT/GFCF	%I_iT/GFCF	%I_oT/X	%I_iT/M
1962	838		2 572		51.0		0.33	1.6	5.0	1.90	6.5
1963	956	+14	2 511	−2	57.6	13.0	0.38	1.6	4.3	2.00	5.3
1964	1 626	+70	3 426	+36	64.1	11.3	0.47	2.5	5.3	3.00	6.3
1965	2 064	+27	3 399	−1	68.0	6.1	0.61	3.0	4.9	3.37	6.1
1966	1 963	−5	3 099	−9	75.3	10.7	0.63	2.6	4.1	2.96	4.8
1967	2 391	+22	3 502	+13	81.4	8.1	0.68	2.9	4.3	3.35	5.1
1968	2 121	−11	2 885	−17	84.3	3.5	0.74	2.5	3.4	2.70	3.7
1969	1 854	−13	4 291	+48	101.8	20.7	0.43	1.8	4.2	1.94	4.3
1970	2 605	+40	7 557	+76	111.0	9.0	0.34	2.3	6.8	2.17	6.4
1971	3 731	+43	5 305	−29	124.6	12.2	0.70	3.0	4.3	2.67	4.0
1972	4 824	+29	4 714	−11	141.2	13.3	1.02	3.4	3.3	3.03	3.1
1973	5 485	+14	6 676	+42	159.7	13.0	0.89	3.4	4.2	2.86	3.5
1974	6 420	+17	10 645	+59	192.5	20.6	0.60	3.3	5.5	2.45	3.7
1975	8 135	+27	9 162	−14	192.7	0.1	0.88	4.2	4.7	2.88	3.5
1976	12 568	+54	10 032	+10	227.3	18.0	1.25	5.5	4.4	3.66	2.9
1977	11 439	−10	11 749	+17	245.6	8.0	0.97	4.6	4.8	2.77	3.0
1978	12 017	+5	15 758	+34	269.7	9.8	0.76	4.4	5.8	2.62	3.6
1979	12 596	+4	16 907	+8	301.4	11.7	0.74	4.2	5.6	2.24	3.0
1980	18 055	+43	19 595	+16	359.3	19.2	0.92	5.0	5.4	3.80	3.4

Sources: I_o, I_i: 'Notes Bleues'—Ministry of Finance
GFCF, X, M: National Accounts
I_o: French gross foreign direct investment, and investment loans, in millions of French francs (MF)
%: Annual rate of increase
I_i: Gross direct investment and direct investment loans made by non-residents in France—millions of francs (MF)
GFCF: Gross fixed capital formation by societies, individual businessmen and credit institutions, in billions of francs

energy. French investment in non-energy mining, agricultural, and commercial activities is negligible. The sectoral distribution of direct investment has changed greatly since 1962.

Considering the period as a whole, the major movement has been the sustained increase in the share of the services sector, at the expense of the energy sector. In comparing these rates of increase to those of the equivalent GFCF, it is remarkable that while I_o flows in oil move in the same direction as those in the domestic GFCF in energy, the fluctuations in industrial I_o investment vary inversely to their domestic counterparts, except in 1972 and from 1975 to 1976. As Table 3.1 shows, I_o in the industrial and services sector has increased faster than domestic GFCF, with the movement being greater in the services sector than for I_o as a whole. This is at least partly a reflection of the accelerating internationalization of French banks (Michalet, 1981).

(b) Foreign activities of French multinationals

After the period of the formation of large industrial groups, which became widespread after 1965, internationalization became the major objective of large French firms. As is the case in most other industrial countries, the economic recession seems to have stimulated this process, and the share of French firms' transactions carried out abroad has grown (Stopford and Dunning, 1983).

(i) The dynamics of multinational growth

Of those firms questioned during a survey carried out by CEREM in 1981 (Michalet and Alii (1983), two-thirds estimated that their foreign markets had grown faster than their domestic markets over recent years, irrespective of whether the production for these markets was located in France or elsewhere. These two forms of access to foreign markets would therefore seem to be complementary with, rather than competitive to each other. The sales of foreign subsidiaries account for between 25% and 70% of sales turnover, according to the firm. The most internationalized firms are to be found in the chemical, engineering, electrical, electronics, durable consumer goods, and transport sectors.

More precise statistics have been calculated for nationalized industries (Michalet and Chevallier, 1983). For example, it is possible to compare, for 1980, the relative importance of exports and foreign production. The relevant data are set out in Table 3.2.

TABLE 3.2   Relative importance of exports to exports plus foreign production of French nationalised firms, by geographical areas, 1962–80

	EEC*	USA	Rest of OECD	IC	OT	Other DC	Total DC
1962	35	11	27	73			27
1963	43	3	24	70			30
1964	44	7	26	77			23
1965	38	2	36	76			24
1966	48	3	23	74			27
1967	38	6	17	61			40
1968	22.5	4.8	15.4	55.8	28.9	15.2	44.2
1969	28.6	3.6	10.5	54.9	22.6	22.5	45.1
1970	25.8	5.2	19.3	54.7	23.6	21.6	45.3
1971	30.1	15.1	14.5	62.0	13.5	24.4	34
1972	37.2	9.3	17.5	67.7	11.8	20.3	32.3
1973	31.4	14.2	15.9	66.7	14.2	19.1	33
1974	37.7	8.4	18.9	67.6	8.3	24.1	32.4
1975	28.9	17.9	17.9	67.1	7.3	25.6	32.9
1976	33.6	14.7	16.7	67.5	5.5	27.0	32.5
1977	31.8	14.0	18.4	65.9	4.0	30.1	44.3
1978	33.1	14.0	21.0	71.5	5.0	24.0	36.0
1979	25.7	19.0	25.0	74.0	5.8	21.0	26.0
1980	28.3	22.0	15.0	68.0	8.2	22.3	31.5

EEC*: Including the UK
Rest of OECD: OECD – (EEC – USA)
IC: Industrialized Countries – Total
OT: French Overseas Territories
DC: Developing Countries
Source: 'Notes Bleues'—Ministry of Finance

Apart from specialized firms in the arms industry, those with the highest foreign production ratio (SS/TO) are also those with the greatest degree of internationalization (Exports + SS/TO). Again, this result suggests that exporting and foreign direct investment are complements to each other. We also reiterate that the strength of this international growth, by whatever means, has developed while the domestic investment by large firms has shown a distinctly downward trend (Bertrand, Mansuy, and Norotte, 1981, p.21).

(ii) The strategy of French multinationals

Data on the geographical spread of French-based MNEs, as derived from direct enquiries, confirms the balance of payments statistics. In particular they continue to direct their activities to the developed economies. Within the OECD area, the strong locational attractions of other EEC member countries seem likely to be consolidated in the later 1970s. But the real growth would appear to have occurred in the United States and, to a lesser extent, in the South European countries, notably Spain and Portugal. As for the Third World, the lack of interest in African countries south of the Sahara is confirmed, the exceptions being Nigeria and South Africa. Currently, Latin America appears the most favoured area for French investment, with Brazil being the most preferred country. The popularity of Argentina, where the level of French penetration is quite high, seems to have peaked, while in Mexico, where the present level is low, interest is increasing. South East Asia also seems set to attract many new French plants in the coming years.

According to Table 3.3, the motives of French businessmen have not greatly changed over the last ten years. Actual presence in a market is always the factor most often quoted to justify a foreign presence vis à vis exports. Nevertheless, it is worth noting that between the two surveys carried out by CEREM, the proportion of replies citing this reason for investment fell quite markedly. French businessmen now seem to be taking other factors into account. *Inter alia* this reflects the changing sectoral composition of FDI, the region in which it is made and the degree of existing multinationalization of the investing firms. For example, in 1970s most French MNEs had only a limited experience of foreign production, and operated only one or two foreign affiliates. By the early 1980s the situation had changed dramatically, and today foreign production is now an integral part of the product and marketing strategy of leading French firms. The dichotomy between the domestic and foreign markets that existed only ten years ago has all but disappeared.

The economic environment in which firms operate has also changed, recession having replaced the high and regular growth of the 1960s. This

TABLE 3.3   Motives for establishing new plants by French MNEs: global results, 1971 and 1981

Motives	Rank 1971	Percentage of total replies	Rank 1981	Percentage of total replies
Importance of presence in a market	1	72	1	87
Protection of local producers by public authorities	2	39	4	31
Exploitation of technical advantage (manufacturing process)	3	37	—	—
Slowing down of demand in French market	4	34	4	31
Geographical diversification to spread risk	5	34	3	35
Seizing a business opportunity			4	31
Nationalistic attitudes of local customers	6	33	5	30
Reduction of transport costs	7	30	—	—
Reduction of wage costs	8	28	8	15
Development of competition in foreign markets	9	25	8	15
Re-export to other countries			9	11
Foreign public authority aid	10	22	10	10
Exploiting a price advantage			8	15
Intervention by foreign government	11	21		15
Reduction of social responsibilities	12	19	—	—
Request of a foreign firm	13	16	8	15
Result of an amalgamation	14	15	—	—
Answering to a foreign competitor established in the foreign market	15	13	—	—
Exploiting a new product				
Re-exporting to France				
French public authority aid			9	11
Slowing down of growth in French market due to growing French or foreign competition			6	21
Exploiting a management advantage	16	12	7	17
Favourable social climate			—	—
Slowing down of growth in the foreign market due to bad adaptation of products			10	10
Reduction in distribution costs	17	10	10	10

NB: Only motives mentioned in more than 10% of replies are registered.
Sources: CEREM enquiries 1971 and 1981, see for example Michalet, C. A. and Delapierre, M., *La multinationalisation des entreprises françaises* (Paris, 1973), and Michalet, C. A. *et al., Nationalisation et Internationalisation: Stratégies de multinationals français* (Paris, La Decouverte, 1983).

current situation explains the appearance of new factors influencing FDI such as the growth of protectionist barriers, recession in the domestic market, and intensified competition in both national and international markets. In this light, the favoured growth areas of the US, other European industrial countries, Japan and the South-Asian NICs are seen as an extension of the French market. The presence of French firms alongside their major international competitors in these major markets is seen as a necessary condition for survival.

As for the developing countries, actual presence in the market is always of primary importance, which can be explained by two main factors: the existence of strong import barriers and intervention by local governments. The existence of a cheap and well-motivated workforce is also relevant in the case of export processing activities.

To sum up, it can be said that the strategy of the internationalization of French firms has been essentially market-oriented, and directed to countries where the actual or potential market size is the greatest. However, this strategy has been pursued in the general context of intensified worldwide competition particularly among large oligopolistic economic groups. It would appear that the North American and EEC markets are considered the most homogeneous, and the most like the French market. The best way of penetrating these markets is to exploit ownership advantages which are specific to French firms, and which arise out of the strength of these firms in their home markets. In due course the exploitation of these O specific advantages in several countries leads French firms to rationalize their output on the basis of product or process specialization. However, the range of goods by French affiliates is not the same for all products, and is usually narrower than that produced in France. However, to the extent that the former consists of the most profitable products, they act as a bridgehead for further market penetration. As this occurs, the competitive advantage of French firms becomes based less on its country-specific characteristics and more on its degree of multinationalization and transaction cost-minimizing capabilities vis à vis other multinational groups.

(iii) Methods of expansion

In the industrialized countries of the Third World, the majority of French affiliates take the form of 'relay subsidiaries rather than 'subsidiary workshops'. We define the first type as subsidiaries replicating at least some of the products produced by their parent company, for sale in the local market (be it national or regional). By contrast, the second type are part of a vertically integrated programme, and supply parts and components which are exported—mainly to their parent companies (Michalet and Delapierre, 1976).

In the European economies and the United States, French firms, often being late arrivals, have entered the market by buying out, or participating in existing firms. In particular, the main trans-Atlantic transactions of the past five or six years have been of this kind.[2]

The growth of this type of French foreign involvement has been accompanied by a marked increase in inter-firm agreements concerning joint production, research, or distribution. We have tried to plot these kinds of agreements for a sample of 19 French industrial groups over the period 1973–80 (Michalet, 1983). Out of 668 cases, 47% involved a foreign partner (or subsidiary). This phenomenon accelerated over the latter part of the last decade. For 14 groups the number of transactions made abroad and/or with a foreign firm was greater than or equal to the number of purely national transactions. Some 85% of the external transactions were concluded with United States or other EEC French firms. According to our survey, this trend will increase in the future.

Foreign investment in France

(a) The development and structure of foreign direct investment

Over the period 1962 to 1980, the rate of growth of foreign investment in France has been very close to that of the gross GFCF by all French firms, each having multiplied by about seven and a half times. A slight acceleration in inward investment is noticeable after 1975, but this has been accompanied by wider annual fluctuations. It should be stressed that domestic and foreign investment do not always rise or fall together; while in the period 1968 to 1976 they were complementary to each other, in other years they seemed to move in opposite directions. This has been particularly apparent since 1976 and is most noticeable in the service and industrial sectors. (Further details are set out in Table 3.1.)

(i) Geographical origin of flows

Table 3.4 shows that about 50% of inward direct investment between 1962 and 1980 came from the EEC; 38% from other OECD countries (of which the US accounted for 13%) and the balance from the rest of the world. The situation was noticeably different in the early 1960s. At that time the United States and the EEC countries both accounted for 28% of investment flows, with the other OECD countries supplying 38% of the total.

TABLE 3.4 Geographical origin of foreign direct investment in France, 1962–80

	EEC*	FRG	GB	Benelux	Italy	USA	Rest of OECD
1962	28.2	5.5	6.4	14.0	2.3	27.7	38.4
1963	33.4	7.5	7.1	15.6	3.2	20.5	39.8
1964	32.7	7.0	7.6	15.6	2.6	27.8	33.5
1965	36.4	8.0	11.3	13.7	3.4	26.6	29.3
1966	32.9	6.9	5.6	17.4	3.0	32.6	25.1
1967	37.1	10.0	7.2	15.5	4.3	34.1	22.1
1968	44.4	21.0	8.9	12.2	2.5	20.2	29.7
1969	35.2	13.7	6.6	12.7	2.5	30.1	30.6
1970	50.7	12.1	8.7	25.7	4.2	25.9	19.9
1971	47.9	12.8	9.0	21.0	4.6	26.0	21.6
1972	49	12.4	11.0	21.0	4.3	22.0	26.7
1973	54.2	10.2	19.6	19.4	4.0	16.0	25.7
1974	52.8	13.6	19.0	18.0	2.7	16.3	27.4
1975	40.6	10.0	10.0	16.0	3.8	17.6	28.0
1976	51.6	12.4	15.0	23.0	3.7	15.0	27.0
1977	48.1	9.5	8.5	26.0	3.2	18.0	26.0
1978	54	13.7	12.7	26.0	5.0	14.6	18.7
1979	52	15.5	13.0	27.0	1.7	13.0	19.5
1980	54	12.0	15.7	23.0	2.6	25.0	22.0

EEC*: Including the UK
RW: Rest of the world, not including Eastern countries
Source: 'Notes Bleues'

The increase in intra-EEC investment has taken place at the expense of America and OECD investment, and has been accompanied by a slight increase in the share of the rest of the world. It is possible to distinguish between two stages in this process of regional restructuring of inward investment. During the 1960s, the OECD share fell while investment by the other three areas remained more or less the same. In the 1970s, the United States share fell, while that of neighbouring EEC countries increased. The first oil crisis had a direct bearing on the regional distribution of inward investment: whereas other European countries reduced their investment by 30%, the rest of the world recorded a threefold increase in their participation. On the other hand, the second oil crisis brought a recovery of the flows without modifying their regional distribution.

In the early 1960s, the two principal foreign investors in France were West Germany and the Benelux countries. Between 1962 and 1970 their shares grew respectively from 6% to 12% and from 14% to 25%. During the 1970s it was the UK which increased its share of French investments the most; its share grew during the period from 8% to 15%. Overall, however, it is the Benelux countries which account for the largest foreign investment stake in France.

(ii) Distribution according to sector

In 1980, inward foreign investment was divided equally between three broad sectors, *viz* manufacturing industry, services, and construction. There is only a negligible foreign involvement in the agriculture, energy, and transport sectors. Since the 1960s, investments in the construction and the service sectors have expanded relative to those in the manufacturing sector. These data are suggestive of a trend in the locational advantage for the French economy which is rather disturbing; *inter alia* they imply that foreign investors prefer to invest in such activities as tourism and building activities rather than in manufacturing, which is still the mainstay of French economic prosperity.

(b) Foreign firms in French industry

At the end of 1980 there were 2196 French firms which had more than 20% of their capital held by foreign firms. These firms, which represented 9% of all French industrial firms, accounted for 18.5% of total employ-

TABLE 3.5   The share of firms with foreign participation in French industry: 1972–80
(in %)

Manufacturing industry excluding energy	1972	1974	1975	1976	1977	1978	1979	1980
Number of firms	6.1	6.7	6.5	6.6	6.5	7.9	8.5	9.0
Employment	18.6	18.1	17.9	18.1	18.0	17.9	18.2	19.3
Total sales	23.5	21.8	21.6	21.8	20.6	21.3	22.5	24.1
Gross value added		22.2	21.9	20.5	20.3	20.1	20.9	22.6
Investments	24.7	23.8	24.5	24.5	24.7	25.1	24.5	29.3
Total industry including energy								
Employment	18.0	17.4	17.4	17.7	17.5	17.3	17.5	18.5
Total sales	25.8	25.8	25.4	26.7	23.6	24.3	25.0	26.6
Investments	24.1	21.7	20.0	19.9	18.5	17.8	17.0	19.1

Source: SESSI: 9 ans d'implantation étrangère, No. 28, p. 45.

ment in French industry, 26.6% of sales and 19.1% of capital expenditure (SESSI, No.28, p.13).

As is shown by Table 3.5, which sets out the changes in these variables over the period 1972 to 1980, the foreign presence in French industry has been remarkably stable.

(i) Foreign penetration by manufacturing sector

In 1980, the manufacturing sectors for which the contribution of foreign affiliates exceeded 30% of all sales were the following:

	%
Computers and data processing equipment	74.1
Agricultural machinery	57.8
Miscellaneous chemicals	53.3
Crude oil and natural gas	51.5
Pharmaceutical products	43.6
Miscellaneous (and other) products	42.1
Oils and animal fats	37.2
Precision and scientific instruments	36.2
Mechanical handling equipment	35.2
Basic chemicals	31.5
Domestic and industrial electronic equipment	30.8
Footwear	30.3

It can be seen from this list that (as in other industrialized countries) foreign subsidiaries tend to be concentrated in the technology-intensive industries. In particular, two groups may be distinguished—first the capital goods industries, particularly the computer and electronic industries and second, the chemical sector, with its upstream activities such as petroleum, and downstream activities such as agro-chemicals and pharmaceuticals.

Secondly, there exist two highly penetrated industries, the technology of which is either fully developed (agricultural machinery) or traditional (footwear). These are two sectors where the high foreign presence is well established, with strong North-American interests in the one case, and Italian interests in the other.

A more detailed industrial classification suggests that in the miscellaneous chemical industries, foreign participation is particularly strong in abrasives, detergents, plant-care products, and photographic and cinematographic products and weak in toilet preparations, adhesives, explosives, and paints. In the electrical and electronics sectors, foreign subsidiaries are concentrated in the manufacture of electric light bulbs and valves, semi-conductors, and radio and TV sets. In precision engineering, foreign firms are most strongly represented in the watch and clock and ball-bearings industries.

Foreign-based MNEs are least active in three types of activities:

(i) Monopoly or quasi-monopoly position of French nationalized firms; electricity (where the foreign participation ratio is 0.2%), aeronautics (0.8%), cars (14.6%).
(ii) Declining activities with low profitability, a tendency for excess capacity, and the presence of a small number of large (and often state-owned) French firms: examples include steel, semi-finished iron products, smelting, glass, metal manufactures.
(iii) Traditional consumer good industries, mainly made up of small firms, such as textile, clothing, leather, wood manufactures, and furniture.

On the whole, the sectors in which the foreign presence is most pronounced are characterized either by high barriers to entry, or by a declining location-specific advantage of the French economy. With the exception of public utility services and, perhaps, cars, these sectors produce mature and standardized goods which are being increasingly relocated in less developed countries. These are also sectors which are sometimes highly subsidized by the state, with a high proportion of nationalized firms.

Turning now to changes in the share of foreign subsidiaries by sector, since the beginning of the 1970s some interesting changes have taken place. First, foreign MNEs have lessened their involvement in industries of low technology and low profitability, noticeably iron ore extraction, steel, semi-finished iron products smelting. In so doing, they have shown a greater capacity for adaptation than their indigenous counterparts, though it must be stated that, relative to French firms, they are allowed greater freedom of action by the government, which has more control over its own firms in counteracting the adverse social consequences of the shutdown of factories. The reduction of the foreign presence in the household durable goods industry also corresponds to a loss of the French economy's location-specific advantage.

Secondly, the decline of foreign penetration in the glass and car industries may be explained by a fall in the ownership-specific advantages of foreign firms (notably Chrysler vis à vis French firms in the car industry, and Owens-Corning vis à vis St. Gobain-Pont à Mousson in the glass industry).

The sectors in which the penetration of foreign subsidiaries has increased during the period generally match with those for which a high index of penetration has already been observed. These include the high-technology sectors of computers and data-processing, associated chemicals, capital goods (including agricultural machinery), machine tools, mechanical handling equipment, and electrical manufacturing of precision instruments. The foreign penetration ratio has also risen in two traditional sectors, *viz* paper and board and footwear.

(ii) Foreign penetration by country

As Table 3.6 shows, foreign penetration is mainly by multinationals originating from the EEC and the USA. The information given in the statistics of investment flows are thus confirmed.

TABLE 3.6   The penetration of affiliates in France according to country of origin
(% of all firms in all industrial sectors–1980)

	Net assets	Employment	Sales	Value added
Belgium	11.9	9.2	8.6	8.1
Holland	4.9	7.0	14.3	7.6
FRG	19.9	15.7	11.4	13.1
Italy.	2.7	2.6	3.0	4.5
UK	11.7	11.4	13.1	10.3
Denmark	0.5	0.1	0.1	0.1
EEC	51.6	46.0	50.5	43.7
Sweden	3.4	2.9	2.0	2.3
Switzerland	15.3	11.5	6.9	9.0
Spain	0.9	0.2	0.1	0.2
Europe	72.0	61.0	59.9	55.6
USA	23.4	33.4	36.2	39.9
Canada	1.1	2.2	1.3	1.5
International control	1.1	2.6	1.4	2.2
Rest of world	2.4	0.8	1.2	0.8
Total	100	100	100	100

Source: See Table 3.7

Overall, European firms account for about 60% of the sales and employment of all foreign affiliates. Of the individual European countries, Germany is the largest investor, followed by Switzerland, the UK, and the Low Countries. But, of all countries, the US remains the single most important investor.

During the period 1972–80 the share of subsidiaries by country of origin remained fairly stable. Nevertheless, whereas between 1972 and 1977 the share of EEC subsidiaries fell and that of American subsidiaries rose (this mainly reflecting the liquidation of Fiat's interest in Citroën), between 1978 and 1980 the reverse movement took place, principally due to the intensification of German and English investments and a deceleration and/or retrenchment of US involvement. As percentages of employment and total sales in industry, the data of the first and last years of the eight-year period are set out in Table 3.7.

TABLE 3.7 Geographical origin of foreign affiliates in all industrial sectors in France 1972 and 1980

	1972		1980	
	Employment %	*Sales* %	*Employment* %	*Sales* %
EEC, of which:	44.0	44.6	46.0	50.5
Belgium–Luxembourg	9.5	9.2	9.2	8.6
Holland	8.5	12.2	7.0	14.3
FRG	8.7	7.4	15.7	11.4
Italy	9.1	7.1	2.6	3.0
UK	8.1	8.4	11.4	13.1
Rest of Europe	27.3	9.7	15.0	9.4
USA	37.2	42.2	33.4	36.2

Source: SESSI: 9 ans d'implantation étrangère, No. 28, Table 10, p. 56.

3.3 INTERNATIONAL COMPETITIVENESS AND FOREIGN DIRECT INVESTMENT

Analysis of inward and outward direct investment is rarely related to the international competitiveness of an economy. The most noteworthy study is that of Dunning (1981) in connection with the UK economy; one of the present authors (Michalet, 1983) has attempted a similar exercise using French data. The methodology of Professor Dunning is based on the distinction between the ownership-specific advantages of MNEs and location advantages of countries, to account for movements in outward and inward investment ($I_o + I_i$) and the ratio between them. This orientation will be adopted in this chapter as far as the statistical data allow. We would, however, emphasize again there are no comprehensive (French) data on the stocks of direct investment and thus it is impossible to accurately calculate rates of profitability.

Before proceeding to a discussion of the interaction between investment flows and international specializations, the recent trends in the I_o/I_i ratio will be traced. A final point will be devoted to the comparative micro-economic performance of foreign subsidiaries.

Equilibrium and disequilibrium of inward and outward flows

(a) Trends in the I_o/I_i ratio

(i) Total I_o/I_i (cf. Table 3.1)

Over the period as a whole the ratio of total I_o to total I_i increased from 0.33 in 1962 to 0.92 in 1980.

Analysis of the series allows three sub-periods to be distinguished:

—before 1968 the average ratio was 0.50;
—between 1968–72 the average ratio was 0.70;
—between 1973–80 the average ratio was 0.75.

The ratio was almost 1 at the end of the period. Precedents exist: it was 1.10 in 1972 and 0.96 in 1976. However, taking account of the varied and discontinuous methods of recording inward and outward flows, only the long-term trend has any real meaning.

Throughout the period (and unlike in the case of Germany) there has been a negative balance on the French direct investment account. It is, however, reducing all the time: in 1980 it was 1.5 thousand million French francs compared to more than 4 thousand million in 1979, 1978, and 1974.

(ii) I_o/I_i according to sector

In the industrial and services sectors I_o/I_i shows the same long-term trend as total flows:

I_o/I_i	1971–2	1973–7	1978–80
Industry	0.85	0.58	0.95
Services	0.90	0.83	0.84

The increase in the I_o/I_i ratio for industrial investments was greater than that for all investments, rising from 0.78 to 1.20 in 1980.

Of the individual industrial sectors two—construction and oil—merit separate treatment as they are both characterized by a very strong imbalance in I_o and I_i. In the case of oil, I_o is much the more dominant and gives a very high ratio. Petroleum I_o represented 30% of total I_o in 1980 and has accounted for one-half of that destined for developing countries since 1974. For example, in the British case, Petroleum I_o averaged around one-quarter of that destined for the OECD area in the mid 1970s and about one-eighth at the end of the decade; in the construction sector, I_i greatly exceeds I_o; in 1980 it represented 30% of all I_i and 50% of that from developing countries.

(iii) I_o/I_i by geographical regions

The balance of the French I_o/I_i ratio between the industrialized economies shows marked differences compared with that between the developing economies.

With developing countries, the ratio of I_o/I_i is greater than one. Inward investments are very small; they represented less than 10% of total investments until 1975 and 11% in 1980. The corresponding outward investment directed to these same countries varied between 30 and 40%. Over the period as a whole, the I_o/I_i ratio has fallen mainly because of a fall in I_o in the Third World. Nevertheless, Latin-America must be distinguished from other developing countries. As the I_o/I_i ratios show, this region continues to be very much in favour of France. While I_i from the Third World is not well documented, it is possible to infer that they are principally concentrated in the construction and banking sector.

TABLE 3.8 Balance of outward and inward investment (I_o/I_i) according to geographical region

	1971–3	1973–5	1976	1977–9	1980
EEC	0.64	0.59	1.08	0.53	0.48
USA	0.59	0.49	1.20	0.9	1.68
Other OECD	0.65	0.50	0.64	0.85	0.76
Rest of the world, of which:	11.00	4.32	3.60	1.64	1.94
Latin America	NA	4.0	7.32	4.2	3.14
Total	0.97	0.67	0.96	0.70	0.92

Source: 'Notes Bleues'—Ministry of Finance.

With the industrialized countries, the ratio of I_o/I_i is generally less than one. For the three geographical areas corresponding to the area of the most industrialized economies, I_o/I_i tended to fall up to 1976 after which a very clear recovery emerges which seems more durable in the case of the USA than for the rest of the OECD. It is nevertheless interesting that the French appear to be one step behind the West Germans in the internationalization process (see also Chapter 4 in this volume).

To conclude, all these data would suggest the French economy is characterized by an intermediary position between the industrialized and the developing countries, but presumably veering towards the former more than (say) in the case of Portugal (see Chapter 11). The competitive advantage of French MNEs is clearer vis à vis the Third World than vis à vis the economies of advanced countries.

(b) I_o/Exports (X) and I_i/Imports (M) ratios

The comparison of trade with direct investment flows raises the question whether they are complementary or substitutable. Before attempting to answer this point, it is important to underline the relative insignificance of capital movements as compared to product trade. During the whole period (as shown in Table 3.9) the ratios of I_o/X and I_i/M were close to 3%. Obviously, like their Japanese counterparts, the French firms are still internationalizing their activities predominantly in the form of trade in goods.

To return to the first question, it is interesting to note that the I_o/X and I_i/M ratios tend to converge over the period. This is the result of a fall of the I_i/M ratio from 6.5% in 1962 to 3% in 1980.

The I_o/X ratio experienced a phase of growth between 1962 and 1976 followed by a decline, bringing the ratio back to 2.2% in 1980. The stability of the I_o/X ratio can be interpreted as confirmation of the interaction between the two forms of international economic involvement: exports attract investments and investments sustain the flows of exports. The first sequence corresponds well to the French case, at least up to 1978.

On the other hand, the fall of the I_i/M ratio reflects the tendency of the rest of the world to substitute exports of goods to France for exports of capital to France, as witnessed by the sustained increase in the penetration of imported products into France.

TABLE 3.9   Relationship of outward direct investment and exports (I_o/X) and inward direct investment and imports (I_i/M) by selected areas and countries (%)

	1971–3		*1973–5*		*1976*		*1977–9*		*1980*	
	I_o/X	I_i/M	I_o/X	I_i/M	I_o/X	I_i/M	I_o/X	I_i/M	I_o/X	I_i/M
EEC	2.1	3.1	2.1	3.4	3.3	2.8	2.0	3.9	2.1	4.0
FRG	1.1	1.8	0.9	2.0	2.0	1.6	1.3	2.5	1.3	2.5
UK	3.2	9.6	5.3	12.3	7.6	7.9	3.7	7.6	2.9	10.0
Benelux	3.4	4.0	2.8	3.9	4.9	3.7	2.3	6.2	2.8	9.5
Italy	1.8	1.5	1.7	1.7	0.8	1.0	1.1	1.2	3.2	0.9
USA	7.9	8.7	9.7	7.5	14.3	5.0	9.7	7.1	19.7	5.4
Total	2.8	3.5	2.7	3.6	3.6	2.9	2.5	3.2	3.8	3.4

Of course, global developments mask individual cases. It is interesting to note the importance of the I_i/M ratio in the case of the UK and the USA. These are also the two principal home countries of MNEs. But in respect of both countries, the French I_i/M ratio shows a downward trend. At the same time, these are the two countries for which the French I_i/X ratio is the strongest. For the non-EEC industrialized countries, French direct investment appears to be a condition for quicker export penetration.

Specialization in industry

(a) A typology by sector

The methodology that will be followed in this section first relates the sector ratios of inward to outward flows to those at an industry level $(I_{ot} I_{it})$. The combination of these ratios leads to the formation of a typology which will distinguish the competitiveness of French MNEs and that of the French economy for a given period. Four types of situations may be identified:

I: I_{os}/I_{ot} rises, I_{is}/I_{it} falls, I_{os}/I_{is} rises. In this example the ownership-specific advantage of French MNEs of the sector has improved; the location advantage of the French has fallen and finally the competitiveness of the sector is reinforced. It is a situation of strong competitiveness with a marked tendency for relocation.

II: I_{os}/I_{ot} falls, I_{is}/I_{it} falls, and I_{os}/I_{is} falls also. When this combination occurs, it indicates the deterioration of the ownership-specific advantage of French firms, a fall in the French location advantage and a drop in world competitiveness of the firms of the sector.

III: I_{os}/I_{ot} falls, I_{is}/I_{it} rises, I_{os}/I_{is} falls. This situation suggests that the competitiveness of the sector is weakening. The comparative advantage is in the French location offered to domestic and foreign firms.

IV: I_{os}/I_{ot} rises, I_{is}/I_{it} rises, I_{os}/I_{it} rises also. This situation corresponds to the convergence of the industry or firm specific advantage of French MNEs and a French locational advantage. This interaction with a not insignificant result demonstrates a slight intra-sectoral specialization.

The application of this typology will be carried out in the following way. First, we shall analyse the share of industrial investment to total investment, then the identification of specialization by sector, and finally we shall examine changes in the international specialization by sector.

(b)   The share of industrial investment (I_{ind}) in total investment

In comparison with all I_o, the share of $I_{o_{ind}}$ fell between 1971–6 (from 42% to 26%) and then rose during the latter years of the period (from 30% to 43%). Similarly, $I_{i_{ind}}$ fell as a proportion of I_i, from 1971 to 1975 (from 50% to 36%); it then rose in 1976–7, but fell back again after 1978.

TABLE 3.10   The evolution of French outward and inward investment 1971–80

	1971	1972	1973	1974	1975	1976	1977	1978	1979	1980
$I_{o_{ind}}/I_{o\,total}$ (%)	42.6	40.4	36.7	25.1	27.6	26.0	30.4	40.2	34.6	43.6
$I_{i_{ind}}/I_{i\,total}$ (%)	50.6	44.6	36.0	35.4	36.3	42.0	38.6	34.2	32.0	33.0
$I_{o_{ind}}/I_{i\,total}$	0.78	0.92	0.87	0.46	0.50	0.60	0.50	0.86	0.80	1.20

As in the case of all investments the $I_{o_{ind}}/I_{i_{ind}}$ ratio was less than one, up to 1980. The ratio fell in the mid 1970s and did not recover its 1973 position until 1978. However, the result for 1980 suggested a strong thrust in the international redeployment of French industry.

(c)   Sectoral specialization

(i)   Development during the period

If we consider firstly I_o by broad sector, we can see (from Table 3.11) that in 1972, the two industries which occupy the most important places are metal-using industries (14.7%) and others (wood, paper and board, construction materials, etc, 15.3%), food and related industries (e.g. drink and tobacco), and textiles and clothing are of negligible importance, while chemicals occupy an intermediate position. At the end of the period, the sectoral hierarchy is the same. Although the relative significance of chemicals has fallen, and is now about the same as textiles, 'others' held second place but its percentage share has fallen greatly and is approaching that of food and related industries which has increased.

As a share of I_i in 1972, metals again occupy first place and this place is kept over the period, but in a decreasing proportion. Chemicals increase their relative share (from 7.7% to 8.9%). The contribution of all other sectors has fallen.

TABLE 3.11 Various inward and outward investment rates, 1972 and 1982

	Industry total %	Metals %	Chemicals %	Food and related %	Textiles %	Others %
1972						
I_{os}/I_o total	42	14.7	9.8	1.0	1.7	15.3
I_{is}/I_i total	50	23.0	7.7	5.0	2.4	11.0
I_{os}/I_{is}	0.78	0.61	1.2	0.20	0.70	1.31
1982						
I_{os}/I_o total	43.6	25.0	3.0	6.0	1.0	8.5
I_{is}/I_i total	33.0	14.0	8.5	4.6	1.4	4.5
I_{os}/I_{is}	1.2	1.66	0.30	1.20	0.60	1.7

For definition of terms, see text.

(ii) Sectoral classification

The analysis of the ownership-specific advantages of French MNEs and/or of the advantage of a French location can be made on the basis of the methodology defined above.

First, the ownership-specific advantage of French firms appears in the sectors in which I_{os}/I_{ot} is increasing while I_i is falling. This is the case of the metals and food and related sectors. Moreover, in both cases, the I_{os}/I_{is} increased during the period. A closer analysis of the fluctuations of I_{os}/I_{is} over the ten years show that they are moving in the same direction for all industries, but with lesser amplitudes when in decline and greater when rising. Metals and food and related industries correspond to Type I situations indentified earlier.

Second, the sectors whose share in the total industrial I_o and I_i is diminishing can be considered as sectors in which the competitiveness of French MNEs and/or the attractions of a French location are declining. This is the case for the textiles and other sectors.

Third, the sectors in which the share of I_o falls relatively and that of I_i increases are those in which is manifested an advantage of localization with loss of competitiveness of French MNEs. This is the case of chemicals; its I_o/I_i has greatly deteriorated during the period. This sector is representative of a Type III situation.

Fourth, comes international sectoral specialization. On the basis of Table 3.12, it is possible to distinguish for each sector the countries in which French MNEs were particularly strongly or weakly represented and/or whose own MNEs were particularly strongly or weakly represented in France. The analysis will deal separately with I_o and I_i, and finally

TABLE 3.12 Share of industrial investments of French inward and outward investment by sector and by zone (in %)

	Total			EEC			West Germany			United Kingdom			Benelux			USA			Rest of OECD		
	I_o	I_i	I_o/I_i	I_o	I_i	I_o/I_i	I_o	I_i	I_o/I_i	I_o	I_i	I_o/I_i	I_o	I_i	I_o/I_i	I_o	I_i	I_o/I_i	I_o	I_i	I_o/I_i
1974																					
Total industrial	32.3	35.4	0.46	28.20	27.4	0.40	71.4	38.2	0.53	7.6	25.0	0.11	9.9	24.0	0.12	69.0	61.0	0.43	32.8	38.0	0.39
Metals	12.0	13.0	0.60	7.50	10.0	0.30	15.6	18.7	0.23	2.0	7.6	0.25	8.1	6.9	0.35	21.6	21.0	0.39	17.0	15.5	0.49
Chemicals	5.0	8.0	0.41	4.60	4.1	0.44	6.3	12.2	0.26	1.1	1.4	0.28	5.3	1.8	0.89	12.0	14.0	0.32	4.8	12.4	0.16
Food and related	2.3	4.4	0.34	4.60	5.3	0.33	12.0	0.6	5.85	2.3	7.8	0.11	1.7	7.1	0.07	2.3	7.7	0.11	—	1.3	—
Textiles	1.5	1.0	1.01	1.16	1.0	0.45	—	—	1.00	1.7	1.4	0.45	10.1	1.3	2.33	—	0.5	—	3.4	1.4	1.02
Others	11.3	8.8	0.83	10.20	7.0	0.57	42.0	6.4	1.80	—	6.8	—	3.3	6.7	0.45	33.0	17.0	0.73	6.8	6.7	0.42
1980																					
Total industrial	43.6	33.0	1.20	61.4	33.0	0.89	65.0	30.0	0.93	50.0	21.0	0.75	27.2	44.0	0.16	55.5	50.4	1.83	40.0	35.0	0.87
Metals	25.0	14.0	1.66	44.0	11.6	1.83	53.0	11.0	2.08	36.0	8.7	1.32	12.6	14.6	0.23	23.0	37.0	1.07	20.7	10.6	1.50
Chemicals	3.0	8.9	0.30	1.3	10.0	0.06	3.5	10.5	0.14	0.4	3.8	0.03	1.1	15.3	0.01	3.5	7.0	0.84	5.7	9.0	0.50
Food and related	6.0	4.6	1.20	5.1	5.0	0.50	1.7	0.1	5.06	2.5	4.6	0.50	6.2	8.4	0.20	14.0	1.4	16.60	3.4	7.6	0.34
Textiles	1.0	1.4	0.60	0.8	1.8	0.80	1.9	3.0	0.27	0.4	0.8	0.16	0.4	0.8	0.13	0.7	—	—	—	1.7	—
Others	8.5	4.5	1.74	10.0	4.3	1.10	4.6	5.3	0.37	10.0	3.0	1.06	6.8	4.8	0.38	13.7	5.3	4.35	9.7	6.0	1.22

the results of the sectoral typology will be compared to those found for the different countries.

Analysis of I_o: the country-specific advantage of French MNEs. French I_o in West Germany in 1974 was highest in others (42.0%) and metals (15.6%). By 1980, I_o of metals had appreciably increased (53.0%) whilst others had fallen to 4.6%. The share of I_o directed to most other industries also fell. French outward investement in the UK was most pronounced in metals at the end of the period (36%), whereas in 1974, petrol occupied the first place (16%); indeed in that year, the leading industrial sector, food and related industries, only accounted for 2.3% of all I_o. Since 1974 there has been an upsurge in the relative share of industrial I_o which has mostly been directed to metals and others. In the Benelux countries, metals occupied first place in 1980 (12.6%) while in 1974 they were second to textiles whose share collapsed in the following six years to 0.4% in 1980. Others and food and related industries increased their participation. This region attracted the lowest share of I_o in 1980 (27%); in 1974 it was Great Britain (7.6%). Metals were still in the lead for I_o in the United States in 1980, taking the lead during the period over others. Food and related industries effected a breakthough between 1974 (2.3%) and 1980 (14.0%). The sectoral hierarchy did not change during the period for the rest of the OECD countries, metals, others and chemicals continuing to be the most attractive sectors for investment. Finally, for Latin America, the ownership-specific advantage of French MNEs is also concentrated in metals, with chemicals a long way behind.

Analysis of I_i: the advantage of a French location (an advantage of competitiveness of foreign MNEs). For I_i coming from West Germany, the advantage of a French location is most evident in the same sectors for the whole period: firstly metals and then chemicals. I_i by UK MNEs is in metals and food and related industries, the latter taking the advantage over the former at the end of the period while the share of others falls sharply. This was accompanied by a weakening of the share of industrial I_i in total I_i, which in 1980, with 21%, is the lowest of the countries/regions considered. MNEs from the Benelux countries seem to have gained an ownership-specific advantage and/or discovered the advantages of a French location for chemicals which came to the top in 1980 (15.3%) whilst they were at the bottom of the list in 1974. Metals and food and related industries remain the two other sectors of preference. United States MNEs increased their share of I_i in metals (37% in 1980, 21% in 1974) and reduced that of others and of chemicals, though without changing the order.

MNEs from the rest of the OECD countries also retain the same preference for investment in the French metals, chemicals and food and related industries. Only this last sector sees its relative importance increase. Latin America is not present in every sector. Chemicals come at the top at the beginning as at the end of the period.

For I_o as for I_i, the metal sector seems to attract the highest share for most countries. But with this exception, 'specializations' both of I_o and of I_i seem to exist between France and the rest of the world.

To pursue this line of investigation further, it may be useful to compare the results obtained across the sectoral typology with the specializations between France and its partners. The differences in relation to the average for each sector will allow us to highlight the characteristics of French competitiveness.

(iii) Sectoral specializations according to countries

First, of all sectors, the French seem to have a comparative investment advantage (I_o-I_i) in metals, other and food and related industries. In the first two of these the advantage of a French location (as shown by the I_i figure) does not change between 1974 and 1980. The characteristics of this type situation are verified for West Germany, the EEC and the rest of the OECD countries in metals. On the other hand, UK and US firms have increased their share of I_i in these sectors. In the case of both countries, metals are now classified as a Type IV situation for which subtle intra-sectoral specializations must have developed. In the case of the Benelux countries, we can see a fall in I_o/I_i despite an upward movement of I_o and I_i. This means that French MNEs have lost their competitiveness relative to other MNEs of this area.

For food and related industries, the average typology is applicable for West Germany, Great Britain, the United States and the EEC. Differences appear for the Benelux countries which come under Type II situations (overall drop in French comparative advantage) and for the rest of the OECD countries which correspond to Type IV situations (intra-sectoral exchanges).

Second, textiles and others can be classified as a Type II situation as far as intra-industry investment between France and Great Britain, the Benelux countries and the rest of the OECD is concerned. If we leave on one side the United States for which I_o and I_i are negligible, we can see two differences, viz, in the case of West Germany, whose MNEs seem more competitive than French ones, and in the case of the EEC where the French advantage is reduced even though the advantage of localization and the ratio I_o/I_i remain on the increase, the results for others vary greatly from one country to another. The typology is verified in the case of the United States and less clearly so in that of West Germany. The variety of cases relates to the extremely heterogeneous nature of this sector.

Third, chemicals are representative of a Type III situation for which only the share of I_o has marginally increased. This is confirmed in the data for the UK, the Benelux countries, the rest of the OECD, and the EEC. Only West Germany and the United States are not considered with the general trend. In the former case, chemicals should be classified in a Type II situation which would reflect the German superiority in this sector. For the United States, despite the drop in I_o and I_i, I_o/I_i is increasing.

3.4 COMPARATIVE PERFORMANCE OF FOREIGN AND FRENCH ENTERPRISES

We now turn to consider a comparison between the performance of the subsidiaries of foreign MNEs and all enterprises in France. In doing so we concentrate on two indices of performance—productivity and the export-/import balance.

Productivity of subsidiaries of foreign MNEs

As Table 3.13 indicates, the apparent labour productivity of the foreign affiliates in France is superior to that of all enterprises. The two ratios used which relate to size (i.e. value added and sales) are higher for foreign subsidiaries, but between 1974–80 they have not evolved at the same rate.

A few general explanations can be offered for the better productivity of foreign subsidiaries: better management, more capital-intensive production techniques, membership of a multinational group allowing the interplay of the effects of 'internalization' (Dunning, 1981; Rugman, 1982). But in the French case, a specific factor must be taken into account. This particular phenomenon is illustrated if we consider the value added/sales ratio.

Here, foreign subsidiaries record a less satisfactory performance than do all French firms. Moreover, the ratio appears to be falling over time. One interpretation of these data is that foreign affiliates, relative to French enterprises, prefer to go for growth of turnover even if this is to the detriment of local productive activity. In turn this suggests inward direct investment is increasingly dependent on imported raw materials, parts, and components for its production.

This observation will be confirmed below by the analysis of the structure of international trade of the foreign enterprises. But we can note that

TABLE 3.13   Selected ratios of performance of foreign affiliates in France and all
French firms, 1974–80

		1974	1975	1976	1977	1978	1979	1980
Constant sample of foreign-controlled firms								
VHT/effectif	(MF)	264	276	321	365	404	490	592
VABCF/effectif	(MF)	78	77	90	98	108	133	149
VABCF/VHT	(%)	29	27	28	26	26	27	25
EBE/VABCF	(%)	42	30	31	28	26	32	29
INV/VABCF	(%)	16	18	14	14	15	14	14
EXP/VHT	(%)					21	23	21
All French firms								
VHT/effectif	(MF)	184	197	226	258	277	334	404
VABCF/effectif	(MF)	62	64	76	84	95	114	131
VABCF/VHT	(%)	34	33	33	32	34	34	32
EBE/VABCF	(%)	34	25	26	25	25	29	27
INV/VABCF	(%)	17	18	16	16	16	17	19
EXP/VHT	(%)					22	23	21

VHT/effectif: total sales/employment (in million francs)
VABCF/effectif: gross value added/employment
EBE: profit margin
INV: investment
EXP: exports
VHT: total sales
Source: SESSI: 9 ans d'implantation étrangère, No. 28, p. 66.

from now onwards this tendency may well intensify. Moreover, the propensity of foreign subsidiaries to invest has fallen relative to that of domestic French enterprises (cf. Table 3.13). The investment of foreign firms
has not followed the upturn in the rates of investment for French industry
as a whole in 1979 and 1980. Our comparison of the 24 sectors distinguished in the report of SESSI suggests that in only 6 is the rate of
investment of foreign enterprises above the average. These are glass, basic
chemicals, agricultural machinery, household equipment, shoe manufacture, and plastic materials.

Beyond these general characteristics, it is possible to note the differences in behaviour among the foreign subsidiaries. To begin with, American subsidiaries are more integrated with the French industrial structure
than are their European counterparts; they are more productive although
they employ, on average, twice as many employees. In short, distance does
not allow them to follow the commercial strategy of European firms.
Secondly, considering all foreign subsidiaries, labour productivity is
greater for small and medium-sized industries than for large enterprises.
The former integrate better than the latter with indigenous firms. Thirdly,

the rate of integration is higher in those sectors in which the foreign penetration is also the highest. In only 5 sectors is the ratio value of labour productivity of subsidiaries superior to that of all industry: pharmaceuticals, agricultural machinery, machine tools, computers and data processing equipment, and construction materials. Only this last sector is not among the most penetrated sectors.

Impact on the export/import balance

In 1979, the proportion of the output exported by foreign manufacturing subsidiaries in France was the same as that for all French firms vis à vis 23%. This reflects a catching up on the part of foreign-controlled enterprises whose export propensity in 1976 was 18%, against 22% for all industrial enterprises (SESSI, p.76).

American and Canadian subsidiaries have a higher propensity to export than European subsidiaries. As a general rule, orientation to export is less strong, the more the subsidiaries are specialized in the production of one good. This finding shows that the very great majority of foreign affiliates are 'relay-subsidiaries'. Their implantation in France is not based on a locational advantage encouraging re-exports. Rather it is the national market which constitutes the predominant motive for the location, and all the more so where the size of the productive unit is large.

If there is comparatively little difference between firms under foreign control and French firms concerning the propensity to export, the situation is very different for imports. In 1977, the proportion of imports of all purchases of foreign subsidiaries rose to 27%, against 15.4% for French enterprises. Taking account of the data on exports, foreign implantation has then had a negative impact on the trade balance. In 1977, for example, the export/import ratio of foreign firms was around 0.73% compared to 1.44% in the case of French industrial enterprises.

Import propensities for subsidiaries are particularly high in the case of equipment goods. Rates are from 36% to 41% in engineering and electrical construction equipment against 11.2% and 11.8% respectively for French enterprises. In the intermediate goods sector as well, the subsidiaries' propensity to import is higher (24.2%) than that of French enterprises (16.6%). The corresponding ratios for consumption goods sectors are 26.9% and 15.1%.

This disequilibrium between exports and imports constitutes a major characteristic of foreign subsidiaries, and confirms the 'relay-subsidiary' character of the majority of foreign implantations. There are also differences in the trading patterns of foreign subsidiaries and French enterprises between region and by product. In the case of exports, foreign subsidiaries are more oriented towards Europe (74.3% of the total) of which the EEC receives 60%, than French enterprises (61.2% and 47.1% respectively). They export less than French enterprises to the United States and more to West Germany. They export less to Latin America, Africa, Asia, and Eastern Europe.

This narrower range of the geographical structure of exports of foreign subsidiaries relative to French enterprises is again revealed in the case of imports. Here too, the subsidiaries are more oriented towards Europe (78% of imports) than French enterprises (70%). They import less from the rest of the world except from the United States. In the case of American subsidiaries, their exports are strongly oriented towards Europe, including non-EEC Europe. In the EEC, they show a preference for the recent members, the highest ranking of which is Great Britain.

No data are available on the intra-firm trade of the French subsidiaries of MNEs. But it is interesting to note that the imports of subsidiaries follow the international specializations of the countries of origin. The comparison between the share of products imported from a country of origin by a subsidiary of the same nationality and the indices of specialization of the exporting country correspond to a certain extent with each other. As one example, we will take the case of Germany, which is France's leading trade partner.

Proportion of imports by German subsidiaries coming from West Germany		*Index of West German export specialization*	
Industry	69.4	Non-electrical machines	1.35
Engineering	88.2	Electrical machines	1.49
Electrics/Electronics	73.1	Transport equipment	1.29
Automobiles	78.1		

3.5   CONCLUSIONS: IMPLICATIONS FOR INDUSTRIAL POLICY

The previous sections have shown that inward and outward direct investment has had a considerable impact on the economic structure of French industry, and that given the right conditions, it could play a critical role in industrial restructuring in favour of the high-technology activities as envisaged by the 9th Plan. Indeed the successful modernization of the French economy is, at least, partly dependent on the recognition that the dimension of international production is as an important component of the external activities of French firms as is trade in goods. Yet up to now the 'foreign constraint' is still conceived of exclusively in terms of the balance and structure of the trade in goods. As a result, a discrepancy exists between the perceptions of the authorities and of businessmen as regards the true role of French industry and commerce in the world economy.

Such a divergence is harmful for the success of a relaunching of 'concentration'; indeed it may have the unintended consequence of a disordered acceleration of the process of internationalization as a reaction to the shortsightedness of the public authorities. The strength of investment abroad by French enterprises has not halted the downward movement of domestic investment. But it is not certain that the inverse sequence might be true. Rather than one taking a stand for or against MNEs, it is far preferable to make an objective assessment of the impact of their activities. It is the best way of appreciating the phenomenon which is likely to play an increasing role in industrial policy. It is therefore helpful, in this perspective, to attempt to retrace the major steps of the evolution of internationalization and to evaluate their consequences for restructuring policy.

First, French MNEs seem to have improved their market position vis à vis their foreign competitors. In this respect the increase in the ratio I_o/I_i is interesting. Whilst it has been traditionally less than one with other industrial economies, it has improved throughout the 1970s, with the United States amongst others. The international growth of French enterprises has indeed accelerated during the latter part of the 1970s. Investment in OECD countries and particularly in the United States constitutes a major feature, while the Third World, with the exception of some of the newly industrialized countries, has become of secondary importance.

The reinforcement of the competitiveness of French enterprises constitutes a second major characteristic of the last decade. This relies on an integration of the multinational dimension in the conception of medium to long-term strategy. This transformation in the entrepreneurial vision is expressed by a more acute appreciation of competition on the world market and by the necessity of identifying gaps, so as to exploit the specific advantages of French firms. This belated disappearance of the frontier between the home and world markets has favoured operations of industrial rationalization rather than a systematic utilization of the effects of internationalization. This orientation probably explains the preference accorded to foreign growth so as to penetrate the markets, and in particular that of the United States. In consequence, French multinationalization arises partly from a financial logic in which the administration of the portfolio of activities has more importance than the construction of a network of productive units integrated into the world ladder. In the face of this offensive by French MNEs, the penetration of foreign investments in France has remained stable. This then is the third tendency.

The increase in the I_o/I_i ratio is due to the increase in I_o with I_i having remained more or less at the same level. French locational advantages have deteriorated except for real estate. This situation does not signify that foreign MNEs have remained inactive. First, they have reinforced their presence in the high-technology sector while they have withdrawn from industries which are in decline or show only weak profitability. In doing so they have shown a capacity for more rapid structural adaptation than French industrial groups.

Secondly, they have increased their share of the national market by an increase in sales fed to a growing degree by imports. On average, foreign MNEs have not systematically sought to enhance their productive capacities. This strategy is characteristic of the neighbouring European MNEs. It is less pronounced in the case of American subsidiaries which are of greater size, more stable, and better integrated into the fabric of local industry. In total I_i seems to have had a negative impact on the French trade balance.

The union of the strategy of French and foreign MNEs allows a supplementary step to be made in the analysis of the impact of internationalization on industrial restructuring. Indeed, everything is occurring as if French MNEs had increased their competitive advantage at the same time as the location advantage of the French economy was diminishing. The convergence of choices of French and foreign firms is worrying: it leads to a weakening of the national productive system. On one hand, international growth seems like a substitute for a reorientation of domestic productive activities.

Indeed the promotion of a strategy of selective industrialization, and the sharing out of activities between firms of the international oligopoly, can lead to the abandonment by firms of certain activities in France. These can be taken up by other groups, French or foreign, or can lead to factory closures. It seems that the foreign MNEs have had more freedom to undertake these operations than the large French groups. State intervention has further slowed down the restructuring actions of these large groups. In consequence, relocalization allows firms to rediscover room for manoeuvre. The world market defines norms for products and techniques of production with which French MNEs can only bring their domestic activities into line with delay. They suffer more heavily from the weight of the reduction of delocalization advantages. On the other hand, foreign MNEs emerge from this problem more easily and can concentrate their efforts in the most profitable sectors where their advantages are the most pronounced. Finally, by extrapolating these tendencies, public authorities might find themselves facing a very difficult situation in which the interests of MNEs, whatever their nationality, were inconsistent with the reinforcement of national industry. On one hand, national MNEs sharpen their competitive advantages so as to develop their activities outside France; on the other, foreign MNEs slow down the development of their productive activities, withdraw from certain sectors and/or endeavour to substitute imports for local production in order to supply the French market. French industrial policy with regard to MNEs has never been explicitly defined. Nevertheless, the major direction during the period 1975–80 was based on the policy of 'redeployment' which encouraged multinational growth in French firms and their alliance with foreign (above all, American) groups. A policy of 'leaving the door wide open' was maintained for foreign investment. One result of this is a strong development of French MNEs, which has already been emphasized, with a tendency towards deindustrialization. Investment abroad has been substituted for domestic investment without the inward foreign investment filling the gap.

The arrival of a government of the left in 1981 saw a reappraisal of industrial policy. The conception of 'networks' was opposed to that of 'commercial leaders', the reconquest of the internal market opposed to worldwide redeployment. Simultaneously, there existed a willingness to fight against the increase in unemployment, while the principal industrial groups, including multinationals, were nationalized. A stronger state interventionism might have led to a policy of slowing down the multinationalization of the groups coupled with a policy of encouraging inward foreign investment. This idea has not been realised, partly because of the resistance of the new directors of the nationalized groups. The current orientation recognizes multinationalization as an essential factor of the competitiveness of enterprises in an open economy. The reinforcement of industrial cooperation between European firms is advocated to the extent that it might provide the basis for a Community industrial policy. In fact, the situation in which investment exchanges are based on subtle specialization could be systematically favoured. Public initiative is aiming to compensate the negative effects of internalization by a voluntary resumption of domestic industrial investment through a mobilization of savings and by a taking into account of the social cost brought about by the restructuring.

If it is wished to safeguard both solidarity and modernization doubtless there is hardly any other policy possible—particularly in the present conditions of world recession. Behind things specific to each nation, in all likelihood there exists a theme common to all economies: that of finding a way out of the crisis. The internationalization of industries in itself does not constitute a solution, as certain people have been led to believe. Indeed it may well aid firms to exploit their full potential. The real problem for the 1980s is to devise industrial and economic policies which might be adapted to the new technological and other developments including the multinationalization phenomenon.

NOTES

1. But see Franko (1976).
2. Examples include Renault-AMC, BSN-Dannon, PUK-Hownet, SG-PM-Certain Teed, Elf-Guelf Oil, and Pernod-Ricard, etc.

REFERENCES

Andreff, W. (1983). *Les multinationales hors la crise,* Paris: Sycomore
Bertrand, H., Mansuy, C., and Norotte, M. (1981). Vingt groupes industriels français et la redéploiement, *Economie et Prévisions,* no. 51, 1981/6
Conseil Economique et social (1981). Les investissements français à l'étranger et les investissements étrangers en France, *Journal Officiel,* no. 3, 25 February
Dunning, J. H. (1981). *International Production and the Multinational Enterprise,* London: Allen & Unwin
De Laubier, D. (1983). Bilan de l'investissement français dans le Tiers-Monde Raport Colloque CERIC, 15–16 December (mimeo)
Franko, L. G. (1976). *The European Multinationals,* London: Harper and Row
Michalet, C. A. and Delapierre, M. (1975). *The Multinationalization of French Enterprises,* Chicago, Academy International Business, published in France in 1974
Michalet, C. A. and Delapierre, M. (1976). *Les implantations étrangères en France: stratégies et structures,* Paris: Calmann-Lévy
Michalet, C. A. (sous la direction de) (1981). *Internationalisation des banques et des groupes financiers,* Paris: Edit. CNRS
Michalet, C. A. and Alii (1983). *Nationalisations et internationalisation: La stratégie des multinationales françaises face à la crise* Paris: Maspéro
Michalet, C. A. and Chevallier, Th. (1983). L'internationalisation des groupes du secteur public élargi (mimeo).
Michalet, C. A. (1983). L'adaptation des stratégies des multinationales à la crise, in A. Cotta and M. Ghertman (eds), *Les Multinationales en mutation,* Paris: IRM-PUF
Michalet, C. A. *et al.* (1983). *Nationalisation et Internationalisation; Stratégies des Multinationales Françaises.* Paris: La Découverte
Michalet, C. A. (sous la direction de) (1984). *L'intégration de l'économie français dans l'économie mondiale,* Paris: Economica
Mucchielli, J. L. and Thuillier, J. P. (1982). *Multinationales Européennes et Investissements croisés,* Paris: Economica
Rugman, A. M. (1982). *New Theories of the Multinational Enterprise,* London: Croom Helm
Savary. J. (1981). *Les Multinationales Françaises,* Paris: PVF-IRM

Stopford, J. and Dunning, J. H. (1983). *Multinationals: Company Performance and Global Trends,* London and Basingstoke: Macmillan

SESSI, Ministère de l'Industrie et de la Recherche (no. 28): 9 ans d'implantation étrangère dans l'industrie (1 January 1974–1 January 1981), Paris: Documentation Français

STISI, Ministère de l'Industrie (no. 10): Importations, exportations et filiales françaises de firmes multinationales, Paris: Documentation Français

STISI, Ministère de l'Industrie (no. 4): Les Exportateurs de l'Industrie Enterprises – Groupes, filiales de groupes étrangers, Paris: Documentation Français

Stoleru, L. (1969). *L'Impératif Industriel,* Paris: Seuil

Vernon R. (ed.) (1974). *Big Business and the State – France,* Harvard University Press

4

The Federal Republic of Germany

4.1 WEST GERMANY'S PARTICIPATION IN INTERNATIONAL TRADE, INVESTMENT, AND TECHNOLOGY TRANSFER

Its history since 1960

(a) Trade

West Germany is poorly endowed with natural resources and unskilled labour, and comparatively rich in real, financial and above all, human capital. Germany thus depends on importing the necessary raw materials and unskilled labour, and real capital-intensive intermediate goods. Additionally, as in other high-income industrialized countries, German consumers also demand differentiated, income-elastic imported products.[1] On the other hand, these imports have to be earned by exporting internationally competitive products which are predominantly human-capital-intensive. Since it is well known that Germany has demonstrated a considerable international competitiveness in world trade we confine ourselves to a few illustrations:

In 1980, German exports and imports were valued at about eight times those in 1960. Over the same period, the contribution of exports to GDP has grown from 15.8% to 23.6%; imports have developed in similar ways. Though exports and imports have been about balanced most of the time, up to the end of the 1970s Germany typically earned an export surplus (Table 4.1). The annual average growth rates of imports and exports has amounted to about 11% per annum which is considerably higher than the appropriate GDP deflator. While the export expansion accelerated in the late 1960s, thus enabling German industry to earn considerably higher export surpluses for some years,

TABLE 4.1   West Germany's international economic involvement since 1960

		1960	1965	1970	1975	1980	Growth[a]
Trade:							
Exports (fob)	billion DM	47.9	71.7	125.3	221.6	350.2	10.5
	% of GDP	15.8	15.6	18.2	21.2	23.6	
Imports (cif)	billion DM	42.7	70.4	109.6	184.3	341.4	11.0
	% of GDP	14.1	15.3	16.0	17.6	23.0	
Long-term private international capital flows:							
Exports	billion DM	−1.4	−2.2	−8.6	−21.9	−27.4	16.0
	% of GDP	−0.5	−0.5	−1.3	−2.1	−1.8	
Imports	billion DM	+2.5	+4.6	+10.1	+2.5	+12.7	8.5
	% of GDP	+0.8	+1.0	+1.5	+0.2	+0.8	
In % of domestic gross fixed investment:							
	exports	−1.9	−1.8	−5.0	−10.5	−8.1	
	imports	+3.4	+3.8	+5.9	+1.2	+3.7	
Payments from/for technology transfer:							
Exports	billion DM	N.A.	0.3[b]	0.5	0.8	1.1	9.4[c]
Imports	billion DM	N.A.	−0.8[b]	−1.3	+2.1	−2.6	8.8[c]

N.A. = not available
[a] Annual average growth rate, 1960–80
[b] 1966
[c] 1966–80 only
Sources: Deutsche Bundesbank; Sachverständigenrat

the import acceleration which followed in the late 1970s ended that golden decade of West Germany's 'excess' export surpluses which in some areas amounted to about 4% of German gross domestic product (GDP).

As in the case of other countries, and in contrast to the neo-classical hypothesis developed by Ohlin (1933) and Samuelson (1948), international trade has not fully substituted for international factor movements in Germany. Foreign labour accounted for up to 10% of West Germany's labour force in the 1970s, while, as Table 4.1 shows, the combined exports and imports of private capital were about 12% of gross domestic fixed investment in Germany in 1980.

(b) Investment

Germany's long-term private international capital outflows rose about twenty times between 1960 and 1980, whereas the corresponding inflows in 1980 rose only fivefold. Thus the international pattern of locational advantages appears to have changed in disfavour of West Germany. While Germany's propensity to import investment capital generally reflects her imports of goods and services, the involvement through direct investment abroad has expanded more rapidly than her export trade.

(c) Technology transfer

The development of West Germany's trade in disembodied technology is surprising for three reasons:

(i) In spite of West Germany's leading position as a producer of technology, income received from the overseas sales of technology is only 0.3% of her exports although, of course, part of the technology exported is embodied in intermediate or final products.

(ii) The expansion of technological exports between 1960 and 1980 was smaller than that of trade in goods and international investment— at a time when the future of German industry was proclaimed as consisting of the export of blueprints, construction plans, etc. (cf. Albach, 1978).

(iii) The import of technology by German firms—as measured by fees and other income from trade in technology—has risen faster than the export of technology.

The determinants

In analysing these determinants we can discern three major dimensions of change:

(i) the change in the volume of international economic involvement of all kinds;

(ii) the change in the relative importance of the various forms of international involvement;

(iii) the change in the composition of industry within the internationally-oriented sector of the German economy

(a) Established research results

Although it seems obvious that these questions should have been subjected to intensive research efforts, some of them have remained unexplored. Although the major German economic research institutes—on behalf of the Federal Government—have started a series of large research projects on the structural change of the German economy,[2] and numerous academic researchers have devoted their efforts to the same subject, the outcome is so far confined to the following aspects:

(1) Empirical research (as documented in the references) has shown that—similar to other industrialized countries—the composition of export-oriented industries in Germany has changed in favour of those sectors which are technology- and/or human-capital-intensive, and which are dominated by relatively large corporations. By contrast, sectors which have experienced increasing import pressure within the complementary international division of labour are typically labour-, real-capital-, and raw-material-intensive with a relatively low level of technology and, in most cases, consist of relatively small firms. Branches, under import pressure in the substitutive sphere of the international division of labour, are similar to those active in the export sector.[3]

(2) As regards the interdependencies between various forms of international economic involvement, only the trade-investment axis has been analysed in any detail. Here, practically all studies have shown that trade and investment usually complement rather than substitute for each other.[4] This parallels research results for other industrialized countries, excepting Japan and the United Kingdom.

Comparatively little attention has been given to the relative importance of technology transfer or to the total international involvement of German firms. Since this is not the subject of this chapter we can only give some tentative explanations.

(b) Technology transfer: Some tentative explanations

(1) The data set out in Chapter 4 show that German trade in technology is both small and unbalanced. However, the balance of payments figures represent only disembodied technology transfer of a very specific kind. There are not only other forms of disembodied technology transfer which appear as trade in services, or are not shown at all (since they consist of barter trade or unreported intra-firm trade); but there is also technology transfer embodied in capital goods and research-intensive products which has grown very much faster than total German international trade.[5]

(2) On the whole, technology transfer complements foreign investment and trade.[6] The sectoral analysis clearly demonstrates that the industries leading in trade and foreign investment (e.g. chemicals, electrical engineering) also account for the bulk of disembodied technology transfer.[7] Like capital exports, technology transfer is concentrated in those branches which possess comparatively high locational advantages in Germany (Reisen, 1982).

(3) The reason for the trade deficit in technology transfer is directly related to Germany's foreign direct investment position. About 75% of Germany's payments for technology are made by foreign affiliates.

By contrast, income from technology exports mainly accrues to German firms without direct investment abroad. However, just as the cross-investment pattern changed in favour of Germany in the mid 1970s, there has been a similar, though weaker, tendency in the balance of disembodied technology transfer. The reduction of the gap between the import and export of technology appears to be closely associated with the acceleration of German direct investment abroad. This holds even more for technology transfer embodied in the trade of capital equipment and research-intensive goods.

(4) Additionally the regional structure of imports and exports of technology can explain part of the unbalanced figures. While Germany receives technology imports almost exclusively from a few other industrialized countries, her own exports of technology to developed and developing countries are distributed in similar proportions to her capital exports. Since technology transfer managed

by non-equity arrangements such as licences is subject to more political risks and barriers in trade with developing countries, suppliers of technology prefer embodied to the disembodied transfer of technology in dealing with these countries. Disembodied technology exports to industrialized countries are thus underreported vis à vis the equivalent imports of technology.

(c) The retardation of Germany's international integration: some explanations

In the two decades 1960–80, Germany became more intensively integrated in the world economy: this is confirmed by the growth of international transactions of all kinds and by the increasing share of trade in Germany's GDP. However, while the trading sector in the German economy has grown relative to the non-trading sector, German international involvement as a whole has grown rather less rapidly than that of her international competitors. Although direct investment abroad accelerated in the 1970s much faster than in other industrial countries (except Japan), German trade has grown less rapidly than total world trade, and as we have seen, the role of disembodied technological transfer of technology is still insignificant. However, bearing in mind the dramatic revaluation of the DM in this period, the substantial increase in some factor prices and the deceleration of German growth rates, one may wonder why (and indeed how) Germany has been able to remain as successful as she has in international trade. We can suggest two reasons:

(1) First, Germany has managed to compensate shrinking international competitiveness due to a rising exchange rate by continued improvements in industrial productivity:[8] although no longer in a leading position, Germany's growth rates of productivity remained above the average for industrialized countries in the 1960s and 1970s.[9].

(2) Second, there seems to be a dual export market for German products, with one market segment being faced by a relatively price-inelastic export demand,[10] and the other by a relatively price-elastic export demand.[11] While the latter market presumably has been protected, in part (and certainly only temporarily) by decreasing relative prices and strong international price competition[12] with resulting shrinking profits or price cost margins,[13] the first market seems to be marked by monopolistic competition. In consequence, while the price increase of German exports in foreign currency due to the

revaluation of the DM seems to have been exhausted, on the whole prices have remained[14] above the competitive level and have been without major repercussions on export volumes.[15] The fact that German export industries' demands for protection of various kinds were relatively weak up to the early 1970s[16] but have intensified since then, supports this contention (Juhl, 1978).

The role of inward and outward investment in particular

(a) The figures

Whereas the ratio between inward and outward foreign direct investment in Germany was about 1.5 : 1 in 1971, by 1981 it had changed to about 1 : 2.5; thus Germany has switched from being a net importer of direct investment to become a net exporter. This change has been most dramatic in the chemical industry where the ratio has fallen (from 2 : 1 to 1 : 2.5), in mechanical engineering (from 4 : 1 to 1 : 1.3) and in transport equipment (from 3 : 1 in 1976 to 1 : 4 in 1981). The improvement in Germany's international direct investment position has been most marked in those industries which also lead in trade in goods and technology as well as in R&D intensity. These industries are also those in which the concentration of inward and outward foreign direct investment is most pronounced. The regional distribution of trade and investment patterns is very similar.[17]

Whereas the cross-hauling patterns of German direct investment have already been described (almost exclusively by Kiera) in German literature, up to now there has not been any study analysing the possible determinants of such patterns.[18] We now analyse some hypotheses advanced to explain cross-country investment patterns to see whether they have any explanatory power for Germany.

(b) The developmental approach

Dunning (1981) has suggested a developmental approach for explaining cross-direct investment patterns. His analysis suggests that Germany should have moved in the 1970s from being a net importer of foreign capital to a net exporter. At the same time, his approach would suggest diverging rather than coinciding sectoral patterns of cross-investment flows while closely complementary *sectoral* concentration patterns prevail in the German case. Thus German foreign investment flows are either determined by factors other than those advanced by Dunning or these patterns exist *within* these sectors of industry, behind the veil of the high level of aggregation.

(c) Market motives and competitive rivalry

Jungnickel *et al.* (1976) have presented questionnaire results pointing to the fact that both inward and outward foreign direct investment in Germany is overwhelmingly motivated by 'market motives'. Thus investment flows in both directions appear to serve a modality of international competition, particularly where it is not profitable or practical to source markets through trade in final products. However, since these motives have been identified as the main driving force for foreign investment in most branches of industry in almost all studies, they hardly allow conclusions specific to the German cross-investment patterns.

By pointing to the market orientation, Jungnickel *et al.* (1976) have

TABLE 4.2   Inward and outward foreign direct investment flows by industry, 1971–81 (in DM million)

Branches of industry	1971		1976		1981	
	Inward	*Outward*	*Inward*	*Outward*	*Inward*	*Outward*
Total	3,986.0	2,667.5	3,064.0	5,056.9	4,044.1	9,824.1
Chemical industry	555.4	271.1	263.8	786.9	476.0	1,177.6
Electrical machinery	267.9	275.2	291.8	529.9	469.7	477.6
Banking	234.9	156.1	532.9	473.8	712.4	1,884.7
Iron and steel	15.5	298.4	51.2	449.3	112.4	8.9
Mechanical engineering	839.2	216.5	301.6	656.8	422.4	556.6
Transport equipment	343.6	266.1	301.0	101.5	361.3	1,339.1
Petroleum	757.6	102.6	36.6	460.1	228.6	544.2
Insurance	N.A.	6.3	N.A.	171.2	N.A.	156.2
Building	N.A.	283.4	N.A.	125.2	N.A.	235.7
Food	34.6	105.6	20.2	76.0	101.7	133.2
Finance	1,001.6	N.A.	328.1	N.A.	450.6	N.A.
Rubber and asbestos	39.0	N.A.	82.0	N.A.	14.3	N.A.

N.A. = not available
Source: Bundesministerium für Wirtschaft.

much in common with other studies. The analyses by Hymer and Rowthorn (1970), Graham (1978) and others stress the oligopolistic rivalry of leading MNEs to protect their market shares either by defensive, export-promoting investments in foreign markets or by retaliatory investment by one nation's firms' in the home countries of those foreign firms which 'had the audacity' to increase competitive pressure by inward investment. Since, however, the industrial sectors engaging in foreign direct investment are typically marked by technological intensity, an above average propensity to invest abroad, large firm size, and high intra-industry concentration rates it seems unsatisfactory to attribute the leading role in cross-hauling to factors which also statistically 'explain' the leading role of a certain group of industries in analysing general propensities to invest abroad.

(d) Protection

Another approach to explaining cross-investment flows is the mutual-tariff-investment-argument which may be developed *inter alia* by Kojima (1978) to explain Japanese cross-investment patterns. If such developed countries install symmetric tariff structures it might be expected that cross-investment would be small in unprotected industries and high in strongly protected branches of industry. However, the analysis of German data does not support such expectations.

(e) Ownership- and location-specific advantages

Dunning's eclectic model (Dunning, 1981) seeks to explain inter-industry foreign direct investment between countries in terms of the balance between the ownership advantages of firms of different nationalities and the location-specific advantages of countries. To what extent can this paradigm be extended to explain the intra-industry activity by MNEs? Since these factors establish the propensity to go abroad in favour of a certain group of industries and since they point to the same set of branches of industry in similarly advanced countries, it is reasonable to expect that the firms which perform industrial activities within these sectors at home will meet each other[19] in international markets and thereby account for the bulk of cross-investment. But, as we shall explain later, such cross-investment is not easily explained by a neo-classical model of international production. Account must rather be taken of the oligopolistic strategy of firms and growth of intra-industry transactions across national boundaries.

4.2   INTERNATIONAL COMPETITIVENESS, ECONOMIC PERFORMANCE, AND THE STRUCTURE OF WEST GERMANY'S INTERNATIONAL CROSS-INVESTMENT

The sectoral concentration of intra-industry FDI: measurement and hypotheses

(a) Measurement problems

Table 4.2 presents data on intra-industry FDI which have been published by the Federal Ministry of Economics. These data are only available at a rather high level of aggregation. However, in the late 1970s the Deutsche Bundesbank developed a new, much more detailed series of foreign investment statistics than previously published. Unfortunately, the data reach back only to 1976 and are not fully comparable with earlier published information. In this chapter we shall therefore confine ourselves to a cross-sectional analysis of cross-investment on two years, 1976 and 1981. The data published give details about foreign affiliates in Germany and German companies abroad in respect of assets, sales, employment, and number of parent firms and subsidiaries; there are sectoral as well as geographical data and, for a reasonably smaller set of items, even matrix presentations.

The data set out in Table 4.2 are based upon these statistics. They again confirm that, within manufacturing, cross-foreign investment is concentrated in the chemical, iron and steel, mechanical engineering, transport equipment, and elctrical engineering industries (but also in mineral oil processing and food as regards inward investment). Outside manufacturing, trade, banking and other services are major two-way sectors of economic activity.

(b) Intra-industry FDI: basic theory and the design of indicators

(1) Since intra-industry foreign direct investment has much in common with intra-industry trade (Dunning and Norman, 1985), it seems advisable to make use of the methods developed for the corresponding foreign trade analysis. Erdilek (1982) has suggested such a modified measure for intra-

industry investment which may be named the cross-investment ratio (CIR):

$$CIR = \frac{(OUTINV + INWINV) - |OUTINV - INWINV|}{(OUTINV + INWINV)}$$

Where CIR is equal to 1 inward and outward investment are the same; and where it is zero CIR = 0 says that there is no cross-investment at all. This indicator can be calculated using various measures of MNE activity, such as Cross-Investment Capital Ratio (CICR), Cross-Investment Sales Ratio (CISR) and Cross-Investment Employment Ratio (CIER). Measuring international involvement by any of these measures suggests similar patterns of involvement by invested capital although different firm sizes and factor intensity by branch of industry cause some minor variations. Throughout the rest of the chapter we shall use the CICR ratio only.

(2) At the first glance, the data suggest an increase in intra-industry FDI; as regards all manufacturing, CICR rose from 0.73 in 1976 to 0.97 in 1981, and this is the inter-temporal pattern typical for almost all branches of industry which basically reflects the relatively faster growth of outward FDI referred to earlier.

(3) The more interesting problem is why some branches of industry approach balanced cross-hauling quicker than others. In this connection, we will observe that the cross-investment ratio as defined above is entirely concerned with the balance, rather than the level, of investment flows and tells us nothing as to whether a country is a net importer or exporter of capital. Take for example the data for transport equipment: This industry's CICR fell from 0.91 to 0.63 between 1976 and 1981. But has cross-investment really fallen? In 1976 inward investment slightly exceeded outward investment but in 1981 outward investment was much higher than inward investment and in value terms both were higher than in 1976. Thus too much should not be read into the ratios. Certainly a ratio of unity has no particular normative implications; it simply represents a border between various stages of development to be passed over by those nations whose outward investment involvement develops more dynamically than their inward investment. Thus a ratio of 0.8 in 1981 could well indicate a more advanced level of development than 0.9 in 1976, if unity has been passed over in between.

In fact, almost all branches of German industry tend to approach, and to exceed, balanced cross-investment patterns. Nations who are more dynamic than others thus seem to pass through a stage of shrinking inter-, but increasing intra-industry investment ratios to a stage of development with decreasing intra-industry and rising inter-industry patterns of involvement in trade in goods as well as in trade in factors of production. The country being in the first stage a net importer (inward > outward investment) becomes a net exporter in Stage 2. These stages may be the named pre-balanced and post-balanced stage of cross-investment; the more dynamically a country developes relative to its competitors, the faster will the country pass through the pre-balanced into the post-balanced stage of cross-investment.

(4) The current situation of any branch of industry with respect to these stages of development can be made more meaningful if the previously defined CIR (CICR) ratio is altered into:

$$\text{MCIR (MCICR)} = (1 - \text{CIR}) \times \begin{array}{l} (-1) \text{ if inward} > \text{outward} \\ (+1) \text{ if inward} < \text{outward} \end{array}$$

The ratios set out in Table 4.3 present the branches according to their MCICR rank and suggest that a perfect balance of cross-hauling = 0; and that the higher the ratio, either positive or negative, the higher the imbalance of outflows and inflows. In analysing these data we shall argue that the current situation of the various branches is due to an interplay of location- and ownership-specific factors. In particular, we offer two specific propositions:

(i) The less important locational factors are likely to be as a determinant of international direct investment, the faster will the corresponding sector of industry tend to pass over to through the post-balanced stage. It is very interesting that the most 'outdated' branches of industry for developed countries, for instance leather and clothing, are leading with respect to cross-hauling dynamics.

(ii) Additionally, the more German investors have acquired ownership advantages and the more these prevail vis à vis locational advantages, the higher will be the cross-hauling between branches (cf. electrical engineering and transport equipment).

Overall, however, the sectoral pattern suggests that the decisive factors determining a branch's dynamic cross-investment position cannot be fully caught since they seem to be as much determined by firm-specific as by industry-specific circumstances.

International comparative advantages and foreign direct investment

Table 4.4 sets out some rank correlation indices, relating intra-industry

foreign direct investment (MCICR) to a number of performance indicators. As the table shows, the simple cross-section comparison of inward
investment, outward investment, and cross-investment ratios, and RCA
figures does not suggest any convincing relationship. If there is any correlation at all, it is rather weak and non-linear. Thus, the question whether
foreign investment is sectorally allocated according to the industries' RCA
position cannot be clearly answered at first glance.

The reason for this lack of association is due to the fact that Germany's
industries' foreign investment and trade positions are determined by a set
of factors such as locational advantages (in raw materials, production,
marketing), ownership advantages of (potential) foreign inward investors,
of domestic investors at home, of domestic outward investors, and of foreign investors at home, which in very different combinations exert diverging influences upon the industries' position. Unfortunately our sample of
observations is too small to allow for serious estimates isolating these different determinants.

Very roughly it may be assumed that—if there are any bilateral interdependencies between RCA and foreign direct investment at all—outward
investment is positively related to RCA, whereas inward investment displays a parabolic function having its minimum at a low positive RCA
value. This suggests that both inward and outward direct investment are
concentrated in industries in which German industry is internationally
competitive (RCA > 0).[20] The higher the industries' competitiveness,
however, the stronger the tendency for Germany to be a net exporter of
investment capital in that particular industry. This is obviously in contrast
with results for Japan and the UK.[21] At the other end of the spectrum,
however, inward investment most exceeds outward in industries in which
Germany is comparatively *dis*advantaged;[22] this is also contrary to the
findings for Japan and the UK.

Intra-industry FDI and sectoral performance

Those industries which lead in cross-investment activities are usually supposed to be marked by mutually reinforcing interconnections with different variables of sectoral performance: foreign direct investment (inward as
well as outward) is assumed to favour, and be favoured by, above average
corporate growth, productivity, and profitability.[23] However, the basic
data upon which this analysis is built fail to support these expectations.
This holds also for almost all of the rank correlations: the results are
summarized in Table 4.4.

TABLE 4.3   Germany's intra-industry investment pattern, 1981: cross-investment
ratios

Pre-balanced	MCICR	Post-balanced	MCICR
Mineral oil	−0.79	Total industry	0.02
Food	−0.69	Manufacturing	0.03
Foundries	−0.68	Earth and stone	0.09
Tobacco	−0.59	Transp. and Comm.	0.10
Rubber	−0.56	Holding companies	0.11
Trade	−0.52	Iron and Steel	0.12
Housing and estate	−0.45	Banking	0.14
Plastics	−0.45	Agriculture	0.17
Fine ceramics etc.	−0.44	Public utilities	0.17
ITM-goods	−0.44	Oil and gas	0.23
Paper, board, print	−0.38	Banking and insurance	0.25
Drawing etc.	−0.34	Mining	0.29
NF-metals	−0.32	Electrical engineering	0.32
Textiles	−0.29	Finance institutions	0.34
Steel and light		Transport equipm.	0.37
metal products	−0.12	Chemical	0.37
Services	−0.09	Insurance	0.48
Mechanical eng.	−0.06	Leather goods	0.52
Wood-working	−0.04	Clothing	0.61
Optics etc	−0.03	Building	0.65
Inward > Outward		Outward > Inward	

Source: Calculated from data published by the Deutsche Bundesbank.

(a) Growth

Sectors in which outward and/or inward investment is concentrated do
not appear to have significantly higher rates of growth of industrial assets
than other sectors. Nor do industries with high MCICR ratios display distinctive growth patterns.

(b) Productivity

The rank correlations tend to suggest a negative relationship between a
sector's level of productivity and its crude cross-investment ratio whereas
it seems to be positively correlated with our adjusted (MCICR) ratios.
However, since the statistical results are insignificant, we can draw only
tentative, cautious conclusions. The indication that outward investment

tends to be the higher relative to inward investment the smaller the industry-specific productivity in Germany (and the corresponding conclusion that inward investment tends to be higher relative to outward, the higher the industry-specific productivity) points to the importance of locational factors influencing the distribution of investment. This would favour the neo-classical rather than the industrial-organization explanations of the allocation of foreign investment. However, this is only part of the answer. The sectoral data clearly demonstrate that there is a dual relationship between productivity and foreign investment; whereas sectors with closely balanced and post-balanced cross-investment relations seem to be marked by a slightly positive relationship between cross-investment and productivity with only a small variance (thus supporting industrial-organization arguments), the opposite is true for clearly pre-balanced industries where remarkably high productivity figures can be observed as coinciding with high inward vis à vis outward investment data. These pre-balanced industries consist of non-ferrous metals and food. Since, however, firms in these industries are in general more influenced by the location of immobile factors than others, they should be omitted. Excluding these a recalculation of Spearman's rank correlation between productivity figures in 1980 and MCICR in 1981 yields a rank correlation as high as $= +0.78$ and significant at 5% level. This clearly supports the view that—in so far as firms are motivated to go abroad at all—the tendency to do so, and to engage in cross-hauling in particular, is the stronger the higher the industry-specific productivity. This also holds for the relationship between productivity and intra-industry investment dynamics. The rank correlation coefficient between productivity in 1980 and MCICR change between 1976 and 1981, re-estimated for the revised sample, was $= +0.71$ (instead of $= +0.25$ in the original sample) and is now significant at a 1% level.

(c) Profitability

The neo-classical model might also be expected to predict that the higher the profitability at home (measured as profits relative to equity capital inclusive of reserves), the stronger will be inward relative to outward investment. Industrial-organization theory, on the other hand, would suggest the opposite is more likely: that higher outward vis-à-vis inward investment can be attributed to the existence of more dynamic and thus more profitable firms in the respective industries. The rank correlations in Table 4.4 unfortunately allow us to make only guesstimates with regard to the MCICR ratio, due to the sample's high variance.

As regards the MCICR ratio, however, a negative relationship between profitability and the industries' cross-hauling dynamics is suggested. Thus the data seem to lend support to the neo-classical hypothesis. Although we do not deny that investors may be prompted to invest because of shrinking profits at home, we do not think this is generally the case. For example, it seems unlikely that the leading branches in foreign investment (chemical industry, mechanical and electrical engineering, transport equipment, iron and steel) should have lost their locational advantage in Germany and suffered from shrinking domestic profits. Even if this may hold for some parts of these industries (which have reached the maturity stage in the product cycle model), Germany's inward investment patterns clearly demonstrate that this group of industries still possesses locational advantages in Germany. This suggests that an alternative explanation is required for the negative correlation between profitability and MCICR.

TABLE 4.4   Performance, structure, and Germany's intra-industry FDI (MCICR measure) rank correlation results

Indicators of performance and structure		MCICR 1976		MCICR 1981		MCICR change (1976 to 1981)	
		r_s	n	r_s	n	r_s	n
Growth of industrial assets, 1975 to 1980				0.11	13	0.14	13
Productivity (sales per man)	1975	−0.36	13			0.29	13
	1980			−0.15	15	0.25	13
Profitability (profits relative to equity capital)	1975	0.32	13			−0.45[a]	13
	1980			−0.12	13	−0.54[b]	13
R&D per employee	(1979)	0.34	16	0.17	16	0.05	16
R&D as a share of sales	(1979)	0.58[c]	16	0.41[a]	16	0.17	16
Second-order technology intensity	(1979)	0.27	16	0.26	16	−0.08	16
SC3	(1979)	−0.31[a]	23	−0.12[a]	23	0.37[a]	23
SC6	(1979)	−0.32[a]	23	−0.14	23	0.36[a]	23
PC3	(1979)	0.35[a]	23	0.35[a]	23	0.20	23
PC6	(1979)	0.35[a]	23	0.38[a]	23	0.24	23

Coefficients significant at the: [a]10%-level
[b]5%-level
[c]1%-level
n = number of observations.
Definition of variables: see text.
Source: Author's calculations from data provided by the Deutsche Bundesbank Bundesverband der Deutschen Industrie (1982), and Monopolkommission (1982).

In this connection it is interesting to note that all industries with *post-balanced* cross-investment flows and *below average* profitability, which have mainly caused the negative relationship even using the MCICR, are strong two-way-investing industries. Perhaps these branches of industry are main investors neither because, nor in spite of, their low profitability level but—on the contrary—their profitability is low *because* these industries are such strong investors: either because they have been remarkably successful in rational international 'tax allocation' (this presupposes a certain minimum level of outward investment) and/or because foreign investors from these branches have earned sufficient tax credits (which have been granted in Germany to German firms having capital investments in the developing countries) as are necessary in order to reduce taxable income. The latter suggestion is even more strongly supported by the negative correlation between profitability and MCICR: since the policy for granting tax credits for outward investment became subject to considerable political dispute in the late 1970s and there was a threat to abolish the tax credit provision,[24] this may have been an incentive to outward investment sensitive to the provision of such tax credits, and may have caused high and rising cross-MCICR ratios coinciding with artificially low (decreased) current profitability.

4.3 CORPORATE RESEARCH AND DEVELOPMENT (R&D), DOMESTIC MARKET STRUCTURE AND WEST GERMANY'S INTRA-INDUSTRY INVESTMENT

R&D intensity and intra-industry investment

(a) The background

Theoretical as well as empirical research in this field suggests that R&D intensity works as a main determinant in explaining corporate success, as well as foreign investment in most advanced countries, and that R&D intensity is a major source of comparative advantage in advanced countries' international trade.

As to Germany, these results have also been reconfirmed in some recent research projects. For example, Blau *et al.* (1982) have re-evaluated the importance of technology intensity for the international competitiveness of German industry. Though the patterns of advantages differ in trade with other advanced countries on the one hand, and from the patterns in trade with newly industrializing developing countries on the other, German industry's competitiveness remains overwhelmingly in the high or medium technology-intensity sectors and German industry still holds second place (next to the USA) in exports in technology-intensive products; moreover, Poensgen *et al.* (1983) have shown that the profitability of German firms has been very much influenced by the firms' R&D efforts quite independently of the particular characteristics of the respective branch of industry.

(b) Measurement problems and empirical results

In face of these research results one should expect clear and convincing interconnections between cross-investments and domestic R&D activities. The following analysis employs three indicators of technology intensity. While R&D expenditures per employee, or as a share of sales, do not require further explanation, something should be said about the indicator 'second-order technology'. This shows the number of 'other' personnel (i.e. other than scientists and engineers) employed in corporate R&D activities per scientist/engineer employed in these activities. While the other indicators then measure differences in technology intensity *between* various industries, the 'second-order technology intensity' also indicates differences *within* various branches with comparable R&D expenditures. The clearly reciprocal relationship between R&D per employee or sales, and this 'second-order' indicator points to the fact that the higher the general technology intensity (by relative R&D expenditure), the higher also is the level of technological human skills which have been made use of in performing corporate R&D.

The sample fails, however, to establish as robust a positive relationship between patterns and cross-investment and technology intensity as might be expected. The elasticity of R&D as a share of sales with respect to MCIR 1976 is as low as 0.5—in spite of the fact that this relation is marked by the highest (and most significant) coefficient of rank correlation from the estimates reported in Table 4.4. The correponding regression estimate reads:

R&D as a share of sales = (3.45 + 3.13 MCICR 1976)

with $R^2 = 0.29$ being rather low, but significant at the 2.5% level. We conclude, then, that the statistical interdependence between various indicators of technology intensity and German cross-investment patterns appears to be rather weak.

(c) Some possible explanations

In spite of these somewhat inconclusive statistical results, the data never-theless seem to suggest some indicative conclusions:

(i) The major two-way-investing industries do not show significantly different technology intensities compared with all industries. Thus, if technology intensity does serve as an important determinant of foreign direct investment, it seems to do so on a by-firm level (or even below) rather than by industry. Firm-specific characteristics with respect to technology intensity would seem to prevail over industry-specific characteristics.

(ii) The most significant results were obtained when using 'R&D expenditures as a share of sales' as an indicator of technology intensity. This relation appears, however, to be systematically overestimated (and this holds for 'R&D per employee', too). It is the very common pattern of behaviour that firms who go multinational have almost all of their R&D activities at home. Thus every foreign investment which is connected with any relocation of production (which comparable domestically active firms would establish at home), will automatically lead to a statistically but only seemingly high technology intensity in favour of those industries which are most likely to engage in FDI. Thus, in order to overcome this structural overestimation, total R&D in relation to world sales (or employees) should be used as an indicator of technology intensity rather than domestic R&D relative to domestic sales (or employees).

(iii) This statistical distortion also explains the somewhat puzzling fact that the functional direction 'cross-investment pattern (1976) to R&D activities (1979)' appears to be more significant than the other way round (i.e. cross-investment patterns 1981 being influenced by R&D activities in 1979), with an appropriate time lag of two to three years. In face of the fact that the importance of cross-investment activities in German industry is still relatively small, a significant impact made by the pattern of cross-investment upon the structure of domestic technology intensity would be hardly conceivable. However, it appears possible as a statistical pretence or distortion caused by the fact that the higher outward investment is vis-à-vis inward, the more marked becomes the industries' technology intensity at home (under comparable conditions and if firms investing abroad behave as they do usually) which seems to be in part a mere algebraic reflection.

(iv) The rank correlations with 'second-order technology intensity' tend to support the conclusion that though there are certainly positive interdependencies between cross-investment activities and technology intensity, these interdependencies have been over-estimated in this sample (using industry data) and have only seemingly suggested a lagged functional dependency of R&D intensity from cross-investment levels by industry.

Domestic market structure and intra-industry investment

(a) Market concentration by sales

Market concentration and foreign direct investment are usually considered to be mutually reinforcing economic factors. This is not only because relatively high market concentration includes the existence of at least a group of bigger firms, and that firm size works as a major determinant of foreign investment,[25] but also, it is usually accompanied by an 'oligopolistic reaction' (Knickerbocker, 1973). This asserts that firms in concentrated markets tend to go abroad as a defensive reaction and in order to re-establish or protect their international oligopolistic position ('follow-the-leader' phenomenon). Thereby, the rising penetration of foreign markets around the world serves as a valve for competitive dynamics artificially suppressed in those markets which have come in between 'established quasi-domestic equilibrium markets'. Additionally, in a second wave, the move of rival firms towards foreign markets usually induces a cluster of suppliers to follow their customers to their new locations. The importance of this phenomenon for Germany's outward investment has been empirically demonstrated in two earlier studies (Juhl, 1980, 1981). Thus it appears reasonable to expect market concentration and cross-investment to be positively correlated.

At first glance, however, the correlations set out in Table 4.4 fail to establish the expected results: the share of the 3 or 6 biggest firms in total sales by industry (SC3 and SC6) is negatively connected with cross-investment. The results are statistically significant even if they appear rather weak. Although supportive statistical evidence is not yet available, two suggestive explanations for this reciprocal correlation will be offered:

(i) First, although West Germany is one of the main capital exporting countries, her share still amounts to about 10% compared, for example, to nearly 50% by the US (see Juhl, 1983). Thus, even if the composition by country of origin of international oligopolies should correspond to the structure of world capital exports by origin, this would result in a structural dominance of inward over outward investment in West Germany in internationally strongly concentrated industries, and hence explain strongly negative MCICR figures with high sales concentration (SC) rates. This holds better the more the national composition of international oligopolies is distorted in disfavour of West Germany.

(ii) Second, an examination of the basic industry data reveals that industries for which highly negative MCICR figures coincide with highly positive SC data consist mainly of those whose connection with the primary sector appears to be rather strong. MNEs in these areas of activity are, however, mainly of non-German origin; or alternatively, that Germany's share in international raw material and associated investment is much less than her share in total international investment (Juhl, 1983). Thus this will quite obviously result in a structural dominance of inward over outward investment in Germany in the corresponding branches of industry.

The surprising reciprocal correlation seems possibly to be caused by some structural biases which presumably have distorted the statistical reflection of the true causal relationships between market concentration and international investment activities. This is also suggested by the positive correlation between cross-investment dynamics and concentration: highly concentrated branches of industry in Germany thus seem to move into the post-balanced stage of cross-investment development faster than others. Bearing in mind that the focus is on exactly that period of time in which German outward investment has increased the most and overtaken inward investment within only a few years, the rank correlation results seem to point to an additional explanation: that is, while Germany up to the early 1970s was a net recipient of transatlantic rivalistic investment (Graham, 1978). German industry has now started to answer this transatlantic challenge and to recover her appropriate role in the network of international oligopolistic activities.

(b) Market concentration, plant size, and coordination skills

Apart from sales concentration, another aspect of market structure has been analysed which is represented by the variable PC, which indicates the number of plants of which, in the corresponding industry, on average each of the 3 or 6 biggest firms consists.

Table 4.4 shows that cross-investment is significantly more developed in those sectors which are most likely to generate multi-plant firms. This stable result is, first, consistent with earlier findings (Juhl, 1979b) suggesting that the sectoral structure of German foreign investment can be explained, by and large, by the sectoral patterns of firm size; second, it is of considerable importance since it suggests that cross-investment is not determined by plant economies of scale, but just the contrary. While it has already been shown that the major determinants of FDI seem to work at a below-industry level of aggregation, this analysis demonstrates that the most important determinants have to be searched for at the level of the firm. This points to the assumption that the sources of corporate advantages upon which foreign investors have to rely consist in those skills which have been acquired at firm-level management, including organization, finance, control, R&D, marketing, planning and the like, which are all part of the firm's transaction cost-minimizing function. An additional asset seems to consist not only in the principal divisibility of the physical production facilities (thus requiring a relatively small minimum-efficient plant size), but in particular in the actual experience of having allocated firm production to various plants. The experience in organizing, planning, controlling, and integrating various units with dozens of different activities (which presumably are at different locations even if within the base country) into one firm network appears to have reinforced the asset power of a firm to expand or diversify its multinationality.

4.4   CONCLUSIONS AND POLICY IMPLICATIONS

Unlike some other chapters in this volume, this chapter has concentrated its attention on the relationship between *cross-investment* and economic structure; rather than considering the effects of inward and outward investment taken separately. The research findings are, however, rather inconclusive from an econometric point of view. Therefore, only a few cautious conclusions and policy implications will be made.

First, German inward and outward FDI, as with exports and technology transfer, is concentrated in only a few branches of industry, the chemical industry, machinery, electrical engineering, and transport equipment. As in some other industrial countries, the sectoral patterns of inward and outward investment (and exports, too) coincide considerably. Locational and country industry-specific determinants thus seem to be of minor importance in explaining German foreign direct investment. This is also suggested by the fact that in outward investment almost always those industries which prevail are those which also reveal comparative export advantages.

Second, the intertemporal development of West German cross-hauling by industry does not appear to be industry-specific. Almost all branches of industry were initially net capital importers; they then experience increasing intra-industry investment, that is, outward investment rising faster than inward investment up to a balanced situation. We then observe decreasing intra-industry investment due to still continuously higher growth rates of outward vis-à-vis inward investment which transform net capital-importing industries into net capital-exporting industries. Since this development pattern is similar for almost all branches of industry, it should be attributed to broadly effective macro-economic events which prevail over industry-specific developments. West Germany's comparatively high outward investment dynamics seem to result from the major changes in Germany's politico-economical environment and from the changes in country-specific production conditions in particular. Although this process has been straightforward up to now, one cannot assume the process is non-reversible, as it depends as much on Germany's relative international competitive position as on her domestic economic environment.

Third, a more detailed analysis by industrial sectors shows that the dynamics of outward vis-à-vis inward investment have been most marked in those industries which have been identified in numerous studies as more or less 'outdated' for industrialized countries. Thus, apart from those sectors which produce some kind of 'non-tradables' and require to have their production facilities near to the place of consumption even in spite of comparative disadvantages, the process of industry's international relocation seems in general to follow the pattern set out by neo-classical international economics. This movement sometimes has been favoured and sometimes distorted by institutional changes, but Germany's policy has followed the principle of capital-export neutrality.

Fourth, while overall the relocation process corresponds to a few macro-economic variables, the sectoral and sub-sectoral pattern is marked by major variations. These result from differences in performance and structure as suggested by industrial-organization theories of foreign direct investment. Deviations from the general trend seem, however, to appear not to stem either from industry characteristics or plant economies; according to the research findings reported in this paper, higher foreign direct investment dynamics are to be attributed to factors effective between industry and plant level. They result from advantages acquired at firm level, including those specific to multinationality *per se,* or acquired by some kind of 'strategic groups' below industry level, and enable those MNEs who possess these advantages to react more elastically to relevant macro-economic changes and challenges. This also includes the ability to relocate only parts of firms and/or industries.

Fifth, our research findings suggest some mutual interdependencies between foreign direct investment and industry structure and performance. But we believe the really decisive factors are twofold:

(i) Macro-economic and environmental variables which give rise to the restructuring of the German economy via changes in industrial structure and performance, via changes in foreign direct investment, and via the more or less intensive and changing mutual interdependence of both.

(ii) Dynamic management assets at firm or perhaps at 'strategic-group' level may exert additional effects upon and via both. These assets open out the field for corporate expansion at home as well as abroad; such expansionary dynamics reshape industrial structure and performance, and make instrumental use of foreign direct investment, even under adverse macro-economic conditions— perhaps they even in part reshape these environmental conditions.

Finally, we believe that in order to meet the needs of the last part of the present century, Germany needs continuous economic growth based upon technological progress; the corresponding structural change is to be accomplished by the provision of millions of essentially new jobs. Germany's FDI has supported the necessary industrial adjustment as far as the direction of this structural change is known: net outward flows have been most marked in 'outdated' industries or industrial facilities. However, no one knows the detailed pattern of future successful industrial activities. Governments and research institutions are not provided with information generally superior to the knowledge of firms, managers, engineers and others. It thus seems questionable whether this adjustment process can be assisted by governmental intervention. This also holds for the policy towards MNE activity. And it proves all the more true if industrial dynamics stem to a considerable degree in firm-specific assets which one can hardly imagine as a proper subject for governmental management and surveillance. If Germany is successfully to meet the challenges of the 1980s and 1990s, she needs a macro-economic environment and general politico-economic climate which is favourable in its attitude to the creation and application of such firm-specific skills. This should be complemented by a stable regulatory framework which encourages successful future industrial activities. As to FDI policy this implies

(i) to continue the policy of capital export neutrality;
(ii) not to retard the relocation of outdated industrial activities via foreign direct investment for myopic short-term employment reasons since this would absorb badly needed economic forces and exaggerate future long-term employment problems;

(iii) to make Germany an attractive location for new inward investment in competitive industrial activities, and in industrial activities
to become internationally competitive by the import of dynamic
ownership-specific skills which challenge and/or complement
domestically developed industrial activities.

NOTES

1. For a detailed empirical analysis see Kriegsmann and Neu (1982).
2. Cf. Rahmeyer (1980).
3. See for example, Baumann *et al.* (1977), Breithaupt *et al.* (1979), and Reisen (1982).
4. See for instance Baumann *et al.* (1977), Breithaupt *et al.* (1979), and Kiera (1976).
5. For some empirical evidence in this connection see Dick and Dicke (1976), Koopmanns
and Matthies (1979), and Deutsche Bundesbank (Monatsbericht, July 1982).
6. The Deutsche Bundesbank (Monatsbericht, July 1980) also mentions potential substitutive effects facing former high (if not excessive) exports. For a similar argument see
Albach (1978).
7. See Koopmanns and Matthies (1979) and Deutsche Bundesbank (Monatsbericht, July
1982).
8. This holds even more in face of the fact that most German exports are invoiced in DM
(cf. Albach 1978; Giesecke, 1977; Juhl, 1978). The role which has been attributed to
'wrong' exchange rates by the Kiel 'school' for explaining the structural change of the
West German economy has been sharply criticized by Riese (1978) who simultaneously
argued that the undervaluation of the DM had not been finished in the early 1970s but
would still persist in the late 1970s and thus explain the remaining export competitiveness of German industry in spite of those major undisputable revaluations.
9. Cf. Hof (1983).
10. Cf. Herrmann (1975) and Albach (1978). Schmidt (1976) has estimated an export price
elasticity of -0.6.
11. Cf. Molsberger (1971).
12. Indicative for this suggestion is the observation that the increase in German export prices in these years has been smaller than the increase in import prices.
13. Cf. Albach (1978).
14. Molsberger (1971) has argued that in some branches (mechanical engineering and scientific and optical goods) this margin has already been passed.
15. Cf. Albach (1978) and Juhl (1978).
16. Even more, German exporters rejected export protection by the federal government (see
Giesecke, 1977; Juhl, 1978).
17. Cf. Kiera (1974, 1977). Erdilek (1982) shows that these branches also prevail in US cross-
investment pattern.
18. Jungnickel *et al.* (1976) is the most appropriate analysis in this connection.
19. They also meet in net capital-importing, less developed countries as competing investors
from different host countries.
20. Agarwal (1978) has shown that the rank correlation between RCA and German outward
investment is $r_s = 0.52$ and that almost all outward investment coincides with German
comparative advantages. Similar results using other indicators have been gained by Juhl
(1979a).
21. See Dunning's study in this volume.
22. Characteristically, this holds for branches like food and mineral oil processing which
require to be located near to the region of consumption regardless of the structure of
locational advantages.

23. For German foreign direct investment cf. Juhl (1979b).
24. Tax credits have indeed been abolished for investment abroad pursued after 31 December 1981.
25. Cf. Juhl (1979b) for the impact of firm size upon West Germany's foreign investment.

REFERENCES

Agarwal, J. P. (1978). Zur Struktur der Westdeutschen Direktinvestitionen in Entwicklungslaendern, *Die Weltwirtschaft*, No. 1, 114–132
Albach, H. (1978). Preisspielraeume und Unterkostenverkaeufe im Export. Ergebnisse einer Diskussion unter den Herausgebern der ZfB. *Zeitschrift für Betriebswirtschaft*, **48**, No. 8, 723–728
Albach, H. (1979). Zur Verlegung von Produktionstaetten ins Ausland, *Zeitschrift für Betriebswirtschaft*, **9**, No. 10, 945–952
Albach, H. (1982). Produktivaetsentwicklung und Risiko, *Zeitschrift für betriebswirtschaftliche Forschung*, **34**, No. 3, 213–224
Amano, A. (1977). Specific factors, comparative advantage, and international investment, *Economica*, **44**, No. 174, 133–144
Baumann, H. *et al.* (1977). *Aussenhandel, Direktinvestitionen und Industriestruktur der deutschlen Wirtschaft*, Berlin
Blau, H. *et al.* (1982). Die technologische Wettbewerbsposition der Deutschen Industrie im internationalen Verleich, *Ifo-schnelldienst*, No. 17–18, 48–59
Breithaupt, K. *et al.* (1979). Analyse der strukturellen Entwicklung der Deutschen Wirtschaft, mimeo, Kiel, 168 pp.
Bundesminister für Forschung und Technologie (1982). *Faktenbericht 1981 zum Bundesbericht Forschung*, Bonn
Bundesministerium für Wirtschaft, *Leistung in Zahlen*, Var. iss., Bonn, var. years
Bundesverband der Deutschen Industrie (1982). *Industrieforschung-Sicherung der Zukunft*, Koeln
Caves, R. E. (1982). *Multinational Enterprise and Economic Analysis*, Cambridge
Deutsche Bundesbank, Monatsberichte, var. iss.
Deutsche Bundesbank, Zahlungsbilanzstatistik, var. iss.
Dick, R. and Dicke, H. (1976). Patterns of trade in knowledge, mimeo
Dunning, J. H. (1981). *International Production and the Multinational Enterprise*, London
Dunning, J. H. and Norman, G. (1985). *Intraindustry Production as a Form of International Economic Involvement: An Exploratory Paper.*
Erdilek, A. (1982). Intra-industry cross-direct foreign investment, mimeo, Washington
Fels, G. *et al.* (1970). Sektoraler Strukturwandel im weltwirtschaftlichen Wachstumsprozess, *Die Weltwirtschaft*, H.1, 49–66
Fels, G. and Weiss, F. (1978). Structural change and employment: the lesson of West Germany, in H. Giersch (ed.), *Capital Shortage and Unemployment in the World Economy*, Tuebingen, 31–53
Gahlen, B. and Rahmeyer, F. (1981). Die Strukturberichterstattung der Wirtschaftsforschungsinstitute. dp IIM/IP 81–26. WZB Berlin
Gerstenberger, W. (1981). Strukturwandlungen unter dem Einfluss weltwirtschaftlicher Verlaenderungen, *Ifo-schnelldienst*, **34**, No. 5, 24–35

Giesecke, H. (1977). Exportfoerderung in der Bundesrepublik Deutschland, *Aussenwirtschaft*, **32**, 275–286

Graham, E. M. (1978). Transatlantic investment by multinational firms: a rivalistic phenomenon, *Journal of Post-Keynesian Economics*, **1**, No.1 82–99

Herrmann, A. (1975). Wirkt jetzt die DM-Aufwertung? *Ifo-schnelldienst*, **28**, No. 22, 7–12

Herrmann, A. and Ketterer, K. H. (1977). Strukturwandel im Aussenhandel der Bundesrepublik Deutschland, *Ifo-schnelldienst*, **30**, No. 11/12, 22–30

Hof, B. (1983). *Produktivitaetdynamik international*, Koeln

Hymer, S. and Rowthorn, R. (1970). Multinational corporations and international oligopoly: the non-American challenge, in C. P. Kindleberger (ed.), *The International Corporation*, Cambridge, pp. 57–91

International Monetary Fund (1982). *World Economic Outlook 1982*, Washington, DC

Juhl, P. (1978). *Struktur und Umfang der deutschen Exportfoerderungspolitik. Eine Bestandsaufnahme*, KAP No. 77, Kiel

Juhl, P. (1979a). *Deutsche Direktinvestitionen in Lateinamerika*, Tuebingen

Juhl, P. (1979b). On the sectoral patterns of West German manufacturing investment in less developed countries: the impact of firm size, factor intensities, and protection, *Weltwirtschaftliches Archiv*, **115**, No. 3, 508–521

Juhl, P. (1980). Industrielle Vorwaertsverflechtungen und grenzueberschreitende follow-up-investitionen, *Konjunkturpolitik*, **26**, No. 5, 308–320

Juhl, P. (1981). Forward linkages and follow-up investment: an input-output analytical approach, *Management International Review/Journal of International Business*, **21**, 64–74

Juhl, P. (1983). *Direktinvestitionen in Entwicklungslandaendern unter dem Einfluss politischer Risiken*, Muenchen

Jungnickel, R. *et al.* (1976). Der Einfluss multinationaler Unternehmen auf Branchenstruktur und aussenwirtschaft der Bundesrepublik Deutschland, mimeo, Hamburg

Kiera, H. G. (1974). Die aussenwirtschafliche Verflechtung der Bundesrepublik durch Direktinvestitionen, *Mitteilungen des RWI*, **25**, No. 3, 147–170

Kiera, H. G. (1976). Die Wirkungen deutscher Direktinvestitionen auf den Aussenhandel, *Mitteilungen des RWI*, **27**, No. 3, 195–216

Kiera, H. G. (1977). Neue Tendenzen in der internationalen Kapitalverflechtung der Bundesrepublik? *Mitteilungen des RWI*, **28**, No. 2, 137–154

Knickerbocker, F. (1973). *Oligopolistic Reaction and Multinational Enterprise*, Boston

Kojima, K. (1978). *Direct Foreign Investment*, London

Koopmans, G. and Matthies, K. (1979). Transfer of technology by German firms, *Intereconomics*, Sept./Oct. 237–242

Kreklau, C. *et al.* (1982). *Staatliche Forschungsfoerderung*, Koeln

Kriegsmann, K. P. and Neu, A. (1982). *Globale, regionale und sektorale Wettbewerbsfaehigkeit der deutschen Wirtschaft*, Frankfurt

Meissner, H. G. (1978). Exportprobleme der deutschen Industrie aus betriebswirtschaftlicher Sicht, *Zeitschrift für Betriebswirtsohaft*, **48**, No. 8, 716–722

Molsberger, J. (1971). Exportwirkungen der DM–Aufwertung von 1969, *Wirtschaftsdienst*, **51**, No. 9, 483–487

Monopolkommission (1982). *Hauptgutachten 1980/81: Fortschritte bei der Konzentrationserfassung*, Baden-Baden

Ohlin, B. (1933). *International and Interregional Trade,* Cambridge, Mass.

Oppenlaender, K. H. (1977). Der gesamtwirtschaftliche Strukturwandel in der Bundesrepublik Deutschland, *Ifo-schnelldienst,* **30**, No. 11/12, 1–13

Poensgen, O. H. and Hort, H. (1983). F & E-aufwand, Firmensituation und Firmenerfolg, *Schmalenbachs Zeitschrift für betriebswirtschaftliche Forschung,* **35**, Jg, No. 2, 73–93

Rahmeyer, F. (1980). Die Strukturberichterstattung der Wirschaftforschungs-institute—Eine kritische Bestandsaufnahme. dp IIM/80–64, Berlin

Reisen, H. (1982). Protektionsstruktur und internationale Wettsbewerbsfaehigkeit der deutschen Industrie, *Zeitschrift für Betriebswirtschaft Ergaenzungsheft* **2**, 47–61

Riese, H. (1978). Strukturwandel und unterbewertete Waehrung in der Bundesrepublik Deutschland, *Konjunkturpolitik,* **24**, No. 3, 143–169

Rothschild, K. W. (1975). Export structure, export flexibility and competitiveness, *Weltwirtschaftliches Archiv,* **111**, No. 2, 222–242

Sachverstaendigenrat zur Begutachtung der Gesamtwirtschaftlichen Entwicklung, Jahresgutachen, var. iss.

Samuelson, P. A. (1948). International trade and the equalisation of factor prices, *Economic Journal,* **58**, 163–184

Schmidt, R. (1976). Die Exporte der Bundesrepublik Deutschland—Eine oekonometrische Analyse auf der Grundlage von Vierteljahresdaten, *Die Welt-wirtschaft,* No. 1, 47–59

Scholz, L. (1977). Ursachen und Ausmass sektoraler Strukturwandlungen in der verarbeitenden Industrie bis 1985, *Ifo-schnelldienst,* **30**, No. 11/12, 31–45

5

Japan

TERUTOMO OZAWA

5.1 INTRODUCTION

Broadly speaking, there are two types of economic policy orientation in market economies: one type encourages a country to base planning of its long-term industrial structures on its dynamic comparative advantage, with an indirect but industry-specific government involvement in the private sector; the other leaves the direction, nature, and pace of structural changes entirely to market forces (i.e. the trial-and-error methods of the market mechanism) and avoids the undertaking of any official projection of structural changes.[1] Japan's orientation has typically been of the first type. Its industrial structure has been altered drastically in response to changes in technological opportunities, availability of resources, and demand conditions by adopting a 'national consensus' approach in which the government plays a significant role as a decision-maker or assisting partner of the private sector. The visible hand of the government has been as important as the invisible hand of the market place in Japan's structural transformation and economic growth. Poor in natural endowments and a latecomer in industrialization, Japan is critically dependent on overseas resources, both physical and technological. Trade, technology absorption and transfers, and direct investment—the three major conduits of commercial relations with the outside world—are the *integral* instruments of Japan's industrial policy.[2]

The theme of this chapter is that Japan has proved more adept than any other industrialized nation in consciously and deliberately both managing and making the best possible use of its ESP (environment, system, and policy) structure and harnessing the forces of OLI (ownership advantages, location advantages, and internalization) system of international production activities for its own benefit.[3] External commercial contacts, notably technology transfer and direct investment, have been used as the crucial means of upgrading the industrial structure—and improving the trade competitiveness—of the Japanese economy; they are not mere haphazard activities incidental to the national economy. This presents an interesting contrast to the approaches pursued by western market economies, particularly those of the United States and the United Kingdom, which are not as conscious as Japan is, at the national economic policy level, of the vital link between foreign direct investment (both inward and outward) and industrial restructuring.

5.2 AN HISTORICAL PERSPECTIVE

After the Second World War Japan became even more wary than it was before the war of direct investments from overseas for fear of foreign domination of domestic industries. In the pre-war years a number of large scale, foreign, wholly or majority-owned ventures existed in Japan; for example, Ford Motor Company and General Motors both set up wholly-owned subsidiaries and assembled automobiles (in 1929 the number of American automobiles thus supplied stood at 36,000, as compared to a mere 437 local ones).[4] General Electric, Westinghouse, and Siemens, who had all operated large scale joint ventures in Japan's heavy electrical machinery industry, became only licensors in the post-war years. The post-war industrial policy was to learn advanced foreign technology as much as possible but to avoid being dependent on direct investment by western corporations.

This general posture of the post-war Japanese economy is well reflected in Table 5.1. Japan, despite its large domestic market supported by the free world's second largest economy, has been the host country for a relatively small amount of foreign direct investment, while it itself has quickly grown to be the third largest overseas investor, next to the United States and the United Kingdom. In 1980, Japan's stock of foreign direct investment amounted to $36,497 million, as compared to a mere $2,979 million of inward investment, the former being *twelve times* the latter. As will be discussed below, such a rapidly enlarged overseas investment has been designed to help to expand Japan's export activities by setting up marketing networks (sales offices, distribution warehouses, customer service facilities, and the like), to secure vital supplies of industrial resources by organizing resource-extractive ventures abroad, and to transfer overseas those segments of manufacturing activities that are no longer suitable to be home-based for a variety of politico-economic environmental reasons.

Japan's dependence on advanced foreign technology, on the other hand, is revealed in its balance of trade in technology; it has been a huge deficit country, paying more royalties and fees overseas than it has

TABLE 5.1 Japan's international balance of direct investments and trade in technology, 1970–80

| | Balance of direct investments | | | | |
| | A. Outward investment | | B. Inward investment | | |
	Value ($ million)	(Cases)	Value ($ million)	(Cases)	A/B (%)
1970	907	(729)	114	(455)	8.0
1971	858	(904)	255	(445)	3.4
1972	2,338	(1,774)	160	(747)	14.6
1973	3,494	(3,093)	167	(756)	20.9
1974	2,395	(1,911)	153	(655)	15.7
1975	3,280	(1,591)	167	(615)	19.6
1976	3,462	(1,652)	196	(652)	17.7
1977	2,806	(1,761)	224	(693)	12.5
1978	4,598	(2,393)	235	(705)	19.6
1979	4,995	(2,694)	524	(704)	9.5
1980	4,693	(2,442)	299	(749)	15.7
1951–80	36,497	(23,948)	2,979	(8,826)	12.3

| | Technology trade | | |
	A. Receipts ($ million)	B. Payments ($ million)	A/B (%)
1970	59	433	13.6
1971	60	488	12.3
1972	74	572	12.9
1973	88	715	12.3
1974	113	718	15.7
1975	161	712	22.6
1976	173	846	20.4
1977	233	1,027	22.7
1978	274	1,241	22.1
1979	342	1,260	27.1
1980	378	1,439	26.3

Sources: The statistics on the balance of direct investments are adopted from MITI (1982), p. 377, and those on technology trade from Japan's Science and Technology Agency (1975, 1982).

received (it is true, however, that in the recent past Japan has become a *net* exporter of technology as far as new contracts are concerned).

It is often said that imports are not a cost but a gain for a trading country; this aphorism applies cogently to Japan's trade in technology. The successful absorption of advanced foreign technology has been the major factor in the miracle of Japan's structural upgrading and post-war economic growth. A burst of innovations triggered by the continual acquisition of new industrial knowledge revolutionized Japanese industry, turned it practically inside out—so quickly, in fact, that the West was ill prepared to realize the magnitude and the full implications of Japan's industrial transformation.

The huge technological gap that existed between Japan and the West, particularly the United States, at the end of the Second World War presented both opportunity and danger—the opportunity to use advanced foreign technologies without starting from scratch, but the danger of domestic industry's being controlled by foreign interests; a 'danger', of course, in the very narrow sense of Japan's nationalistic viewpoint.

Thus, fearful of the possible foreign domination of industry yet eager to absorb advanced technologies from the West, the government restricted foreign direct investment at home but encouraged technology imports through licensing agreements. As a result, for Japanese industry licensing has become a far more important vehicle of knowledge transfer than direct investment.

5.3   TECHNOLOGY IMPORTS, INWARD DIRECT INVESTMENT, AND CAPITAL FORMATION

The regulatory authority of the government over technology acquisition and inward direct investment lay in two pieces of legislation: the Foreign Exchange Control Law of 1949, which was designed to regulate the use of foreign exchange reserves (say, for remittance of royalties and profits), and the Foreign Investment Law of 1950, which concerned an 'orderly' influx of foreign capital and technology for the purpose of developing domestic industry and improving its international payments position.[5] The preamble of the latter enunciated two major goals of the Japanese economy: 'the self-support and sound development of the Japanese economy' and 'the improvement of the international balance of payments'. These objectives clearly meant the development of both import-substituting and export-competitive industries with a minimum of foreign capital (ownership) participation. In order to screen applications for technology imports and inward direct investment, the Foreign Investment Council was set up as the central administrative organ.

Technology imports

A *dual structural* approach was initially taken in Japan's industrial and trade strategy in the 1950s: the traditional, labour-intensive light manufacturing industries, notably textiles and clothing, were *export* industries that had strong comparative advantages and earned precious foreign exchange Japan badly needed, while the modern, capital-intensive, heavy and chemical industries were still largely in the stage of *import substitution*, with domestic production made possible by imported foreign technologies. The latter were heavily protected as 'infant' industries.

The acquisition of advanced foreign technologies was therefore initially aimed at the development of the heavy and chemical industries, *viz* the producer-goods sector of the Japanese economy. During the 1950s, for example, the government approved 1,029 technology import contracts (class A),[6] out of which 218 (21.2%) were secured by the non-electric machinery industry, 217 (21.1%) by the electric machinery industry, 198 (19.2%) by the chemical industry, and 94 (9.1%) by the metals industry (including steel)—these four industries alone accounting for 70.6% of the total (see Apendix Table 5.A1).

These imported technologies, examined in detail elsewhere,[7] triggered a series of capital investments in new production facilities not only by those manufacturers who purchased technologies but also by other closely related firms through business linkages. In fact, a vigorous investment boom ensued throughout Japanese industry by way of the familiar multiplier/accelerator mechanism. The phenomenon of 'investments creating more investments' was observed throughout the Japanese economy. Clearly, Japan's economic growth during the 1950s and the early part of the 1960s was led more by the investments induced by imported technologies than by exports or anything else.

To site some specific evidence, as much as 27.7% of the investment made by technology-importing firms in machinery and equipment (excluding buildings and other overhead plant facilities) in the manufacturing sector as a whole was *directly* necessitated by imported technologies during the 1950s. A further breakdown of the manufacturing sector itself reveals that the ratio was as high as 41.6% for chemicals, 25.8% for electrical machinery, 14.9% for non-electric machinery, 16.4% for iron and steel, 16.3% for transport equipment, and 5.4% for textiles (this relatively small ratio for textiles is understandable, since it was already a well-established industry).[8]

The time series regression analyses relating the value of imported technology-based investments in machinery and equipment at the firm level (independent variable) to the total value of investments in machinery and equipment made by technology-importing firms (dependent variable) over the 1950–60 period show high correlation, particularly in those industries that acquire a relatively large number of foreign technologies, confirming the strong 'investment creating more investment' effect of technology imports.[9] Another set of statistics also shows that the sales of licensed manufactures (i.e. products manufactured under licence) were heavily concentrated in domestic markets: in 1960, for example, 89.9% in electrical machinery, 94.3% in non-electrical machinery, 85.8% in chemicals, 86.0% in iron and steel, 94.6% in transport equipment, and 43.4% in textiles—convincing evidence that licensed manufactures were initially designed mostly to meet the rising demands for such products at home, replacing otherwise importable foreign manufactures. (On the other hand, although the sales of licensed manufactures in export markets were small in proportion, such exports were nevertheless increasingly important components of Japan's exports in some industries: in 1960, the exports of licensed manufactures accounted for 50.2% of total exports in electrical machinery, 8.8% in non-electrical machinery, 24.3% in chemicals, 35.6% in iron and steel, 1.5% in transport equipment, and 6.0% in textiles.)[10]

In short, evidence for the 1950s illustrates the fact that imported technologies clearly led to the structural upgrading of Japanese industry by way of capital investment, which expanded domestic productive capacities and resulted in import substitution—and later on, gradually, in the export expansion of modern manufactures.

Stepped-up research and development and engineering (R, D&E)

Needless to say, Japan's technological borrowing was (and is) not mere imitation. Japanese firms imported 'seed technologies' and commercialized them through adaptive R, D&E, creating in the process many significant improvements, particularly in the area of production processes. The ratio of technology import payments (royalties and fees for technology purchase contracts with foreign enterprises) to R&D expenditures rose throughout the 1950s, reaching a record high of 18.5% in 1960, but has been on the decline ever since. *This pattern strongly suggests the growing importance of indigenous R&D efforts vis-à-vis imported technologies since 1960.* In fact, a so-called 'research centre boom' took place in Japan during the first half of the 1960s in which central research facilities were set up by large corporations on the model of American research centres. And R&D expenditures more than tripled, from ¥250 billion in 1965 to ¥800 billion in 1970. Yet Japan's R&D efforts were not necessarily competing with imported technologies; as a matter of fact, a large amount of R&D money was spent on adapting and commercializing imported technologies.[11] Following the substantial liberalization of controls on technology imports in June 1968, the number of technology purchase contracts began to rise sharply: it jumped from 638 (Class A contracts) in 1967 to 1,061 in 1968 and continued to climb to a record high of 1,916 in 1972. Such an increased influx of technology imports itself no doubt led to a rise in adaptive R, D&E.

Because of stepped-up research activities on the part of Japanese firms it is no longer clear how much imported technologies themselves contributed to Japan's industrial expansion in the 1960s and the 1970s. Unfortunately, from 1960 on there are no comparable data available on licence-induced investments, licensed manufactures and other details as for the 1950s. But there is little doubt that imported technologies continued to play a key role, if one of diminishing importance, in facilitating Japan's industrial restructuring throughout the 1960s and the 1970s.

At the aggregate level, indeed, we can still detect a very close correlation between the number of foreign technologies acquired (X) and the amount of capital investments in the private sector (Y in billion yens) over the 28 year period from 1950 to 1978:[12]

$$Y = -877 + 8.28 \times \quad (r^2 = 0.94)$$
$$(0.145)$$

Although the above simple regression equation implies that the number of foreign technologies acquired is an explanatory variable, while the amount of capital investments is a dependent variable, the direction of causation clearly runs two ways. Imported technologies necessitated the purchase of advanced machinery and equipment and other new plant facilities, but the output capacity, thus improved and expanded, not only generated more need for new technologies but also increased the capacity to absorb such technologies. In addition, a multitude of favourable factors other than imported technologies no doubt contributed to the rapid capital build-up in Japanese industry.

Inward direct investment

There are three interesting features in the trend of inward direct investment. First of all, throughout the 1950s the annual amounts of such investment were one digit million dollar figures (with the sole exception of 1951); in the 1960s the annual amount fluctuated between $22 million and $70 million (that is two digit million figures); but in the 1970s three digit million figures were recorded year after year, with the highest, $524 million, in 1979. This no doubt mirrored the phenomenal expansion of the Japanese economy in each past decade and the sharply rising interest of foreign firms in advancing into Japan by way of direct foreign investment.

Second, foreign investments in Japan were, in the beginning, almost entirely in manufacturing (more than 90% until the mid 1960s), and only later on were they increasingly made in the tertiary sector, notably in the area of commerce and foreign trade (in 1980, for example, the tertiary sector came to account for as much as 36.9%) (see Appendix Table 5.A2). This pattern, as will be seen below, contrasts with that of Japan's outward investments, which were highly commerce-oriented from the very beginning.

Third, within manufacturing itself, it was the 'basic material' type sector (metals, chemicals, petroleum, rubber, ceramics, and textiles) that first attracted inward foreign investment, while the 'fabricating/assembly' type sector (electrical machinery, non-electrical machinery, transport equipment and precision machinery) grew more and more important as host sectors later on. The former sector, for example, captured as much as 85.0% of the total value of inward investments in manufacturing during the 1950–55 period, 76.3% during the 1956–60 period, 74.5% during the 1961–65 period, and 70.5% during the 1966–70 period—the first two decades in which import substitution and export promotion of the basic materials industries were the primary feature of Japan's industrial transformation.

Yet inward direct investment, on the whole, has not been quantitatively important for Japanese industry. For example, the market share of foreign-affiliated enterprises (that is, in circumstances where at least 25% of the equity of an enterprise is owned by foreign interests for the purpose of management participation) has been insignificant in all manufacturing industries except petroleum and rubber products. For the manufacturing sector as a whole, the market share of foreign-affiliated enterprises is currently less than 5%, although it has gradually risen from 2.5% in the mid 1960s, mainly on account of inward investment in the automobile industry. The petroleum and rubber product industries have been most actively participated in by foreign-affiliated enterprises, but their position declined from about 60% in petroleum and about 20% in rubber products in the mid 1960s to about 40% and 10% respectively, by the beginning of the 1980s.

Since there has not been much change in the relative position of foreign-affiliated enterprises over the past decades, recent statistics are used to examine their operational behaviour. Two major operational characteristics are observable in Table 5.2. First, foreign-affiliated enterprises are relatively more asset-intensive (i.e. capital-intensive) and less employment-intensive (i.e. less labour-using) than local enterprises. In all the three broad categories of industry shown, the shares of foreign-affiliated enterprises in assets are much higher than those in employment. Secondly, their

TABLE 5.2 Shares of foreign-affiliated enterprises in sales, profits and assets in Japan (%)

	1974	1975	1976	1977	1978	1979	1980
All industries							
Sales	1.9	1.9	2.1	2.2	1.9	2.0	2.1
Profits after tax	2.0	2.0	4.2	4.9	3.8	3.3	3.3
Assets	2.1	2.0	2.1	2.2	2.0	2.2	2.1
Employees	1.0	0.8	0.9	1.0	1.0	1.0	0.8
Manufacturing							
Sales	3.7	3.9	4.6	4.7	4.2	4.4	4.7
Profits after tax	3.5	5.2	7.4	8.3	6.9	5.0	5.0
Assets	4.1	3.9	4.5	4.6	4.2	4.6	4.5
Employees	1.8	1.5	1.9	2.0	1.9	2.0	1.6
Petroleum							
Sales	NA	29.4	34.3	34.4	33.0	33.2	38.1
Profits after tax	NA	NA	50.3	66.5	92.6	50.9	62.9
Assets	NA	29.6	31.3	30.5	29.4	31.4	33.6
Employees	NA	21.3	21.5	21.3	21.0	22.4	22.0

Source: Compiled from MITI (1983), pp. 32–34.

shares in profits are much higher than those in assets, an indication of their higher profitability in comparison with local corporations.

These two characteristics do indeed corroborate the well known feature of large Western multinational corporations: their possession of firm-specific advantages cultivated in research-based, capital-intensive, oligopolistic industries. Their firm-specific advantages are thus translated into the higher profitabilities of their operations.

In fact, it is Western multinationals' possession of corporate advantages in the form of superior production technology and marketing skills—and their monopolistic control of supply sources, as was the case with petroleum—that compelled the Japanese government and industry to accept their insistence on direct investment (if not under 100% ownership, then in joint ventures with local Japanese firms) rather than licensing arrangements as a way of exploiting such advantages. This fact is reflected in the findings of a survey taken by the Japanese Ministry of International Trade and Industry (MITI) in 1967 on the motives of both Japanese and foreign parties with respect to foreign-affiliated enterprises in Japan: 229

Japanese manufacturers out of the 246 surveyed (93%) said that acquisition of technology was a primary motive for accepting foreign capital, and 172 identified it as *the* most important reason. On the other hand, 79% of the responding foreign partners (326 of the 414 foreign partners surveyed) explained that the primary reason was 'growth potential of the Japanese market'.[13]

As far as ownership is concerned, the majority of foreign-affiliated enterprises in manufacturing are either 50–50 (evenly-owned) or minority foreign-owned joint ventures. In 1980, only 19.9% of them were wholly foreign-owned, and 68.2% of them were either 50% owned (41.8% occurrence) or less than 50% owned (26.4% occurrence). In contrast, foreign-affiliated enterprises in the tertiary sector are more frequently majority foreign-owned. For example, in commerce (wholesale and retailing) 67.9% were either wholly-owned (51.9% occurrence) or more than 50% owned (16.0% occurrence).[14]

The predominance of joint ventures is clearly a result of the past government policy of restricting foreign ownership to 50% or less in manufacturing but of allowing majority ownership in wholesale marketing and small scale retailing. In some cases, however, foreign investors themselves no doubt preferred joint ventures in order to take advantage of local resources.

In short, the prime reason for hosting foreign direct investment has been the acquisition of the latest foreign technologies, which the Japanese (especially the government) preferred to purchase under licensing agreements, whenever practical. But foreign manufacturers became more interested in capital participation as they were increasingly attracted to the growth of the Japanese market, and as they saw in it a superior way of exploiting their corporate advantages (both licensable and non-licensable) in that rapidly growing market. Indeed, the growth-induced nature of inward investment is reflected in the fact that the import orientation of foreign-affiliated enterprises in securing raw materials and inputs is, on the whole, much stronger than their export orientation in marketing outputs, although there some industrial variations. (In 1980, for example, for foreign-affiliated enterprises as a whole the ratio of imported inputs to total inputs in value was 59.7%, while the ratio of exports to total sales was 7.3%.)[15] Through the medium of direct investment, some important production and marketing knowledge has been transplanted into Japan, technologies that foreign enterprises are willing—and able—to transfer only in 'bundled' form. These foreign operations did not remain technological enclaves, however, because they were usually forced to take the form of joint ventures for the very purpose of facilitating knowledge transfers to the Japanese partners.

5.4 STRUCTURAL CHANGES AND OVERSEAS INVESTMENT

Strong trade orientation

Japan visualizes itself as a trade dependent nation. Since it has a relatively large population but a very limited endowment of natural resources, its industrialization was designed to make itself a workshop importing raw materials from overseas, processing them into finished goods at home, and exporting them back to the world. But by the end of the 1960s, paradoxically, its successful development of heavy and chemical industries had turned Japan, one of the world's most resource scarce countries, into one of its most resource consuming countries. Japan soon became the world's leading importer of many resources: it now takes about 40% of the world's iron ore imports, 25% of its coal and copper ore, 20% of its bauxite, and 10% of its timber.[16]

In order to pay for these imported resources Japan must export. The 'two-way' trade imperative has thus been the cornerstone of Japan's industrial policy, and so far trade has been assigned the primary role, overseas investment only a supplementary or supportive one. Japan's overseas investments are therefore concentrated in commerce and resource extraction to promote its trade and to secure overseas supplies of natural resources. At the end of March 1980, for example, as much as 41.6% of the total value of Japan's overseas investments were made in the tertiary (mainly trade-related commerce) sector, and 23.1% in the primary sector (2.6% in agriculture, forestry and fishery; and 20.5% in mining).[17] Thus, on the whole, Japan's overseas investment has so far been complementary with exporting and importing (pro-trade), rather than competing or substituting (anti-trade),[18] although, as will be seen below, an export-replacing type of investment has recently emerged in some manufacturing sectors.

Industrial shedding—and upgrading

Japan's structural changes in rapid sequence from low value-added industrial sectors to higher value-added ones (initially, from primary to secondary industry, then from light manufacturing to heavy and chemical manufacturing activities, and more recently from resource and energy-intensive, basic-materials sectors to knowledge-intensive, fabricating/assembly sectors) have brought a swift rise in labour productivity and wages. Shifting patterns of trade competitiveness and sectoral resource reallocation have been the dominant features of this process, and Japanese manufacturers' advance overseas has inevitably been influenced to a significant degree by these changes in their macro-economic environment.

In the very early post-war period, Japan depended solely on labour-intensive, light manufacturing industries to earn foreign exchange while it was striving to build up heavy and chemical industries through technological assimilation and import substitution. In other words, *location-specific factors* (especially abundant labour supply and undervalued yen) constituted the basis of Japan's initial export competitiveness, while *ownership-specific advantages* (technologies) were being imported and assimilated into the modern, capital-intensive industries.[19] But the very success of developing the latter and the accompanying high economic growth as a whole led to a sharp rise in wages and to acute shortages of workers, particularly young factory workers, that is to say, *a successful industrial transformation in effect destroyed the location-specific advantage of early post-war Japan.* Labour tightness adversely affected traditional labour-intensive manufacturing activities, especially those of small and medium-sized enterprises in light manufacturing industries (whose trade competitiveness was built on the relatively low cost labour available in early post-war Japan and the undervalued national currency). Hence Japan's exports of labour-intensive manufactures to the West, particularly to the US, began to decline. These manufactures included such simple products as cotton textiles, toys, wigs, metal tablewares, umbrellas, baseball gloves, rubber and plastic footwear, and the like. Most of these sundries were exported by Japan's trading companies.

It was against this background that Japanese manufacturers began to transfer labour-intensive production to neighbouring developing countries in which they were able to find an abundant supply of labour. In many instances Japanese trading companies took the initiative to shift the manufacturing activities of small and medium-sized enterprises by investing jointly and offering the necessary services for overseas production and marketing. A sharp rise in the value of yen in the early 1970s (loss of another location-specific advantage in Japan) rang the knell for Japanese exports of light manufactures.

Indeed, it was during the 1971–73 period that Japan's first overseas investment boom occurred. Direct foreign investment, which was $907 million in 1970 and $858 million in 1971, jumped to $2,338 million in 1972 and $3,494 million in 1973, increasing the cumulative total from $4,435 million in 1970 to $10,267 million in 1973 (see Table 5.1). This means that the investments made in 1972 and 1973 alone more than doubled the then existing stock of Japan's overseas investment. At the end of September 1971, furthermore, 33% of Japan's overseas manufacturing ventures were made by small and medium-sized enterprises (with paid-in capital worth 50 million yen or less), and 88% of these small scale ventures were concentrated in other Asian countries. The lower value-added (so-called 'sunset' industries, which are *comparatively disadvantaged*) end of Japan's manufacturing activities was thus transplanted on to the soil of developing Asian countries.[20] For example, four major labour-intensive industries that had a large number of small and medium-sized enterprises (textiles, metal products, electrical machinery and sundries) together accounted for as much as 65.5% of the total number (and 55.4% of the total value) of new overseas investments made during the two-year period 1972–73. And these ventures were set up mostly in other Asian countries: 64.3% of them in textiles, 69.2% in metal products, 81.8% in electric machinery, and 75.4% in sundries.[21]

To recapitulate, Japan's first investment boom in manufacturing during the early 1970s was caused not by a sudden endowment of ownership-specific advantages in Japanese firms including small ones, but by the loss of home-based, location-specific advantages (availability of low cost labour and the undervalued yen) and by the discovery of new location-specific factors suitable for their offshore manufacturing in developing countries.

Protectionism induced investment

Japan's overseas investment continued to record a high level of activity throughout the 1970s, but toward the end of the decade and at the start of the 1980s there were two step jumps that can be identified as the second overseas investment boom. Beginning in 1978, annual overseas investment exceeded the 4 billion dollar level, and 1981 saw a sudden rise to $8,906 million from the previous year's $4,693 million. The cumulative total at the end of 1981 was $45,403 million.

In contrast to the first manufacturing investment boom, which was characterized by the concentration of activities in relatively simple (that is, technologically unsophisticated) types of consumer products such as textiles, electrical appliances and sundries, the subsequent high level of investment activities (during the second boom in particular) increasingly involved technologically more sophisticated producer goods such as chemicals, metals, industrial machinery and electronics components, as well as high income consumer products such as automobiles and processed foods.[22]

A ban on imports of completed automobiles and enforcement of the local content requirements in developing countries led to Japanese investment in knock down assembly operations and automotive parts manufacturing. In newly industrializing countries, especially South Korea, Hong Kong, Singapore, Taiwan, and Brazil, rapid industrialization increased the demand for intermediate industrial goods, attracting a large number of investments by Japanese capital goods producers.

There was also a shift in Japan's overseas manufacturing activities from a heavy concentration in developing Asian countries towards a diversification into advanced countries, particularly into the United States and Europe. Most of these manufacturing ventures were induced by the rising clamour against Japan's export penetration of Western countries' markets. By the early 1970s the composition of Japan's exports had changed dramatically from labour-intensive, technologically standardized manufactures (represented by textiles) towards capital-intensive, technologically sophisticated manufactures (best exemplified by electronics products), which were more directly competitive with the core manufacturing activities of the West. Unexpectedly, moreover, the first oil crisis and the subsequent multiple hikes in oil prices touched off an explosive growth in the demand for Japanese sub-compact cars, especially in the United States; Western consumers discovered that Japanese cars were both efficient in fuel consumption and reliable in mechanical engineering. The image of 'made in Japan' products became a symbol of high quality and reliability—a clear reflection of Japan's successful industrial restructuring towards knowledge-intensive, fabricating/assembly-type industries.

Here Japanese manufacturers have accumulated production advantages not only in the form of *production technology* (based on both imported knowledge and indigenous research activities) but also—and more significantly—in *organizational technology* (e.g. the widespread practice of quality control circles and the type of inventory management known as 'just in time' inventory control). The former offers ownership-specific advantages, while the latter relates to location-specific advantages *internal to* Japanese industrial relations and organization—and culture. Thus, while Japan lost the old set of location advantages suitable for labour-intensive manufacturing, it created a new set of location advantages ideal for sophisticated manufacturing.

At the moment, the creation of technological and organizational advantages is proceeding in mutually supportive fashion, leading to a favourable innovation and manufacturing environment in Japan. The best (first-best) option for Japanese manufacturers who wish to exploit corporate advantages in knowledge-intensive manufacturing is, therefore, to produce at home and export to overseas markets. Yet this avenue is now increasingly blocked by protectionism overseas. Hence, under the pressure exerted by foreign countries to produce locally, many of Japan's export-competitive manufacturers, particularly in electronics and automobiles, have lately been forced to experiment with direct local production as the second best strategy. As a result of manufacturing environments less favourable overseas than at home, Japan's new manufacturing ventures in other industrialized countries are reportedly barely breaking even in most cases. Of Japanese manufacturing ventures in the United States, for example, it has been said that many, indeed all except a handful, are 'marginal to disasters' in their operation.[23] Their profitability is often supported only by the use of intermediate inputs (of parts and components) imported from Japan. In other words, their ownership advantages, brought in through the medium of direct investment, are not sufficiently large to compensate for the 'costs of being alien' (relative to local firms) in overseas manufacturing, not to speak of offsetting for operating in an unfavourable overseas manufacturing environment (as compared to the one at home). In fact, the industries in which Japanese enterprises have recently been compelled to set up manufacturing (at the moment, mostly assembly operations with partial production of components overseas) are exactly those knowledge-intensive, fabricating/assembly industries for which they are still expanding home-based, comparative advantages in trade by building up their ownership advantages in technology (as will be seen in section 5.5 below).

Degree of multinationalization and integrated (intra-company) operations

As shown in Table 5.3, at the end of March 1979 the accumulated value of Japan's outward investment amounted to 12.4% of the total value of paid-in capital of Japanese corporations at home (column A). This ratio may be interpreted as a measure of outward multinationalization of the Japanese economy. A breakdown by industry reveals that it is the mining sector that is the most multinationalized (49.1%), followed by textiles (47.8%), non-ferrous metals and related products (30.6%), transport machinery (20.1%), timber, pulp and paper products (TPP) (18.4%), and electrical machinery (17.2%). Thus a resource-securing activity ranks first, and labour-intensive manufacturing industries (textiles and metal products) second, a pattern compatible with Japan's changing macroeconomic environment.

The measures of Japanese multinational enterprises' (MNEs) trade dependence and intra-company trade are presented in columns B and C. Those in mining, non-electrical machinery, electrical machinery, transport machinery and precision machinery all show both a high (i.e. above average) degree of export dependence (20.0, 22.3, 31.6, 38.4 and

TABLE 5.3   Indicators of outward multinationalization, trade dependence, and intra-company trade (at the end of March 1979)

	A. Outward multi-nationalization	B. Japanese MNEs' exports (X)		C. Japanese MNEs' imports (M)		D. Overseas ventures' procurements			E. Overseas ventures' sales		
	Cumulative value of overseas investment/total value of all firms' paid-in capital at home (%)	(1) X from home/total sales (%)	(2) Intra-company X (%)	(1) M/total Sales (%)	(2) Intra-company M (%)	(1) L[a] (%)	(2) T[b]	(3) J[c]	(1) L[a] (%)	(2) T[b]	(3) J[c]
Agriculture, forestry and fishery	20.0	4.5	27.3	20.6	51.2	65.3	19.1	15.6	38.1	15.2	46.7
Mining	49.1	20.0	31.6	8.3	71.5	12.6	85.7	1.7	26.3	12.6	61.2
Manufacturing	14.1	21.1	26.2	14.3	16.2	34.9	9.1	56.0	78.6	15.5	5.9
1. Food	5.1	0.7	62.1	21.1	3.2	92.6	5.1	2.3	54.6	23.7	21.7
2. Textiles	47.8	13.3	4.3	9.7	9.7	55.9	22.1	22.0	68.6	26.1	5.3
3. Timber, pulp and paper	18.4	4.6	0.7	21.1	31.1	94.3	3.5	2.2	35.1	23.1	41.9
4. Chemicals	12.5	9.3	22.9	4.4	11.9	49.9	15.9	34.2	80.8	14.6	4.6
5. Steel	13.8	28.2	3.6	34.5	14.4	17.3	22.0	60.7	85.5	14.1	0.4
6. Non-ferrous metals and related products	30.6	8.1	10.4	37.3	2.5	12.4	14.2	73.4	85.3	9.9	4.8
7. Non-electrical machinery	5.1	22.3	26.9	2.0	38.1	28.7	3.0	68.3	88.6	9.7	1.7
8. Electrical machinery	17.2	31.6	48.8	3.8	61.0	33.6	5.8	60.6	81.2	14.0	4.8
9. Transport machinery	20.1	38.4	26.2	1.1	5.2	19.5	0.3	80.2	90.6	6.3	3.1
10. Precision machinery	8.0	49.4	45.0	3.8	47.6	9.7	8.1	82.2	54.0	35.2	10.8
11. Sundries	5.6	5.8	43.6	28.2	20.3	25.9	8.9	65.2	73.8	16.1	10.1
Commerce	12.1	19.5	28.7	11.5	49.5	34.2	21.0	44.8	49.0	18.6	32.4
Other	2.3	10.8	1.5	1.8	10.0	66.6	14.0	19.5	94.5	4.4	1.1
Total	12.4	19.7	26.6	12.2	36.5	34.6	19.6	45.9	55.7	17.5	26.8

[a] Local market.
[b] Third country market.
[c] Japan.

Source: Compiled from MITI (1980).

Statistics are based on the results of a questionnaire survey of 1,307 responding companies, whose total value of overseas investment accounted for 85.3% of the total cumulative value of Japan's overseas investments in 1979.

49.4%, respectively) and a high degree of intra-company exports from parent companies to their overseas ventures (31.6, 26.9, 48.8, 26.2 and 45.0%, respectively). Although Japanese MNEs in food and sundries are not strongly export-oriented, they exhibit a very high level of intra-company export activities (62.1 and 43.6%, respectively). An opposite pattern is observable in steel: Japanese MNEs are fairly export-oriented (a 28.2% export sales ratio), but their intra-company exports are insignificant (3.6%).

As far as imports are concerned, Japanese MNEs in agriculture, forestry and fishery (AFF), TPP, steel, non-ferrous metals and related products and sundries (all resource-dependent industries except sundries) are highly import-dependent, but those in AFF and TPP alone show a high degree of intra-company imports from overseas ventures to their parent companies. More interestingly, Japanese MNEs in mining, non-electric machinery, electric machinery, precision machinery and commerce are not comparably import-dependent, but are highly dependent on intra-company imports, indicating the active procurement of raw materials and/or intermediate imputs (except those in commerce, which procure mostly either raw materials or finished products) from their overseas ventures.

All in all, Japanese MNEs in mining (i.e., resource-based industry), non-electric machinery, electric machinery and precision machinery (i.e. high value-added industries) are active *both* in intra-company exports (31.6, 26.9, 48.8 and 45.0%, respectively) and intra-company imports (71.5, 38.1, 61.0 and 47.6%, respectively), a strong indication of *vertically integrated operations*.

How closely Japan's overseas ventures are tied to their parent companies (or the Japanese market) is indicated also by the overseas ventures' sources of procurement (column D) and their sales markets (column E). As might be expected of resource-scarce Japan, its overseas ventures in AFF, food and TPP procure a large portion of their materials from local markets (65.3, 92.6 and 94.3%). They were set up to take advantage of abundant local supplies of resources. Those in textiles also show a high ratio of procurement from local sources (55.9%), reflecting the local availability of intermediate inputs (fibres and fabrics) abroad.

But what is distinct is the fact that the overseas ventures in steel, non-ferrous metals and related products, non-electric machinery, electric machinery, transport machinery, precision machinery and sundries all show a very high procurement ratio from Japan (60.7, 73.4, 68.3, 60.6, 80.2, 82.2 and 65.2%, respectively). This indicates an active intra-company shipment of plant machinery and equipment, as well as intermediate inputs and semi-finished products which are fabricated or assembled in local markets.

On the whole, Japan's overseas ventures are strongly local market-oriented, except in AFF, mining and TPP. This is shown in column E. Those in AFF, mining and TPP export 46.7, 61.2 and 41.9% of their products, respectively, to Japan; they essentially serve as procurement outposts for Japanese industry.

5.5 STRUCTURAL UPGRADING AND TRADE IN TECHNOLOGY

Earlier Japan's imports of technologies were discussed. Since adaptive research and commercialization were required to process imported technologies, Japan's effort to absorb advanced foreign technologies in turn stimulated—and gave the 'learning by doing' effect to—a high level of R, D&E in Japanese enterprises. Besides, industrial restructuring towards knowledge-intensive industries itself naturally made Japanese industry more active in research than ever before. How quickly Japan's R&D activity intensified can be seen in terms of R&D expenditures as a ratio of national income: it was a mere 0.8% in 1953, but reached 1.4% in 1960, 2.0% in 1970, and finally 2.4% in 1980, thereby attaining a level comparable with that in other industrialized countries (2.6% for the United States in 1980 and 2.7% for West Germany in 1979).[24]

The net outcome of stepped-up R&D efforts was the growth of new industrial knowledge, both as the by-products of adaptive effort and as the fruits of original research, and an expansion in exports of 'Japanese' technologies. At the same time, technology imports, which reached a record high of 2,450 contracts (both Class A and Class B) in 1973, have been declining ever since—an indication of a narrowing technology gap. As a result, Japan's receipts from technology exports have been increasing at a much faster pace than its payments for technology imports, improving the balance of trade in technology considerably. In 1970, for example, the ratio of receipts to payments was 13.6%, but in 1981 it was 31.4%. In fact, as far as new technology contracts are concerned, Japan has been enjoying a net trade surplus ever since 1973: the ratio of receipts to payments in 1980 was as high as 2.7 for new contracts.[25]

Sectoral analysis reveals another interesting feature: as shown in Table 5.4, it is the fabricating/assembly industries (which are knowledge-intensive and whose comparative advantage is *expanding*) that still show *substantial net deficits*, whereas it is the basic materials industries (which are resource and energy-intensive and whose comparative advantage is *stagnant, declining, or even negative*) that are currently exhibiting either *a*

TABLE 5.4 Japan's technology trade, R&D intensity, and changes in comparative advantage by industry

	Technology trade, 1980 Receipts/payments (%)	R&D intensity R&D expenditure/sales (%)	Changes in comparative advantage ratio,[b] 1970–79 (%)
All industries	0.66	1.48	
Manufacturing	0.57	1.73	+1
Fabricating/assembly type			
Non-electrical machinery	0.32	1.90[a]	+8
Electrical machinery	0.37	3.71[a]	+7
Transport machinery	0.54	2.34[a]	+8
Precision machinery	0.29	3.02[a]	+6
Basic material type			
Iron and steel	2.23[a]	1.14	+3
Textiles	1.42[a]	0.77	−4, except apparel (−11)
Chemicals	0.81[a]	2.55[a]	+1
Glass, clay and stone products	0.83[a]	1.30	0
Non-ferrous metals	0.99[a]	1.03	−2
Metal products	0.28	1.15	+1
Other manufactures	0.39	1.16	Not available
Construction	9.38	0.46	Not available

[a]More than average for the manufacturing sector.
[b](Exports−Imports)/Total domestic outputs.
Source: Technology trade and R&D intensity are compiled from Science and Technology Agency (1982) and comparative advantage ratios from MITI.

substantial surplus or a near surplus (except metal products); that is, a more favourable position that the average for the manufacturing sector as a whole, in technology trade. The basic materials industries have already reached maturity and are currently in the stage of *relative contraction* at home, with their R&D intensity (measured in terms of R&D expenditures as a ratio to sales) lower than the average for the manufacturing sector (except chemicals). On the other hand, the fabricating/assembly industries are still in the *vigorous growth* (or *catching up*) stage, stepping up both technology imports and their R&D activities, with their R&D intensity much higher than the average.[26]

Another significant feature is that as much as 60% of Japan's receipts from technology come from developing countries, particularly in Asia and the Middle East (which account for 34% and 15%, respectively). Japan's technology exports to developing countries are mostly 'carried' through the medium of either direct foreign investment or comprehensive turnkey projects (or plant exports), rather than through 'pure' licensing agreements, that is, sales of technology *per se*. The fact that the construction industry has by far the largest surplus, with receipts as much as nine times payments, attests to the prevalence of those technology exports associated with turnkey projects and infrastructural ventures for economic development in developing countries, notably in the Middle East.

5.6 SUMMARY AND OVERALL ASSESSMENT

Japan has turned many of its adversities into advantages. Resource indigent as it is, it has striven to make the most of the post-war liberal trade environment that existed outside Japan for both commodities and technology, and has succeeded in the attempt. Japan has swiftly undergone triple structural changes—from the primary to the secondary sector, from light manufacturing to heavy and chemical industrialization, and from material-intensive to knowledge-intensive manufacturing activities. Massive technological absorption from the West, stimulated by the opportunity to fill a huge technology gap, has been primarily responsible for the development of brand new industries and the obsolescence of existing industries introduced, it seemed, only yester-year—an incessant process of industrial renovation.

In order to pay for the imported industrial resources and food, Japan initially made the best use of its existing factor endowment and situational advantages (namely home-based, location-specific advantages in the form of disciplined, low-cost labour and the undervalued yen) to manufacture and export labour-intensive products. In the meantime it made every effort to upgrade its industrial structure by fostering heavy and chemical industries with the introduction of the latest technologies from overseas (which eventually resulted in the development of ownership advantages at the firm level). Here, apprehensive of the possible foreign domination of domestic industries, the government restricted inward direct investment and instead encouraged the purchase of advanced technologies under licence (that is, the importation of foreign ownership advantages in 'unbundled' form). As a result, inward direct investment has been relatively insignificant in Japanese industry except in petroleum and rubber products.

The government's policy of acquiring technology through licensing as much as possible, however, necessarily required adaptive R,D&E on the part of technology-importing Japanese firms for the very reason that foreign firms were hindered from providing 'ready-made' technologies via direct investment. Hence the Japanese themselves had to carry out adaptive research, product and process engineering, designing, marketing, and all other commercialization efforts. In this sense the government's insistence on licensing created the 'learning by doing' effect in R, D&E and generated technological momentum in Japanese industry. Many significant improvements on imported technologies were introduced; alternative ways of achieving certain technical results were discovered. Technology gap-filling efforts, moreover, led to high rates of economic growth via capital investment, a growth environment that in turn created favourable opportunities to embody many more new ideas in production and marketing. The net result has been a snowballing causation between technological progress and economic expansion. Thus, because of the technological absorptive and adaptive capacity of Japanese industry,[27] *foreign ownership advantages have successfully been translated into home-based ownership advantages*, advantages that now constitute the basis of Japan's new comparative advantages in the fabricating/assembly industries, and of Japan's rising technology exports.

In the beginning, Japan's overseas investments were essentially a consequence of its swift structural changes and economic growth. A rapid rise in productivity and wages caused by the successful development of capital-intensive heavy and chemical industries and a subsequent sharp appreciation of the yen inevitably destroyed the initial set of location-specific factors supportive of Japan's exports of labour-intensive, technologically standardized manufactures. Those Japanese manufacturers, particularly small and medium-sized ones, operating in traditional light manufacturing industries such as textiles, metal products and sundries, therefore had to adapt themselves to a changing macro-economic environment by upgrading their products qualitatively, by diversifying into new industrial sectors, or by shifting production to labour-abundant developing countries where they could find a production environment suitable to their labour-intensive manufacturing activities. Many chose the third option. Thus those Japanese industries that underwent the greatest comparative disadvantage turned out to be the ones in which Japan's overseas manufacturing investments first became most active.

Japan also invested extensively in the trade-supportive commercial sector abroad and in overseas resource extraction. These investments were designed to enhance Japan's comparative advantage in manufactures by facilitating its overseas marketing and to reduce its comparative disadvantage in resources by opening up more supply sources abroad.

The growth of new ownership-cum-location advatages in Japan's fabricating/assembly industries (notably automobiles and electronics) has more recently generated another wave of manufacturing investments overseas, mostly in response to protectionism in overseas markets. At the moment, these ventures are basically assembly-type operations, serving as conduits for exports of intermediate products (as seen in Table 5.3, column C), although pressures upon them to procure or produce parts and components locally are increasing. These overseas manufacturing investments, emanating from the industries in Japan with new comparative advantages, are thus partially export-replacing (i.e. offer substitutability between exports and foreign direct investment), but their adverse impact on Japanese exports has not yet been seriously felt.

Japan's technology exports have recently been expanding at a fast rate —faster, in fact, than its technology imports, particularly in basic materials industries such as steel, textiles and basic chemicals, reflecting the ongoing restructuring of Japanese industry towards more knowledge-intensive industries, industries of the R&D intensive, fabricating/assembly type.

In sum, technological transfers and direct investments, inward and outward, have been both the facilitators and the concommitants of Japan's rapid structural transformation. In other words, these forms of international economic involvement have so far proved to be macroeconomic congruent with Japan's industrialization and economic growth, although some fear of their adverse 'boomerang' effect on national economic interests has lately been expressed in certain manufacturing industries, particularly in the basic materials sector, notably steel and textiles. Yet as far as Japan's overseas ventures are concerned, this fear is perhaps not justified (as evidenced in Table 5.3, column E).

NOTES

1. For a brief analysis of the pros and cons of these two different approaches, see OECD (1983), p. 13.
2. John H. Dunning, for example, observes: 'One might examine how far existing competitiveness of a country might be improved by more, less or a different kind of trade and international production . . . As far as I am aware [the Japanese] are the only country which explicitly incorporates foreign direct investment and production into their industrial and technology strategy.' See Dunning (1982).
3. The concepts of the ESP structure and the OLI system are discussed in Chapter 1 of this book.
4. Arisawa *et al.* (1967), pp. 359–60.
5. Japan's post-war programme of technology imports is examined elsewhere. See, for example, Ozaki (1972), Henderson (1973), Ozawa (1974), and Peck (1976).
6. Technology purchase contracts were classified into two categories: Class A and Class B. Class A comprised those contracts that had an effective life of more than one year, with payment of royalties guaranteed to be made in foreign currency, and Class B covered those that called for royalty payments in the Japanese yen or were less than one year in contract duration.
7. See Ozawa (1974), Chapter 3.
8. *Ibid.,* pp. 37–41.
9. *Ibid.,* p. 42
10. *Ibid.,* pp. 44–51. A regression analysis between changes in Japan's export share in the world market (dependent variable) and the number of foreign licences acquired (independent variable) for 1953–60 is made in Ozawa (1968).
11. About one third of R&D expenditures over the 1957–62 period was, for example, spent to adapt and commercialize imported technologies, MITI (1963).
12. The number of foreign technologies acquired includes both Class A and B contracts.
13. MITI (1968), p. 274.
14. MITI (1983a), p. 86. For an analysis of foreign-affiliated ventures in Japan in the 1950s and the 1960s, see Komiya (1972).
15. MITI (1983a), p. 37 and p. 39.
16. MITI (1982), p. 405.
17. MITI (1980), p. 14.
18. This characteristic has been emphasized by Kojima (1973, 1978) and has been elaborated upon by Ozawa (1979a, 1979b) and Kojima and Ozawa (1984).
19. For an elaboration of these advantages, see Dunning (1981).
20. See Kojima (1978), Chapter 4 and Ozawa (1979a), Chapter 3.
21. MITI (1978), p. 108.
22. Kojima (1983/84).
23. Ohmae (1983).
24. Japan's Science and Technology Agency (1970, 1975, 1982).
25. Japan's Science and Technology Agency (1983).
26. These dualistic features of Japanese industry are emphasized in Ozawa (1983).
27. The socio-cultural and historical factors of Japan's absorptive and adaptive capacity are discussed in Ozawa (1981).

REFERENCES

Arisawa, H. *et al.* (1967). *Nippon Sangyo Hyakunenshi* [The One-Hundred-Year History of Japanese Industry], Vol. 1, Tokyo: Nippon Keizai Shimbun

Dunning, J. H. (1981). *International Production and the Multinational Enterprise*, London: Allen & Unwin

Dunning, J. H. (1982). Domestic and National Competitiveness, International Technology Transfer, and Multinational Enterprise, mimeograph

Henderson, D. F. (1973). *Foreign Enterprise in Japan: Laws and Policies*, Chapel Hill, N.C.: University of North Carolina Press

Kojima, K. (1973). A macroeconomic approach to foreign direct investment, *Hitotsubashi Journal of Economics*, **16**

Kojima, K. (1978). *Direct Foreign Investment: A Japanese Model of Multinational Business Operations*, London: Croom Helm

Kojima, K. (1983/84). Japanese direct foreign investment and economic development in the Asia Pacific region, *Korean Journal of International Studies*, **15**, 39–53

Kojima, K. and Ozawa, T. (1984). Micro- and macro-economic models of direct foreign investment: Toward a Synthesis, *Hitotsubashi Journal of Economics*,**5**, June, 1–20

Komiya, R. (1972). Direct foreign investment in postwar Japan, in P. Drysdale (ed.), *Direct Foreign Investment in Asia and the Pacific*, Canberra: Australian National University Press

MITI (Ministry of International Trade and Industry) (1963). *Gijutsu Doko Chosa Hokokusho* [Report on the Trend of Technology], Tokyo: MITI

MITI (1968). *Gaishikei Kigyo* [Foreign-Affiliated Enterprises], Tokyo: MITI

MITI (1978). *Wagakuni Kigyo no Kaigai Jigyo Katsudo* [Overseas Business Activities of Japanese Enterprises], No.7 Report, Tokyo: Government Printing Office

MITI (1980). *Wagukuni Kigyo no Kaigai Jigyo Katsudo* [Overseas Business Acitivities of Japanese Enterprises], No. 9 Report, Tokyo: Government Printing Office

MITI (1982). *Tsusho Hakusho* [White Paper on International Trade], Tokyo: Government Printing Office

MITI (1983a). *Gaishikei Kigyo no Doko* [Trend of Foreign-Affiliated Enterprises], Toky: Toyo Hokisha

MITI (1983b). *Tsusho Hakusho* [White Paper on International Trade], Tokyo: Government Printing Office

Ohmae, K. (1983). Management style: the mixed scorecard of Japanese management abroad, *International Management, Europe*, July

Organization for Economic Cooperation and Development (OECD) (1983). *Positive Adjustment Policies: Managing Structural Change*, Paris: OECD

Ozaki, R. S. (1972). *The Control of Imports and Foreign Capital in Japan*, New York: Praeger

Ozawa, T. (1968). Imitation, innovation, and Japanese exports, in P. B. Kenen and R. Lawrence (eds), *The Open Economy: Essays on International Trade and Finance*, New York: Columbia University Press

Ozawa, T. (1974). *Japan's Technological Challenge to the West, 1950–1974*, Cambridge, Mass.: MIT Press

Ozawa, T. (1979a). *Multinationalism, Japanese Style: The Political Economy of Outward Dependency*, Princeton, NJ: Princeton University Press

Ozawa, T. (1979b). International investment and industrial structure: new theoretical implications from the Japanese experience, *Oxford Economic Papers*, **31**.

Ozawa, T. (1981). Technology transfer and Japanese economic growth in the postwar period, in R. Hawkins and A. J. Prasad (eds), *Technology Transfer and Economic Development*, Greenwich, Conn.: JAI Press

Ozawa, T. (1983). Macroeconomic Factors Affecting Technology Inflows to and Outflows from Japan: The Postwar Experience, paper presented at the Conference on International Technology Transfer: Concepts, Measures, and Comparisons, New York, 2–3 June

Peck, M. J. (1976). Technology, in H. Patrick and H. Rosovsky (eds), *Asia's New Giant: How the Japanese Economy Works*, Washington, DC: Brookings Institution

Science and Technology Agency (1970, 1975, 1982). *Indicators of Science and Technology*, Tokyo: Science and Technology Agency

Science and Technology Agency (1983). *1982 Kagaku Gijutsu Hakusho* [White Paper on Science and Technology], Tokyo: Government Printing Office

APPENDIX TABLE 5.A1   Japan's technology imports (Class A), 1950–80 (in number of licensing contracts. % in parenthesis)

Industry SIC^a	1950–4	1955–9	1960–4	1965–9	1970–4	1975–80	Total
Chemicals 261–269	82 (18.1)	116 (20.2)	280 (13.7)	678 (17.3)	1,048 (12.6)	808 (10.3)	3,012 (13.0)
Petroleum and coal prod. 271–279	15 (3.3)	36 (6.3)	62 (3.0)	146 (3.7)	299 (3.6)	176 (2.2)	734 (3.2)
Ferrous and non-ferrous metals 311–327	38 (8.4)	56 (9.7)	96 (4.7)	181 (4.6)	201 (2.4)	147 (1.9)	719 (3.1)
Metal products 331–339	6 (1.3)	20 (3.5)	74 (3.6)	124 (3.2)	225 (2.7)	217 (2.8)	666 (2.9)
Machinery 341–349	98 (21.6)	120 (20.9)	589 (28.9)	1,021 (26.0)	1,973 (23.8)	1,759 (22.4)	5,560 (24.0)
Electrical machinery 351–359	108 (23.8)	109 (19.0)	469 (23.0)	664 (16.9)	1,251 (15.1)	1,451 (18.5)	4,052 (17.5)
Transport equipment 361–369	42 (9.3)	34 (5.9)	94 (4.6)	209 (5.3)	438 (5.3)	391 (5.0)	1,208 (5.2)
Precision equipment 371–377	0	8 (1.4)	48 (2.4)	125 (3.2)	261 (3.1)	304 (3.9)	746 (3.2)
Food, tobacco 181–194	0	1 (0.2)	8 (0.4)	58 (1.5)	260 (3.1)	151 (1.9)	478 (2.1)
Textiles 201–219	24 (5.3)	33 (5.7)	83 (4.1)	172 (4.4)	794 (9.6)	1,060 (13.5)	2,166 (9.4)

Ceramics (glass, stone and clay) 301–309	10 (2.2)	8 (1.4)	45 (2.2)	81 (2.1)	206 (2.5)	134 (1.7)	484 (2.1)
Other manufactures 391–399	21 (4.6)	27 (4.7)	168 (8.2)	398 (10.1)	1,187 (14.3)	1,070 (13.6)	2,871 (12.4)
Construction 15–17	10 (2.2)	6 (1.0)	17 (0.9)	39 (1.0)	129 (1.6)	84 (1.1)	285 (1.2)
Others A–D, G–N	0	1 (0.2)	6 (0.3)	30 (0.8)	23 (0.3)	94 (1.2)	154 (0.7)
Total	454 (100.0)	575 (100.0)	2,039 (100.0)	3,926 (100.0)	8,295 (100.0)	7,846 (100.0)	23,135 (100.0)

[a]SIC: Standard Industrial Classification, Japan.
Source: Compiled from Science and Technology Agency (1960, 1975, 1982).

APPENDIX TABLE 5.A2 Foreign direct investment in Japan by industry, 1950–80 ($1,000. % in parentheses)

Industry SIC^a	1950–5	1956–60	1961–5	1966–70	1971–5	1976–80
Manufacturing	a26,804 (92.9%)	a61,804 (98.9%)	a167,812 (92.8%)	a269,390 (83.1%)	a695,592 (77.0%)	a1,092,101 (73.8%)
Machinery 241–359	4,033 (13.9)	14,622 (23.4)	42,806 (23.7)	79,581 (24.6)	240,679 (26.6)	268,922 (18.2)
Metals and metal prod. 311–339	2,219 (7.7)	3,082 (4.9)	11,249 (6.2)	41,620 (12.8)	35,941 (4.0)	57,343 (3.9)
Chemicals 261–269	4,635 (16.1)	24,436 (33.1)	38,643 (21.4)	81,897 (25.3)	162,286 (18.0)	402,489 (27.2)
Textiles 201–209	592 (2.1)	99 (0.2)	788 (0.4)	4,350 (1.3)	7,056 (0.8)	1,642 (0.1)
Petroleum 271–279	14,149 (49.0)	10,019 (16.0)	64,894 (35.9)	37,157 (11.5)	107,523 (11.9)	216,961 (14.7)
Rubber and leather prod. 28–29	847 (2.9)	7,319 (11.7)	5,830 (3.2)	6,194 (1.9)	7,112 (0.8)	169
Glass, clay and stone products 301–309	329 (1.1)	2,227 (3.6)	2,437 (1.3)	7,818 (2.4)	14,388 (1.6)	58,724 (4.0)
Food 181–193	—	—	1,165 (0.6)	10,773 (3.3)	54,629 (6.0)	26,606 (2.0)
Other manufacturing	b	b	b	b	65,978 (7.3)	59,245 (4.0)
Commerce and foreign trade	1,646 (5.7)	81 (0.1)	4,387 (2.4)	22,708 (7.0)	139,596 (15.5)	195,228 (13.2)
Services	139 (0.5)	111 (0.2)	297 (0.2)	5,386 (1.7)	42,882 (4.7)	58,623 (4.0)
Construction and real estate	76 (0.3)	215 (0.3)	148 (0.1)	239 (0.1)	2,975 (0.3)	19,536 (1.3)

Transportation and communication	163 (0.6)	144 (0.2)	174 (0.1)	3,103 (0.9)	7,074 (0.8)	1,671 (0.1)
Warehousing	6	—	—	167	—	24,926 (1.7)
Others	13	139 (0.2)	7,917 (4.4)	23,060 (7.1)	15,259 (1.7)	87,419 (5.9)
Total	28,847 (100.0)	62,494 (100.0)	180,735 (100.0)	324,053 (100.0)	903,378 (100.0)	1,479,504 (100.0)

[a]Standard Industrial Classification, Japan.
[b]Included in 'Others'.
Source: Compiled from MITI (1983a).

APPENDIX TABLE 5.A3 Japan's foreign direct investment by industry, 1951–81 ($1,000. % in parenthesis)

Industry SIC^a	1951–62	1963–7	1968–71	1972–3	1974–8	1979–81
Manufacturing	191,477	301,921	727,045	2,021,058	3,897,177	7,716,538
	(36.3)	(34.8)	(24.7)	(38.1)	(33.7)	(34.3)
Food	6.168	20,479	43,027	97,249	195,589	365,882
181–194	(1.2)	(2.4)	(1.5)	(1.8)	(1.7)	(1.6)
Textiles	36,169	54,464	162,968	488,375	543,293	442,593
201–219	(6.9)	(6.3)	(5.5)	(9.2)	(4.7)	(2.0)
T, P & P^b	50,747	61,908	150,679	98,982	264,603	198,595
220–229	(9.6)	(7.1)	(5.1)	(1.9)	(2.3)	(0.9)
Chemicals	2,249	13,509	50,440	460,329	842,135	1,485,393
261–269	(0.4)	(1.6)	(1.7)	(8.7)	(7.3)	(6.6)
Metals	38,011	48,594	100,903	297,658	565,817	2,089,456
341–347	(7.2)	(5.6)	(3.4)	(5.6)	(4.9)	(9.3)
Machinery	13,308	24,552	52,853	121,809	300,669	588,004
341–349	(2.5)	(2.8)	(1.8)	(2.3)	(2.6)	(2.6)
Electrical machinery	5,371	17,083	80,324	224,754	520,110	1,207,024
351–359	(1.0)	(2.0)	(2.7)	(4.2)	(4.5)	(5.4)
Transport equipment	26,578	47,092	26,768	121,733	316,256	821,160
361–369	(5.0)	(5.4)	(0.9)	(2.3)	(2.7)	(3.6)
Sundries	12,876	14,240	59,083	110,169	348,705	518,431
	(2.4)	(1.6)	(2.0)	(2.1)	(3.0)	(2.3)
A, F and F^c	10,777	25,672	66,265	125,408	329,527	460,277
	(2.0)	(2.9)	(2.3)	(2.4)	(2.9)	(2.0)
Mining	224,738	218,212	908,681	1,422,586	2,896,775	4,294,820
	(42.6)	(25.2)	(30.8)	(26.8)	(25.0)	(19.1)

Commerce	45,477 (8.6)	113,568 (13.1)	369,940 (12.6)	661,271 (12.4)	1,764,341 (15.2)	3,628,472 (16.1)
Banking and insurance	18,405 (3.5)	117,595 (13.6)	234,620 (8.0)	475,459 (9.0)	847,743 (7.3)	1,575,257 (7.0)
Other services	36,816 (7.0)	90,337 (10.4)	638,542 (21.6)	604,564 (11.4)	1,837,001 (15.9)	4,850,739 (21.5)
Total	527,690 (100.0)	867,305 (100.0)	2,945,093 (100.0)	5,310,346 (100.0)	11,572,564 (100.0)	22,526,103 (100.0)

[a]Standard Industrial Classification, Japan.
[b]Timber, pulp, and paper.
[c]Agriculture, forestry, and fishery.
Source: As for Table 5A2.

6

Canada

STEVEN GLOBERMAN

6.1 INTRODUCTION

Canada is an important representative of the set of smaller industrialized countries that face international competition from countries enjoying larger domestic markets; however, it is unique among all industrialized countries in the substantial percentage of private-sector assets owned and controlled by foreigners. The degree of foreign ownership and control of economic activity in Canada is substantially higher than in any other industrialized country. Canada's close economic, geographic and cultural ties to the United States also contribute to making the Canadian experience with foreign direct investment (FDI) unique.

In keeping with the other contributions in this volume, the broad purpose of this chapter is to evaluate the impact of FDI on the structure and economic performance of the Canadian economy. In particular, the analysis evaluates whether patterns of inward and outward FDI promote a distribution of economic activity consistent with Canada's comparative advantage. Under the simple principle of comparative (trading) advantage, any such specialization encouraged by the FDI process would be likely to contribute to increased real incomes in Canada. The chapter also addresses the issue of whether or not FDI encourages a more efficient use of Canadian factors of production within individual sectors of the economy, either by leading to the displacement of less efficient firms by more efficient units, or by stimulating increased efficiency throughout a given economic sector.

The overall impact of inward FDI on Canada's international competitiveness is important not only for its impact on real incomes but also for Canadian government efforts to 'restructure' the Canadian economy. In particular, both the federal and provincial governments have emphasized the importance of improving Canada's merchandise trade performance, especially in highly processed goods.[1] An overall assessment of the MNEs' role in Canada, as well as the formation of policies towards

MNEs, depends greatly upon the perceived relationship between inward FDI and Canada's trade competitiveness. While the efficiency impacts of FDI will bear upon this relationship, a more direct evaluation is desirable. A direct examination of the FDI-trade competitiveness relationship is undertaken through standard statistical techniques and is described in a later section.

Since efficiency and increased trade competitiveness may only be aspects of governmental economic priorities, the chapter also includes a brief consideration of how FDI has contributed to achieving another major priority of the Canadian government: increased indigenous technological innovation accompanied by greater domestic expenditures on R&D. The chapter concludes with an evaluation of the policy implications of the foregoing analysis.

6.2   AN HISTORICAL OVERVIEW OF FDI

Despite a heavy reliance on external capital (prior to the First World War), foreign ownership and control of Canadian business (apart from railways) was not great in the half-century following Confederation, because much of it came in the form of debt securities, rather than equity. Between 1914 and 1930, US direct and portfolio investment in Canada grew rapidly. US investors showed a greater interest in direct investment than those in the United Kingdom. Thus, in 1930, foreign long term investment in Canada amounted to slightly more than $7.6 billion. Of this amount, approximately 32% represented FDI, of which about 80% was of US origin (Government of Canada, 1972, p. 13). The US investors tended to concentrate in specific sectors, in particular the extractive and processing industries, automobile manufacturing, pulp and paper production, non-ferrous metal mining and refining, and the manufacture of electric apparatus and supplies.

Canadian direct investment abroad was extremely modest compared to inward FDI in the approximate half-century following Confederation. Specifically, the book value of Canadian direct investment abroad amounted to less than $500 million in 1926. This represented about 30% of the total value of Canadian assets abroad (Brecher and Reisman, 1957, p. 89). Two especially noteworthy aspects of early Canadian direct investment abroad include the relatively small number of Canadian companies involved, and the fact that many of these companies were controlled by non-residents.

6.3 STATISTICAL DESCRIPTION OF FDI PATTERNS

Table 6.1 reports the book value of net assets owned by Canadian companies abroad, along with the book value of net assets owned in Canada by foreign investors.[2] Perhaps the most notable feature of the data presented is the predominant growth of the inward capital investment stake over the period 1945–65, followed by the predominant growth of the outward capital investment stake in the post-1965 period. This pattern is underscored by the following statistics: from 1945 to 1965, the average annual compound rates of growth of the inward and outward capital investment stakes were 9.69% and 8.27% respectively. From 1965 to 1978, the comparable rates of growth were 5.25% and 7.90%, respectively. As a result, the ratio between the inward and outward capital stake fell from a maximum value of 4.93 in 1965 to 2.97 in 1978.

TABLE 6.1   Book value of foreign direct investment
($ millions)

Year	Canadian direct investment abroad	Foreign direct investment in Canada
1945	720	2,713
1955	1,751	7,728
1965	3,523	17,356
1970	6,200	26,358
1974	9,210	36,385
1976	11,491	40,311
1978	16,253	48,288
1979	NA	54,260

Source: Statistics Canada, *Canada's International Investment Position*, various issues.

Table 6.2 reveals that as a proportion of Canada's gross national product (GNP), the combined inward and outward capital stake $(K_i + K_o)$ has ranged from around 38% in 1965 to around 28% in 1978. The relative significance of the inward capital stake has declined fairly consistently from 1970 onward, while the outward capital stake (after remaining fairly constant over most of the post-war period) began to increase relative to GNP in the latter half of the 1970s.

An examination of investment flows (i.e. changes in the capital stakes, or I_i and I_o) shows fairly sizeable annual fluctuations relative to GNP, as well as relative to imports (m) and exports (x). While there appear to be cyclical patterns in these series, no secular trends are apparent. In particular, outward and inward investment flows became increasingly important relative to exporting and importing in the latter half of the 1970s.

TABLE 6.2   The significance of outward and inward investment for the Canadian economy: selected indicators

Year	K_o	As a % of GNP K_i	I_o	I_i	As a % of trade $I_{o/x}$	$I_{i/m}$
1945	6.1	23.1				
1955	6.5	28.7				
1965	6.4	31.3				
1970	6.3	30.8	0.18	0.85	1.43	9.7
1971	6.9	29.6	0.36	1.65	1.5	7.2
1972	6.4	28.1	0.17	1.56	0.69	6.5
1973	6.3	26.6	0.91	2.61	3.5	10.4
1974	6.2	24.7	0.07	2.38	3.4	8.4
1975	6.4	22.6	0.04	0.61	3.3	2.2
1976	6.0	21.1	—	1.53	2.1	5.8
1977	6.4	20.9	—	1.61	3.7	5.9
1978	7.1	20.9	0.09	1.97	4.5	6.7

Source: Statistics Canada: *Canada's International Investment Position*, various issues, *Canadian Statistical Review*, various issues, and *Canadian Balance of International Payments*, various issues.

TABLE 6.3   Distribution of outward and inward direct capital stake by geographical area

		Outward capital stake $ (millions)	%			Inward capital stake $ (millions)	%
1945	US	455	63	1945	US	2,304	85
	UK	54	9		UK	348	13
	Other	211	29		Other	61	2
1955	US	1,302	74	1955	US	6,513	84
	UK	131	8		UK	890	12
	Other	318	18		Other	325	4
1965	US	2,041	59	1965	US	14,059	81
	UK	482	14		UK	2,033	12
	Other	946	27		Other	1,264	7
1978	US	8,898	55	1978	US	38,348	80
	UK	1,512	9		UK	4,476	9
	Other	5,843	36		Other	5,404	11

Source: Statistics Canada, *Canada's International Investment Position*, various issues.

The geographic distribution of Canada's outward and inward capital stakes is shown in Table 6.3 for selected years. The United States is clearly the dominant source of inward direct investment, as well as the primary destination of outward direct investment. The relative importance of the

TABLE 6.4   Distribution of outward and inward direct capital stake by sector

	Canadian direct investment abroad *($ millions)*						
Year	*Manufacturing*	*Petroleum and natural gas*	*Mining*	*Utilities*	*Merchand.*	*Financial*	*Other*
1945	337[a]	138		239			6
1955	993[a]	291		438			20
1965	2,111 (61%)	242 (7%)	253 (7%)	407 (12%)	155 (5%)	165 (5%)	136 (4%)
1978	4,587 (31%)	1,611 (11%)	784 (15%)	538 (20%)	357 (8%)	829 (14%)	192 (2%)

	Foreign direct investment in Canada *($ millions)*						
Year	*Manufacturing*	*Petroleum and natural gas*	*Mining*	*Utilities*	*Merchand.*	*Financial*	*Other*
1945	1,359 (50%)	138 (5%)	240 (9%)	375 (14%)	202 (7%)	339 (12%)	60 (2%)
1955	3,434 (44%)	1,754 (23%)	811 (11%)	320 (4%)	538 (7%)	706 (9%)	165 (2%)
1965	7,255 (42%)	4,600 (27%)	2,017 (12%)	301 (2%)	1,061 (6%)	1,694 (10%)	428 (3%)
1978	20,265 (42%)	11,329 (23%)	4,219 (9%)	632 (1%)	3,722 (8%)	6,155 (13%)	1,906 (4%)

[a]Industrial and commercial.
Source: Statistics Canada, *Canada's International Investment Position*, various issues.

US share of Canada's inward capital stake declined slightly over the post-war period, while the relative importance of other countries' stakes increased. In a corresponding fashion, the relative importance of the United States as the destination of outward direct investment declined significantly over the period 1955 to 1978, while the outward capital stake in EEC countries and Central and South America became relatively more important.

As noted in the introduction, the direct investment process can have a substantial impact upon allocative efficiency to the extent that inward and outward capital flows promote a movement of resources out of economic activities in which Canada has a long run comparative disadvantage and into those in which Canada enjoys a long run comparative advantage.

The sectoral distribution of inward and outward capital stakes, reported in Table 6.4, provides some preliminary data against which to evaluate the empirical relevance of locational and ownership determinants of direct investment flows. Almost one third of the book value of the total inward capital stake in 1978 (and approximately 37% of the book value of foreign owned assets in non-financial industries) represented foreign ownership in the petroleum and natural gas and mining sectors. By comparison, the book value of total capital employed in the petroleum and mining industries was less than 25% of the total book value of capital employed in all non-financial industries. Thus, the resource extraction industries were disproportionate recipients of direct investment inflows over the post-Second World War period, although their relative importance apparently peaked around 1965.

Slightly over one quarter of the book value of the total outward capital stake in 1978 (and around 30% of the outward stake in non-financial industries) was concentrated in the petroleum, natural gas and mining industries. This represented almost a doubling in the relative importance of this sector as the destination of the outward capital stake compared to 1965. Over the same period, the relative importance of manufacturing industries as the destination of direct investment abroad declined almost 50%.[3]

6.3   HYPOTHESES RELATING INWARD FDI TO ECONOMIC STRUCTURE AND PERFORMANCE

The Canadian literature relating direct investment to industrial structure and performance has primarily focused on inward FDI. In this regard, Saunders (1982) identifies two broad schools of thought: the Nationalists and the Continentalists.

The Nationalist position

The Nationalists argue that inward FDI exacerbates any allocative inefficiencies that are promoted by tariff and non-tariff barriers to trade. Specifically, by reproducing the (primarily) US oligopoly industrial structure in
small, protected Canadian markets, foreign-owned firms are responsible
for fragmenting domestic markets and preventing domestically owned
firms from realizing extant economies of scale. Implicit (and sometimes
explicit) in this argument is the notion that foreign-owned firms can enter
domestic industries more easily than Canadian-owned firms, otherwise
inward direct investment would have no marginal significance to the
extent of 'overcrowding' in domestic industries. Among other advantages,
advertising spillovers from the United States into Canada have been identified as providing unique marketing advantages for US-based companies
in the Canadian economy.[4]

The hypotheses that foreign-owned firms enjoy a competitive advantage
in domestic markets owing to the possession of intangible 'marketing'
assets is consistent with findings that foreign ownership levels are
positively correlated with advertising to sales ratios in samples of
Canadian industries.[5] It is also consistent with a finding that high
advertising intensity and R&D intensity in an industry apparently restrict
the entry of domestically owned firms into Canadian industries but do not
restrict the entry of foreign-owned firms.[6]

What is noteworthy about the Nationalists' argument is their tolerant
attitude towards the domestic tariff, notwithstanding their acknowledge-
ment that (by attracting direct investment) it indirectly promotes inefficiency and reduces the competitiveness of domestic industries. Evidently,
the Nationalists believe that while the tariff may induce allocative inefficiencies (at least in the short run),[7] inward direct investment imposes
unique inefficiencies, in addition to the allocative effects of the tariff, by
pushing domestic firms backwards along a downward sloping cost function; however, to the extent that domestic protection encourages inward
FDI, the 'overcrowding' of domestic industries is not independent of tariff
and non-tariff protection.

Another reason is posited by the Nationalists for why the presence of
MNE affiliates leads to Canadian industries becoming increasingly
uncompetitive over time in the world market. It rests on the notion that,
while the transfer of technology and (or) marketing-based assets from
parent companies to their Canadian affiliates is socially less costly in the
short run than producing those assets indigenously, in the long run
Canadians are deprived of the opportunity to develop their skills at innovation.

With terms-of-trade allegedly shifting in favour of 'high technology' activities, American subsidiaries are seen as perpetuating Canada's technological dependence, thereby preventing the 'necessary' creation of a dynamic comparative advantage in the growth industries of the future.[8] Thus, the presence of American subsidiaries in Canada is seen as contributing to the 'wrong' types of goods being produced over time in the domestic economy, and to higher costs for the goods that are produced domestically.[9] More directly, it is alleged that MNE affiliates are often prevented by their parent companies from exporting, even when they enjoy a comparative advantage in world markets. Similarly, MNE affiliates are often forced to import from sister affiliates, even when lower cost domestic sources of supply are available.

The Continentalist position

The Continentalists maintain that the tariff and other barriers to trade are the main source of structural inefficiency in the Canadian economy. Specifically, protectionism is seen as encouraging production in import-competing activities in which Canada enjoys neither a static nor a dynamic comparative advantage. Furthermore, they argue that excessive product differentiation and the use of less than minimum efficient scale plants can only persist in the presence of domestic barriers to trade. Given the existence of domestic trade barriers, inward direct investment is seen as promoting allocative and technical efficiency in the domestic economy.

In the Continentalists' argument, incoming direct investment promotes allocative efficiency via the displacement of less efficient Canadian producers by more efficient foreign producers. In addition, existing domestic producers are encouraged to perform at higher levels of efficiency by the poised competition of potential entry reinforced by periodic actual entry of foreign firms into domestic markets.

Beyond the influence of the tariff, other market imperfections are alleged to encourage the internalization of the ownership advantages enjoyed by foreign firms.[10] In this framework, the introduction of new technologies, improved marketing techniques and other intangible assets underlying foreign firms' ownership advantages might be delayed or blunted if inward direct investment flows were blocked or otherwise discouraged. Therefore, the Continentalists attribute an important role to inward direct investment in improving the technical efficiency of Canadian industries.

Unlike the Nationalists, the Continentalists do not ascribe much general importance to anti-competitive motives for direct investment. As a consequence, the latter have no great concern that the Canadian subsidiaries of MNEs will deliberately choose inefficient factor input combinations or forgo opportunities to exploit the locational advantages of the Canadian economy. For example, they do not put much stock in the argument that Canadian subsidiaries are prevented by their parents from competing in world markets, even when Canadian affiliates are the most competitive sources of supply, since that form of behaviour would be inconsistent with global profit maximization by MNEs. For a similar reason, the Continentalists reject the argument that the indigenous production of R&D and other inputs is discouraged by the MNE parent, even when internal rather than external sourcing is the most efficient route for its Canadian affiliate to pursue.[11]

6.4 HYPOTHESES RELATING OUTWARD FDI TO ECONOMIC STRUCTURE AND PERFORMANCE

In contrast to the case of inward FDI, discussion of the allocative and competitive consequences of outward FDI tends to be understated and somewhat less focused. The primary concern raised is that Canadian firms invest abroad in order to maintain worldwide dominance in natural resource markets, even though equally profitable opportunities exist to invest domestically.[12] In the context of a model of efficient international production, Canadian multinational resource companies have been accused of transferring resources from areas enjoying a locational advantage to areas suffering a locational disadvantage. All other things the same, such behaviour is inconsistent with an efficient allocation of domestically owned resources.

On the other hand, if overseas investment did assist in pre-empting entry and preserving higher price-cost margins for Canadian-owned firms, it might be viewed as efficient in a pecuniary sense, even though it did not follow along the lines dictated by locational advantage. However, this qualification is of dubious relevance, since in most areas Canadian direct investment is marginal relative to the activities of US, European and Japanese multinationals. This qualification is especially relevant for manufacturing industries, although a 'terms-of-trade' argument for outward direct investment cannot be as readily dismissed in specific resource activities such as nickel mining.

Direct investment undertaken by Canada's leading manufacturing companies has also been criticized along the lines of Kojima's critique of US multinationals. Specifically, a concern has been raised that in the few high technology activities in which Canada is currently internationally competitive, outward direct investment (especially to the United States) may contribute to the erosion of Canada's competitive advantage, particularly if domestic R&D activities are transferred to foreign markets.[13] The transfer of technological capabilities by Canadian MNEs is therefore seen by some as 'trade-diverting' and as undermining Canada's dynamic comparative advantage in industries enjoying increasingly favourable terms of trade.

Supporters of outward direct investment argue that it may be a means of perpetuating the competitive advantage enjoyed by specific Canadian firms in the world market. For example, the establishment of R&D facilities abroad is suggested to be required in high technology industries in order to keep Canadian management abreast of technological and other competitive developments in foreign markets. It is also argued that where tariff and non-tariff barriers preclude exports, sales by foreign subsidiaries facilitate lower unit costs of domestic production by allowing indivisible inputs to be utilized over longer output runs.

Some Canadian managers argue that, in fact, their transfer of activities from Canada to foreign markets was motivated by considerations of locational advantage. For example, the chairman of Northern Telecom has stated that his firm's expansion in the United States was motivated by increasing costs in Canada relative to the United States in virtually all input categories, including labour, capital, construction and even R&D.[14]

6.5 EVIDENCE RELATING FDI TO ALLOCATIVE AND TECHNICAL EFFICIENCY

As noted above, both the Nationalists and the Continentalists tend to agree that tariff and other trade distortions have promoted a distribution of inward FDI that is inconsistent with Canada's locational advantages, at least in manufacturing industries; however, there is fundamental disagreement between the two schools on the relationship between inward FDI and efficiency within sectors. There is also a concern that outward FDI is inconsistent with the locational advantage of Canadian industries.

Allocative efficiency

Existing studies are quite consistent in their conclusions that Canada's comparative advantage lies very heavily on the land and natural resource side in relation to her major trading partners, and to a lesser degree on capital stocks. Canada's comparative disadvantage lies in scale, technology, and skill-intensive activities relative to her major trading partners, in particular the United States and Japan.[15]

The pursuit of locational advantage would therefore dictate, all other things constant, that the inward capital stake be concentrated in the resource sector and in manufacturing industries that are resource-intensive. Conversely, the outward capital stake should be concentrated in industries that are intensive users of highly skilled labour and whose production functions are characterized by significant economies of scale.

There are several substantial problems in evaluating the locational determinants of FDI flows. One is that the aggregation level of the available data may mask significant intra-industry capital flows and therefore obscure the correspondence between locational advantage and FDI that would be identified at more detailed industry levels. A second is that government policies, in pursuit of distributional or other social objectives, may alter the outcome of 'economically directed' international capital flows. A third potential problem is that the sectoral distribution of inward and outward capital stakes reflects the joint influence of both locational and ownership advantage. Identification of the influence of locational advantage, *per se*, requires disentangling the joint impacts of these two factors.[16]

In light of these complications, it is not surprising that the distributions of inward and outward capital stakes reported in Table 6.4 fail to provide strong support for the relevance of locational determinants of FDI flows. Indeed, as noted above, substantial inward and outward capital stakes in the natural resource and manufacturing sectors are, on the surface, inconsistent with a strong influence of locational determinants. In particular, the significant outward capital stake in the resource extraction sector is seemingly at odds with the strong consensus view of Canada's comparative advantage in natural resource-based industries.

Product differentiation is an unlikely general explanation for observing both inward and outward FDI flows in the resource sector. Nor is sectoral aggregation likely to be a significant source of bias. There is some indirect evidence to suggest that while Canadian resource companies enjoy ownership advantages in certain activities, they suffer ownership disadvantages in other activities. For example, the ratio of net profits before taxes to total equity averages 0.23 for Canadian-owned mining firms over the period 1973–75, while this ratio averaged 0.16 for foreign-owned mining companies operating in Canada over the same period. On the other hand, the ratio of net profits before taxes to total equity averaged 0.18 for Canadian-owned petroleum companies and 0.33 for foreign-owned petroleum companies.[17]

To be sure, the existence of a significant outward capital stake in the resource industries is not necessarily inconsistent with Canada's comparative advantage in that sector. Higher expected returns, on average, to resource investments in Canada do not preclude the existence of more profitable investments (on the margin) abroad. Nor do they preclude Canadian firms from investing abroad to achieve geographical diversification. However, empirical evaluation of these possibilities cannot proceed at an aggregate statistical level.

Some additional perspective on the motives of Canadian multinationals for undertaking outward direct investment is provided by a survey and case analysis prepared by Litvak and Maule (1981). Before reviewing some of their results, it might be pointed out that Canada's outward capital stake is highly concentrated in a few large firms. As an illustration, in 1974, sixteen large Canadian enterprises accounted for about 67% of the total outward capital stake.[18] Canada's investment in the resource sectors of developing countries is dominated by the activities of four firms: Inco, Falconbridge, Noranda, and Texasgulf.[19]

In their case study of Inco's investment in Guatemala to extract lateritic nickel, Litvak and Maule (1981, pp. 80–82) argue that Guatemalan nickel deposits were cheaper to mine than deposits in Canada in the early 1970s, before energy prices took off. Furthermore, Guatemalan nickel is less pure than Canadian nickel, and investment in different types of nickel ore was becoming essential to meet shifts in market requirements. Litvak and Maule conclude that Inco's investment in the Indonesian lateritic nickel deposits was motivated by similar considerations, but with the additional fact that by being associated with Japanese investors, Inco would be able to penetrate the Japanese market both for sales of nickel and, through forward integration, for sales of processed metal products.[20]

In a similar vein, Inco's refinery in Wales, and its rolling mills and metal fabrication plants in the United States and Britain, were aimed at servicing within protected markets for which exporting opportunities were highly restricted. Alcan's strategy of investing in US fabrication facilities was also apparently dictated by the fact that US tariffs on fabricated aluminium products were higher than on primary aluminium, thereby making expansion of fabrication in Canada (as opposed to the United States) an unrealistic alternative.[21] Thus a substantial portion of outward FDI in the resource sector has apparently been motivated by trade barriers on processed metals.

The distribution of the inward capital stake in Canada's manufacturing industries shows a fairly clear anti-locational advantage bias. More specifically, Postner (1979, p. 109) identifies machinery, textiles, electrical products, rubber products, non-metallic minerals, chemicals, metal products and publishing as suffering the greatest comparative disadvantage among all manufacturing industries in 1970.[22] At the same time, six of these seven industries (with the exception of metal fabricating) had inward capital stakes that exceeded the median value for all manufacturing industries (i.e. 55.2%).

This anti-locational advantage pattern of inward FDI in Canada's manufacturing sector suggests that some additional factors are influencing foreign firms' decisions to exploit their competitive advantages by establishing domestic subsidiaries. Several empirical studies have identified a positive relationship between foreign ownership intensity, on the one hand, and advertising and technological intensity, on the other hand, in Canadian manufacturing industries. These findings are taken as indirect support for the hypothesis that the possession of intangible assets (such as R&D knowledge or trademarks) can best be exploited through their internalized transfer within the multinational network. The preponderance of studies have also identified a significant positive relationship between the level of tariff protection in an industry and the industry's inward capital stake.[23] Thus, the available evidence appears to suggest that market imperfections (including government-imposed distortions) offer the most general explanation of the pattern of inward FDI in Canada's manufacturing industries.[24]

Detailed data on the distribution of Canada's outward capital stake are unavailable for manufacturing industries. However, the overwhelming bulk (around 90%) of Canada's outward capital stake in manufacturing industries in 1976 was located in four industries: beverages, non-ferrous metals, wood and paper products and iron products.[25] Interestingly, these are all industries in which Canada's resource base provides a comparative advantage.[26] Thus the outward capital stake in manufacturing industries also appears to be against the pattern dictated by locational advantage.

In short, the available evidence strongly suggests that the distribution of Canada's inward and outward capital stakes in manufacturing are largely inconsistent with the pattern dictated by underlying comparative advantage.

Intra-sectoral and technical efficiency

Where market-related or government-imposed barriers to trade encourage the substitution of direct investment for exporting (or importing), allocative efficiency can still be improved as a consequence of the extension of ownership advantage. In particular, if foreign-owned firms displace less efficient, domestically-owned firms in Canadian industries, inward FDI promotes a movement towards the economy's production possibilities frontier. While ownership advantages must be presumed to underlie direct investment flows—especially those that are anti-locational advantage in nature—the relevant issue is whether the advantages derive from superior efficiency or from market power. With regard to the latter point, it has been argued that access to a stream of monopoly rents allows multinational managers to pursue non-pecuniary objectives, including an indulgence in empire-building through investing abroad, even when it is cheaper to produce at home and export to foreign markets. In related versions of this argument, large firms invest abroad in order more effectively to forestall entry by local firms and thereby protect rents being earned in overseas markets.[27]

Inward FDI might also promote technical efficiency and, thereby, the increased competitiveness of domestic industries by encouraging domestic firms (not displaced by inward FDI) to operate more efficiently, that is at lower costs for all possible output levels. This potential impact has been identified in the literature under the broad heading of 'spillover' efficiency benefits.[28] These spillover benefits can materialize in a number of ways. For example, incoming FDI, by promoting increased competition, can encourage the faster adoption of new technology by domestic managers. Increased competition might also encourage domestic firms to reduce the diversity of their product lines in order to capture extant product economies of scale.[29] Technical efficiency might also be improved if foreign subsidiaries are quicker (or better able) to implement new production techniques developed abroad.

(a) Evidence on FDI and intra-sectoral allocative efficiency

The consensus of findings reporting that foreign-owned firms outperform domestically owned firms, other things constant, supports a conclusion that allocative efficiency in Canadian industries will improve to the extent that MNE subsidiaries displace Canadian-owned firms.

In one relevant study, Shapiro (1980) compared the financial structure and performance of 750 of the largest domestically and foreign-controlled manufacturing firms in Canada covering the period 1968 to 1972. He found that US controlled firms are generally more profitable than either Canadian or other foreign-controlled firms and this result holds for most size classes. In addition, US controlled firms exhibit a lower standard deviation of profit rates. Shapiro concludes that US controlled firms possess a profitability advantage above and beyond that associated with market power, as it is traditionally measured. That is, it presumably reflects real efficiency advantages.

Interestingly, other foreign-owned firms are not found by Shapiro to enjoy a profitability advantage over domestically-owned firms. Shapiro (p. 98) interprets this finding as possible evidence that non-US MNEs, as recent arrivals, may not yet have begun to exploit the efficiency advantages gained through internalizing resource transfers within the MNE network. A complementary interpretation, following along the lines of Kojima, is that non-US MNEs adopt a longer run perspective on their participation in the Canadian economy. Hence they incur substantial expenses over extended periods of time to develop an appropriate infrastructure for doing business in Canada, e.g. nurture a cadre of reliable, local suppliers. The impact of non-US direct investment in Canada might therefore be realized in the form of an improved overall industry performance for a substantial period of time before the non-US investors begin to realize above average profits.

Raynauld (1972) provides some additional evidence to support an assertion that foreign-owned firms are more efficient than their domestically owned counterparts. Specifically, Raynauld found that, for a sample of 2,000 manufacturing establishments located in Quebec in 1961, value added per worker in a foreign-owned plant was approximately 1.5 times the value added per worker in an English Canadian-owned plant and about 1.8 times the value added per worker in a French Canadian-owned plant. This is consistent with more recent Statistics Canada (1977) data indicating that value added per employee is higher in US controlled than in Canadian-controlled plants for an overwhelming majority of Canadian manufacturing industries.

It should be cautioned that the precise sources of the labour-productivity advantages of foreign-owned plants are not identified in the above mentioned studies; therefore, it cannot necessarily be concluded that total factor productivity is higher in foreign-owned plants. Indeed, since foreign-owned establishments are typically larger and more capital-intensive than their domestically owned counterparts, the former would be expected to enjoy higher labour productivity, *ceteris paribus*.

(b) Evidence on FDI and technical efficiency

The bulk of the evidence supporting the argument that inward FDI has promoted technical efficiency in Canadian industries consists of findings that attributes of efficient performance are positively correlated with the extent of foreign ownership across domestic industries. For example, Gupta (1979) found for a sample of Canadian manufacturing industries that excess capacity—measured as the percentage of plant capacity less than minimum efficient scale—was negatively related to the percentage of assets owned by foreigners in an industry.

Koutsoyiannis (1981) investigated the effects of the activities of MNE subsidiaries on price and cost levels in 20 two digit manufacturing industries in Canada over the period 1962–75. She concludes that the competitive pressure supplied by foreign subsidiaries has had a favourable impact on the prices of manufacturers. Specifically, prices have tended to vary inversely with the amount of foreign ownership. Furthermore, foreign subsidiaries have exerted a downward pressure on the costs of Canadian manufacturing industries.[30]

To be sure, the available evidence linking technical efficiency to inward FDI indicates that the relationship is, at best, a modest one. Indeed, several recent studies question the existence of any such relationship. In one such dissenting study, Bernhardt (1981) compared the relative productivity of Canadian industries to comparable US industries for 1966 and 1972. He found no relationship between relative productivity and foreign ownership in 1966, and a negative relationship between the two variables in 1972. The negative relationship disappeared, however, once a measure of technological intensity was included in the estimating equation. Furthermore, an interaction term between technological intensity and foreign ownership was positively related to the relative productivity variable. Bernhardt interprets this result as evidence that foreign ownership promotes the diffusion of technology into domestic Canadian industries.

In another study questioning the efficiency-promoting effects of inward FDI, Saunders (1980) examined the ratio of physical value added per employee in Canada to physical value added per employee in the United States for 84 matched three digit industries for the year 1967. Saunders found that relative productivity was significantly negatively associated with foreign ownership. He adduces several possible explanations for this:

(1) In the case of industries dominated by Canadian-owned firms, recent tariff reductions—by exposing the industry to greater competition from imports—would tend to cause the most inefficient firms to be eliminated, thus improving observed productivity. However, industries dominated by foreign-owned firms would largely escape this competitive influence, since the source of the potential imports would in most cases be the parent firms who would be unwilling to sacrifice their fixed investment in production facilities in Canada.

(2) The marketing strength of foreign-owned firms might enable the survival of inefficiently small production units, particularly in consumer goods industries.

Saunders acknowledges in his interpretation of the evidence that the foreign ownership variable is undoubtedly proxying structural influences not fully captured by the other explanatory variables.

A problem with the available evidence is that one cannot be sure that causation runs strictly from foreign ownership to improved efficiency and not vice-versa. It should be recalled that the distribution of Canada's inward capital stake at the two digit manufacturing level was concentrated in industries where Canada suffered a comparative disadvantage. However, these industries might still enjoy higher absolute levels of productivity than location-advantaged industries.

A more exacting test of the influence of inward FDI on technical efficiency might examine whether industries characterized by high foreign ownership levels enjoyed lower rates of productivity growth. Such a test would focus more closely on the core of the nationalist critique of foreign ownership, namely, that it provides short term efficiency gains at the expense of long-run economic performance. This critique is essentially an hypothesis about the impact of inward direct investment on dynamic (or long run) competitive advantage. A more specific hypothesis is that the failure of foreign subsidiaries to innovate and export aggressively leads to a long run deterioration of the competitive position of domestic industries. In the following section, the relationship between FDI and the international competitiveness of Canadian industries is considered.

6.6 FDI AND THE INTERNATIONAL COMPETITIVENESS OF CANADIAN MANUFACTURING INDUSTRIES

For a variety of reasons, it can be argued that the international competitiveness of a domestic industry is a reasonably good measure of its productivity performance, holding constant extant opportunities to improve productivity and economic performance. In effect, the relative trade performance of an industry indicates how well domestic managers in that industry have taken advantage of changes in underlying knowledge about production and marketing conditions compared to managers in counterpart industries located abroad. The measure of relative trade performance employed in this study is a net trade balance ratio defined as:

$$\text{RCA}_{it} = \frac{X_{it} - M_{it}}{(X_{it} + M_{it})}$$

where X_{it} is the value of exports of the ith industry in period t, M_{it} is the value of imports and RCA_{it} stands for revealed comparative advantage.

The trade performance of Canadian manufacturing industries

The available data limited the sample to 38 manufacturing industries.[31] Two RCA indexes were calculated: one for the years 1960 and 1961 (averaged) and one for 1980 and 1981 (averaged). While data on exports and imports are available for earlier years, it was felt that a twenty year period was sufficient to identify secular changes in international competitiveness. The calculated indexes are reported in the first two columns of Table 6.5. It can be seen that in the period 1960–61, only 9 industries had positive RCA values; in the period 1980–81, a slightly greater number (12) had positive net trade balances.

The relevant empirical issue of concern is whether the change in RCA between the two periods is related to the extent of foreign ownership in an industry. Several earlier studies focused on the relationship between foreign ownership and the trade performances of Canadian industries. Safarian (1969) found no consistent tendency for foreign subsidiaries to export more or less than domestically-owned firms, holding other relevant factors constant, although the former are more intensive importers than the latter, especially from their parent companies. Hanel (1976) examined the determinants of relative exporting intensity for 14 two and three digit Canadian manufacturing industries through multiple regression analysis. He found that an increase of foreign (US) control not accompanied by an increase in research intensity and/or an increase of labour productivity worsened an industry's relative export performance.

Columns (3) and (4) report two measures of foreign ownership: the percentage of an industry's assets owned by US investors (USO_i) and the percentage owned by other foreign, non-US investors (OFO_i). The US ownership stake was specified separately from the other foreign ownership stake in order to test Kojima's (1978) hypothesis that American MNEs do little to promote the long run competitiveness of host industries in comparison to Japanese and possibly other foreign MNEs.

The foreign ownership shares are for 1972.[32] Since this represents the midpoint of the sample period, a simultaneity bias running from changes in RCA to changes in foreign ownership cannot be ruled out. However, the magnitude of this potential bias is mitigated by the fact that foreign ownership shares across industries tend to be fairly stable over the sample

TABLE 6.5   RCA indices and foreign ownership

Industry	(1) RCA 1980/81	(2) RCA 1960/61	(3) Assets US-owned (%)	(4) Assets owned by other foreigners (%)
1. Bakery products	0.625	−0.428	17.45	55.62
2. Soft drinks	−0.515	−0.979	40.70	1.11
3. Breweries	0.519	0.792	—	28.70
4. Distilleries	0.416	0.665	—	29.97
5. Tobacco products	−0.317	−0.752	11.95	72.80
6. Leather products	−0.546	−0.407	18.41	4.25
7. Rubber products	−0.815	−0.813	74.83	19.00
8. Cotton and wool mills	−0.637	−0.803	10.21	3.94
9. Synthetic textiles	0.657	0.045	77.96	10.68
10. Fertilizers	0.805	0.461	52.24	8.14
11. Paints and related	−0.721	−0.844	65.82	12.46
12. Petroleum refining	0.546	−0.812	74.47	25.24
13. Wire products	0.229	−0.681	43.81	14.32
14. Hardware	−0.400	−0.602	51.21	3.93
15. Clay products	−0.624	−0.625	14.91	9.35
16. Glass products	−0.963	−0.947	28.11	4.87
17. Cement products	0.687	0.334	—	83.33
18. Motor vehicles	−0.111	−0.407	95.41	0.50
19. Aircraft and parts	−0.131	−0.300	50.35	38.96
20. Communication equipment	0.259	−0.789	39.72	6.31
21. Radio and TV	−0.701	−0.876	46.57	24.26
22. Heat equipment	−0.374	−0.406	31.93	0.46
23. Refrigeration equipment	−0.578	−0.891	66.63	—
24. Small appliances	−0.433	−0.657	0.10	—
25. Ind. electricity	−0.269	0.416	91.79	5.87
26. Major appliances	−0.598	−0.844	46.85	0.70
27. Battery	−0.529	−0.719	74.56	25.44
28. Scientific and professional	−0.443	−0.854	71.33	3.26
29. Household furnishings	−0.606	−0.865	10.31	0.71
30. Soaps and cleaning	−0.571	−0.942	76.91	18.80
31. Toiletries	−0.746	−0.785	69.10	12.74
32. Jewelry	−0.524	−0.866	47.90	0.58
33. Toys	−0.514	−0.730	40.38	5.80
34. Pharmacy	−0.479	−0.577	65.37	20.41
35. Publishing and printing	−0.564	−0.853	6.57	11.17
36. Veneer/plywood	0.461	0.581	41.03	1.17
37. Sash/door	0.170	0.572	3.90	2.00
38. Pulp and paper	0.930	0.828	32.32	13.97

Source: Columns (1) and (2); Statistics Canada, *Exports and Imports of Canada*, Ottawa: Queen's Printer, various issues.
Columns (3) and (4); Calculated from CALURA data provided to the author by Professor Lindsay Meredith.

period. Furthermore, there is no strong evidence that foreign-owned firms were concentrated in especially favoured (in terms of RCA) domestic industries at the start of the sample period. For example, the simple correlation coefficient between $RCA_{60/61}$ and USO_i is -0.280, while the same coefficient for $RCA_{60/61}$ and OFO_i is 0.176. Thus, the inward capital stake originating in the United States (the dominant source of inward direct investment) concentrated in competitively disadvantaged industries.[33]

The determinants of changes in RCA[34]

In estimating a relationship between changes in RCA and the foreign ownership intensity of industries, it is necessary to hold constant other factors that influence RCA and that are not statistically independent of foreign ownership. A full development of the estimating model is provided elsewhere.[35] In this section, the broad highlights of the model are outlined.

Three standardizing variables are included in the initial estimating equation: VAL_i is the percentage growth in the value of shipments of the corresponding US industry over the period 1960–80. This variable is taken to be a measure of the potential growth in US demand for products provided by the ith Canadian industry. While value of shipments includes imports, in most industries, the bulk of all shipments are domestic. All else constant, VAL should be positively related to the change in RCA; $ENINT_i$ is the ratio of fuel and electricity costs to the value of shipments in 1973. The variable was included to reflect the potential subsidies enjoyed by energy-intensive industries resulting from the Canadian government's policy of keeping the domestic price of oil and gas well below the world price in the post-1973 period; $CONTAR_i$ is a simple multiple of two statistics: the calculated Herfindahl index for the ith industry in 1965 and the industry's effective tariff rate in 1961. The CONTAR variable is taken to be a structural measure of the market power enjoyed by domestic producers. It should be negatively related to the change in RCA.

For purposes of estimation, $RCA_{1960/61}$ was included as a right hand-side variable. Thus, the basic relationship estimated through ordinary least squares is given in equation (5.1):

$$RCA_{80/81} = f(RCA_{60/61}, USO_i, OFO_i, VAL_i, ENINT_i, CONTAR_i) \quad (5.1)$$

The results from estimating equation (5.1) as a linear relationship are reported as equation one in Table 6.6. The main finding is that holding constant durable factors contributing to an industry's international com-

TABLE 6.6 Regression results[a]

Equation	Constant	$RCA_{60/61}$	USO	OFO	VAL	ENINT	CONTAR	UST	USNT	OFOT	OFONT	$\bar{R}^2$	F
							Variables						
One (38 observations)	−0.394 (−2.66)	0.652 (7.40)	−0.001 (−0.55)	0.007 (2.82)	0.104 (3.18)	0.009 (1.30)	0.010 (0.47)					0.709	1602
Two (38 observations)	−0.343 (−2.20)	0.639 (7.20)			0.095 (2.83)	0.008 (1.15)	0.003 (0.13)	0.001 (0.50)	−0.002 (−1.03)	0.001 (0.17)	0.008 (2.81)	0.710	12.31
Three (38 observations)	−0.609 (−3.87)	0.467 (4.28)			0.133 (4.17)	0.007 (1.14)	0.040 (1.76)	*USA* −0.001 (−0.20)	*USNA* −0.003 (−1.31)	*OFOA* 0.012 (3.90)	*OFONA* 0.001 (0.139)	0.753	14.50
Four (37 observations)	−0.436 (−3.27)	0.667 (8.43)	−0.001 (−0.64)	0.005 (1.85)	0.114 (3.88)	0.009 (1.36)	0.024 (1.18)					0.757	19.69
Five (37 observations)	−0.592 (−4.04)	0.518 (4.98)			0.134 (4.52)	0.007 (1.22)	0.044 (2.06)	−0.001 (−0.26)	−0.003 (−1.32)	0.008 (2.66)	0.001 (0.102)	0.777	16.66

[a] A t-value is shown in parenthesis below each coefficient.
$\bar{R}^2$ is the adjusted (for degrees of freedom) coefficient of determination.

petitive advantage, that is by including $RCA_{60/61}$ as a right hand-side variable, US ownership is unrelated to an industry's net trade balance; however, the extent of ownership by non-US foreign investors is positively and significantly related to an industry's RCA.

A possible explanation of the statistical insignificance of the USO variable is that the core skills of US-owned companies reside in their technological expertise. Therefore, if US MNEs can be expected to promote the international competitiveness of Canadian industries, this effect is most likely to be identified in so-called 'technology-intensive' industries. This hypothesis was tested by estimating separate slope coefficients for the USO variable for two groups of industries, where the groups were divided based upon subjective determination of discrete inter-industry differences in technological opportunity.[36] Two US ownership variables are therefore specified in equation two: UST_i, which takes the observed values of USO for 10 'technology-intensive' industries and zero values otherwise, and USNT, which takes the observed values of USO for the other 28 industries and zero otherwise.[37] The OFO variable was re-specified in a similar fashion.

Regression results are reported in equation two in Table 6.6. The UST coefficient, while positive, is statistically insignificant.[38] On the other hand, while the coefficient for OFOT is statistically insignificant, the coefficient for OFONT remains significant at very high levels of confidence. Taken as a whole, the results indicate that only non-US foreign ownership contributes to increased international competitiveness of domestic industries and that contribution is restricted to industries that are not technology-intensive.

Since technological intensity has been a traditional source of comparative disadvantage for Canada, the foregoing results suggest that inward FDI has failed to contribute significantly to a 'restructuring' of Canada's traditional industrial strengths and weaknesses. This suggestion was examined more explicitly by dividing the total sample into two sub-samples: the 19 industries enjoying above-average RCA values for 1960/61 and the remaining 19 industries. Then, separate slope coefficients were estimated for the USO and OFO variables, much along the lines described in equation two. Statistical results are reported in equation three, where the coefficient reported for UST is the slope coefficient for the above average industries, while the coefficient reported for USNA is the slope coefficient for the below average industries. OFOA and OFONA are similarly interpreted. The results for equation three strongly support a conclusion that non-US foreign ownership encourages the increased competitiveness of comparatively advantaged industries only, thereby providing some indirect Canadian support for a version of the Kojima hypothesis.

Examination of the residuals from equations one–three indicate that the bakery industry exerts a substantial influence on the results. This is confirmed in equations four and five, which represent re-estimation of equations one and three, respectively, with bakery products deleted from the sample. Nevertheless, while the magnitudes of the OFO and OFOA coefficients decline, they remain statistically significant at acceptable levels.[39]

Other evidence on foreign ownership and industrial restructuring

Notwithstanding arguments that R&D is a means to an end and not an end in itself, it is clear to all observers that the performance of increased R&D is a strong priority of the Canadian government. Coupled with granting their subsidiaries world product mandates, MNEs in Canada have come under increased pressure to do more domestic R&D. Indeed, policies have been advocated under which only subsidiaries enjoying full responsibility for the development, production, and marketing of a single product on a worldwide scale would be eligible to receive R&D grants.

Rugman (1983) has recently criticized the government's policy focus on stimulating R&D and world product mandating as being inconsistent with the MNEs motivation to internalize complex transactions. Moreover, he notes that the export and R&D performances of the 22 largest US subsidiaries in Canada are comparable to or even better than the performances of the largest Canadian-owned MNEs. And at least 9 of the 22 US subsidiaries in Rugman's sample increased their ratios of R&D to sales over the period 1979–82.

Thus, it may be fair to say that MNE subsidiaries in Canada have been taking action to restructure Canada's competitive advantages away from resource-based activities and towards what might be argued are technology-based activities. There is also anecdotal evidence that major US subsidiaries in Canada are embracing with increased acceptance (if not enthusiasm) the concept of world product mandating;[40] however, as the results summarized in Table 6.6 indicate, inward FDI (to date) has not altered Canada's fundamental RCA pattern.

Whether increased R&D performance and the granting of world product mandates can lead to a desired restructuring of Canadian industries is questionable. There are a number of case studies, including the aircraft industry, that testify to the futility of trying to 'engineer' changes in Canada's pattern of comparative advantage through substantial increases in government support of R&D activities.[41]

Rather than being economic in nature, the motive for promoting indigenous R&D on the part of economic nationalists appears rooted in the desire to generate 'high technology' employment in Canada and substitute away from the services of foreigners, especially Americans. This also tends to explain the mercantilistic bent of economic nationalists with respect to so-called technology-intensive industries. On the one hand, such technological autocracy is consistent with rent-seeking behaviour described in public choice models of government intervention. Specifically, some of the most strident proponents of technological sovereignty are owners and managers of aerospace, computer and related organizations. On the other hand, technological virtuosity might be in the nature of a collective consumption good, much the same as sending athletes to international competitions, which Canadians are perfectly ready to pay for in terms of a lower standard of living.

Obviously it is extremely difficult to distinguish empirically between these two competing arguments. Moreover, given the commitment of all political parties in Canada to promote indigenous R&D and to encourage import-substitution in high technology products, the value of making a distinction is somewhat moot. The point remains that Canadian politicians are concerned with the behaviour of foreign subsidiaries perhaps as much as with their performance. On the basis of collective 'revealed preference', one must conclude that the perceived benefits of Canada's inward capital stake might increase if foreign subsidiaries engaged more intensively in indigenous R&D and exporting, even if it led to reduced inward FDI and reduced allocative and technical efficiency.

6.7   CONCLUSIONS AND POLICY IMPLICATIONS

The most contentious policy debate in Canada has surrounded the appropriate treatment of inward FDI. This contention has been exacerbated by the absence of strong and persuasive evidence regarding the impacts of inward FDI on the efficiency and competitiveness of the Canadian economy. The evidence, including some presented in this paper, suggests that the beneficial impacts may be specific to particular economic activities and to particular groups of foreign investors. While the beneficial impacts of FDI may seem surprisingly mild, at least to those impressed with the importance of internalizing the transfer of technology and management knowhow, it is consistent with the broad position of mainstream (Continentalist) Canadian economists, who have argued that the performances of both MNE subsidiaries and Canadian-owned firms are largely conditioned by Canada's general competitive and economic environment.

While the somewhat ambivalent evidence regarding the impact of MNEs on allocative and technical efficiency serves as grist for the Nationalists' mill, it would be a mistake to conclude that restrictions on inward FDI and policies designed to reduce existing levels of foreign ownership would necessarily be in the national interest. One major complication to a welfare analysis of inward FDI is the fact that the behaviour of MNEs is often a response to government policy. For example, it is apparent that inward FDI is promoted by government-imposed trade barriers. Presumably these trade barriers are imposed to encourage economic activity in location-disadvantaged sectors. In this case, inward FDI may be consistent with public objectives, although the latter may be inconsistent with economic efficiency.

A broad implication of this observation is that MNEs, like domestically-owned firms, respond to incentives in the general economic environment. If the incentives encourage inefficient forms of behaviour, policy-makers should not assign blame (in a causal sense) to the foreign investor. The appropriate policy response would be to determine whether MNE behaviour is consistent with other primary policy objectives. If it is not, the incentive structure should be examined and, if necessary, modified.

A second complication is that restrictions imposed on inward FDI or on MNE subsidiaries may beget retaliatory restrictions on trade flows (or on flows of portfolio capital) which impose substantial costs on the host economy. In the Canadian case, there is no doubt that the US government has been strongly vexed by Canada's National Energy Policy and the Foreign Investment Review Agency. Both institutions are justifiably seen as placing US subsidiaries at a competitive disadvantage relative to domestically-owned firms. Threats of trade retaliation have been raised in the US Congress in response to these perceived violations of trade principles.

It must also be cautioned that identification of the impacts of inward FDI is plagued by theoretical and empirical complexities. In particular, the very potential for entry through the direct investment process may have salutory effects on efficiency. Indeed, a sufficient threat of entry might ensure that domestically-owned firms perform at least as efficiently as MNE subsidiaries would if the latter actually entered domestic industries; however, potential entry is not easily measured. Nor is it necessarily coincident with actual entry patterns. Furthermore, implicit assumptions about the independence of employment and savings rates from direct investment flows may be inappropriate. For example, inward FDI might mobilize otherwise unemployed labour resources and domestic savings, yielding broad macro-economic benefits not captured by statistical analyses of the sort described in Sections 6.5 and 6.6.

Normative conclusions with respect to outward direct investment are quite obscure in the Canadian context given the dearth of evidence on the economic impacts of Canada's MNEs. To date, the Canadian government appears convinced that outward direct investment is complementary to indigenous R&D performance by allowing Canadian companies to spread R&D 'overhead' expenditures over greater volumes of output. Furthermore, the government has expressed no great concern that overseas investment is significantly displacing Canadian exports. Rather, it seems persuaded that the existence of tariff and non-tariff barriers to trade contribute to making exports and outward direct investment mutually exclusive alternatives. Against this perspective, outward direct investment may be presumed to be welfare-improving.

In light of the foregoing evidence and disclaimers, it seems prudent to interpret the Canadian evidence as a caution against expecting 'too much' from foreign and home-based MNEs. Government attention is probably better focused on 'infrastructure' policies designed to promote efficient behaviour of all economic units in its jurisdiction, whether foreign or domestically-owned.[42] As well, it cautions against the wisdom of national and local governments aggressively competing for inward FDI through tax incentives and the like. The burden of proof should rest on MNE managers to demonstrate that their inward FDI will create net social benefits that justify public sector incentives.

NOTES

1. For a recent statement of this policy emphasis, see 'Ontario eyes more exports', *The Globe and Mail*, 14 December, 1983, B2.
2. These figures are exclusive of exchange rate movements.
3. A disproportionate amount of Canadian direct investment abroad (in 1978) was concentrated in the utilities sector, although this statistic primarily reflects Brascan's large investment position in Brazil's utility system. Since that time, Brascan has sold off its utility affiliate.
4. The empirical relevance of advertising spillovers from the United States into Canada is addressed in Meredith, forthcoming.
5. See Caves (1974). In a more recent study, Saunders (1982) confirms that advertising intensity in a Canadian industry and R&D intensity in the corresponding US industry are positively and significantly related to the extent of foreign ownership in Canadian industries; however, the strongest influence of foreign ownership appears to be the extent of multi-plant development in the corresponding US industries.
6. See Gorecki (1976).
7. Recently, arguments have emerged purporting to demonstrate that the domestic tariff can encourage a long run, dynamic comparative advantage in industries characterized by learning and scale economies. See, for example, Curtis (1983).
8. A similar criticism of American MNEs can be found in Kojima (1978). Kojima argues that, unlike the Japanese, American MNEs do not transfer core skills to the host economy.
9. For a relatively terse statement of the Nationalists' position, see Starks (1978).
10. The internalization theory of direct investment is discussed in Rugman (1980).

11. A summary of the Continentalist argument can be found in Globerman (1979a).
12. This argument is made by Langdon (1980).
13. This concern is discussed in Starks (1978), pp. 53–55.
14. Starks (1978), p. 53. The various positions tend to assume that domestic employment levels are independent of outward FDI flows. Moreover, there is no reference to the potential for external diseconomies to outward FDI; that is decreasing returns to infra-marginal investments caused by additional outward capital flows.
15. For evidence on these points, see Daly (1979) and Postner (1979).
16. This effort will, in turn, be complicated by the interactive nature of locational and ownership advantage. Specifically, locational advantage may, in many cases, underlie ownership advantage.
17. The relevance of this comparison rests on the assumption that profitability differences reflect ownership advantages.
18. Litvak and Maule (1981), p. 11.
19. The latter is a recently acquired subsidiary of the Canada Development Corporation. See Langdon (1980), p. 38.
20. Sales of nickel from Canada to Japan were limited by the Japanese tariff on refined nickel as opposed to the free entry of nickel in matte. Langdon (1980), p. 38, acknowledges that prior to unexpected escalations in both fuel and capital costs, Inco's overseas mines were less costly than Canadian mines; however, he credits Inco's overseas investments at least partially to a market foreclosure motive.
21. See Litvak and Maule (1980). Alcan's US investments were also encouraged by the larger size of the American domestic market, combined with transportation costs, which facilitated the capture of extant scale economies through the establishment of US plants.
22. Postner also argues there is no reason to believe that, by the year 2000, these industries will have reversed their positions as the leading comparatively disadvantaged sectors.
23. For a review of much of this evidence, see Globerman (1979a).
24. Some evidence that inward direct investment is positively related to Canadian efficiency relative to US efficiency is provided in Caves *et al.* (1977).
25. Litvak and Maule (1981), p. 8.
26. Postner (1979), pp. 109–110 identifies wood products, paper products, and base metals as Canadian industries enjoying a long run comparative advantage. The beverage industry largely reflects the activities of Seagram's and Hiram Walker, two large distillers. The domestic grain crop can be suggested to underlie, at least in part, the latter firm's competitive advantages.
27. This argument is developed in Langdon (1980).
28. See, for example, Globerman (1979b).
29. Excessive product diversity has been cited by many Canadian economists as a barrier to higher productivity. The failure of domestic firms to specialize is, in turn, credited to the existence of protected oligopolies in the Canadian economy. For a full exposition of this theme, see Daly and Globerman (1976).
30. In fact, Koutsoyiannis concludes that the primary benefits of inward FDI on domestic prices and costs have been realized from increased competition which forced inefficient local firms to close down, rather than from direct increases in technical efficiency.
31. In particular, there is a problem in matching industries over this period owing to changes in the Standard Industrial Classification Code.
32. The USO and OFO variables are calculated from unpublished data collected under the Corporation and Labour Union Returns Act. The earliest data available is for 1972. The author thanks his colleague, Lindsay Meredith, for making these data available to him.
33. This observation is consistent with other findings discussed in Chapter four of this volume.
34. Professor Tom Pugel made especially helpful suggestions for this section of the paper.
35. See Globerman (1983).
36. The definition of sub-samples was guided by inter-industry differences in indices of technological opportunity reported in Globerman (1973) and references therein.
37. The 10 'technology-intensive' industries include: rubber products, synthetic textiles, fertilizers, petroleum refining, motor vehicles, aircraft, communications equipment,

214 Multinational enterprises, economic structure & international competitiveness

glass products, scientific and professional instruments and pharmaceuticals. It should be noted that the results were quite insensitive to alternative lists of technology-intensive industries.
38. Furthermore, an F test does not allow rejection of the restriction that the UST and USNT coefficients are equal.
39. The positive sign for the CONTAR variable is contrary to expectations. It is possible that the variable is acting as a proxy for multiplant economies of scale, although evaluation of this explanation is beyond the scope of the present study. It is also worth noting that the motor vehicle industry was deleted from the sample to determine if the Auto Pact made this industry's experience with FDI unique. The results deleting the industry were virtually identical to those with the industry included.
40. Science Council of Canada (1980).
41. For a discussion of several case studies, see Palda (1984).
42. These include policies designed to promote competition and efficiency in contracting, macro-economic stability, educational achievement and so forth.

REFERENCES

Bernhardt, Irwin (1981). Sources of productivity differences among Canadian manufacturing industries, *Review of Economics and Statistics*, **63**, 503–512
Brecher, Irving and Reisman, S. S. (1957). *Canada-U.S. Economic Relations*, Ottawa: Royal Commission on Canada's Economic Prospects
Caves, Richard (1974). Causes of direct investment: foreign firms' shares in Canadian and United Kingdom manufacturing industries, *Review of Economics and Statistics*, **56**, 279–293
Caves, R. E., *et al.* (1977). *Studies in Canadian Industrial Organization*, Royal Commission on Corporate Concentration Study No. 26, Cambridge: Harvard University, mimeo
Curtis, D. C. A. (1983). Trade policy to promote entry with scale economies, product variety and export potential, *Canadian Journal of Economics*, **XVI**, 109–121
Daly, D. J. (1979). *Canada's Comparative Advantage*, Discussion Paper 135, Ottawa: Economic Council of Canada
Daly, D. J. and Globerman, S. (1976). *Tariffs and Science Policies: Applications of a Model of Nationalism*, Ontario Economic Council Research Study Number 4, University of Toronto Press
Globerman, Steven (1973). Market structure and R&D in Canadian manufacturing industries, *Quarterly Review of Economics and Business*, **13**, 59–67
Globerman, Steven (1979a). *U.S. Ownership of Firms in Canada*, Montreal: C. D. Howe Research Institute
Globerman, Steven (1979b). Foreign direct investment and 'spillover' efficiency benefits in Canadian manufacturing industries, *Canadian Journal of Economics*, **XII**, 42–56
Globerman, Steven (1983). Foreign Ownership and Canada's International Trade Competitiveness, Simon Fraser University, mimeo
Gorecki, Paul (1976). The determinants of entry by domestic and foreign enterprises in Canadian manufacturing industries: some comments and empirical results, *Review of Economics and Statistics*, **58**, 485–488

Government of Canada (1972). *Foreign Direct Investment in Canada*, Ottawa: Information Canada

Gupta, Vinod (1979). Optimal capacity and its determinants in Canadian manufacturing industries, *Review of Economics and Statistics*, **61**, 506–512

Hanel, Peter (1976). *The Relationship Existing Between the R&D Activity of Canadian Manufacturing Industries and Their Performance in the International Market*, University of Sherbrooke, Department of Economics, mimeo

Kojima, Kyoshi (1978). *Direct Foreign Investment*, New York: Praeger

Koutsoyiannis, A. (1981). The impact of multinational firms, *Economia Internazionale*, **XXXIV**, 356–375

Langdon, Steven (1980). *Canadian Private Direct Investment and Technology Marketing in Developing Countries*, Hull, Quebec: Supply and Services Canada

Litvak, I. A. and Maule, C. J. (1980). Canadian outward investment: impact and policy, *Journal of World Trade Law*, **14**, 310–328

Litvak, I. A. and Maule, C. J. (1981). *The Canadian Multinationals*, Toronto: Butterworths

Meredith, Lindsay (forthcoming). U.S. multinational investment in Canadian manufacturing industries, *Review of Economics and Statistics*

Palda, Kristian (1984). *Industrial Policies Toward Innovation*, Vancouver: The Fraser Institute

Postner, Harry (1979). *Canada and the Future of the International Economy: A Global Modeling Analysis*, Discussion Paper No. 129, Ottawa: Economic Council of Canada

Raynauld, Andre (1972). The ownership and performance of firms in Gilles Paquet (ed.), *The Multinational Firm and the Nation State*, Toronto: Ryerson Press

Rugman, Alan (1980). Internalization as a general theory of foreign direct investment: a reappraisal of the literature, *Weltwertschaftlichs Archiv*,**116**, 365–379

Rugman, Alan (1983). *The Behaviour of U.S. Subsidiaries in Canada: Implications for Trade and Investments*, paper prepared for the Second Annual Workshop on US-Canadian Relations, University of Western Ontario, 18–19 November

Safarian, A. E. (1969). *The Performance of Foreign-Owned Firms in Canada*, Montreal: Private Planning Association of Canada

Saunders, Ronald (1980). The determinants of productivity in Canadian manufacturing industries, *Journal of Indsutrial Economics*, **XXIX**, 167–184

Saunders, Ronald (1982a). Continentalism and economic nationalism in the manufacturing sector: seeking middle ground, *Canadian Public Policy*,**VIII**, 463–479

Saunders, Ronald (1982b). The determinants of inter-industry variation of foreign ownership in Canadian manufacturing industries, *Canadian Journal of Economics*, **XV**, 77–84

Science Council of Canada (1980). *Multinationals and Industrial Strategy: The Role of World Product Mandates*, Ottawa: Science Council of Canada

Shapiro, Daniel (1980). *Foreign and Domestic Firms in Canada*, Toronto: Butterworths

Starks, Richard (1978). *Industry in Decline*, Toronto: James Lorimer

Statistics Canada (1977). *Foreign Ownership and Control of Canadian Manufacturing Establishments*, Ottawa: Information Canada

7

Sweden

BIRGITTA SWEDENBORG*

7.1 INTRODUCTION

Sweden is a small and highly industrialized economy, which has relied heavily on international exchange for its economic development. The small size of the domestic market has impelled Swedish industry to sell in foreign markets to exploit the advantages of large scale production. Today, exports are roughly 50% of manufacturing and a quarter of GNP.

Although exporting has always been the major avenue for penetrating foreign markets for Swedish industry, the growth of exports was early on accompanied by the establishment of foreign manufacturing facilities. Many of today's large Swedish MNEs had set up a network of manufacturing affiliates abroad by the early 1920s, some dating back as far as the late nineteenth century. Today about a third of Swedish industry's total foreign sales is supplied from manufacturing plants abroad. Relative to its size, Swedish manufacturing industry ranks as one of the most multinational in the world.

Swedish industry is a substantial *net* foreign investor in that investment abroad by Swedish firms is several times larger than investment in Sweden by foreign firms. For example, in 1978 the combined manufacturing employment of Swedish MNEs at home and abroad was 76% of total manufacturing employment compared to 6% for foreign manufacturing affiliates in Sweden. An analysis of the impact of MNEs on the Swedish economy must therefore focus mainly on the effect of outward investment.

This chapter will explore the inter-relationship between international trade, production abroad by Swedish firms and production in Sweden by foreign firms, and how this bears on the comparative advantage of Sweden and the international competitiveness of Swedish industry. In doing so it will draw on the large body of data on especially Swedish but also foreign multinational enterprise activity which has been collected in Sweden from 1960 onwards and which has been analysed in a number of, mainly, Swedish studies.[1]

* I am indebted to Professor R. E. Lipsey of the National Council of Economic Research for valuable comments and criticisms on this paper.

The chapter is organized as follows. It starts by providing a cursory theoretical framework and a description of Sweden's international investment position. This is followed by a description of the industry and country pattern of outward and inward investment as well as a more formal analysis of the determinants of international production. The second part of the chapter deals with the effects of foreign production on resource allocation and efficiency in Sweden, especially those due to changes in MNE exports and R&D activities. Here the focus is almost exclusively on the effects of outward investment. Finally, there is a summary and evaluation of international investment in the Swedish context.

The analytical framework

The analysis in this chapter is based on the notion that international trade and production by multinational firms can only be explained by merging traditionally separate strands of theory: international trade and location theory, to explain the location of production and trade flows, and industrial organization theory and the theory of the firm, to show why production is undertaken by home country firms rather than foreign firms. This view of international production and MNEs, which owes much to the early contributions of Hymer (1960), Kindleberger (1969) and Caves (1971), has been set out succinctly by Dunning (1981) under the heading of the eclectic theory of international trade and production. Swedenborg (1979) has used it to explain the international involvement of Swedish firms. Caves (1983) gives an excellent analytical survey of the theoretical and empirical literature to date.

Briefly, the theory states that the location of production, and hence trade flows, is determined by each country's comparative advantage in production and by barriers to factor and product mobility. Thus the relative factor endowment of countries, the proportions in which factors are used in different industries and natural and artificial barriers to trade are characteristics of industries and countries respectively which simultaneously determine the location of production and whether a particular country exports, imports, or merely produces for the home market in a particular industry.

Given that locational factors favour production in a country, that production will be undertaken by foreign firms (MNEs) whenever, due to their ownership, they possess an advantage over domestic firms which enables them to produce at lower cost. The advantage must be such that it is relatively more mobile across national boundaries within a firm than between firms. Technological, managerial and sales know-how are intangible assets which often have these properties. They are specific to the firm in the sense that it can earn a higher rate of return on its asset, say technological know-how, by exploiting this itself than by transferring it to other firms in the form of patents or licensing agreements. The reason is that transfer is associated with information, transaction and monitoring costs. Whenever such costs are low, or local firms have offsetting advantages, patent sales, licensing and managerial contracts will take the place of production by MNEs. To the firm then, exports, foreign production and licensing are alternative ways in which it can exploit its advantage in foreign markets.

What, then, are the implications of this theory for the pattern of outward and inward investment? Should one expect the industry pattern of exports and outward investment to be the same? What about inward investment?

Different hypotheses have been advanced. Some (e.g. Kojima, 1978), argue that home country firms invest abroad in industries in which the home country is losing its comparative advantage, while foreign firms invest in industries in which the home country is developing comparative advantage. Others (e.g. Hirsch, 1976) argue that outward and inward investment will tend to be in the same industries in all countries (due to industry differences in R&D and advertising intensity). Each has merit—as a partial explanation.

The theory implies that it is a bit more complicated than these hypotheses suggest. Country comparative advantage and trade barriers should determine the pattern of a country's exports, while firm-specific advantage should determine whether production at home *and* abroad is undertaken by home country firms. It implies the following relationships:

$$\text{Exports} = f_1(\text{O advantage, L advantage, trade barriers abroad}) \qquad (1)$$
$$\qquad\qquad\quad + \qquad\quad + \qquad\qquad\qquad -$$

$$\text{Outward DI} = f_2(\text{O advantage, L advantage, trade barriers abroad}) \quad (2)$$
$$\qquad\qquad\qquad + \qquad\quad - \qquad\qquad\qquad +$$

so that:

$$\text{Exports/Outward DI} = f(\text{L advantage, trade barriers abroad})$$
$$\qquad\qquad\qquad\qquad\qquad + \qquad\qquad\quad -$$

$$\text{Inward DI} = f_3(\text{O advantage, L advantage, trade barriers at home}) \quad (3)$$
$$\qquad\qquad\qquad + \qquad\quad + \qquad\qquad\quad +$$

Note that O-specific advantages in equations (1) and (2) refer to those enjoyed by home country firms and in equation (3) to those enjoyed by foreign firms. Note, too, that if the O-specific advantage of firms of different national origin were in the same industries, equation (3) implies that the share of foreign firms in an industry would be indeterminate. The reason is that country comparative advantage and trade barriers affect home country firms and foreign firms equally.[2]

Equations (1)–(3) show that the hypothesized pattern of trade and direct investment depends on which set of explanatory variables are deemed most important. However, if all play a role, there is no way that the industry pattern of exports and inward and outward investment will be the same. The first term tends to make the pattern of exports and outward direct investment the same, while the second and the third terms tend to make it different. Inward direct investment potentially differs from outward direct investment because of all three terms.

Sweden's international direct investment position

Sweden's investment abroad is, of course, small relative to the foreign investment of larger countries. But it is far from insignificant when set in relation to the size of the Swedish economy. Sweden ranks as the ninth largest foreign investor in absolute terms and as the fifth most multinational country if foreign investment is related to GNP (SOU, 1982: 15, p.7). It would rank even higher if the comparison were limited to the manufacturing sector, since Sweden's foreign investment is relatively concentrated in manufacturing.

Investment by other countries in Sweden, by contrast, is relatively small. In 1982 the flow of outward investment was more than four times the flow of inward investment. Similarly, employment in Swedish manufacturing affiliates abroad was four times larger than employment in foreign-owned affiliates in Sweden.

Although international investment by Swedish firms has a long history, Sweden's position as a relatively sizeable net foreign investor has been strongly accentuated since the late 1960s. Since then foreign investment in Sweden has practically stagnated (in real terms), while Swedish investment abroad has continued unabated (Fig. 7.1). While employment in Swedish manufacturing affiliates abroad   1965–78 increased from 16% to 26% of domestic manufacturing employment, foreign manufacturing employment in Sweden grew from 3% to 6%—a rapid growth rate, but from a low level (Table 7.1).

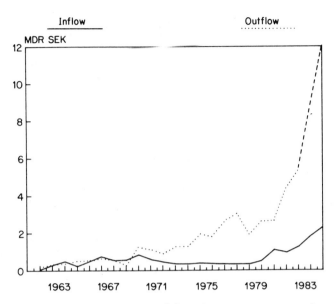

FIG. 7.1 *Outward and inward direct investment, current prices*
Source: Bank of Sweden
Note: Data for 1983 and 1984 refer to permissions granted for direct investment by the Bank of Sweden in 1982 and 1983. Actual investment follows such permissions with roughly a one year lag. For additional data on investment flows and stocks, see Appendix.

Two main factors explain Sweden's position as a significant net foreign investor. First, as an industrialized, high-income country, Sweden is relatively well-endowed with capital, especially the human capital, which lies at the bottom of the foreign investment process. As Dunning (1981) has shown, GNP per capita is strongly and positively correlated with inter-country differences in the propensity to invest abroad.

TABLE 7.1   MNE manufacturing employment in Sweden and abroad 1960–78

	1960	1965	1970	1974	1978
All manuf. in Sweden	880,260	938,915	921,780	929,200	874,230
Swedish MNEs	—	325,980	395,990	431,740	416,235
% of Swedish manuf.	—	35	43	46	48
Foreign affiliates of Swedish MNEs	105,510	147,805	182,650	219,625	227,825
% of Swedish manuf.	12	16	20	24	26
Foreign MNEs in Sweden	—	28,290	41,850	50,000	51,000
% of Swedish manuf.	—	3	4	5	6

Source: Swedish MNEs from Swedenborg (1982); Foreign MNEs from Samuelsson (1977) and SCB, 1981.

Second, the small size of the Swedish market forces Swedish firms to export at an early stage of growth in order to reap economies of large scale production. It also forces them to produce abroad, when that is the more profitable way of serving foreign markets, to reap the economies of large firm size. (Economies of firm size are related to the large fixed cost of investment in R&D, advertising, and a sales and distribution network.) Thus, small Swedish firms are more export-oriented and more prone to invest abroad than are US firms of comparable size (Swedenborg, 1979, Ch. 6).

The small Swedish market may also explain the relatively modest involvement of foreign firms in the Swedish economy. Production on an efficient scale in most industries in Sweden requires firms to have substantial exports. But in those industries where Sweden has a strong comparative advantage, favouring Sweden as a production location, Swedish MNEs are particularly strong, leaving little room for foreign-based MNEs (Samuelsson, 1977, pp. 102–103). The incentive to produce in Sweden mainly for import substitution, on the other hand, is reduced by Sweden's free trade policy.

A third factor which may have contributed to the divergent trends in outward and inward investment since the late 1960s is an overvalued Swedish exchange rate, which has made Sweden a relatively less attractive location for production. Persistent current account deficits, starting in 1969, eventually forced Sweden to devalue by a total of 50% (against its own trade-weighted currency basket) in the years 1977–82.[3]

Finally, a note on how Swedish regulatory policy has affected foreign direct investment. Sweden regulates such investment as part of its foreign exchange controls and requires that firms wishing to invest abroad seek permission from the Bank of Sweden to do so. Until recently such permission was granted—in principle—only if terms could demonstrate that the investment would have a positive effect on the Swedish trade balance. As a practical matter, however, permission was almost always granted for investment by manufacturing firms. Consequently, the regulation has hardly affected either the level or the composition of foreign manufacturing investment either in or outside of Sweden (Swedenborg, 1980).

7.3 EXPLAINING SWEDEN'S INTERNATIONAL INVOLVEMENT

Comparative advantage and the pattern of international production

According to equations (1)–(3) above, total foreign sales by Swedish firms should be determined both by Sweden's comparative advantage as a producing country *and* by the firm-specific advantage of Swedish firms as producers. The choice between the two sources of supply should be determined by locational factors (relative production costs and trade barriers). The same should hold for foreign firms. That means that foreign firms will exploit Sweden's comparative advantage as a producing country but will tend to be relatively large only in industries where Swedish firms have a competitive *dis*advantage. Is this consistent with the actual pattern?

Table 7.2 gives the breakdown of outward manufacturing investment (measured by employment) and Swedish exports by industry. Two features stand out. The first is that the pattern of Swedish production abroad *broadly* follows that of exports. The second is that the divergence between the two is explainable by factors affecting locational choice.

TABLE 7.2   Industry pattern of Sweaish production abroad 1970 and 1978 (%)

Industry	Manufacturing empoyment abroad % distribution 1970	1978	Swedish exports % distribution 1970	1978	Manufacturing employment abroad in % of manuf. empl. in Sweden 1970	1978
Food, drink, and tobacco	1	1	2	2	3	3
Textiles, clothing, etc.	2	2	4	3	4	11
Paper, pulp	2	4	} 18	13	8	15
Paper products, printing, etc.	2	6		3	7	27
Chemicals, rubber, etc.	14	8	6	9	38	26
Primary and fabricated metals	10	12	19	15	13	20
Machinery	43	34	18	18	61	63
Electrical machinery	18	21	8	8	45	62
Transportation equipment	2	8	15	16	4	15
Other manufacturing	6	4	10	13	8	8
All manufacturing	100	100	100	100	20	26

Sweden's comparative advantage is held to lie in the machinery industry (especially non-electrical machinery) and in the transportation equipment, metals, and paper and pulp industries. In the engineering industries it is based on Sweden's relative endowment of skilled labour, while in the metals (mainly steel) and paper and pulp industries, it is based on the country's relative endowment of iron ore (at least historically) and of forests.

These industries together accounted for 73% of manufacturing exports and 85% of foreign production in 1978. But foreign production is much more concentrated in the electrical and non-electrical machinery industries than are exports (55% compared to 26%). The reason, presumably, is that these are relatively 'footloose' industries, that is production must not be located close to a raw materials source or to the final market. Thus, although Sweden may have a comparative advantage in these industries, changes in trade barriers or relative costs can easily tip the balance in favour of a foreign production location.

The metals and paper and pulp industries, on the other hand, are dependent on locating close to the natural resource. Foreign production in these industries, as a consequence, is almost entirely in the less natural resource-intensive end of production, that is, in fabricated metals and in paper products respectively. This pattern is reinforced by the presence of substantial economies of scale in the earlier stages of production.

It is worth noting that the Swedish chemicals industry is declining in importance as a foreign investor, which contrasts sharply with the picture in other countries. It reflects the fact that Swedish foreign investment in that industry was historically dominated by match production (the Swedish Match Company had, at one time, a world monopoly), which has since stagnated. Today the pharmaceutical industry accounts for a growing share of the industry's foreign investment.

These points about the chemical industry suggest two caveats in interpreting the current industry pattern of foreign production. One is that the current pattern depends on dynamic historical factors and not only on current factors. The other is that industry aggregates may conceal important intra-industry differences as well as unique characteristics of single, dominant firms. The latter is particularly true of small countries like Sweden.

Turning next to foreign investment in Sweden, Table 7.3 shows that it, too, is relatively concentrated in those industries in which Sweden has a comparative advantage. Metals, non-electrical and electrical machinery account for over 50% of foreign employment, which is higher than in other host countries.[4] However, foreign production is not large relative to those industries in Sweden, suggesting that foreign producers do not have ownership-specific advantages *vis-à-vis* Swedish producers.

In the food products and chemical industries, by contrast, foreign producers do seem to have such a competitive advantage, as seen by their high share of employment. These are industries in which Swedish firms have not developed a competitive advantage—as revealed by their low export and foreign production propensities—and foreign firms have moved in to fill the gap.

In sum, both outward and inward investment seem to call for a

TABLE 7.3 Industry pattern of foreign production in Sweden 1970 and 1977 (%)

Industry	Foreign manuf. empl. in Sweden % distribution		Swedish exports % distribution		Foreign in % of manuf. employment in Sweden	
	1970	1977	1970	1978	1970	1978
Food, drink, and tobacco	9	15	2	2	6	10
Textiles, clothing, etc.	7	3	4	3	4	3
Paper, pulp	3	} 5	} 18	13	2	} 3
Paper products, printing, etc.	4			3	3	
Chemicals, rubber, etc.	22	19	6	9	14	14
Primary and fabricated metals	13		19	15	4	
Machinery	19	} 52	18	18	6	} 6
Electrical machinery	16 } 48		8	8	10	
Transportation equipment	0		15	16	0	
Other manufacturing	7	4	10	13	2	2
All manufacturing	100	100	100	100	5	6

two pronged explanation: one that explains the industry distribution of foreign production in terms of locational factors and one that explains it in terms of the competitive advantage of the investing country's firms.

Table 7.4 gives the breakdown of outward investment by region or country. It shows that Swedish manufacturing is highly concentrated in the industrial countries and, within these, Western Europe, especially the EEC.

Comparing Swedish foreign investment with that of other countries one finds that Swedish investment is relatively more concentrated in countries with which Sweden has traditional commercial ties, such as the Nordic countries. US and UK investment is relatively more concentrated in other English-speaking countries with which they have such ties. For the US this share was over 50% in 1970 (over half of which was in Canada), for the UK it was over 60%, while for Sweden it was only 30% (where the group of English-speaking countries includes the US, the UK, Canada, Australia, New Zealand, and South Africa), (Swedenborg, 1979, Ch.3).

Table 7.4 also shows that the ratio of foreign production to total sales by Swedish firms varies significantly between countries. That ratio is highest in Latin America (65%), in the original EEC countries (47%) and in North America (46%), that is, in major markets where Swedish firms

TABLE 7.4   Country pattern of Swedish production abroad compared to Swedish exports 1970 and 1978 (%)

Region/country	Employment		Swedish exports		Foreign production in % of total sales[a]	
	1970	1978	1970	1978	1970	1978
Industrial countries						
EEC[b]	58	54	53	47	32	39
of which:						
Great Britain	8	10	13	11	—	—
Denmark	4	3	11	9	—	—
Other EEC	46	41	29	27	42	47
EFTA[b]	10	9	23	20	14	16
of which:						
Norway, Finland	6	5	18	16	(12)[d]	(14)[d]
Other EFTA	4	4	5	4		
Other Europe	1	3	2	7	13	33
North America	7	11	8	8	37	46
of which:						
USA	5	9	6	6	—	—
Other industrial countries[c]	4	3	3	3	33	38
Developing countries						
Africa, Asia	8	3	6	12	18	4
Latin America	12	17	4	3	49	65
All countries	100	100	100	100	29	34

[a]See definition in Table 7.3.
[b]EEC and EFTA membership as in 1978. In 1970 Great Britain and Denmark were members of EFTA.
[c]South Africa, Australia, New Zealand, Japan.
[d]Nordic countries, i.e. Norway, Finland, and Denmark.

have encountered tariffs or non-tariff barriers to exporting. The ratio is lowest within EFTA, of which Sweden is a member.

Loosely, then, the evidence suggests that 'traditional commercial ties', trade barriers, and host country size are country characteristics which affect the choice between exports and foreign production in serving foreign markets. Similarly, it seems possible, in a very general way, to explain the industry pattern of exports and foreign production by industry characteristics such as factor proportions (natural resource intensity, labour skill intensity), economies of large scale production (favouring concentrated production), and product tradeability.

The next section will show that these tentative conclusions hold up in a more rigid test of the underlying hypotheses. It will also show how characteristics of firms explain differences among firms in the volume of foreign production and exports.

Determinants of international production by firms

The theory of international production is ultimately a theory of the size and growth of firms, since it is only by bringing in the notion of an ownership-specific advantage that one can explain why foreign production is undertaken by MNEs rather than by local firms. Hence it is appropriate to test a theory of the growth of the international firm on data for individual firms.

TABLE 7.5 'Degree of multinationality': Swedish MNEs 1978 by ratio of foreign sales to total sales

Foreign sales in % of total sales	Number of firms	Foreign sales (Skr millions)	Average foreign sales (Skr millions)	Foreign production in % of foreign sales
0–20	9	164	18	49
21–40	19	2,123	112	46
41–60	28	22,533	805	43
61–80	40	55,055	1,376	49
81–100	14	33,960	2,426	63
All	110	113,835	1,035	52

Note: Foreign sales are total sales less consolidated sales in Sweden. Foreign production is sales by foreign affiliates less imports from Swedish parent.

Firms differ in size and they differ in the degree to which they export and produce abroad. Table 7.5 shows how Swedish MNEs in the manufacturing sector differ in the degree to which they sell in foreign markets, while Table 7.6 shows how they differ in the degree to which they

TABLE 7.6   'Degree of multinationality': Swedish MNEs 1978 by ratio of foreign production to total sales

Foreign prod. in % of total sales	Number of firms	Foreign prod. (Skr millions)	Average foreign prod. (Skr millions)
1–20	26	703	27
11–20	32	6,437	201
21–40	28	13,922	497
41–60	20	26,369	1,318
61–80	4	11,714	2,928
All	110	59,145	538

Note: See Table 7.5.

produce abroad. The former is a measure of their international competitiveness, while the latter depends on factors affecting locational choice.

The data show a wide dispersion among firms. They also show that, on average, Swedish MNEs are highly dependent on foreign markets for their sales, while manufacturing is still predominantly in Sweden. Of these firms 75% sold more than 40% of their output abroad, while only 20% had such a large share of their total output abroad. Foreign production by this latter group was also large in absolute terms, which reveals how, in a small country, a very limited number of MNEs account for a very large part of total investment. In the Swedish case, the 20 largest MNEs account for some 85% of total foreign manufacturing. The dominance of a few large MNEs should not be taken to mean that foreign investment is a large firm phenomenon, however. It is not (cf. Swedenborg, 1979, Ch. 6).

How well does the theory of international production set out in equations (1)–(3) above explain differences between firms in relative volume of foreign sales and production? Table 7.7 presents the results of regression analysis across firms and across countries in which these firms have manufacturing affiliates. The dependent variables are the propensities to sell and to produce abroad (and in individual countries) and correspond to the ratios in Tables 7.5 and 7.6. The propensity to sell abroad has been divided into the propensity to supply the foreign market through exports (SX) and the propensity to supply it through local production (SQ).

The independent variables are characteristics of firms and of their industries to explain inter-firm differences and characteristics of countries to explain inter-country differences. Firm variables are measures of a firm-specific advantage, namely R&D intensity (RD) and labour skill intensity (LS). Industry variables are variable factors affecting location, namely, capital intensity (KL), economies of scale (SC, average plant size), and natural resource intensity (NR, a dummy for the paper and pulp and steel industry). Country variables are two measures of foreign demand, namely market size (GDP) and income per capita (GDP_{cap}), and a measure of relative costs (w_j/w_H, affiliate wage level relative to parent wage level). In addition there is a variable, YR, showing the age of the foreign affiliate to take account of the fact that it takes time to grow large and that the present size of the affiliate also depends on when it was first started up (dynamic historical factors). YR may also be a measure of accumulated learning by doing, since that, too, is a function of time.

RD and LS are expected to have a positive effect on both exports and foreign production volumes and KL, NR, and SC to have a positive effect on exports and a negative effect on foreign production (since KL and NR are related to Sweden's comparative advantage and since SC should favour concentrated production in the home country). GDP and GDP_{cap} are expected to have a positive effect both on exports and on foreign production. Relative wages, however, are ambiguous, depending on the extent to which they show differences in labour costs in productivity. Relative wages and income per capita are highly correlated.

Basically, the results in Table 7.7 are consistent with the hypotheses. In the analysis across firms, RD and LS positively affect both export and foreign production propensities, although a high R&D intensity biases firms more towards exporting than towards producing abroad.[5]

Domestic natural resource endowment has the predicted positive effect on exports, while scale economies have the predicted negative effect on foreign production. Since there is a high multi-collinearity between NR, SC and KL (the paper and pulp and steel industries are characterized both by large plant size and by high capital intensity), only one of the variables is significant in each equation.

Finally, YR, as expected, has a positive effect on foreign production and no effect on exports. Its high explanatory power shows how important it is to take account of each firm's history to understand its present performance.

The analysis across countries shows that country size and income per capita *or* the wage level have a positive effect on *both* exports and foreign production. This result indicates that Swedish firms tend not only to sell but also to produce where the market is. The latter might capture the effect of barriers to trade, which is an important missing variable in the regressions.

To sum up, the regression analysis is consistent with hypotheses generated by the theory on international production. Exports and foreign production are indeed explainable by the kind of firm and industry characteristics that the theory suggests. The explanatory variables that have been included explain 25%–40% of the variation in the propensity to

TABLE 7.7 Determinants of foreign sales and foreign production by Swedish MNEs. Cross sections over firms and over firms and countries in 1978. (Log form)

Indep. var.	(a) Firms Dependent variable			(b) Firms and countries Dependent variable		
	$\frac{SX+SQ}{SH}$	$\frac{SX}{SH}$	$\frac{SQ}{SH}$	$\frac{SX+SQ}{SH}$	$\frac{SX}{SH}$	$\frac{SQ}{SH}$
Const.	-6.23** (-2.49)	-1.98	-6.80** (-2.09)	-4.39** (-1.59)	-8.86** (-2.64)	-0.23
RD	0.30** (3.94)	0.43** (4.99)	0.26** (2.92)	0.14** (2.17)	0.39** (5.18)	-0.05
LS	1.80** (3.21)	0.85 (1.33)	1.75** (2.40)	0.91** (1.60)	0.13	0.43
KL	-0.05	-0.15 (-1.00)	-0.21 (-1.31)	-0.08	-0.26 (-1.43)	-0.01
NR	1.50** (3.21)	2.49** (4.58)	0.70** (1.31)	1.83** (5.11)	2.83** (6.20)	1.22** (3.17)
SC	-0.12 (-1.04)	-0.02	-0.22 (-1.63)	-0.23** (-2.62)	0.03	-0.36** (-3.81)
YR	0.75** (2.53)	0.18	1.52** (4.45)			
GDP				0.29** (4.79)	0.15** (1.99)	0.41** (6.08)
GDP$_{cap}$				-0.05	0.72** (3.64)	-0.38** (-2.29)
w_j/w_H				0.50** (2.21)	0.04**	0.82** (3.32)

YR$_j$				0.52** (2.53)	−0.01	0.84** (3.79)
DF	105	107	99	321	322	346
R^2	0.42	0.37	0.39	0.23	0.25	0.23
F	12.88**	10.35**	10.38**	10.50**	12.19**	11.31**

The numbers in parentheses are *t*-statistics: $t < 1$ not shown.
***indicate significance at the 10% and 5% levels respectively. R^2 is not corrected for degress of freedom (DF).

Definition of variables:

(SX + SQ)/SH	=	foreign sales/domestic sales.
SX/SH	=	exports/domestic sales.
SQ/SH	=	manufacturing affiliate net local sales/domestic sales.

In 7(a) the above variables refer to total activities abroad, in 7(b) they refer to activities in individual countries of foreign manufacturing.

RD	=	R&D-sales ratio.
LS	=	labour-skill measure (average wage and salary level in parent company).
KL	=	capital-labour ratio.
NR	=	dummy variable for paper and pulp, and iron and steel industries.
SC	=	scale economies (average plant size, weighted by parent's industries).
YR	=	age of foreign affiliate (1978 less year of establishment).
GDP	=	gross domestic product of country *j*.
GDP^{cap}	=	per capita GDP of country *j*.
w_{ij}/w_H	=	ratio of foreign to domestic wages (affiliate wages relative to parent wages).

sell and to produce abroad. That is high for cross-sectional analysis. It is also high for an analysis based on individual firm data.[6]

Regression analysis has also been used to explain the share of foreign firms in Swedish industry (Samuelsson, 1977). Separate regressions were estimated for US and European firms (in 126 industries). The most salient results of this analysis are the following. The presence of European firms in an industry had a negative effect on the share of US firms in the same industry and vice-versa. The presence of Swedish MNEs in the industry had a negative effect on both. This supports the point made above that the competitive advantages of investors from different countries are not in the same industries.[7] In line with this, US firms were competitive in industries characterized by high technical personnel intensity and a high propensity to export, while European firms were competitive in industries characterized by high advertising intensity and oriented toward the domestic market.

An important and unconventional (cf. Caves, 1983, Ch.2) conclusion that emerges from this analysis is that MNEs from different countries do not have a competitive advantage in the same activities. Although there may be a two way investment flow in many industries, sometimes in narrowly defined sub-industries, there is a pattern of specialization in international production just as there is in international trade. This specialization pattern depends both on the comparative advantage of the investing country and on the ownership-specific advantage of its firms. It seems likely that the two are related, in so far that through specialization in accordance with home country comparative advantage firms acquire firm-specific know-how in production and marketing which they can exploit in a foreign production location.

7.3   THE IMPACT OF INTERNATIONAL PRODUCTION ON ECONOMIC STRUCTURE AND INTERNATIONAL COMPETITIVENESS

How does international production impinge on the Swedish economy? Does it lead to increased specialization and international exchange or just the opposite? By what mechanism does foreign production by home country firms affect the home economy and the host economy? The foregoing analysis does not answer these questions, but it provides a necessary first step in analysing them.

The first thing to note is that it is not legitimate to infer anything about the effects of MNEs simply from the fact that they are concentrated in certain industries and are more research-oriented than domestic firms.[8]

These may be characteristics of MNEs, but they do not necessarily imply anything about the effects of foreign production.

Essentially the question we are interested in answering as set out in the introductory chapter is: what would happen to economic structure *if* international production by MNEs were not allowed? That is, what would be the effect of a policy which effectively constrained firms from producing (or increasing their production) abroad?

Theoretically, as noted earlier, exports, foreign production and licensing a foreign producer are alternative ways in which a firm can exploit its competitive advantage in foreign markets. The profit-maximizing firm will choose the most profitable alternative, which in the case of exports and foreign production is the least cost source of supply (Horst, 1973, 1978). Foreign production allows the firm to lower its prices and increase its foreign sales more than it otherwise could have. An unambiguous effect of larger foreign sales is that the investing firm will be larger overall. However, domestic production may increase or decrease, depending on whether the positive effect of a lower price abroad on the firm's complementary exports is sufficiently large to offset the negative effect on substitute exports (Horst, 1973, 1978; Swedenborg, 1979).

These are the mechanisms by which domestic production and allocation can be affected by allowing firms the option of producing abroad. Is larger firm size 'good'? Does it matter if the effect on exports is positive or negative?

Increased exports *per se* are not a goal for policy—even though the policy debate often seems tinged with mercantilist ideas. But to the extent that increased exports reflect increased specialization in accordance with country comparative advantage, they should imply higher efficiency and incomes in the exporting country. Then, if exports increase as a result of allowing firms to produce abroad, it is a sufficient condition for a positive effect on the home country.

Exports may not be affected at all—for example because trade barriers are in any case prohibitive or because the alternative to foreign production by home country firms is the same production abroad by other firms. If that is the case, foreign production implies a corresponding increase in the size of the investing firm. Output abroad increases, but domestic output is unchanged.

What are the effects of larger firm size on allocative efficiency in the home country? They derive from economies and diseconomies of firm size (as opposed to plant size). The beneficial effects have been stressed most and, at least for MNEs from a small country, probably rightly so. The economies of firm size have to do with investment in R&D, advertising, and a sales and service network which benefits the entire firm regardless of where production is located. R&D results are mobile within the MNE, an advertising campaign in a particular market benefits both exports and foreign production, sales outlets and service functions display indivisibilities and depend positively on the volume of sales in each market. The larger the sales volume over which the fixed investment cost can be spread, the more profitable the investment and the more will be invested. And increased investment in, for example, R&D enhances the competitiveness of domestic operations.

The question of how foreign production by Swedish MNEs impinges on allocative efficiency in Sweden will be evaluated below by analysing the effect on Swedish exports and the indirect effect on the volume of R&D. In the latter context the extent to which licence and patent sales are an alternative to foreign production will also be addressed.

The effect via exports

A number of studies in recent years have sought to determine the effect on home country exports of allowing firms to produce abroad.[9] The problem which has plagued all these studies has been to determine 'what would have happened in the alternative position when foreign production is not allowed'. Or put in a different way: to establish the partial effect on exports of an exogenous change in foreign production due to a regulatory policy.

Different studies have grappled with the problem in different ways. Some have calculated an interval between what the most 'pessimistic' and 'optimistic' *assumptions* regarding the alternative to foreign production would mean. Others have tried to make informed judgments on the basis of individual case studies, interviews, etc. Still others have used single equation regression estimates and hoped, or argued, that the simultaneity problem is not severe. In studies of Swedish foreign production the present author used a two stage estimation procedure to deal with the simultaneity problem and determine the partial effect of an *exogenous* change in foreign production. It was found that a single equation estimate on cross sectional data tended to overestimate the positive effect of foreign production on exports.

Table 7.8 summarizes the results of a two stage, least squares analysis of the effect of allowing firms the option of producing abroad on the exports of the same firms to different countries.[10] The elasticity of exports with respect to foreign production is the estimated regression coefficients in the log equations. It shows the percentage change in the relative volume of exports when the relative volume of foreign production increases by 1%. The derivative shows the absolute change in exports when foreign production increases by $1.

TABLE 7.8   The estimated effect of an increase in foreign production by $1 on the exports of the average firm to the country of production (Combined cross section and time series analysis)

Variable[a]	Mean	Elasticity[b]	Derivative[c]
$\dfrac{SQ}{SH}$	0.0654		
$\dfrac{SX}{SH}$	0.0275	−0.07 (−0.61)	
$\dfrac{SXS}{SH}$	0.0033	−0.42 (−1.36)	−0.02
$\dfrac{SXC}{SH}$	0.0096	0.81 (5.43)	0.12

[a] $\dfrac{SQ}{SH}$ = affiliate net local sales/home country sales.

$\dfrac{SX}{SH}$ = exports/home country sales.

$\dfrac{SXS}{SH}$ = non-complementary or 'substitute' exports/home country sales, where non-complementary exports are exports to others than manufacturing affiliates in country j.

$\dfrac{SXC}{SH}$ = complementary exports/home country sales, where complementary exports are exports to manufacturing affiliates in country j.

[b] Equals the estimated regression coefficients in the log equations; t-values in parentheses.
[c] Calculated for mean values.

Note: The table shows the results of estimation on combined cross section and time series data (for 1965, 1970, 1974, 1978), since this comes closest to answering what the effect of increased production *over time* is on individual firm exports.
    Table 7.8 builds on the same regressions as in Table 7.7 estimated on combined cross-section and time series data. See Swedenborg (1982), Chapter 7, for further details.

The effects on complementary and non-complementary exports have been estimated separately. The former should, if anything, be positive, while the latter should be zero or negative. The results are consistent with these expectations. They show a negative, though weak, effect on non-complementary exports and a positive and highly significant effect on complementary exports. The calculated net effect is that total exports to a country increase by 0.10 dollars (0.12 − 0.02) when foreign production increases by $1.

The estimated effects may appear small, especially in view of the heated debate over employment effects of foreign production in many investing countries. But they are neither surprising nor unreasonable in view of what underlies them. Ultimately, they depend on the price elasticity of demand at home and abroad and the elasticity of export supply. If the price elasticity of demand is high, that is if firms compete in a market with many sellers of similar products, which Swedish firms presumably do in foreign markets, the effects cannot be very large. Then, increased foreign production has a small effect on foreign price and, thereby, a small effect on Swedish exports.

At the same time, the fact that the estimated effects are non-zero is equally noteworthy, in so far as it lends additional support to the underlying theory of international production. The reason is that non-zero effects imply less than perfectly competitive conditions, which, in turn, is consistent with the idea of a firm-specific competitive advantage.

The results imply that the alternative to foreign production by home country firms is not exports by the same firms. In the absence of foreign production the foreign market would largely have been lost to the firm. Only 2% of the sales supplied through foreign production could 'in the alternative position' have been supplied through exports from Sweden. The remaining 98% represents a net increase in the firm's foreign market share. To this should be added the increase in complementary exports induced by foreign production.[11]

The effect on resource allocation in Sweden is as follows. The investing firm increases its output of products complementary to foreign production and decreases its output of products which compete with or are independent of foreign production. Since the net effect is increased exports, the change should represent a move towards increased specialization and higher efficiency.

A plausible story one can tell about this is a version of the product-cycle theory. The product mix and production technology of firms undergo constant change. The R&D and skill intensive part of output, in which the home-based parent has a competitive advantage, remains in the home country, while other, though complementary, output is moved abroad. The MNE still has a knowledge advantage in organizing the output that is located abroad, but the production process itself has become sufficiently standardized to be sensitive to relative wage differences and trade barriers.

What about the effects in the rest of the economy? Could increased foreign production by Swedish MNEs displace exports by other Swedish firms, so that the overall effect on Swedish exports is negative? What can be said of the overall effect on resource allocation?

In order for there to be a direct effect (negative or positive) on non-MNE exports, the exports of these firms have to compete with or be complementary to foreign production by MNEs. Such effects are, however, likely to be of second order magnitude. For one thing, the number of Swedish producers, especially competitors, in most industries is small relative to the number of producers abroad.

Even if non-MNEs are not directly affected by foreign production, they will be affected by the higher growth of MNEs in Sweden. Assuming full employment at the outset, more rapid expansion in one sector of the economy must mean less rapid expansion (or contraction) in another sector. Competition between firms for factors of production will see to that. Assuming, also, continuous balance in the balance of payments, that contraction must either mean increased imports or decreased exports, or both, from non-MNEs.

To conclude: the effect of allowing firms the option of producing abroad is increased specialization in accordance with both country- and ownership-specific advantages. This is true whether foreign production is motivated by differences in relative costs between countries or by the presence of artificial or natural barriers to trade—*given that these barriers exist*. Of course, if all artificial barriers to trade (tariffs, government regulation or preferential treatment) could somehow be eliminated, world efficiency would probably be raised. It is quite possible, too, that in such a world there would be more trade and less foreign production by MNEs. But that is not the point at issue.

The location of R&D; effects via R&D and/or licensing

In 1978 Swedish MNEs accounted for over 70% of the total R&D in the manufacturing sector. This may be compared to their share of manufacturing employment and exports, which was 47% and 58% respectively. MNEs are highly research-oriented and, as argued here, there is a reason for this. R&D-oriented firms are most likely to become multinational, because an ownership advantage based on R&D results can be exploited regardless of location.

Here we will explore three other questions. The first is where Swedish MNEs locate their R&D activities. The second is how R&D depends on firm size and, hence, on whether firms are allowed to produce abroad. The third is the extent to which licence and patent sales, in practice, are alternatives to foreign production in exploiting a technological advantage.

A common viewpoint in Swedish policy discussion about MNEs is: 'We don't mind if Swedish firms locate some production outside Sweden, so long as they keep the more advanced, innovative production in Sweden.' The presumption is that advanced, R&D-intensive production would generate higher incomes in the country and possibly, too, higher growth.[12]

Whether it does have these effects depends, of course, on whether Sweden has a comparative advantage in R&D production. If it does not, it would be more efficient to import R&D results. Whether firms in fact choose to locate such production in Sweden depends not only on Sweden having such a comparative advantage but also on whether or not it is distorted by the tax system and trade barriers. If Sweden has a comparative advantage in production which requires highly skilled labour, and if the Swedish tax system does not distort this by taxing such labour relatively more than other countries do, and if other countries do not impose trade barriers with a view to attracting this particular production, *then* it is likely that the more advanced production will be maintained in Sweden.

As seen earlier, Swedish firms have a competitive advantage in R&D-intensive production and a high R&D intensity leads both to higher exports and to higher foreign production (cf. Table 7.7). But how about R&D production itself? Where is that located?

Table 7.9 shows that R&D activities are predominantly located in Sweden: 86% of total R&D of MNEs in 1978. Moreover, this share has been constant since 1970. The decline (from 91%) between 1965–70 was primarily due to one major MNE moving its entire R&D operation to another country. Thus, while production and employment abroad have steadily increased relative to total MNE production and employment, R&D abroad has remained remarkably constant. Why?

TABLE 7.9   The share of R&D production located in Sweden. Swedish MNEs
1965–78
(%)

	1965	1970	1974	1978
R&D in Sweden relative to total RD	91.4	85.6	86.0	85.9

Note: R&D is defined as expenditures for R&D and includes both company R&D and R&D commissioned by the company. The figures refer to MNEs which existed throughout the period.

One straightforward reason is simply that the Bank of Sweden has been reluctant to grant permission for firms to move their R&D operations abroad—reflecting the above mentioned view that it would be beneficial to retain such production in Sweden.[13] However, it is not clear to what extent this has been a binding constraint. Most firms would probably retain their R&D in Sweden anyway. There are advantages to keeping R&D relatively concentrated in one country and also to keeping it close to major manufacturing units, which for most firms means a Swedish location. Only a small number of very large MNEs, which have more production abroad than in Sweden, might have preferred a foreign location.

Turning now to the second question: do Swedish MNEs carry out more

R&D than they would have if they had not been allowed to produce abroad? Table 7.10 shows three different measures of R&D intensity. The first measure relates total R&D expenditures, regardless of where R&D is carried out, to total company sales. The second relates total R&D to the sales of the Swedish parent groups, that is, to net domestic sales plus exports. A result of foreign production, then, is that total R&D relative to production in Sweden is higher, which is also apparent in the Table. Assuming that R&D costs reflect R&D results and that the latter are available throughout the MNE, then it is the second measure which should affect the competitiveness of the Swedish-based firms. The more R&D they can draw on, the more competitive they become internationally.

TABLE 7.10   R&D intensity according to alternative measures. Swedish MNEs 1965–78
(%)

	1965	*1970*	*1974*	*1978*
Total R&D/total sales	1.84	2.15	2.22	2.30
Total R&D/Swedish parent sales	2.48	3.01	3.25	3.77
Swedish R&D/Swedish parent sales	2.27	2.53	2.77	3.23

Note: Total sales is consolidated total sales. Swedish parent sales is consolidated domestic sales plus exports.

The third measure shows R&D carried out in Sweden relative to Swedish production. It is included only to illustrate that measured R&D intensity is lower if one overlooks the fact that Swedish firms also have access to the R&D which they undertake outside Sweden.

The table shows that the R&D intensity of Swedish MNEs—by all measures—has increased steadily in the 1965–78 period. The most rapid increase is in the second measure, since production in Sweden has not increased as rapidly as total production by these firms.

The difference between overall R&D intensity (measure 1) and the Swedish parent R&D intensity (measure 2) is 1.47 percentage points. If the overall R&D intensity of 2.3% is the R&D intensity which would have characterized Swedish firms in the absence of foreign production, then this difference could be said to be an 'effect' of allowing foreign production. But that assumes (i) that the volume of R&D depends only on firm size and (ii) that foreign production is a net addition to total output, that is that firms 'in the alternative position' would not be larger in Sweden. Both are complex questions. Nevertheless it has been argued that firm size is an important determinant of the volume of R&D and, in the previous section, it was shown that foreign production constituted a net increase in the firm's sales. A cautious interpretation of this is that at least part of the 1.47 percentage point difference between the two measures is the result of allowing foreign growth, and that Swedish R&D intensity may be as much as 65% higher than it would otherwise have been.

The implications of this are considerable. Referring back to Table 7.7, a 1% increase in R&D intensity leads to a 0.4% increase in Swedish exports. A crude calculation would then indicate that Swedish exports (relative to domestic sales) could be as much as 26% higher (0.4% × 65%) as a result of this indirect effect of foreign production. Obviously, such an effect could easily dwarf the more short run direct effects on exports of allowing foreign production.

The third question to explore is the extent to which licensing is an alternative to foreign production. It is related to the last point. If firms could get the same return on their R&D investment (and other intangible assets) by licensing a foreign producer as they do through direct investment, then foreign production is not a necessary condition for increased R&D. However, that would assume that foreign production and licensing are perfect substitutes, which is hardly the case. Much knowledge, including that generated by R&D, is not in a form which is easily packaged and sold in the market. Information, transaction and monitoring costs have to be incurred.

Table 7.11 shows that, in practice, Swedish MNEs do not choose licensing to any significant degree. Almost all of their income from sale of licences, patents, 'know-how', etc., came from majority-owned affiliates or minority interests abroad. Only a quarter came from sale to independent foreign producers.

The income from selling licences, etc., to foreign affiliates covered 9% of total MNE expenditures for R&D in 1978. Adding to this the R&D carried out and paid for by foreign affiliates, the contribution of affiliates to total R&D expenditures amounts to 23%. That roughly corresponds to their share of total MNE production in the same year (25%), which means that affiliates, on average, paid 'their' share of R&D costs. However, that average conceals considerable individual variations. Most firms do not, in fact, charge affiliates directly for their use of R&D or other services provided by the parent.

The income from selling licences, patents and know-how to independent foreign firms amounted to only 4% of total MNE expenditures for R&D (150/3,629 Skr million). It seems unlikely that such income could be increased sufficiently to compensate the lost income from foreign affiliates 'in the alternative position' of no foreign production. The actual choice made by MNEs seems to prove that they are a more efficient vehicle for the international transfer of technology than are transactions through the market—a point which has been stressed throughout this chapter.

Table 7.11   Income from and payments for licences, patents, royalties and
'know-how'. Swedish MNEs 1970–78
(Skr millions)

	1970	1974	1978
Total income of Sw. parent		316	557
of which:			
foreign affiliates	111[a]	200	333
foreign minority interests		25	33
other foreign firms		64	150
Total payments by Swedish MNEs	99	128	172
of which:			
abroad	54	70	98

[a]Only manufacturing affiliates.

Finally, some words about the balance of 'technology' (broadly defined) trade for Swedish MNEs and foreign MNEs in Sweden. As seen in Table 7.11 total *purchase* of licences, know-how, etc., is smaller than the corresponding sales. Purchase was less than a third of income from sales, while purchases from abroad were less than a fifth of income from abroad. The balance of such international payments is much more positive for Swedish MNEs than for the rest of the manufacturing sector—a reflection of the greater research orientation of Swedish parent companies. The balance for foreign affiliates in Sweden, by contrast, is much more negative than for the rest of manufacturing, reflecting a similar reliance by foreign affiliates on their parents in the home country (SCB, 1978).

7.4 SUMMARY AND POLICY IMPLICATIONS

The growth of MNEs has raised a number of policy issues in investing and host countries alike. In Sweden, as in most other major investing countries, concern initially centred around the effects of the investment outflow on the balance of payments. Subsequently, it has shifted to the effects of foreign manufacturing by Swedish MNEs on Swedish exports, on the level and structure of employment in Sweden, and on the overall competitiveness of Swedish industry. In the 1970s these concerns were translated into the regulations governing direct investment. Thus, investment abroad was allowed only if firms could persuade the central bank that the investment would have a beneficial effect on the Swedish trade balance and, hence, indirectly on employment in Sweden. Although actual practice was liberal and the trade balance requirement was formally dropped in 1981, the underlying issues remain politically very much alive.

The empirical questions addressed in this chapter are, of course, highly geared to policy issues and, by way of summary, some of the policy implications of the analysis for Sweden will be repeated.

This chapter has shown that the pattern of both outward and inward direct investment is consistent with the notion that direct investment occurs because, (i) foreign production is a cheaper source of supply and, (ii) because MNEs have an advantage or set of advantages which allows them to produce abroad at lower cost than their competitors could. This implies that direct investment leads to a more efficient allocation of resources both between countries in accordance with location comparative advantage and between firms in accordance with ownership-specific advantage. Only to the extent that direct investment is primarily motivated by *artificial* barriers to trade (tariffs, regulations, etc.) does direct investment imply a less efficient allocation of resources between countries. In order to raise efficiency, policy should be aimed at removing such trade barriers. Controls on direct investment induced by such trade barriers, however, would merely be to attack one symptom rather than the cause of the inefficiency. Allowing direct investment at least guarantees allocative efficiency between firms, that is, that production inside tariff walls is carried out by the most efficient producer.

According to the empirical results, Swedish exports are somewhat larger than they would have been in the absence of foreign production. This, perhaps surprising, finding is related to the above point. To the extent that foreign production substitutes for Swedish exports, the decline in exports would have occurred even without foreign production by Swedish firms. The reason is that the main determinant of the change in exports is the change in relative production costs and trade barriers, not the change in MNE production. Thus, if foreign tariffs are raised, Swedish exports will decline, but they will decline by less than they would have done if Swedish firms had not increased their output abroad.

The effect on 'restructuring' and employment in Sweden is entirely derivative from the effect on exports. A positive effect of foreign investment on the investing firm's exports means that this firm will be larger and, hence, increase its employment more than it otherwise would have. The increased demand for labour and other inputs by this firm will lead to a higher price of the kind of inputs used relatively intensively by this firm. Since Swedish foreign investors are characterized by a relatively high R&D and skill intensity, income redistribution should be in favour of skilled labour.

Policy discussion as well as academic studies of 'the effect of foreign production on exports' are sometimes couched in terms like 'foreign production implies an export of job opportunities', as if the *level* of employment in a country depended on MNEs rather than on economic policy. That is highly misleading. The only effect that can reasonably be credited to MNEs—at least in the longer run—is on the *allocation* of resources (jobs) within the country and on incomes.

To be sure, resource reallocation is associated with adjustment costs and may imply temporary unemployment. But the reallocation of resources brought on by MNE activity is, as emphasized above, extremely marginal compared to that caused by the underlying changes in international cost and demand conditions to which MNEs and others respond. It can also be argued that MNEs actually reduce adjustment costs in that much of the required reallocation (from activities where profitability is declining to those where it is rising) takes place *within* the firm.

Probably the most important effects of allowing MNE growth are indirect and long run, however. Through international production firms can grow larger than they would otherwise have done. This, in turn, allows them to invest more in R&D, advertising, and a sales and distribution network, since these costs can be spread over larger sales volumes. Such investment enhances the firm's competitiveness in both its domestic and its foreign operations. In this chapter the positive effect on Swedish exports of increased R&D investment has been quantified to some extent. To this should be added the positive effect of increased advertising and an expanded network of foreign sales and service affiliates.

In the space of one chapter it is not possible to analyse or even touch on all the concerns regarding MNE growth that have been voiced in policy discussions. Indeed, even without space limitations, analytical treatment of all the issues is probably a hopeless task. Caves (1983, p. xi) observes that he knows 'of no subject in economic policy in which the issues that excite public discussion bear so little relation to the welfare issues identified by normative economics'. In other words, they are not related to MNEs as such or they do not directly or indirectly affect the level or distribution of real income either between countries or within them.[14]

This chapter has focused on some of the more important effects identified by economic analysis and relevant for a country like Sweden and the analysis has shown that, in general, these effects are positive. In short, it has shown that there are important efficiency gains from inter-firm specialization through MNE production just as there are from inter-country specialization through trade. On these grounds, and in the case of Sweden, it establishes a strong argument for a non-interventionist policy towards MNE involvement.

NOTES

1. Most of the data on Swedish direct investment have been collected by the Industrial Institute for Economic and Social Research in Stockholm and have been analyzed by Swedenborg in a number of earlier publications (1973, 1975, 1979, 1981, 1982). Whenever a data source on Swedish direct investment is not given in this chapter, the source is that data bank or one of those studies.

   Data on foreign investment in Sweden have also been collected by the above institute (and analyzed by Samuelsson, 1977) as well as by the Central Bureau of Statistics (SCB). Recently, a series of studies, commissioned by the government, on the impact of MNE production on the Swedish economy have brought together data from old and new sources (SOU, 1981: 43, 1982: 15, 1982: 27, 1983: 16, 1983: 17).

   This note cannot exhaust the list of both major and minor studies devoted to the problem of MNEs in Sweden. Among non-Swedish studies Lipsey and O'Connor (1982), Lipsey, Kravis, and Roldan (1982) should be especially mentioned.
2. The theory explains the determinants of country comparative advantage. But what are the determinants of firm-specific advantage? Elsewhere this author has argued that country- and firm-specific advantage are related in that country comparative advantage can lead to firm-specific advantage through learning by doing. That is, firms will acquire relatively more know-how in industries in which home country firms specialize. This, in turn, explains why the industry pattern of foreign production by different countries differs (Swedenborg, 1979. Ch. 3).
3. The current account deficit means that Swedish direct investment abroad has not been matched by a real capital transfer, as this would have required a corresponding current account surplus.
4. Swedenborg (1979) compares the outward investment of Sweden, the US and the UK. For a comparison between the structure of inward investment is Sweden and that of other advanced countries see Clegg (1985).
5. This fits the product-cycle theory of trade and investment, which states that innovative firms can exploit their knowledge advantage through exporting and that foreign production follows when the output has become more standardized. Horst (1978) shows similar results for US firms.
6. Similar results have been obtained in cross sectional analysis based on 1974 data and in combined cross section and time series analysis. See Swedenborg (1979, 1982) for more detail on the underlying model and the regression analysis.
7. It should be noted that Samuelsson does not himself draw that conclusion, but rather the opposite. He puts more stress on the fact that 'a knowledge advantage' explains foreign investment regardless of source country.
8. SOU, 1982: 15 found this to be true of Swedish MNEs as well as for foreign affiliates in Sweden compared to purely domestic firms.
9. Reddaway *et al.* (1968) for the UK, Hufbauer and Adler (1968), US Tariff Commission (1973), Lipsey and Weiss (1981), Horst (1978), Stobaugh *et al.* (1972), Frank and Freeman (1978) to mention some of the better known for the US and SOU, 1981: 33, SOU, 1981: 43, SOU, 1982: 15 aside from my own studies, Swedenborg (1979, 1982, the latter also published as SOU, 1982: 27), for Sweden.
10. The analysis is based on the same kind of equations as in Table 7.7. In the first step the value of foreign production is estimated using the SQ equation. In the second step, the estimated value of SQ $(S\hat{Q})$ is inserted in the SX equation. $S\hat{Q}$ is exogenous in the second equation and its coefficient shows the partial effect of an exogenous change in foreign production on exports. For proof that the model is identifiable and capable of estimation, see Swedenborg (1979, Appendix A).
11. The magnitudes cannot, of course, be stated with such exactness. What one can say is that with 95% probability the net effect is between 0.04 and 0.16 dollars when foreign production increases by $1. The important thing is, however, that it is probably small and probably positive.
12. This viewpoint permeates a recent government study on MNE impact on Sweden. See SOU, 1983: 17.

13. As noted earlier, the Bank of Sweden administers the regulations governing Swedish outward and inward investment. Until recently firms applying for permission to invest abroad had to demonstrate that the investment would have a positive effect on exports or permission would not be granted. Investment in foreign R&D production could not fulfil this requirement, at least not in any direct way. But more importantly, permission has not been granted because it has been considered 'good' if R&D production were retained in Sweden.

14. In his excellent survey (1983, Ch. 10) Caves shows that most, if not all, the policy issues which devolve from economic analysis deal not with total world income but with the distribution of income between and within countries. Political pressure to interfere with MNE growth can, therefore, be explained by a wish to alter the distribution of income.

REFERENCES

Caves, R. E. (1971). International corporations: the industrial economics of foreign investment **38**, *Economica*, February

Caves, R. E. (1983). *Multinational Enterprise and Economic Analysis*, Cambridge: Cambridge University Press

Clegg, J. (1985). *The Determinants of International Production: A Comparative Study of Five Developed Countries*, Ph.D. thesis University of Reading

Dunning, J. H. (1981). *International Production and the Multinational Enterprise*, London: Allen & Unwin

Frank, R. H. and Freeman, R. T. (1978). *Distributional Consequences of Direct Foreign Investment*, New York: Academic Press

Hirsch, Seev (1976). An international trade and investment theory of the firm, *Oxford Economic Papers*, **28**, July

Horst, Thomas (1973). The simple analytics of multinational firm behaviour, in M. B. Connolly and A. K. Swoboda (eds), *International Trade and Money*, London: Allen & Unwin

Horst, Thomas (1978). American exports and foreign direct investment, in F. C. Bergsten, T. Horst and T. H. Moran, *American Multinationals and American Interests*, Washington: Brookings Institution

Hufbauer, G. C. and Adler, M. F. (1968). *Overseas Manufacturing and the Balance of Payments*, Washington: Tax Policy Research Study No. 1, Treasury Dept.

Hymer, S. H. (1960). *The International Operations of National Firms: A Study of Direct Foreign Investment*, Ph.D. thesis 1960 and Cambridge, Mass: MIT Press, 1976

Kindleberger, C. P. (1969). *American Business Abroad. Six Lectures on Direct Investment*, New Haven: Yale University Press

Kojima, K. (1978). *Direct Foreign Investment: A Japanese Model of Multinational Business Operations*, New York: Praeger

Lipsey, R. E. and O'Connor (1982). Swedish Firms Acquired by Foreigners: A Comparison of Before and After Takeover, NBER Working Paper No. 1082, November

Lipsey, R. E., Kravis, I. B. and Roldan, R. A. (1982). Do multinational firms adapt factor proportions to relative factor prices? in Krueger, A. O. (ed.) *Trade and Employment in Developing Countries: 2, Factor Supply and Substitution*, Chicago: The University of Chicago Press

Lipsey, R. E. and Weiss, M. Y. (1981). Foreign production and exports in manufacturing industries, *Review of Economics and Statistics*, **63**, November

Reddaway, W. B., Potter, S. J. and Taylor, C. T. (1968). *Effects of UK Direct Investment Overseas: Final Report,* Cambridge: Cambridge University Press

Samuelsson, H. F. (1977). *Utländska direkta investeringar i Sverige* (Foreign Direct Investment in Sweden), Stockholm: Industriens Utredningsinstitut

SCB (1981). *Utlandsägda företag,* SM 1981: 5

SCB (1978). *Export av tjänster,* Promemorior från SCB 1978: 7

SOU, 1981: 33. *Effekter av investeringar utomlands. En studie av* sex industrier. (Effects of Investment Abroad. A Study of Six Industries.) Expert Report from the Commission on Direct Investment

SOU, 1981: 43. *De internationella investeringarnas effekter. Några fallstudier* (Effects of Investment Abroad. Some Case Studies). Expert Report from the Commission on Direct Investment

SOU, 1982: 15. *Internationella företag i svensk industri* (International Firms in Swedish Industry). Expert Report from the Commission on Direct Investment

SOU, 1983: 16. *Sysselsättningsstrukturen i industriella företag. En studie av utvecklingen i svensk industri 1966–80* (Employment Structure in Swedish Manufacturing 1966–80). Expert Report from the Commission on Direct Investment

SOU, 1983: 17. *Näringspolitiska effekter av internationella investeringar* (Effects of International Direct Investment). Final Report of the Commission of Direct Investment

Stobaugh, R. *et al,* (1972). *U.S. Multinational Enterprises and the U.S. Economy: A Research Study of the Major Industries that Account for 90 Per Cent of U.S. Foreign Direct Investment in Manufacturing,* Boston: Harvard Graduate School of Business Administration

Swedenborg, B. (1973). *Den svenska industrins investeringar i utlandet* (Swedish Manufacturing Investment Abroad), Stockholm: Industriens Utredningsinstitut

Swedenborg, B. (1975). Svenska, amerikanska och engelska utlandsinvestering några jämförelser (Swedish, US and UK investment abroad: some comparisons), in Lundgren, N. (ed.), *De internationella koncernerna och samhällsekonomin,* Stockholm: Rabén & Sjögren

Swedenborg, B. (1979). *The Multinational Operations of Swedish Firms. An Analysis of Determinants and Effects,* Stochholm: Industriens Utredningsinstitut

Swedenborg, B. (1980). Valutaregleringen och direkta investeringar (The Foreign Exchange Control Act and foreign direct investment), in *Valutareglering och ekonomisk politik* (SOU, 1980: 51)

Swedenborg, B. (1982). *Svensk industri i utlandet. En analys av drivkrafter och effekter* (Swedish Manufacturing Abroad. An Analysis of Determinants and Effects), Stockholm: Industriens Utredningsinstitut. Also published as SOU, 1982: 27

US Tariff Commission (1973). *Implications of Multinational Firms for World Trade and Investment and for U.S. Trade and Labour,* Washington: TL Publication 537

APPENDIX TABLE 7.A1   Net outward and inward direct investment in Sweden
1961–82
(million Skr at current prices)

	Outward	*Inward*
1. 1961	154	64
2. 1962	310	280
3. 1963	338	463
4. 1964	483	203
5. 1965	528	450
6. 1966	612	719
7. 1967	569	524
8. 1968	229	542
9. 1969	1,225	799
10. 1970	1,103	557
11. 1971	900	423
12. 1972	1,256	325
13. 1973	1,267	320
14. 1974	1,913	357
15. 1975	1,812	323
16. 1976	2,578	17
17. 1977	3,016	313
18. 1978	1,888	312
19. 1979	2,596	476
20. 1980	2,648	1,054
21. 1981	4,322	915
22. 1982	5,243	1,225

APPENDIX TABLE 7.A2   Some basic data on the role of foreign direct investment
in the Swedish economy
(Skr million current prices)

	1960	1965	1970	1978
GDP	72,190	113,450	172,230	412,450
Exports		20,540	35,150	98,210
Manuf. employment	880,260	938,910	921,780	874,230
Swedish MNEs in manufacturing				
Employment:				
in Sweden	—	325,980	395,990	416,230
in foreign manufacturing affiliates	105,510	147,805	182,650	227,820
in foreign sales and service affiliates	—	23,220	39,790	73,385
Foreign manufacturing affiliates				
Total assets	3,830	8,030	15,610	47,260
Swedish capital stake	—	3,010	5,300	14,130
Sales	—	8,530	16,038	56,990
Imports from Sw. parents	—	1,180	2,680	9,390
Exports:	—	1,010	2,770	13,700
of which to Sweden	—	120	400	1,950
Foreign MNEs in Sweden				
Employment:				
in manuf. affiliates	—	28,290	41,850	—
in other affiliates	—	11,320	15,660	—

Sources: Data on Swedish MNEs from the data bank of Industriens Utredningsinstitut.
Data on foreign MNEs in Sweden from Samuelsson (1977) and SCB (1981).

8

Belgium

DANIEL VAN DEN BULCKE

8.1 IMPORTANCE OF OUTWARD AND INWARD DIRECT INVESTMENT FOR THE BELGIAN ECONOMY: THE HISTORICAL BACKGROUND

Outward direct investment

An examination of the historical records shows that Cockerill of Belgium put up its first foreign manufacturing plant in Prussia in 1815. This pioneering venture in textile machinery was also probably the first foreign investment by any European firm (Franko, 1976). Although the Kingdom of Belgium was only founded in 1830 and John Cockerill was a British expatriate who built a steel mill in Liège, this early subsidiary is symbolic of the past prominence of outward foreign direct investment for a small and young country which played a major role in the industrialization of Europe and the world and is now confronted with important structural problems of its own.[1] It has been estimated that Belgian investment abroad reached $684 million in 1985 and $2 billion in 1914 (Alloo, 1953). This represents about 4.5% of the estimated world stock of FDI in 1914 (Dunning, 1983). Recent UN calculations indicate that Belgium's share in the direct investment total of all developed market economies was 1.3% in 1978 (UN CTC, 1983).

From 1880 to 1914, 1,189 companies took up the special legal status of a Belgian *société anonyme* which carried out most or all of its activities abroad. In 1914, 680 of these firms, which started out in railway construction and branched out into heavy metallurgy and mining, were still in existence.

The Société Générale played a very important role in the expansion of the world's railway network, especially through its subsidiary Société Belge des Chemins de Fer which had sizeable interests in France, Germany, and Austria. Before the First World War broke out, Belgium controlled 140 railway companies and 65 steel mills in developing countries. In total,

557 Belgian firms had been established in the lesser developed countries of that time, as compared with about 130 subsidiaries in the industrial countries (Frère, 1947).

Belgian investment abroad suffered a major setback when it lost its 161 companies located in Russia, as a result of the revolution of 1917. The Société Métallurgique Russo-Belge employed no less than 25,000 people. Belgian firms had been responsible for half of Russia's glass production, a third of its heavy metal products and a quarter of its coal. The First World War also caused important losses for Belgian companies in Germany, Austria, and France.

Except for the Belgian Congo (now Zaire), the inter-war period saw a retrenchment of Belgian foreign investment abroad. An important step for the Belgian expansion in Africa was the establishment in 1886 of the Compagnie du Congo pour le Commerce et l'Industrie (CCCI). Although 212 companies had been established in the Belgian Congo before 1914, it was only in 1910 that the first industrial ventures were set up. While investment in the Belgian Congo increased gradually during the inter-war period, a really strong expansion only occurred after 1945.

When the Belgian Congo acquired its independence in 1960, most colonial companies had their administrative headquarters located in Belgium, while their social and economic activity took place in Zaire, and 60% of these 500 firms transferred their assets to Zairan subsidiaries. After 1965 the 'zairization' or nationalization of foreign companies was promulgated. However, during the mid 1970s the Zairan economy was doing so badly that most of these foreign companies were returned to their previous owners. Even today, more than half of the Belgian affiliates in developing countries of its largest MNE are located in Africa, with half of them in Zaire. The African orientation of Belgium's largest MNE is highlighted by the fact that only one out of five of the MNEs originating in eighteen industrial countries has subsidiaries in Africa (UN CTC, 1983).

Since the beginning of the 1970s Belgian direct investment abroad has started to rise again. There are even indications that it is growing faster than other Western European countries. From 1965 to 1967 the flow of Belgian direct investment abroad represented 1.7% of the total Western European flow. During 1974–6 and 1977–9 this proportion increased to 3 and 5.5% respectively. While Belgian direct investment abroad varied around 1% of its own gross capital formation before 1970, it reached 2.5% during the 1970s, which is about the average for the rest of the developed market countries.

It was also at the beginning of the 1970s that the Belgian authorities decided to encourage outward direct investment. First, the public investment company Société belge d'investissement international (SBI) made it possible to subscribe to the equity capital of Belgian foreign subsidiaries and to grant loans at the going rate of interest in the Belgian capital market for five to ten years' maturity. Secondly, the government authorities allowed the Office National du Ducroire (OND) to insure against political risks and other catastrophes. In comparison with most other developed countries, Belgium was rather late in setting up these facilities. To the extent that commercial ventures abroad grow into industrial subsidiaries (Newbould, Buckley, and Thurlwell, 1978), the decision to allow the Foreign Trade Office (1975) to intervene in the establishment expenses of a foreign sales subsidiary indirectly assisted foreign direct investment. In 1979, new directives were issued concerning the tax treatment of Belgian nationals carrying on an activity in non-European countries for which there were no double-taxation conventions. Finally, in July 1981, the Belgian Office of Development Cooperation created a development cooperation fund (Fonds de Cooperation au Développement) which allows Belgian bilateral assistance to be used as loans to or shareholdings in Belgian firms established in developing countries. This new instrument is, however, restricted to semi-public or public enterprises in the developing countries and to national or regional development banks.

Inward direct investment

The stock of inward direct investment in Belgium was estimated at $9.6 billion in 1978, that is twice as high as the stock of Belgian outward direct investment. From 1967 to 1978 the stock of foreign direct investment in Belgium increased more rapidly than in Western Europe and the developed market economies as a whole. The contribution of the flow of direct investment to gross fixed capital formation, which rarely surpassed 2% for all developed market economies and never got higher than 3% for Western European countries, varied in Belgium between 5 and 8.5% from 1967 onwards. The ratio between the annual flows of inward and outward direct investment for all market developed economies oscillated, for practically the whole period 1965-1979, between 0.4 and 0.8, thereby indicating that outgoing flows surpassed incoming capital flows. For Western Europe, this ratio between inward and outward flows was close to one until 1975, but came down afterwards. Except for 1979, inward investment in Belgium has been at least two to three times as important as that of outward investment.

Quite rightly the Bureau du Plan considers the multinationalization of Belgian industry as one of its main structural characteristics. In 1975, subsidiaries of foreign companies provided 33% of total employment in 'he

Belgian manufacturing sector. These same subsidiaries accounted for 44% of Belgian industry's sales. Over one half (55%) of the foreign subsidiaries established in Belgium come from the partner countries belonging to the European Community. American enterprises reached 36% of the total number of foreign subsidiaries and 40% of their total industrial employment. Some American firms (e.g. Bell-ITT) have been in Belgium for about a hundred years. Whereas on average barely 3.7% of all enterprises in 1975 had at least 10% of their equity capital owned by foreigners, the proportion was 50% for enterprises with over 1,000 employees and 48% for those with between 500 and 999 workers (Van Den Bulcke *et al.,* 1978).

During the 1960s and the beginning of the 1970s the rate of growth in Belgium was quite high. From 1960 to 1974 GNP in real prices nearly doubled. Crucial to this favourable development was the modernization of the West European economies which followed the founding of the European Economic Community and the resulting strong demand for the products of Belgian heavy industry, notably steel, non-ferrous metals, chemicals, and glass. Because of its central geographical position in Western Europe and its favourable investment climate—which received an extra push from the government assistance provided under the so-called expansion legislation (1959, 1966, 1970)—many foreign, especially American, enterprises flocked to Belgium during this period. Although the general aims of the expansion laws were to stimulate the national and regional economy by creating jobs and launching a technological renewal, and the various incentives applied to all firms, the evidence points to foreign MNEs responding to these stimuli more positively than local firms. This was first because the new foreign plants had greater mobility to locate in the regions offering the greatest advantages. Secondly, as the most important incentives under the expansion legislation were of a financial nature (especially interest subsidies) the more capital-intensive MNEs were encouraged relative to the local firms (Van Den Bulcke *et al.,* 1971; Yannopoulous and Dunning, 1976).

The changed conditions of economic growth since 1973–4 have posed many difficulties for Belgian industry. To quote from a recent publication:

> With a very open national economy, oriented largely towards European export markets, Belgium has been strikingly vulnerable to slackening demand for heavy industry goods. Steel, not surprisingly, has been the most dramatic case. In addition, high wages and salaries, a relatively strong currency during much of the 1970s—with a Belgian franc effectively within the orbit of the Deutsche Mark—and an increasingly strained and expensive social security system, have led to high labour costs by international standards. And this has been a factor working against new foreign investment, which would anyway have been less buoyant than in the 1960s. (Bank Brussels Lambert, 1983).

The comparison between the pre- and post-crisis period clearly shows how the rate of economic growth broke down (7.1% for 1965–73 and 1.2% for 1973–8). The less rapid growth of exports after 1973 (2.9% as compared with 10.3% between 1965–73), together with an increase in imports, caused disequilibrium in the trade balance. Industry, which was considered as the propellant of economic growth, slowed down to such an extent that de-industrialization became a serious worry (Jacquemin, 1976). From 1973 to 1978 Belgian industry lost over 200,000 jobs, or one-sixth of its workforce. That the share of manufacturing industry in total employment decreased from 33% in 1970 to 25.9% in 1979, was, however, mainly due to the bad performance of indigenous firms. While the net annual rate of growth of new employment creation by foreign subsidiaries (excluding take-overs) between 1968 and 1975 amounted to 5.1% and added 80,000 jobs, Belgian firms registered an annual loss of 1.7% which was equivalent to the elimination of more than 90,000 positions. From 1975 to 1978 another 120,000 jobs were lost by Belgian firms (annual rate of growth of -6.3%). During the same period, foreign subsidiaries still succeeded in withstanding the aftermath of the crisis ($+2,400$ jobs and an annual rate of growth of 0.2%) (Van Den Bulcke and Halsberghe, 1979). Although Belgian MNEs played a role in the loss of industrial employment[2] there are some indications that in the metal sector the uninational firms and especially the holding companies were the main cause for the continuation of the loss of jobs. However, from 1978–80 the foreign subsidiaries in the metal sector also started to shed jobs. Yet their employment performance compares favourably with that of domestic firms (Fabrimetal, 1981).

In 1975, subsidiaries of foreign MNEs employed about 331,000 workers in Belgium. When the jobs provided by Belgian MNEs in Belgium itself (155,000) are added to this, it can be seen that almost half (48%) of the workers in Belgian manufacturing industry were employed either by a foreign or a Belgian MNE. That MNEs dominate Belgian manufacturing is also illustrated by the fact that 45% of the 522 largest Belgian manufacturing companies in 1978 were foreign affiliates, three-quarters of which were in the metal and chemical sector. Of these larger enterprises 13% were Belgian MNEs, with half of them in metals, while 42% were local uninational firms.[3]

Multinational enterprises also proliferate in the Belgian service sector. The evidence is rather patchy, however. In 1977, 50 of the 88 Belgian commercial banks were controlled from abroad. Although these foreign banks employed only 8% of the total jobs in the banking sector, because they engage in wholesale banking, they accounted for about one-third of all assets and liabilities. Out of a total of 150 advertising bureaux only 23 were foreign-owned but they accounted for two-fifths of total employment, two-thirds of total sales, and one-third of all accounts. These foreign offices generally offer a more complete and sophisticated package of services than their local competitors. In the insurance sector, the leading firms are of Belgian origin. Yet the foreign insurance companies represent two-thirds of the total number of firms and about two-fifths of the total premiums (Van Den Bulcke *et al.*, 1978). Belgium has also attracted a relatively high number of American regional office headquarters in and around Brussels. The employment provided by these offices, in both the broad and the narrow sense, has been estimated at 15,000 to 20,000 jobs in 1979 (Van Den Bulcke and Van Pachterbeke, 1984).

8.2   INDUSTRIAL DISTRIBUTION, SIZE AND CONCENTRATION OF INWARD AND OUTWARD INVESTING FIRMS IN BELGIUM

Industrial distribution

Using employment data, Table 8.1 shows that chemicals (including rubber and petroleum) and metals are the most multinationalized industrial sectors, as foreign and indigenous MNEs taken together provide respectively 80 and 60% of the employment in these sectors (1975). About half of the employment in non-metallic minerals and about one-third in food, beverages and tobacco also results from the activities of MNEs. In textiles and clothing, wood and paper and other industries the contribution to sectoral employment by foreign and domestic MNEs amounts to about 20%.

The comparison between the relative distribution of employment of foreign-owned subsidiaries and the relative distribution of the total Belgian manufacturing industry on the basis of a so-called concentration coefficient, gives some idea of the sectoral specialization of this former group of firms. A coefficient which is higher than 1 shows that foreign subsidiaries are relatively more present in a particular sector than Belgian and foreign firms combined. The sectors which in 1975 registered a coefficient of 1.5 or more are electronics (2.4), tobacco (2.3), transport equipment (2.1), rubber and petroleum (1.9), chemicals (1.7), and paper (1.5). Foreign enterprises are much less involved in iron and steel (0.2), textiles and clothing (0.4), beverages (0.4), food (0.6), and machine construction (0.7). Apart from chemicals, and food and beverages, where these concentration coefficients had been as high as 2.6 and 1.7 in 1968, no major changes have

TABLE 8.1   Multinational enterprises and their share in Belgian manufacturing
employment (1975)

Sectors	(1) Foreign subsidiaries		(2) Belgian MNEs[c]		(3) = (1) + (2) All MNEs	
	N^a	$\%^b$	N	$\%^b$	N	$\%^b$
Food, beverages and tobacco	23.2	22	14.6	13	37.9	35
Textiles and clothing	22.8	13	15.2	9	38.0	22
Wood and paper	15.1	19	3.5	4	18.6	23
Chemicals, rubber and petroleum	60.4	57	24.3	23	84.7	80
Non-metallic mineral products	20.8	29	13.5	19	34.4	48
Metals	186.9	40	80.2	18	267.0	60
Other industries	2.2	18			2.2	18
Total	331.4	33	151.3	15	482.8	48

[a]Thousand employees.
[b]As percentage of *total* employment in the manufacturing sectors.
[c]Employment in Belgium only.
Source: D. Van Den Bulcke *et al.* (1978).

occurred since 1968 (Van Den Bulcke *et al.,* 1978). Within the group of
foreign subsidiaries, American groups dominate in rubber and petroleum,
transport equipment, machine construction, and pharmaceuticals. EC
parent companies are relatively more present in chemicals, non-metallic
minerals, and textiles and clothing.

Table 8.2 presents the share of foreign-owned enterprises in the total
sales of Belgian manufacturing industries using the NACE 2-digit code.
The table also distinguishes between US and EC subsidiaries. Mineral oil
refining (78%) and electrical engineering (87%) show the highest participation coefficients for foreign subsidiaries.

If one ranks the Belgian manufacturing industries on the basis of the
NACE 3-digit code according to their relative importance and the share of
total sales being realized by foreign subsidiaries, one finds that those sectors in which the foreign share is more than 50% represent almost two-
fifths (37.5%) of the total sales of foreign-owned enterprises. Most of the
sub-sectors of the chemical industry (including petroleum and rubber) and
of electrical and mechanical engineering, as well as several branches of the
transportation equipment sector, belong to this strongly controlled group.
The remaining chemical and engineering branches, as well as some sub-
sectors out of metal products and food and beverages, take up a middle

TABLE 8.2   Share of foreign enterprises in the total sales of Belgian manufacturing industries (NACE 2-digit) (1975)

NACE 2-digit code	Sectors	All foreign subsidiaries %	US subsidiaries %	EC subsidiaries %
14.	Mineral oil refining	77.7	42.5	35.2
22.	Production and preliminary processing of metals	16.1	1.8	12.1
23.	Extractions of minerals	3.1	—	3.1
24.	Non-metallic minerals	21.0	4.1	16.9
25.	Chemicals	55.8	21.8	34.0
26.	Man-made fibres	66.3	59.2	7.1
31.	Metal articles	20.2	9.2	11.0
32.	Mechanical engineering	57.7	47.1	10.6
33.	Office and data processing machinery	29.7	25.6	4.1
34.	Electrical engineering	87.3	34.6	37.5
35.	Motor vehicles and parts	54.7	40.4	14.3
36.	Other means of transport	17.0	3.2	9.2
37.	Instrument engineering	30.8	22.3	7.2
41–42.	Food, beverages and tobacco	22.5	6.9	11.5
43.	Textiles	11.3	4.0	7.3
44.	Leather goods	7.8	7.4	0.3
45.	Footwear and clothing	17.3	5.4	10.7
46.	Timber and wood	1.3	0.1	1.2
47.	Paper, printing and publishing	30.4	8.5	21.9
48.	Rubber and plastics	59.8	37.0	22.8
49.	Other manufacturing	2.6	1.5	1.1

Source: Sleuwaegen and Van Den Bulcke (1983).

position as between 25 to 49.9% of their sales are carried out by foreign
subsidiaries. This smaller, moderately controlled intermediate group
represents only 13% of total sales by foreign-owned subsidiaries in
Belgium. The other sectors, with a foreign participation ratio of less than
0.25, account for half of the total sales of foreign affiliates. This group is
dominated by the more traditional sectors such as textiles, footwear and
clothing, lumber, wood and furniture, production and preliminary processing of metals, mineral and metal products, and food and beverages. Foreign subsidiaries clearly thrive best in the technologically more advanced
sectors where ownership advantages tend to be of the utmost importance.
They account for more than three-quarters of total sales in agricultural
machinery, telecommunications and electronic equipment, steel tubes,
radio and TV sets, manufacture of plant equipment, mineral oil refining,

and motor vehicles and engines. In another twelve sub-sectors the share of foreign-owned enterprises surpasses 50% of total sales.

The presentation of the sectoral distribution of foreign subsidiaries gave a first indication of the product and process structure of foreign-owned subsidiaries. A more direct comparison indicates that, compared with Belgian firms, foreign subsidiaries produce more semi-finished products and raw materials (Haex, Halsberghe, and Van Den Bulcke, 1979). This phenomenon is probably linked to the extensive intra-group trading by MNEs. Moreover, a comparison of a relatively large sample of 100 companies which provided data for the surveys of 1968 and 1976 showed that the number of producers of semi-finished and raw materials had actually increased more rapidly than for finished products. This points to the conclusion that relatively more foreign subsidiaries have been given a specific role in the global sourcing system of the multinationals. According to some authors, the establishment and development of the EEC has encouraged a processs of Europeanization of activities by rationalizations on a horizontal basis, to achieve economies of scale through a more advanced division of production (Fishwick, 1982).

Size

It is generally acknowledged that foreign subsidiaries are relatively larger than domestic firms. This is confirmed for Belgium by several sets of data. First, evidence from a survey carried out on foreign direct investment in Belgium (Van Den Bulcke *et al.*, 1978) shows that foreign-owned industrial enterprises employed on average 343 people as compared with only 37 for all enterprises in Belgian manufacturing industry. Foreign subsidiaries surpassed the national average in all sectors. Secondly, the average size of foreign firms, measured by total sales in 1975, shows that domestically-controlled enterprises achieved only 0.02 billion Belgian francs for all foreign subsidiaries and 0.94 for US and 0.63 for EC firms (Sleuwaegen and Van Den Bulcke, 1983).

Thirdly, a highly representative sample of 221 Belgian firms (including 30 Belgian MNEs) and 262 foreign subsidiaries,[4] which was limited to companies with at least 20 employees in 1976, showed that foreign subsidiaries, with an average of 595 employees, provided more than twice as many jobs per company as Belgian uninational firms (251 employees), although Belgian MNEs brought the average employment size for all Belgian firms up to 720. The same sample indicates that the average annual sales in 1976 were four times as high in foreign subsidiaries than in uninational firms (1.89 billion Belgian francs as compared with 0.47 billion Belgian francs). Inclusion of the activities of Belgian MNEs in

Belgium brings this turnover (1.37 billion Belgian francs) for the total sample much closer to that of foreign subsidiaries (Haex, Halsberghe, and Van Den Bulcke, 1979).

To find out to what extent these differences could be attributed to differences among and within sectors two other analyses were carried out. First the average size per company was calculated as if foreign subsidiaries had the same sectoral distribution as local uninational firms. Although the size of foreign subsidiaries is almost halved (down to 0.96 billion Belgian francs), this is still almost twice as high as for uninational firms. American subsidiaries averaged 2.1 billion sales per year before the similation procedure and remained the largest group of subsidiaries at a level of 1.2 billion Belgian francs (as compared with 0.77 for EC companies) after the elimination of the sectoral differences. A second method to isolate the effects of differences due to the industry composition from the intra-industry differences is the so-called shift and share technique which is often used in regional studies (Sleuwaegen and Van Den Bulcke, 1983). Table 8.3 confirms that the differences between foreign-owned and domestic firms within industries, that is after correction for sectoral mix effects, are an important factor. The differential component, indicating the differences within industries, is much larger than the proportional component, which is based on differences due to industry composition. The negative sign of both these components results from the fact that the smaller domestic enterprises were used as the reference group, while the foreign subsidiaries were regarded as the norm group.

TABLE 8.3   Average size in terms of annual sales of foreign and Belgian enterprises: a shift and share analysis (1976)
(Bel. f millions)

	Comparison between domestic and foreign enterprises[a]	Comparison between US and EC subsidiaries[b]
Average size		
Reference group	23.63	936.70
Norm group	745.78	629.86
Nominal difference	722.15	306.84
Proportional component	− 193.83	310.57
Differential component	− 526.40	− 22.62
Specific component		
Reference group	− 1.91	− 9.69
Norm group	0	28.58

[a]Domestic firms: reference group; foreign firms: norm group.
[b]US subsidiaries: reference group; EC subsidiaries: norm group.
Source: Sleuwaegen and Van Den Bulcke (1983).

The differences between US and EC subsidiaries are almost entirely explained by the different industrial composition of the industrial ventures originating within these countries. The negative sign of the differential component means that, on average, affiliates of EC subsidiaries are larger within certain industries. The specific component has to do with the absence of certain enterprises in particular industries.

Concentration

MNEs have acquired a substantial share of the Belgian market. About one in four foreign manufacturing subsidiaries estimated that they controlled half or more of the Belgian market for their most important product. Only one out of seven Belgian uninational enterprises considered themselves to have a market share of more than 50%. If Belgian MNEs are included one out of five Belgian enterprises dominate more than half of their local market. American subsidiaries more often hold a relatively large slice of the Belgian market than the EC firms. The construction of a matched sample of 93 foreign and domestic firms, and the ensuing result that slightly more Belgian than foreign firms held a market position of 50% or more, indicate that dominating market positions of foreign subsidiaries are sectorally determined and oligopolistic situations occur more frequently in some sectors than others. In non-metallic minerals and electronics, not one Belgian firm attained a market share of 30% for its products, while 38 and 60% of the foreign subsidiaries in these sectors had control of such a large market share (Haex, Halsberghe, and Van Den Bulcke, 1979).

Together with the share of foreign enterprises in the 3-digit NACE sectors, Table 8.4 presents the C_4 concentration ratio, that is the share in total sales of the four largest enterprises. As high C_4 ratios occur both at the beginning and at the end of the ranked sectors, it can be concluded that concentration is not only high in sectors dominated by foreign subsidiaries. The correlation coefficients between, on the one hand, foreign control as measured by the share of total sales, and on the other hand three of the most often used concentration indices confirm this. For C_4 the correlation coefficient amounts to 0.334, while for the Herfindahl index and the entropy measure respectively 0.330 and -0.358 is found. The aggregate results of different concentration measures indicate that multinational firms are not of major importance for the market structure in Belgium. With the exception of mineral oil refining and man-made fibres, where the concentration among the individual firms is much more important than between the groups of US and EC subsidiaries and domestic enterprises, for the other sectors the reverse situation applies, which indicates that the concentration among these groups is more important than within the groups.

TABLE 8.4 Share of foreign enterprises in the total sales of Belgian manufacturing industries and concentration coefficients
(NACE 3-digit) (1975)

Rank: Sector (NACE 3-digit)	Percentage share of foreign subsidiaries	C_4 concentration measure	Entropy measure
Strongly controlled sectors ($C_4 > 50$ p.c.)			
1. Agricultural machinery (321)	99.0	0.98	1.15792
2. Telecommunications and electronic equipment (344)	99.0	0.91	2.02173
3. Steel tubes (222)	85.9	0.98	1.88100
4. Radio and TV sets (345)	83.4	0.94	2.94100
5. Manufacture of plant equipment (325)	79.2	0.78	3.94900
6. Mineral oil refining (140)	77.6	0.92	2.81400
7. Motor vehicles and engines (351)	75.6	0.83	4.02800
8. Basic industrial chemicals (251)	73.7	0.59	4.56500
9. Tobacco (429)	71.4	0.75	3.25700
10. Processing of plastics (483)	69.4	0.69	6.00100
11. Aerospace equipment (364)	67.5	1.00	2.68600
12. Electrical industrial appliances (343)	64.7	0.52	4.34500
13. Machinery for food, chemical and related industries (324)	63.3	0.53	4.43300
14. Pharmaceutical products (257)	61.6	0.60	4.76500
15. Glass products (247)	61.1	0.80	2.58472
16. Transmission equipment (326)	60.0	0.58	3.69900
17. Rubber products (481)	53.6	0.78	3.12200
18. Other chemical products (256)	52.9	0.65	4.67300
19. Electrical machinery (342)	51.9	0.85	3.71100
Moderately controlled sector ($25 < C_4 \leqslant 50$ p.c.)			
20. Paint industry (255)	47.3	0.74	4.80000
21. Soap, detergents and toiletries (258)	43.3	0.70	4.22900
22. Other food products (423)	37.5	0.94	5.86800
23. Tools and finished metal goods (except electrical) (316)	33.9	0.44	6.40100
24. Vegetable and animal oils (411)	31.7	1.00	2.89100
25. Boilers and sheet metal containers (315)	29.5	0.89	5.96500

TABLE 8.4 *(continued)*

Rank: Sector (NACE 3-digit)	Percentage share of foreign subsidiaries	C_4 concentration measure	Entropy measure
26. Cables and wires (341)	28.6	1.00	2.38500
27. Machine tools and equipment (322)	28.4	0.64	5.45600
28. Dairy products (413)	26.8	0.83	5.59500
29. Cocoa, chocolate and sugar confectionery (421)	25.2	0.80	5.46100
Less controlled sectors ($C_4 \leqslant 25$ p.c.)			
30. Wine production of fresh grapes (425)	24.8	1.00	2.48600
31. Cement products for construction (243)	24.5	0.72	6.89000
32. Clay products (241)	23.9	1.00	6.39500
33. Cement, lime and plaster (242)	23.7	1.00	2.89400
34. Foundries (311)	22.5	0.88	5.52300
35. Electrical domestic appliances (346)	22.0	0.73	5.20100
36. Ready made clothing (453–454)	20.7	0.41	4.97629
37. Semi-finished wood products (462)	19.2	1.00	4.86100
38. Processing of fruit and vegetables (414)	18.8	0.97	4.45700
39. Carpets and other floor coverings (438)	18.5	0.71	5.46900
40. Alcohol distillation (424)	17.6	1.00	4.33400
41. Production of non-ferrous metals (224)	16.7	0.84	3.38500
42. Textile machinery (323)	16.3	0.93	2.70600
43. Structural metal products (314)	15.1	0.64	7.98100
44. Railway and tramway rolling-stock (362)	14.5	1.00	1.39600
45. Drawing and cold rolling of steel (223)	14.2	0.92	3.47500
46. Soft drinks (428)	14.0	1.00	4.42400
47. Furs and fur goods (456)	13.1	1.00	0.85240
48. Silk (433)	12.8	1.00	3.58600
49. Household textiles (455)	12.7	0.81	5.57600
50. Ceramic products (248)	12.2	1.00	4.48200
51. Cork and other plaiting materials (466)	11.3	1.00	5.34300
52. Iron and steel (221)	10.9	1.00	2.49100
53. Brewing and malting (427)	10.7	1.00	5.74200

Source: Sleuwaegen and Van Den Bulcke (1983)

8.3   IMPACT ON INDUSTRIAL STRUCTURE OF INWARD AND OUTWARD INVESTMENT

Motives and development of inward and outward investment

In theory, a distinction can be made between first-stage and second-stage impact of MNE activity on market structure (Dunning, 1981). The available evidence in the Belgian case, however, does not allow such neat distinctions. Besides, even if the behaviour of foreign affiliates should be distinctive, it is often difficult to draw conclusions as to their effects on market structure.

An earlier survey of the motives of new foreign industrial enterprises locating in Belgium since the end of the Second World War showed that the labour market situation, infrastructure and central geographical location, the fiscal system, government incentives, and credit facilities were most often quoted as positive factors (respectively 46, 40, 38, 37, and 36% of the 261 responding firms (Van Den Bulcke *et al.,* 1971)). A second survey indicated that between 1968 and 1976 only minor changes in the ranking of these factors had occurred. The advantageous central location of Belgium in the European Economic Community and Western Europe, which had already been the main attraction for US investors before 1968, came out on top as it was cited by 62% of the 90 responding MNEs. That the quantitative and qualitative aspects of the labour market were less highly ranked was probably due to the economic crisis. In both the 1968 and 1976 surveys the advantages offered by national and regional government authorities ranked quite high in the scale of preference of foreign MNEs to locate in Belgium. The average wage level which became increasingly negative for location in Belgium was largely compensated by the high productivity of Belgian workers. In fact, labour productivity ranked second in the 1976 survey and was quoted by more than half of the responding subsidiaries (Halsberghe and Van Den Bulcke, 1978).

A third and more recent survey, which also included commercial enterprises, largely confirmed the above findings. Belgium's central geographical position was quoted as positive by three out of four foreign subsidiaries, while several other infrastructural and most labour market aspects (availability and qualifications) were mentioned by 40–50% of the responding companies (Vlaams Economisch Verbond, 1981). It should be stressed that access to other EC countries is closely linked with the favourable locational advantages of the Belgian economy.

According to the Ministry of Economic Affairs, 1,263 industrial enterprises and 12,093 trade and service sector enterprises were set up in

Belgium between 1959 and 1981. Between 1959 and 1963 an average of 50 foreign-controlled industrial enterprises had been established per year. For the periods 1964–8 and 1969–73 the annual average was as high as 70 firms. While nearly 80 new firms were set up in 1974, the number of new foreign industrial establishments fell, compared to the preceding periods, by a half in 1974–8 to only 35 per year. Since then the number of new plants being put up by foreign MNEs has continued to diminish (Van Den Bulcke, 1983a).

Although this development of receding new foreign direct investment is not restricted to Belgium, it is much more vulnerable to shifts in the investment policy of MNEs. Data from the National Institute of Statistics suggest that from 1970 to 1976 about 80% of all *new* industrial investment was made by foreign subsidiaries. In 1977 this proportion was down to 40%. Although there was a rise to over 50% in 1979, the share of foreign firms in new Belgian industrial investment decreased again in the following years. Not only did foreign subsidiaries put up less investment funds in general, their higher capital intensity resulted in a smaller contribution to new employment. During 1970–5 foreign subsidiaries had provided over half of the newly created jobs in Belgian industry. While foreign MNEs still made a little over a half of new investment in 1979, they contributed only one-tenth of the new jobs.

The number of foreign subsidiaries established by Belgian MNEs expanded tremendously during the 1970s. About half of all existing foreign subsidiaries in 1975 had been set up in the preceding five-year period. Of the foreign affiliates of Belgian MNEs in the metal sector which existed in 1981, 30% had been set up after 1978, while three out of five had been launched after 1971. Although undue weight should not be given to the responses of the top managers of MNEs about their reasons for investing abroad, the survey method provides some interesting indications. A detailed study of the location motives of 30 Belgian MNEs showed that marketing factors dominated in both developed and developing countries as they were mentioned for 43 and 32% of all subsidiaries. Cost factors took second place and were relevant for 16% of the subsidiaries in industrial countries and 26% in developing countries. Investment climate, the advantages of internationalization and trade barriers were less important. Within the group of market factors, those mentioned most frequently were the need to acquire better market knowledge (8.5% of the subsidiaries) or to maintain a market position (7.5%), or to increase the existing market share (7.5%). However, cost elements such as lower wages (7%) and transport costs (6.5%) which come into fourth and fifth position, rank first and second for the developing countries. In 1975, only 13% of all foreign subsidiaries were located in developing countries. Almost two-thirds of all Belgian subsidiaries were established within the

European Community. It should also be mentioned that about half of the 96 Belgian industrial parent companies were actually binational firms as they had production sites only in Belgium and one foreign country. Not more than 16 Belgian MNEs owned plants in five or more countries (Haex and Van Den Bulcke, 1979).

Method of entry

It has been stated that internalization is 'a powerful motive for take-overs or mergers and a valuable tool in the strategy of oligopolists' (Dunning, 1981). MNEs more often acquire existing companies than indigenous firms as they use take-overs as a means to penetrate local markets. While green-field entry brings in a new competitor, a take-over leaves concentration initially unchanged. 'Entry by acquisition can have a pro-competitive significance if the MNE picks up and revives a failing business or uses its non-production assets to make the acquired company more effective' (Caves, 1982).

Although it is hard to draw general conclusions about market structure on the basis of the method of entry, the following considerations have to be taken into account. First, there has been an increasing tendency to use acquisitions as a route for foreign MNEs to penetrate the Belgian market and for Belgian MNEs to acquire a foothold in other industrial countries. During 1973–5, 38% of the foreign subsidiaries in Belgium resulted from the take-over of a local company. The share of acquisitions was only 30% for those MNEs which entered during 1969–72 and even less during previous periods. The tendency for a gradual increase of acquisitions as a method of entry to the Belgian market was evident for both US and EC subsidiaries (Van Den Bulcke *et al.*, 1978). During 1968 and 1975, 57,000 jobs lost the Belgian identity as local enterprises became foreign-owned by acquisition. This employment shift represented 17.7% of the total employment in foreign-owned enterprises in 1975. Two-thirds of these employment changes resulting from take-overs were carried out by EEC enterprises, while 28% was due to US initiatives and only 6% by firms from other countries. Take-overs in the opposite direction, that is of foreign subsidiaries by Belgian firms, occurred much less frequently and involved only 6,250 jobs (of which 55% were in former US firms) (Van Den Bulcke and Halsberghe, 1979).

Secondly, there are indications that after an initial decline in employment, due to restructuring and rationalization efforts, foreign acquisitions succeeded in increasing their employment after only a few years (Van Den

Bulcke *et al.,* 1971). Yet foreign acquisitions have performed less well in terms of employment expansion than green-field investments. As compared with the existing employment level of 1968, newly built plants had in 1975 realized a net expansion of about 60% as compared with 11% for take-overs. During 1975–6 a negative employment effect was registered as the employment expansion of some acquired enterprises was eliminated by the losses in other enterprises that had been taken over.

Thirdly, to the extent that companies which would otherwise have run into serious difficulties are taken over, the real effect of take-overs is more positive and can be compared with green-field investments. Only about one out of five cases of foreign acquisition which took place before 1968 was the result of the one-sided initiative of a foreign MNE. Since then there have been several cases in Belgium where foreign MNEs were the only candidates for the take-over of ailing companies, even after an active government search. In one-third of all cases the initiative was taken by the indigenous company, while in another quarter the take-over was the result of a mixed initiative by the local and the foreign enterprise. The three most important reasons for indigenous companies to approach foreign MNEs with a proposal for take-over were internal financial problems (38%), shortage of capital for expansion (29%), and the need for new products (17%) (Van Den Bulcke *et al.,* 1971). Belgian firms which took the initiative to sell out to foreign MNEs did so because they needed the financial means and the technological knowhow to safeguard their market position or to continue their expansion. Without this foreign intervention, and assuming that no Belgian enterprise could have replaced the foreign MNE, this results in a positive contribution to the Belgian economy.

Comparative performance of foreign subsidiaries, domestic firms, and Belgian multinationals

A previous section enumerated the major locational advantages of the Belgian economy: central location, labour market, and government policy towards foreign companies. The ownership advantages which are necessary for foreign firms actually to invest abroad have been characterized as being of three main types (Dunning, 1981). The first stems from size, monopoly power, and better resource usage. As it has already been shown that foreign subsidiaries are generally larger than indigenous Belgian firms and that a certain number are situated in highly concentrated industries and thus have a certain market power, in the next paragraphs special attention will be given to the study of the use of resources or the economic performance.

The second type of ownership leverage has to do with the fact that subsidiaries, contrary to uninational firms, do not always have to bear their full costs as they benefit from many of the endowments (e.g. R&D and marketing) of the parent company.

The third type of advantage is an extension of the previous two and is derived specifically from the multinationality of the company. The more globally an MNE is oriented the more it should be able to take advantage of different factor endowments and market situations. Multinational subsidiaries should thus not only be better performers than indigenous firms, but there should also be differences among foreign affiliates according to the degree of multinationality. Although this latter point will not be dealt with, there are indications that the performance of foreign subsidiaries in Belgium is related to the increasing global strategy of MNEs.[5]

(a) Discriminant analysis

Starting from a list of 64 economic, financial, and behavioural characteristics in a highly representative sample of 170 foreign subsidiaries and 170 indigenous firms, a discriminant analysis was carried out to isolate the most distinctive features of the foreign enterprises (Haex, Halsberghe, and Van Den Bulcke, 1979). Discriminant analysis allows us to deal with many characteristics at the same time and can be used to classify enterprises in sub-groups on the basis of their respective scores. After a number of tests 20 variables were selected for a detailed analysis. These are set out in Table 8.5.

The results of this analysis showed that there were indeed distinctive differences between foreign subsidiaries on the one hand and Belgian enterprises on the other hand. In a confusion matrix only 14% of the Belgian firms were wrongly labelled as foreign subsidiaries, while 21% of the foreign enterprises were classified as indigenous firms. Further details are set out in Appendix 8A at the end of this chapter. The restriction of this analysis to uninational enterprises instead of including all Belgian firms did not significantly change the results.

It is rather remarkable that the sectoral distribution gives very similar results for the simulated and actual classification, at least with the exception of the metal industry. The most discriminating variables are competitive pressure, use of R&D of other firms, the rate of profitability, and the sales per employee as a measure of productivity. Each of these factors was highly discriminating for all of the companies and for four out of the five large sectors out of Table 8.5. The skill ratio (employees as a percentage of total personnel) was also an important discriminating factor. The market share was only important for the chemical industry while R&D orientation and intensity was relevant only to firms in the metal sector.

When Belgian MNEs are compared with uninational firms, the variables with the highest discriminating values were financial strength (share of self-financing and debt ratio and solvency ratios), R&D and advertising intensity, export ratio, sales per employee and, to a lesser extent, the rate of return.

TABLE 8.5   Most important discriminating variables between foreign subsidiaries and local firms in Belgium (1976)

Variables	All sectors	Metals	Wood and paper	Non-metallic minerals	Chemicals	Food and beverages
K_1 : competitive pressure between 1970–6	×	×	×	×	×	
K_2 : market share					×	
K_3 : research activity		×				
K_4 : use of R&D from other firms	×	×	×	×		×
K_5 : R&D expenditures as % of sales		×	×			
K_6 : trade union membership					×	×
K_7 : wages as % of total sales					×	
K_8 : average wage level of workers						
K_9 : average level of salaries of employees						
K_{10}: employees as % of total personnel	×	×	×			×
K_{11}: women as % of total personnel			×	×		×
K_{12}: marketing personnel as % of total personnel			×	×	×	
K_{13}: advertising expenditures as % of total sales						
K_{14}: relative importance of self-financing					×	×
K_{15}: credit capital as % of total capital		×				×
K_{16}: long-term credit capital as % of net fixed assets	×			×	×	×
K_{17}: profit rate (profits before tax as % of sales)	×	×	×	×	×	
K_{18}: financing ratio (net fixed assets compared with total long-term capital)			×		×	
K_{19}: rate of return			×	×		×
K_{20}: sales per employee	×	×	×		×	×

Source: Haex, Halsberghe, and Van Den Bulcke (1979).

(b) Matched sample

Using a parallel sample of 36 companies in mechanical engineering, the authors of a British study in which the comparative efficiency of foreign affiliates and indigenous firms was examined concluded that foreign affiliates performed less well, particularly with respect to exporting and labour productivity (Solomon and Ingham, 1977). However, a more extensive parallel sample of 93 companies covering several sectors in the Belgian economy points to a generally better performance of multinational subsidiaries.

Table 8.6 illustrates that multinational subsidiaries generally realize a higher level of *productivity,* not only as far as the global sample is concerned but also when the matched or parallel sample and the simulated averages are calculated. This conclusion applies both to sales per

TABLE 8.6   Sales and value added per employee in Belgian and foreign-owned enterprises (1976) (Bel. f. millions)

	Sales per employee	*Value added per employee*	
		Cost method[a]	*Sales minus purchases*
Global sample			
Belgian enterprises[b]	1.89	0.62	0.83
Belgian uninational enterprises	1.87	0.53	0.77
Foreign enterprises	3.24	0.80	1.05
American enterprises	3.42	0.85	1.09
EEC enterprises	3.00	0.75	0.99
Matched sample			
Belgian enterprises	1.82	0.85	0.76
Belgian uninational enterprises	1.87	0.57	0.77
Foreign enterprises	2.16	0.65	0.91
Simulated average[c]			
Belgian uninational enterprises	1.87	0.53	0.77
Foreign enterprises	2.20	0.66	0.94
American enterprises	2.63	0.66	1.11
EEC enterprises	1.97	0.58	0.91

[a]Cost method (wages + depreciation allowances + profits before tax + interest + rent).
[b]Including Belgian MNEs.
[c]Calculated as if the foreign enterprises had the same sectoral distribution as Belgian uninational enterprises.
Source: Haex, Halsberghe, and Van Den Bulcke (1979).

employee and to value added per employee. Although the matched sample and the simulated average diminish this supremacy of foreign-owned subsidiaries, their productivity remains generally much better than for local companies. The superiority of foreign subsidiaries is evident in practically all sectors and size categories. Only in the more traditional sectors of food and textiles were the differences rather small. American subsidiaries achieve a higher productivity than EEC firms and confirm the results of our 1968 study in which it was already noticed that productivity was higher for the American companies.

In 1976, the average rate of return on turnover (profits before tax as a percentage of sales) was almost 4% for foreign enterprises as compared with 2% for Belgian uninational firms and 1.65% for all Belgian enterprises, that is including Belgian MNEs. The calculation of a matched sample and the simulated average confirm again that the supremacy of the foreign subsidiaries cannot be attributed to sectoral specialization. The higher profitability of foreign subsidiaries is largely due to the rate of profitability of 6.4% of American firms, which is almost three times as high as for EC affiliates (2.4%). Food and beverages are the only sector where Belgian enterprises surpass foreign firms (3% as compared with 0.7%) mainly because of the poor performance of subsidiaries from the EC partner countries (Haex, Halsberghe, and Van Den Bulcke, 1979).

The rate of profitability of 0.18% on net assets in 1978 of the 282 largest indigenous Belgian firms is little different from that for the 236 largest foreign subsidiaries in Belgium (0.23%). However, even with these small rates of profitability both groups realized an average profitability which was almost three times as high as the 0.08% achieved by the 214 uninational firms. The 68 Belgian MNEs that were included in the Belgian total performed about the same as the foreign subsidiaries. While American subsidiaries registered a profitabilty of 0.95%, EC affiliates actually incurred a negative rate of 0.59%. As the above results were largely influenced by a small number of enterprises which registered losses of 300 or more million Belgian francs per company, the elimination of 7 Belgian MNEs and 4 foreign subsidiaries leads to an increase of the average profitability to 2.05% for Belgian MNEs, 1.65% for American firms, and 0.55% for EC subsidiaries. Contrary to expectations, outward investors do not originate in those sectors with lower rates of profitability. The assumption that foreign-owned subsidiaries engage in activities with higher profit rates is, however, confirmed.

Foreign investors also tend to concentrate in sectors with high skill ratios as they need qualified employees to valorize their ownership advantages in the host countries. There is clear evidence that multinational subsidiaries in Belgium employ relatively more white-collar workers than domestic firms. As this higher skill ratio is also typical for foreign-owned subsidiaries in the parallel sample, the simulated averages, and in all size categories, it can be concluded that the observed differences are not exclusively due to sector and size characteristics. Transport equipment and electronics are too dominated by foreign subsidiaries to offer valid points of comparison. It should be added that no relevant differences were found as to the employment of university graduates as a percentage of total white-collar workers. Yet American subsidiaries employ a slightly higher proportion of university graduates in both the global and the matched sample (Haex, Halsberghe, and Van Den Bulcke, 1979).

Belgian multinationals and Belgian uninational firms employ about the same proportion of white-collar workers as a percentage of total personnel. However, in chemicals and metals, the sectors which take up about three-quarters of Belgian investment abroad, Belgian MNEs surpass their uninational competitors. While Belgian MNEs employ relatively more university graduates than uninational firms in both the global and the matched sample, Belgian uninational companies have engaged relatively more employees with technical degrees. In this latter case the differences are not due to multinational character as the matched sample shows practically the same ratio for multinational and uninational Belgian firms. The original difference is to be explained by the substitutability of university and technical graduates (Haex and Van Den Bulcke, 1979). These findings confirm the Kojima thesis that inward direct investment takes place in sectors with higher skill ratios than domestic firms. Outward direct investment, on the other hand, originates from sectors where the skill ratio is very similar to that of uninational domestic enterprises (Kojima, 1978).

8.4   INTERNATIONAL COMPETITIVENESS

Competitive pressure

Survey evidence from the mid 1970s suggests that foreign-owned subsidiaries occupy a stronger competitive position than indigenous firms (Haex, Halsberghe, and Van Den Bulcke, 1979). First, relatively fewer foreign affiliates were exposed to strong competitive pressure from developing countries (15% as compared with 30% for local companies in the global sample and 17 and 24% in the matched sample). Secondly, only about one out of three foreign subsidiaries was confronted with competition from Belgian firms compared with one out of two of the matched uninational Belgian companies. Thirdly, while about 40% of the foreign

MNEs complained about the increasing competitive pressure during the period 1970–6, more than half of the Belgian firms experienced similar problems. About one out of three foreign subsidiaries actually registered an improvement in their competitive position during the first half of the 1970s, as against only one out of five indigenous companies. Fourthly, foreign subsidiaries were relatively less concerned about the effects of mounting wage costs on their competitive situation than were Belgian firms. That these latter differences are largely sectorally determined is illustrated by the fact that the important distinctions in the global sample are eliminated with the calculation of a parallel sample of foreign and local companies.

More than half the surveyed multinational subsidiaries regarded their belonging to a multinational group as a definite competitive advantage. Special mention was made of their privileged access to R&D facilities and patents of the multinational group, their use of brand names made familiar by the promotion strategy of the parent company, and their cheaper purchases of raw materials, semi-finished products and parts because of their participation in the global sourcing policy of the group.

Foreign trade intensity

While in 1976 Belgium registered a negative trade balance of 80 billion Belgian francs in the manufacturing sector, a representative sample of foreign-owned subsidiaries realized a positive contribution to the trade balance of almost 70 billion Belgian francs. The contribution of inward foreign direct investment to the trade balance was positive in all sectors, except rubber and petroleum, and food and beverages. According to the matched sample the contribution of foreign companies was twice as high as for uninational Belgian firms. The average trade balance effect for foreign firms was equally much higher than for Belgian companies.

Foreign subsidiaries and Belgian MNEs greatly outperform uninational Belgian firms in exporting. The export ratio (exports as percentage of sales) was 68% for multinational subsidiaries and 50% for uninational firms. When Belgian MNEs are included the export ratio for Belgian firms increases to 61%. However, the import ratio (imports as percentage of purchases) was almost twice that of Belgian firms. Moreover, although the export ratio of foreign subsidiaries remained practically unchanged, at about two-thirds, between 1968 and 1976, the import ratio rose from two-thirds to four-fifths, mainly under the influence of EC subsidiaries. The main reason for the increase in the import ratio for EC subsidiaries was the rise in their intra-group sales from two-fifths of their total exports in 1968 to practically two-thirds in 1976. The globalization of European MNEs also resulted in an expansion of the share of intra-group exports during 1968–76 from 37% in 1968 to 53% in 1976. Conversely, intra-group imports by foreign subsidiaries fell back from 57% to 48% between 1968 and 1976. It would appear there were no major differences in export intensity either in 1968 or 1976 according to the degree of multinationality of foreign firms (Van Den Bulcke and Halsberghe, 1981).

Competitive tactics

In view of the high export performance of foreign subsidiaries, there is little reason to suppose that Belgium's trade activity has been greatly diminished by the export restrictions as imposed by foreign MNEs. Yet the fact remains that certain markets are declared inaccessible to the subsidiary as they are reserved for the parent company or other subsidiaries. Almost three out of four US affiliates in Belgium, about two out of three Dutch, British, and French affiliates and half of the German firms were not allowed to sell in the market of their respective parent countries. Markets in other industrial countries, and East Bloc countries were generally prohibited for one-fifth to half of the foreign subsidiaries from different nationalities. Of course, it must be accepted that some of these market limitations are a reflection of high transport costs or other trade barriers to exports, and that the Belgian subsidiaries themselves often get the assurance that their own privileged market (which often is the whole EC market) will not be invaded by the parent company or other subsidiaries (Van Den Bulcke, 1971).

Outward investment and export performance

Declarations about Belgian commercial policy by politicians and government officials have repeatedly stressed that foreign direct investment abroad should be stimulated in order to increase Belgian exports.

Associated exports of semi-finished products, parts and finished products from a sample of Belgian MNEs to foreign subsidiaries amounted to 14% of their total exports. Most of these exports were finished products that were sold without any transformation by the subsidiary abroad. An extrapolation from the sample to the total population of Belgian MNEs showed that these exports in 1976 represented 2.5% of total Belgian exports.

Part of these exports would undoubtedly have been realized without the subsidiaries acting as export platforms, so that this effect cannot be attributed solely to Belgian outward direct investment.

A regression analysis of a sample of 210 of the largest Belgian industrial companies composed of 83 uninational Belgian firms, 80 foreign subsidiaries and 47 Belgian MNEs, showed on the one hand a small negative correlation between exports and the presence of an industrial establishment abroad, and on the other a slight positive correlation between exports and membership of a foreign multinational group. The multinational character of Belgian enterprises had a negative influence in all sectors, although the relationship is not significant in metals. In order to eliminate the effect of heteroscedasticity, the analysis was also carried out according to size of total sales. This calculation pointed to a non-significant negative correlation for Belgian MNEs with sales lower than $50 million and a significant positive effect (at the 0.15 level) for Belgian MNEs with sales of more than $50 million (Van Den Bulcke, 1980).

8.5 RESEARCH INTENSITY

The tendency for MNEs to concentrate their research and development efforts in their country of origin typically worries countries with a high degree of inward direct investment. However, the available evidence for Belgium suggests that the R&D activities of foreign MNEs is not insignificant.

First, it should be noted that in 1976 two out of five foreign subsidiaries in Belgium were engaged in R&D. While almost half of American MNEs were active in research, only about a third of the parent companies from the EC countries had launched R&D programmes in Belgium. Yet the percentage of enterprises that carry out research is on balance slightly smaller among foreign subsidiaries than Belgian enterprises, at least when sectoral differences are eliminated by the matched sample and the simulation method. The percentages are 37 and 35 for foreign and 43 and 44 for Belgian firms. Secondly, the number of foreign companies conducting research has increased from 27% in 1968 to 39% in 1976. Also within a representative group of 100 foreign subsidiaries that participated in both surveys a greater number had actually initiated research programmes during this same period.

Thirdly, bearing in mind that foreign subsidiaries strongly rely on the research experience of their parent companies, it is surprising to find that their research expenditures as a percentage of turnover are not that much lower than for Belgian uninational firms (1.52 as against 1.77%). Indeed, the American subsidiaries perform better than the average as they spent 2.17% of their sales on R&D, as opposed to only 1.09% for EC firms. Also, when the research orientation is measured by comparing research personnel to total personnel, foreign-owned enterprises score higher than their local counterparts. However, normalizing for the different sectoral distribution of foreign and indigenous firms, only in the chemical sector do the former out-perform the latter.

Two considerations which are often made are that, on the one hand, the research efforts of multinational subsidiaries are merely adaptive, and on the other hand, that even if research activities are carried out in the host country they are strongly controlled from abroad.

Belgian firms do indeed channel their efforts somewhat more towards research into new products (85% as against 72% for foreign subsidiaries). Although foreign firms orient their research more to adapting products already manufactured by their parent companies to the local market, the differences from uninational companies are fairly small.

As to the decision-making R&D authority of foreign subsidiaries in Belgium, it has to be admitted that the determination of the research programme is decided upon in a decisive manner by the parent company in more than half of all cases (Van Den Bulcke and Halsberghe, 1984). Only in 15% of all foreign subsidiaries was the subsidiary able to programme its own research activities. That decisions about the decentralized research activities are among the most centralized decisions within MNEs not only has to do with the fact that R&D is the basis of many of the MNEs ownership advantages, but also with its important strategic role and the necessity of a close interface with top corporate management.

Belgian MNEs also practise a research approach which consists of centralizing the actual R&D programme within the home country, while keeping the research programmes of their subsidiaries within a short rein. Belgian MNEs are only more research-intensive than uninational firms in the chemical sector, however.

8.6   STRUCTURAL ADJUSTMENTS AND POLICIES

The slowdown in economic growth which became noticeable from the 1973–4 crisis onwards, the new technological division of labour, and the technological evolution are compelling Belgium, like the other industrial countries, to make structural reforms, concentrating on its relative strengths. Belgium's position is hampered by the greater concentration of her output in traditional industries with low growth, which are also those under heavy competitive pressure from the new industrial countries. Yet, taking this into account, Belgian industry has over the last decade conducted a more positive restructuring of its manufacturing base than some of its major European competitors. In view of the strong influence of multinational enterprises, the question arises as to the role of these firms in the restructuring of the Belgian economy.

Investment and disinvestment policy by multinational enterprises

Analysis of the different statistical series available in Belgium concerning investment by foreign subsidiaries clearly points to two major shifts of policy by MNEs (Van Den Bulcke, 1983a). First, as the impact of the crisis spread, the number of new investment projects fell and investment was concentrated in existing firms. Secondly, new activities were characterized by high capital intensity in existing firms. These two observations apply to both Belgian and foreign firms. However, in foreign subsidiaries, rationalized investment was more geared to saving labour. As a result of their investing in increased productivity, the share of foreign investment in Belgian domestic gross capital formation remained virtually unchanged between 1970 and 1978.

In the wake of the economic crisis, the number of foreign firms which have disinvested has greatly increased. MNEs move more swiftly than indigenous firms in closing a subsidiary or a division as they have a greater range of options. Contrary to uninational firms, closures of subsidiaries do not necessarily jeopardize the main activity of MNEs. Where necessary, MNEs may wholly or partly shift their unprofitable plant or division to other countries.

This is confirmed by the fact that in 1975–6, immediately following the crisis, closures were more frequent amongst foreign subsidiaries than among Belgian firms. As the crisis continued, not only were the number of closures by foreign subsidiaries observed to fall, but also the gap between the relative closure ratios (number of closures expressed as a percentage of total plants) of foreign firms and of Belgian firms narrowed. That relatively fewer employees were shed following disinvestment in foreign firms than in Belgian companies was due to the relatively higher capital intensity of the former. The fact that the loss of jobs due to plant closures also fell amongst Belgian firms and became comparable to foreign subsidiaries, is likewise due to the fact that as more labour-intensive firms were closed, the labour intensity of the remaining Belgian firms was reduced.

Most disinvestments, by foreign as well as Belgian enterprises, were carried out in textiles, metal, and food. About one-third each of the number of firms closed between 1975–81 were concentrated in the sectors of textiles and metal and about one-tenth in food. In relation to the number of existing firms, the rate of closure was highest for foreign subsidiaries in textiles, food, and wood and paper. Especially in the immediate post-crisis years, foreign MNEs disinvested relatively more than Belgian companies in these sectors.

Belgian government policy towards multinational enterprises

The first Belgian legislation on the expansion of the economy dates from the 1950s. This, and subsequent legislation, encouraged the modernization and restructuring of the Belgian economy and fostered a highly favourable investment climate which attracted numerous MNEs to Belgium. Although the Expansion Acts were not implemented in a discriminatory way—as is the case with all Belgian industrial policy measures—foreign subsidiaries, through their high mobility and capital intensity, have made a valuable contribution towards achieving the objectives of the legislation. However, since the crisis began the government authorities have felt bound to involve the *expansion* legislation to support *ailing* companies in order to protect employment. This of course left fewer funds available to finance an economic 'relance'.

In the meantime, the emphasis of industrial policy has shifted towards aiding restructuring. Instruments have been developed which enable private firms engaging in restructuring to receive assistance with innovation and marketing amongst others. In addition, national and regional bodies have been given power to support new initiatives and assist ailing firms by means of government shareholdings.

Two recent initiatives (1982) with special relevance to MNEs are the so-called 'employment zones' and 'coordination centres'. The first provides special incentives for new companies which are set up in designated zones, and are located in areas of high structural unemployment. The activity of a particular enterprise in these 'employment zones' must consist either of research involving products or the manufacture of or service in technologically advanced sectors such as data processing, software technology, micro-electronics, telecommunications, robotics, bio-engineering, and automated office systems. Total employment is limited to 200 employees. The special incentives which are granted consist of a ten-year tax holiday for corporate income taxes (which was brought down from 48 to 45%) and privileged treatment of foreign researchers and executives (e.g. exemption from social security contributions).

The second measure grants special advantages to MNEs setting up and maintaining so-called 'coordination centres' in Belgium. To qualify as a coordination centre a company must centralize and develop a number of service activities (e.g. marketing, advertising, insurance, scientific research, accounting, data processing, foreign exchange operations) on behalf of and for the exclusive use of the controlling multinational group which must have consolidated sales of at least 10 million Belgian francs and capital and reserves of one million Belgian francs.

Although both measures have employment-creating objectives, for example the companies involved must employ at least 10 persons after two years of activity, the main priority goes to technologically innovative firms and is a belated recognition that radical industrial restructuring is necessary to the future prosperity of the Belgian economy.

With regard to the 'exit' of multinational subsidiaries, the mitigation of the social impact of the disinvestment decisions by MNEs has been a major preoccupation for the Belgian government. To make the social consequences of restructuring acceptable, welfare funds have been set up to pay supplementary compensation to the workers affected by certain closures. The government authorities have themselves intervened directly in certain cases to safeguard the interests of workers in the subsidiaries of multinationals by, for example, insisting on the enforcement of the OECD code (e.g. Badger, Antwerp), by seeking a potential candidate to acquire a subsidiary the multinational wanted to divest (e.g. British Leyland, Seneffe), or by taking a shareholding in a firm threatened with closure because of the bankruptcy of its parent company (e.g. Fairey, Gosselies).

Thanks to its central geographical location within the European Community, its excellent infrastructure facilities and good transport potential, the level of skill of its workers and an overall favourable business climate, Belgium has been a centre of attraction for multinational subsidiaries since the 1960s. Although the economic crisis of the 1970s compelled firms to revise their investment projects to some degree, if not to delay or cancel them altogether, foreign subsidiaries remain largely predominant because they have stood up better to the crisis than national firms and they still play an important part in the Belgian economy. Foreign subsidiaries remain to the fore in economic changes and have been swifter and more thorough than indigenous firms in carrying out rationalization investment and in reshaping their policies.

When explaining the objectives of Belgian industrial policy, the government has stressed that the small number of Belgian MNEs, as compared with other small industrial countries, presents them with a handicap. In 1977 the government made official its policy of foreign direct investment abroad, a number of years after this policy was actually started. As has been illustrated in this chapter, the advantages of investing abroad should not be seen so much in terms of favourable employment and export effects, but rather as a means to sharpen the competitive power of its indigenous enterprises. Instead of an indiscriminate promotion policy, the Belgian government should be aware of the fact that, in the short run, outward investment may lead to a reduction in employment and exports, and that only if appropriate adjustment measures are taken by the government will the beneficial affects work out in the long run (Van Den Bulcke, 1983b).

NOTES

1. Cockerill Sambre (CS) has developed into one of the major industrial and political problems in the Belgian economy. The political dimension is a consequence of its location in the highly unionized centres of Liège and Charleroi and the objections from the Flemish part of the country to putting up funds for a company with continuing and huge losses. In 1983 CS employed about 23,000 people in its parent company and another 11,000 in its Belgian subsidiaries. Another 40,000 jobs indirectly depend on CS ongoing activity. It is to some extent ironic that the Belgian government, who became the major shareholder to save the enterprise, felt obliged to bring in as consultant Jean Gandois—a French expatriate manager who is the former president of the French nationalized MNE Rhône Poulenc—to restructure a company which was originally founded by a British expatriate.
2. It has been estimated that Belgian foreign direct investment abroad resulted in an employment loss between (according to different assumptions) 9,350 and 33,000 jobs. The fact that a number of important indirect effects could not be taken into account led to the conclusion that the eventual loss would be small and the long-term effects (competitive strengths) might even be positive (Haex and Van Den Bulcke, 1979).
3. These largest 522 manufacturing firms figured on the 'Top 3000' (published by *Trends* magazine) and listed companies with sales of at least 500 million Belgian francs (Haex, Halsberghe, and Van Den Bulcke, 1980).
4. The 'global sample' represents, on the one hand, 27% of all foreign-owned enterprises in Belgium and 40% of their total sales and employment, and on the other hand 13% of all Belgian multinational firms with more than 50 employees and about 20 and 25% respectively of their total sales and employment.
   The 'matched sample' tries to eliminate the sector differences between foreign subsidiaries and Belgian firms by 'pairing' a foreign firm with a Belgian firm on the preconditions of similarity in sub-sector, employment size, and age group.
   The 'simulated totals and averages' calculated the foreign-owned subsidiaries as if they had the same sectoral distribution as the Belgian uninational enterprises.
5. This aspect is elaborated upon in Van Den Bulcke and Halsberghe (1981).

REFERENCES

Alloo, R. (1953). Le rôle des banques et des capitaux belges dans le développement des pays étrangers, *Revue de la Banque,* no, 3–4

Bank Brussels Lambert (1983). The Promotion of Technological Innovation in Belgium at National and Regional Levels, *Report from Brussels,* April, pp. 1–3

Bertin, G. (1967). *L'investissement international,* Paris: PUF

Caves, R. E. (1982). *Multinational Enterprise and Economic Analysis,* Cambridge: Cambridge University Press

Dunning, J. H. (1981). *International Production and the Multinational Enterprise,* London, Allen and Unwin

Dunning, J. H. (1983). Changes in the level and structure of international production: the last one hundred years, in M. C. Casson, (ed.), *The Growth of International Business,* London: Allen and Unwin

Fabrimetal (1981). *Plaats van de buitenlandse bedrijven in de metaalverwerkende industrie,* Brussels: mimeo

Fishwick, F. (1982). *Multinational Companies and Economic Concentration in Europe,* London: Gower

Franko, L. (1976). *The European Multinationals,* London: Harper and Row

Frère, L. (1947). *Etude historique des sociétés,* Brussels

Haex, F. and Van Den Bulcke, D. (1979). *Belgische Multinationale Ondernemingen,* Diepenbeek: LEHOC-VWOL

Haex, F., Halsberghe, E. and Van Den Bulcke, D. (1979). *Buitenlandse en Belgische Ondernemingen in de Nationale Industrie,* Ghent: Serug

Haex, F., Halsberghe, E., and Van Den Bulcke, D. (1980). *Financiële Structuur en resultaten van buitenlandse filialen,* Economisch en Sociaal Tijdschrift, no. 2, 233–254

Halsberghe, E. and Van Den Bulcke, D. (1978). Buitenlandse en industriële bedrijven in Vlaanderen, Wallonië en Brussel, *GERV-Bulletin,* no. 19, December, 93–124

Jacquemin, A. (1976). Le phénomène de désindustrialisation et la Communauté européenne, *Revue économique,* no. 6, November, 985–999

Kojima, K. (1978). *Direct Foreign Investment,* London: Croom Helm

Newbould, G. D., Buckley, P. J., and Thurlwell, J. (1978). *Going International: The Success of Smaller Companies Overseas,* London: Associated Business Press

Sleuwaegen, L. and Van Den Bulcke, D. (1983). Multinational Enterprises and Industrial Market Structure in Belgium. A Statistical Decomposition Analysis, Leuven: KUL-CES (paper)

Solomon, R. F. and Ingham, K. P. (1977). Discriminating between MNC subsidiaries and indigenous companies: a comparative analysis of the British mechanical engineering industry, *Oxford Bulletin of Economic Statistics,* May

United Nations, Center Transnational Corporations (1983). *Salient Features and Trends in Foreign Direct Investment,* New York: United Nations

Van Den Bulcke, D. *et al.* (1971). *De buitenlandse ondernemingen in de Belgische industrie,* Ghent: Serug

Van Den Bulcke, D. *et al.* (1978). *Multinationale Ondernemingen in de Belgische economie,* Ghent: Serug

Van Den Bulcke, D. (1980). Export Activities of Multinational Enterprises in Belgium, in M. R. Czinkota and G. Tesar, *Export Management: An International Context,* New York: Praeger, pp. 149–173

Van Den Bulcke, D. (1983a). *Restructuration industrielle et entreprises multinationales,* Brussels: Ministry of Economic Affairs

Van Den Bulcke, D. (1983b). Belgian industrial policy and foreign multinational corporations: objectives versus performance, in W. Golberg (ed.), *Governments and Multinationals,* Cambridge, Mass.: Oelgeschlager, Gunn and Hain, pp. 219–248

Van Den Bulcke, D. and Halsberghe, E. (1979). *Employment Effects of Multinational Enterprises: A Belgian Case Study,* Geneva: International Labour Office
Van Den Bulcke, D. and Halsberghe, E. (1981). Degree of Multinationality and Foreign Headquarter-subsidiary Relationship in a Belgian Context, Stockholm: Stockholm School of Economics (Working paper)
Van Den Bulcke, D. and Halsberghe, E. (1984). *Employment Decision-Making in Multinational Enterprises: Survey Results from Belgium,* Geneva: International Labour Office
Van Den Bulcke, D. and Van Pachterbeke, M. A. (1984). *European Headquarters of American Multinational Enterprises in Brussels and Belgium,* Brussels: ICHEC
Vlaams Economisch Verbond (1981). *Enquête buitenlandse vestigingen,* Antwerp: VEV
Yannopoulos, G. and Dunning, J. H. (1976). Multinational enterprises. Locational strategies and regional development, *Regional Studies,* **10**.

APPENDIX 8.A1　Confusion matrix of the global discriminant analysis of foreign subsidiaries and Belgian firms (1976)

I. *Belgian firms[a] and foreign subsidiaries[bc]*		*Estimated distribution*	
		Belgian firms[a]	Foreign subsidiaries
Actual distribution	Belgian firms	86	14
	Foreign subsidiaries	21	79
II. *Belgian uninational[d] firms and foreign subsidiaries[ef]*		*Estimated distribution*	
		Belgian uninational firms	Foreign subsidiaries
Actual distribution	Belgian uninational firms	85	15
	Foreign subsidiaries	19	81
III. *Belgian uninational firms and Belgian MNE[gh]*		*Estimated distribution*	
		Belgian uninational firms	Belgian MNEs
Actual distribution	Belgian uninational firms	94	6
	Belgian MNEs	0	100

Source: Haex, Halsberghe, and Van Den Bulcke (1979) and Haex and Van Den Bulcke (1979).
[a]Including Belgian MNEs.
[b]N = 173 for Belgian and foreign firms.
[c]F value 3.85, significant at the level of 0.01.
[d]N = 161 Belgian uninational firms.
[e]N = 173 foreign subsidiaries.
[f]F value 3.93, significant at the level of 0.01.
[g]Only the larger uninational firms were included.
[h]F value 17.38, significant at the level of 0.01.

9

Korea

BOHN-YOUNG KOO

9.1 INTRODUCTION

Korea has achieved remarkable economic progress during the past two decades (1962–82), registering over 8% real GNP growth per annum. With this high growth, the nation's industrial structure has undergone significant changes, transforming Korea from a backward agricultural nation to a semi-industrial modern state.

The purpose of this chapter is to examine the role foreign direct investment (FDI) has played in bringing about the marked changes in Korea's economic structure.[1] Although the pattern of out-going investment by Korean firms is also briefly surveyed, its effects on changes in Korea's economic structure are not comprehensively analysed, as the scale of Korean multinational activity is still very small, particularly in the manufacturing sector, which is the main object of our study.

The next section will briefly summarize the changes in Korea's economic and industrial structure during the past two decades and discuss the major industrial policies followed by the government during the period. This is followed by an analysis of the relationship between changes in the industrial structure and changes in trade patterns.

Section 4 will review the patterns of FDI and discuss foreign investment policies followed by the Korean government during the period. The fifth section will then critically examine the interrelationship between industrial structure, comparative advantage, and foreign investment, so as to gain further insight into the causes and the nature of FDI in Korea and to investigate the effects of the operation of the affiliates of foreign MNEs on allocative efficiency in Korea.

The sixth section will analyse various behavioural differences between Korean and foreign affiliates in order to draw some implications concerning the effects of FDI on sectoral or technical efficiency in Korea. The seventh section will test Dunning's hypothesis on the relationship between net outward foreign investment and stages of development (Dunning, 1981) and then briefly examine the characteristics of outward investments made by Korean firms. The final section concludes the chapter with some policy observations.

9.2 OVERVIEW OF THE CHANGES IN KOREA'S ECONOMIC AND INDUSTRIAL STRUCTURE

In 1962 Korea was still in the process of recovering from the Korean War, and was heavily dependent on foreign aid for its survival. The domestic savings ratio, savings to gross national product (GNP), was only 3.3%, while the ratio of foreign savings, which was mostly in the form of US aid, was 10.7%. Per capita GNP stood at only $87.

The economic structure was naturally very much underdeveloped, with the primary sector accounting for 36.6% of GNP, and the manufacturing sector for only 14.2%. Exports were negligible, amounting to only $55 million in 1962, and more than two-thirds of these were primary products.

Since then, Korea's economic structure has undergone immense changes, owing mainly to the government's consistent outward-oriented economic policies of the past two decades. Exports increased at the remarkable rate of 35% per annum during the period (in value terms), reaching $21.9 billion in 1982, while per capita GNP increased to $1,678. Accordingly, the share of exports increased from only 5.1% of GNP in

TABLE 9.1   General economic indicators of Korea: 1962 and 1982

	Unit	1962	1983
GNP	$ billion	2.3	66.0
Per Capita GNP	$	87	1,678
Merchandise exports	$ billion	0.05	21.9
Merchandise imports	$ billion	0.4	24.3
Total exports to GNP[a]	%	5.1	40.3
Total imports to GNP[a]	%	16.6	41.2
Domestic savings to GNP	%	3.3	22.0
Foreign savings to GNP	%	10.7	4.6
Industrial Structure[b]	%		
Primary		36.6	16.9
Mining and Manufacturing		16.2	30.0
(Manufacturing)		(14.2)	(28.5)
Services		47.1	53.1

[a]Includes commodity and services.
[b]Based on the distribution of the value added.
Source: Economic Planning Board, *Major Statistics of Korean Economy*, 1983.

1962 to 40.3% in 1982. Over the same period the share of imports also increased from 16.6% of GNP to 41.2% (Table 9.1).

The industrial structure underwent significant changes during the period. The share of the primary sector decreased from 36.6% of GNP in 1962 to 16.9% in 1982, while the share of the manufacturing sector increased from 14.2% to 28.5%. Thus, the manufacturing sector came to far outweigh the primary sector in importance, when viewed in terms of their respective contributions to the nation's value added.

These changes in the pattern of Korea's economy were brought about mainly by changes in her trade patterns. Particularly fast growth in exports of manufactured goods was one of the key factors behind the striking changes in Korea's industrial structure. The share of manufacturing goods in total exports increased from 27% in 1962 to 94% in 1982; and the share of exports in total sales of manufactured goods increased from a mere 1.2% to over 29% over the same period. As a result, the manufacturing sector grew rapidly in importance and, within this sector, trade-related industries grew much faster than non-trade-related industries.

The role of government policies

What were the government policies which brought about the changes just described? A review of the role of the government is essential, not only to understand how changes in Korea's industrial structure were brought about, but also to analyse their effects on the patterns of FDI which appeared later in Korea.

In 1962, the Korean government consciously embraced an outward-looking industrialization strategy and has pursued this strategy consistently for the past two decades. Adoption of an outward-looking strategy was perhaps inevitable for Korea, as the country was deficient in most natural resources and had only human resources in abundance. In order to promote industrialization, the government has wielded a comprehensive influence on the economy through various regulations and incentives. Although we do not propose to give details of all the industrial policies adopted by the Korean government, at least three important policy lines, which were generally maintained throughout the period, should be noted.[2]

First, in order to promote exports, various incentives were introduced, including income tax reductions for export-related earnings (abolished in 1973), free imports of export-related raw materials or equipment, preferential financing for export-related activities (abolished in 1982), and generous wastage allowances for imported raw materials (reduced in 1973). Above all, except in the late 1970s, reasonable exchange rate adjustments were made throughout the period.

Until the end of the 1970s, export promotion was the government's top priority. Export targets were set up for each year and regular monthly export-promotion meetings chaired by the President of the Republic were held to maintain the export orientation of private entrepreneurs.

Second, to encourage inflows of foreign capital, the Foreign Capital Inducement Act was introduced in 1960. Since Korea lacked the necessary domestic savings, she had to finance her investment by borrowing from foreign countries. Based on the Act, the government guaranteed the repayment of foreign loans and provided tax and other incentives to foreign investors and licensors of foreign technologies. Sometimes, explicit guarantees of profits or markets were made to large foreign investors to attract them to Korea. At the same time, two free export zones were established in 1970 and 1974. However, for most of the period the Korean government maintained relatively restrictive foreign investment policies, so most foreign capital came in the form of loans rather than direct investment.

Third, to facilitate the modernization of Korea's industrial structure, the government provided various tax and financial incentives for investments in industries deemed important by the government. Promotional laws were introduced, which specified the incentives and eligible products in such industries as electronics, shipbuilding, steel, machinery, and petrochemicals.

Many industrial parks were set up to help the growth of these industries, and for major projects the government sometimes intervened directly in the planning of individual plants, selection of plant operators (owners), and in the operation of the plants.

In summary, the pattern of industrialization which has emerged in Korea over the past two decades has been strongly influenced by government policies, although these policies have been influenced by (as well as influencing) changes in the nation's comparative advantage position and the level and structure of markets.

More recently, there has been a fundamental change in the way the government manages the economy. Realizing that heavy-handed government intervention had introduced many undesirable biases in the economy, the government began to reduce its intervention in the early 1980s and to introduce more competition in the economy through liberalization of imports and direct foreign investment and through abolition of government subsidies or incentives. The effects of these changes have not yet become apparent; we shall therefore only allude to them again in the final section of the chapter.

9.3 INDUSTRIAL STRUCTURE AND TRADE PATTERNS IN KOREA

The industrial structure of an economy changes as its level of income grows. Usually, as per capita income rises, the importance of the primary sector decreases, while that of the industrial sector increases. However, depending on the character of the industrialization strategies adopted, considerable differences in the speed and pattern of industrial changes are likely to be observed.

In the case of Korea, the outward-oriented industrialization strategy adopted in the early 1960s brought about rapid changes in the nation's industrial structure. Therefore, we need to look at the changes in Korea's export and import patterns more closely before we analyse the effects of FDI on structural change.

Korea's export growth began with exports of simple labour-intensive products like garments, plywood, footwear, and wigs. However, the proportion of most of these products reached its peak in the early 1970s, and since then exports of more capital- and skill-intensive products such as cement, tyres, steel, electronics, and fabricated metal products have began to grow faster.

By 1980, exports of simple labour-intensive products had declined further in importance, and the heavy and chemical industries came to account for almost half of all merchandise exports. Among others, steel, ships, electronic products, and fabricated metal products became Korea's newest major export items. The textile industry still claimed 21% of total exports (or 27% of total merchandise exports) in 1980, but, due to a considerable decline in the contribution of clothing in total textile exports, the product mix of the textile exports had changed significantly from that of the early 1970s.

The share of primary goods in total exports declined sharply and consistently during the period, as a result of much faster growth of exports of manufactured goods. By 1980, primary goods accounted for less than 4% of total exports. Similarly, the share of the services sector in total exports declined considerably during the period, although it tended to rise again during the late 1970s, because of an increase in the value of sea and air transportation activities.[3]

Thus, since the early 1970s Korea's export pattern has been characterized by a steady increase in the proportion of exports of manufactured goods; and among manufactured goods, a marked shift from labour-intensive to more skill-intensive products.

Unlike exports, imports into Korea were tightly controlled by the government throughout the period. In consequence, for the most part only raw materials to be used in producing export goods, or materials that were in short supply domestically, and capital goods which could not be supplied by domestic producers were allowed to be imported.

Even by 1980, when significant import substitution had been accomplished in Korea, the chemical, metal, and machinery industries still accounted for 78% of imports of total manufactured goods, although structural changes had occurred within each industry in accordance with their growth.

The share of primary goods in total imports fluctuated during the period, depending on the annual rice harvest and the price of oil. Recently, however, due to the rapid rise of oil prices, the share of primary goods has increased again, reaching 36% in 1980. But generally, imports of services have remained small throughout the period.

Changes in Korea's industrial structure were the inevitable consequence of these changes in her export and import patterns and the concurrent changes in her domestic demand pattern, which occurred as a result of increasing income levels.[4] For example, the growth of the fabricated textile products industry up to 1973 and its subsequent stagnation were the direct result of changes in the export volume of textiles; the same appears to have been true of the wood products industry (due to stagnation of plywood exports at a later stage). The consistent growth of the rubber products, fabricated metal products, and electronics industries also came mainly from continued export growth in these industries.

For some sectors, growth both of exports and of domestic demand has increased their relative importance. Examples are the basic chemicals, plastic products, and steel industries, while for other industries expansion in domestic demand has been the main reason for growth. Examples are the synthetic resins and rubber, petroleum refining, non-ferrous metal, and the business services industries.

Overall, import substitution appears to have had considerably less influence than either domestic demand or exports on changes in industrial structure. The growth of industries like chemical yarns (particularly between 1963 and 1980), chemical fertilizers, and petroleum (particularly between 1963 and 1973) has been the result of import substitution, but for many other industries import substitution was not directly related to the relative growth of the industry for three main reasons.

First, although import substitution occurred for some products, in any one industry, often imports had to be continued or even increased for other products of the same industry. This resulted in the growth of the industry, but caused no decrease in the industry's share in total imports. Examples are basic chemicals, steel, general machinery, electrical machinery, and precision equipment.

Second, for some industries import substitution resulted in an increase in imports of parts and components. Again, although the industry grew there was no decrease in import share. Examples again are general machinery, electrical machinery, and precision equipment.

Third, for some other industries, import substitution did not result in the relative growth of the industry, because either the speed of growth in the industry's exports or domestic demand was below that of the whole economy. Examples of this situation are fabrics (between 1973 and 1980), and drugs and cosmetics.

Basically, if imports had not been strictly controlled by the government, there might have been a closer negative relationship between changes in imports and changes in industrial production. However, as noted earlier, imports were tightly controlled; in consequence, their patterns did not closely reflect the comparative advantage position of Korean industries.

Our conclusions regarding the relative influence of exports, imports, and domestic demand on changes in domestic industrial structure have already been confirmed by Kim (1980) in his comprehensive study on the sources of industrial growth in Korea. As the purpose of this chapter is not so much to examine the relationship between industrial structure and trade patterns as that between economic structure and direct foreign investment, we have not carried out any further statistical analysis here.

9.4 INDUSTRIAL PATTERN OF FDI IN KOREA

In order to analyse the effects of FDI on Korea's industrial structure, we must first examine its changing level and composition over the past two decades. The relevant details are set out in Table 9.2.

FDI in Korea first began in the area of import substitution of key raw materials. The first foreign affiliate was set up in 1962 by an American textile firm named Chemtex, to produce nylon filaments. It was soon followed by investments in petroleum refining and chemical fertilizers. Until 1968, FDI in those three import-substitution industries (chemical yarns, chemical fertilizers, and petroleum products) explained 74.4% of all FDI in Korea. Other foreign subsidiaries were established in the non-metallic mineral products, hotels, and finance sectors. The period between 1963 and 1968 was a period of first-stage import substitution and the beginning of export-led growth in Korea.

Import-substituting FDI continued into the early 1970s in other areas such as non-synthetic yarns, basic metals, and petrochemicals. At the same time, some foreign investments were allowed in some basically domestic-market-oriented industries, such as food processing, paper products, pharmaceuticals, and automobiles.

TABLE 9.2   Industrial distribution of cumulative foreign direct investment in Korea (in %)

	1963	1968	1973	1978	1980
Agriculture, fishery, and mining	0.0	0.8	0.5	0.6	0.6
Manufacturing	100.0	88.8	91.8	80.8	73.5
Food Processing	0.0	0.4	1.7	1.2	2.1
Beverages	0.0	0.0	0.0	0.1	0.1
Tobacco	0.0	0.0	0.0	0.0	0.0
Chemical fibre and yarns	7.7	8.4	3.8	3.0	2.7
Other fibre yarns	0.0	1.2	19.8	9.9	0.3
Fabrics	0.0	0.6	2.6	1.3	1.2
Fabricated textile products	0.0	0.0	2.2	1.5	1.4
Leather and leather products	0.0	0.0	0.4	0.4	0.4
Wood and wood products	0.0	0.2	0.4	0.2	0.2
Paper and paper products	0.0	0.0	1.1	0.6	0.6
Printing and publishing	0.0	0.0	0.1	0.1	0.1
Basic chemicals	0.0	0.0	1.7	7.7	11.3
Chemical fertilizers	0.0	40.8	6.0	4.9	4.5
Drugs and cosmetics	0.0	0.5	0.4	0.6	0.6
Plastics products	0.0	0.0	1.1	0.7	0.6
Synthetic resins, rubber and other chemical products	0.0	1.1	4.0	7.8	7.6
Petroleum products	91.3	25.2	10.4	7.9	4.2
Coal products	0.0	0.0	0.0	0.0	0.0
Rubber products	0.0	0.0	0.2	0.4	0.5
Non-metallic mineral products	0.0	6.8	4.4	2.0	1.9
Basic metal products	0.0	0.0	2.7	2.7	3.4
(Steel products)	(0.0)	(0.0)	(1.7)	(1.7)	(2.4)
Fabricated metal products	0.0	0.1	2.2	2.9	4.4
General machinery	0.0	0.5	3.5	3.9	4.1
Electrical machinery	0.0	0.0	1.4	1.8	2.5
Electronic and communication equipment	0.0	1.1	11.5	12.0	12.2
Transportation equipment	0.0	0.0	7.7	4.9	4.4
(Shipbuilding)	(0.0)	(0.0)	(0.3)	(1.0)	(1.0)
(Automobiles)	(0.0)	(0.0)	(7.4)	(3.5)	(3.4)
Precision equipment	0.0	1.1	1.1	1.1	1.3
Other manufacturing	1.0	0.8	1.4	1.1	1.0
Services	0.0	10.4	7.7	18.6	25.9
Hotel	0.0	4.3	3.5	12.0	13.5
Transportation and warehousing	0.0	0.0	0.6	0.1	1.7
Finance	0.0	5.2	1.7	4.1	4.7
Business services	0.0	0.9	1.8	2.4	6.0
Other services	0.0	0.0	0.0	0.0	0.0
Total	100.0	100.0	100.0	100.0	100.0
($ millions)	(7.5)	(50.2)	(339.0)	(879.6)	(980.0)

Note: The distribution has been based on the remaining balance of FDI in the year.
Source: Ministry of Finance.

However, as Korea's political and social stability became established and her location-specific advantage as a site for sourcing-type investments became better known, foreign firms began to set up processing plants to exploit Korea's low-cost and highly productive labour. Investments in electronics explained the bulk of such investment, but there were also export-platform-type investments in areas like cotton yarns, garments, plastic products, and some machine parts.

Thus by 1973 the foreign investment pattern in Korea had already become quite diversified. The share of chemical yarns, fertilizer, and petroleum-refining industries in total FDI declined sharply from 74.4% in 1968 to only 20.2% in 1973. On the other hand, the electronics industry came to account for 11.5% of total FDI; the non-synthetic yarns industry for 19.8%; the chemical industry (basic chemicals, drugs and cosmetics, synthetic resins and rubbers, plastics products and other chemical products, but excluding fertilizers) for 7.3%; and the broadly-defined machinery industry (including fabricated metal products, electrical and non-electrical machinery, transport equipment, and precision equipment, but excluding electronics) for 15.9%. This period from 1968 to 1973 was a period of continuous import substitution and export growth in Korea.

During the middle and latter part of the 1970s, foreign firms were more attracted to the heavy and chemical industries. By 1980, the chemical industry (excluding fertilizers) claimed 20.1% of all FDI, the broadly-defined machinery industry, 16.7%, and the electronics industry, 12.2%. The share of synthetic yarns, chemical fertilizers and petroleum products, which were the major areas for FDI, continued to decline during this period, reaching 11.3% by 1980.

At the same time, Korea witnessed increased FDI in the services area; indeed its share of all FDI rose sharply from 7.7% in 1973 to 25.9% in 1980. Investments in hotels accounted for more than half of this, followed by those in business services and finance.

Government policy towards FDI

The foreign investment policies followed by the government up to 1980 were generally restrictive. Although it offered tax and other incentives for approved foreign investors, the approval procedures were tightly controlled.

Basically, FDI was permitted only where the entry of foreign firms was considered compatible with the development strategies the government was following. For example, as export promotion was the major policy objective during the whole period, export-oriented affiliates were allowed almost without restriction. For many large-scale import-substituting projects, the government often directly intervened in their planning and operation through public corporations, as noted earlier. FDIs were not allowed in most domestic consumer goods industries, particularly in cases where the government believed that a viable indigenous producer existed.[5]

One means used to control the inflow of foreign investment has been the placement of restrictions on the extent of foreign ownership. Especially since about 1973, majority foreign ownership has been allowed only in special cases, such as for export-oriented or highly technology-intensive projects or for projects by Korean residents abroad or located in free export zones.[6]

These restrictions have been more rigidly applied in the case of FDI in the services sector, than in the manufacturing sector. Exceptions include FDI for building large-scale hotels to promote tourism. Some joint-venture merchant banks were also allowed, as a means to promote the inflow of foreign capital; while in some specialized business service areas such as computer or machinery leasing FDI was valued as a means of gaining information technology. Except for these areas, however, FDI has been rarely allowed in service industries.

Since restrictions on the inflow of foreign investment were widespread in Korea, it is natural that a good economic theory to explain satisfactorily the overall pattern of FDI in Korea is hard to find. Indeed most theories of FDI implicitly assume a non-interventionist government policy. However, since this frequently is not the case, particularly in developing countries, it is not surprising that these explanations are found wanting.

In the case of Korea, for example, as the consumer durable goods market was mostly closed to foreign investors, and since the market for labour-saving producer goods has been relatively small, there have been few instances of FDI, which could be explained by Vernon's product cycle model (Vernon, 1966, 1971). Radios, TVs, refrigerators, washing machines, elevators, and tyres are all being produced by domestic firms in Korea, and even the automobile market has been dominated by a domestic firm, rather than by a joint venture with a multinational car manufacturer.

Of course, some sourcing-type investments in the field of electronics may be considered as examples of Vernon's model, but in his study, income-elastic and labour-saving consumer or producer goods, not their parts, are the chief objects of explanation. Furthermore, the product cycle model cannot explain the bulk of other import-substituting investments in Korea.

Similarly, Caves' (1971, 1974) explanation of the causes of horizontal FDI is also only of limited validity in the case of Korea. Caves, adopting the industrial-organization approach, argued that direct foreign investments are likely to be found most frequently in differentiated oligopolistic industries. In Korea, however, because of government restrictions, FDI in industries where the market structures are differentiated oligopolies has been the exception rather than the rule. Food processing (2.1%), beverages (0.1%), paper products (0.6%), drugs and cosmetics (0.6%), and automobiles (3.4%) fall into this category; but FDI in these industries explained only 6.8% of total cumulative foreign investments at the end of 1980.[7]

Therefore, we can say that basically only two types of direct FDIs existed in Korea, one of which substituted for imports of raw materials and the other which exported most of its products. In the latter case, since the main purpose of the FDI was to exploit Korea's relatively low labour cost, inputs were imported in many cases.

Lastly, we have made a comparison of US and Japanese investment patterns in Korea, in order to examine Kojima's hypothesis (Kojima, 1978) regarding differences in behaviour between American and Japanese foreign investors. Kojima argued that most Japanese manufacturing investments in developing countries were made in industries where Japan was losing its comparative advantage, while most American investments were made in the highly technology-intensive and oligopolistic industries where the US had a comparative advantage.

As such, Japanese FDIs facilitated the restructuring of the Japanese economy, while at the same time helping the host countries to develop industries in which they have comparative advantage. On the other hand, American FDIs tended to increase the balance of payments difficulties and unemployment problems in the US, by reducing American exports to the host countries, while providing little help to the host countries in the exploitation of their potential comparative advantages.

A cursory examination of Japanese and American investment patterns in Korea, set out in Table 9.3, generally confirms Kojima's hypothesis. US investments have been relatively more concentrated in such Korean industries as basic chemicals, chemical fertilizers, petroleum products, automobiles and business services. These are all industries in which Korea does not enjoy a comparative advantage at this stage. On the other hand, Japanese investments have been relatively more concentrated in textiles, metal products, machinery, electronics, and hotels. Most of these are industries in which Korea currently enjoys or is expected to enjoy a comparative advantage in the near future. Therefore, in general, Kojima's argument seems valid in the case of Korea.

Nevertheless, his generalization appears to be a little too sweeping. First, there have been many cases of Japanese investment in technically advanced industries. Secondly, much of American investment in Korea

TABLE 9.3   Percentage industrial distribution of cumulative American and Japanese investments in Korea (end 1980)

	US (%)	Japan (%)
Agriculture, fishery, and mining	0.7	0.4
Manufacturing	81.5	72.5
Food processing	1.0	3.1
Beverages	0.3	0.0
Tobacco	0.0	0.0
Chemical fibre and yarns	0.0	4.5
Other fibre yarns	0.0	0.2
Fabrics	0.1	2.2
Fabricated textile products	0.2	2.0
Leather and leather products	0.0	0.6
Wood and wood products	0.0	0.4
Paper and paper products	0.4	0.8
Printing and publishing	0.0	0.1
Basic chemicals	24.6	5.7
Chemical fertilizers	13.3	0.4
Drugs and cosmetics	0.4	0.2
Plastics products	0.0	1.1
Synthetic resins, rubber and other chemical products	8.4	8.7
Petroleum products	8.6	0.0
Coal products	0.0	0.0
Rubber products	0.1	0.8
Non-metallic mineral products	0.7	2.5
Basic metal products	0.7	2.7
(Steel products)	(0.5)	(2.3)
Fabricated metal products	3.1	5.1
General machinery	1.8	5.7
Electrical machinery	0.6	3.2
Electronic and communication equipment	8.1	16.2
Transportation equipment	8.0	2.9
(Shipbuilding)	(0.2)	(1.7)
(Automobiles)	(7.7)	(1.2)
Precision equipment	0.6	1.7
Other manufacturing	0.1	1.7
Services	17.9	27.1
Hotel	1.9	22.6
Transportation and warehousing	3.4	0.8
Finance	1.4	0.3
Business services	11.2	3.4
Other services		0.0
Total	100.0	100.0

Note and Source: same as in Table 9.2.

has been made in the essential import-substituting industries, rather than in differentiated oligopolistic (consumer goods) industries; thus they have had little adverse effect on resource allocation. Thirdly, for a rapidly growing economy like Korea, the scope of so-called complementary investments becomes limited, as the nation's comparative advantage position changes so rapidly.

For example, Korea's comparative advantage has moved from simple labour-intensive products like wigs, plywood, garments, and consumer electronics (assembly) to more capital- and skill-intensive products like steel, ships, electronic parts, and fabricated metal products. For many of these skill-intensive products, the Korean products compete directly with Japanese products in the world market. Thus the so-called complementary investment by Japanese producers argued by Kojima becomes less likely. The recent relative decline of Japanese investment in Korea appears to have been partly the result of this changing nature of the comparative advantage between the two countries.

9.5 INDUSTRIAL STRUCTURE, COMPARATIVE ADVANTAGE, AND FOREIGN INVESTMENT

Now that we have reviewed the changes in the patterns of industrial structure, trade, and direct foreign investment in Korea, we are ready to examine more systematically the interrelationship among them.

First, let us re-examine the relationship between trade patterns and patterns of FDI. According to our cursory examination of FDI patterns in Korea, it first began in import-substituting industries and then gradually moved to export industries. However, at a later stage, it moved back to (second stage) import-substituting industries like chemicals and machinery.

Table 9.4 clearly shows the changing industrial distribution of FDI in Korea, through examining the propensity to export by foreign affiliates. Although FDI in export-oriented industries was marginal until 1968, it grew rapidly between 1968 and 1973. However, since 1973 FDI in import-substituting industries has grown faster than that in export-oriented industries. In 1973 FDI's export orientation was even stronger than domestic firms when viewed in terms of its industrial distribution. However, for other years, the national average has been always higher than the FDI-weighted average.

TABLE 9.4   Export/sales ratios in industries
where FDI occurred 1963–80

	Average export/sales ratios	
	FDI Weighted	Total average
1963	0.3	3.8
1968	4.3	8.6
1973	24.3	22.5
1978	19.3	23.6
1980	18.5	23.4

This structure of FDI has been a direct result of the Korean government's foreign investment policy. As stated earlier, the Korean government has tried to maximize the contribution of foreign affiliates to Korea's economic growth by only allowing them to operate where their expected contribution was compatible with the development objectives the government was pursuing. Therefore, the pattern of FDI in Korea has closely followed the character of industrialization strategies being followed.

1973 was a turning point in Korea's industrialization process, because in that year the government began to pursue actively the development of import-substitution in the heavy and chemical industries. Consequently, the growth of export-oriented FDI has been relatively stagnant since then.

What is the meaning of the pattern of FDI paralleling Korea's industrialization strategy? Does it imply a closer relationship between the pattern of FDI and Korea's comparative advantage? The answer is a definite no.

Although export-oriented foreign affiliates were allowed to produce in Korea almost without restriction, it does not follow that the pattern of FDI will necessarily have a close relationship with the patterns of either exports or comparative advantage in Korea. In order to invest in a foreign country, foreign firms need to be tempted not only by that country's location-specific advantages, but also to enjoy ownership and specific advantages over local producers.

For many export-oriented industries in Korea, foreign firms did not possess even the basic ownership advantages. Even for the consumer electronics, steel and shipbuilding industries, which have become Korea's major exporting industries at a later stage, foreign firms' ownership advantages were limited to certain lines of products in the industry or certain processes in production.

Therefore, foreign firms' export-oriented investments had to be limited to certain offshore export-platform-type industries, where they enjoyed favoured access to inputs or markets, and this is why, in Table 9.4, FDI firms appear less export-oriented than domestic firms (except for 1973), although their propensity to export in individual industries has been generally higher.[8]

By contrast it is evident that foreign firms possessed substantial owner-ship-specific advantages in most import-substituting industries. But here the restrictions imposed by the Korean government greatly reduced the possibility of internationalization of these advantages. The result then was less FDI than might otherwise have been the case in such industries as computers, consumer electronics, industrial machinery, automobiles, and precision equipment.

When foreign firms had strong ownership-specific advantages such as technical or managerial superiority, or favoured access to inputs or mar-kets, they were either allowed majority foreign ownerships or they came in without majority ownership with the conviction that they could still appropriate some economic rent from their advantages. Examples include FDI in industries like petroleum refining and fertilizers in the early stages of Korea's development and in petro- and fine chemicals, and some heavy machinery in recent years. As noted earlier, FDI was not allowed in most domestic-market-oriented consumer goods industries.

What then might we conclude about the effects of FDI on changes in Korea's industrial structure? We noted earlier that Korea's industrial structure has been strongly affected by changes in the patterns of exports and domestic demand and hardly touched by changes in the pattern of imports. We have noted also that because of constraints placed on it by the Korean government FDI had little to do with the patterns of either Korean demand or its comparative trading advantage. There is thus the strong implication that the influence of FDI on changes in Korea's econ-omic structure has been very marginal.

TABLE 9.5   Relationship between FDI and trade patterns[a]

| | Correlation coefficients between FDI and: | | |
	Exports	Imports	RCA[b]
1968	− 0.0957	0.0320	− 0.2070
1973	− 0.0003	0.2725	− 0.0079
1978	0.0437	0.3214*	− 0.1524
1980	0.1951	0.5129**	− 0.2706

[a] Patterns of FDI, exports and imports refer to industrial percentage distribution.
[b] RCA, defined as (exports − imports)/(exports + imports).
Notes: The year 1963 has been omitted because there was FDI only in three industries.
* and ** denote that the relationship is significant at 10% and 1%.

Although the data are very limited we attempted some statistical exercises to check the validity of the preceding arguments. First, we ran a correlation analysis between the pattern of FDI in manufacturing industry and the patterns of exports, imports, and revealed comparative advantage (RCA) for four different years (cf. Table 9.5).

As earlier hypothesized, patterns of FDI had no close correlation with patterns of either exports or RCA. All the relationships were statistically not significant even at the 10% level. At the same time the data do suggest that over time the negative correlation between patterns of FDI and RCA has tended to increase. We believe that this reflects the move away from export-oriented towards import-substituting type FDI since 1973. This trend is also confirmed by the growing positive relationship between the pattern of FDI and that of imports over the last 8 years. However, as import substitution gains momentum and imports into Korea become more liberalized in future, this relationship between imports and FDI is likely to be weakened.

Another test of the relationship between patterns of FDI and trade used the market share of foreign affiliates, in individual industries as the dependent variable. Our results are set out in Table 9.6.

TABLE 9.6   Relationship between foreign affiliates' share of total sales and skill ratios, 1980

	Propensity to Export	RCA	Skill Ratio
Foreign affiliates share in sales	0.0416	−0.0836	0.1791

As would be expected, the share of foreign affiliates in the total sales for the industry was not related at all to propensity to export, RCA, or indeed in this case to the skill ratio (here represented by the proportion of administrative and technical workers to total workers), which has been used as an indicator of the technological intensity of a particular industry.

In summary then, the relationship between patterns of FDI and exports or comparative advantage in Korea has not been significant. On the other hand, due to an increase of FDI in large importing sectors, some significant positive correlation existed between patterns of FDI and imports, although this relationship is expected to become less significant in the future. We would emphasize, however, that the reasons for these findings have as much to do with government policy towards inward direct investment as with allocative efficiency of foreign affiliates in Korea. Given a different or non-interventionist policy on the government's part (see, for example, the Singapore case study), the impact of FDI on resource disposition may have been quite different.

9.6 COMPARATIVE PERFORMANCE OF FOREIGN AND DOMESTIC FIRMS

Some statistical findings

The participation of foreign-owned firms in an economy may not only affect allocative efficiency through altering the distribution of industrial investment, but also affect technical or sectoral efficiency, both directly through their own activities and indirectly through the spillover effects on indigenous firms in the host country. Both data and conceptual problems, however, make examining sectoral efficiency much more difficult than examining allocative efficiency.

Data on the performance of foreign firms are scarce in most countries, and particularly so in developing countries. In the case of Korea, however, some data are available on the performance of foreign affiliates from a survey carried out by the government in 1979.[9] These include the capital/labour ratios, financial structures, profitability, and value-added ratios of foreign firms from 1974 to 1978. Since similar data are available on all domestic firms it is possible to make some assessment on the distinctive character of FDI in these years.

Table 9.7 compares the average performance of all firms existing in Korea with that of foreign affiliates in 1978. The table shows that the latter, on average, were more capital-intensive, more skill-intensive (higher wages), less profitable, less debt-ridden, and produced more value added.

TABLE 9.7 Comparative performance of domestic and foreign firms (1978)[a]

	All firms[b]	Foreign firms	Statistical significance of difference[c]
Total assets per capita (W million)	9.0	23.3	P. > 99
Wage rate (W '000 per year)	1420	2319	P. > 99
Value added to net sales (%)	24.6	36.3	P. > 99
Value added per capita (W million)	2.8	3.0	P. > 50
Net profit to total assets (%)	4.98	3.64	P. > 95
Total debt to net worth (%)	366.8	97.6	P. > 99

[a]Comparison has been restricted to the manufacturing sector only.
[b]As all firms include foreign firms, their performances do not refer to the performances of domestic firms proper. However, as the proportion of foreign firms had been small (particularly in terms of number), bias due to this misrepresentation should be negligible.
[c]P. > 99 means that the difference in the performance of foreign and domestic firms was statistically significant at 1% level. The formula used to check the statistical significance of difference was $z = (Xf - X)/(sf/\sqrt{n})$, where $\overline{Xf}$ and $\overline{Xa}$ refer to the average performance of foreign and all firms, sf is standard deviation of performance of foreign firms and n is sample number of foreign firms.

However, as the relative importance of direct foreign investments differed among industries, the differences in performance may have been the result of different weight of FDI by industries. But to what extent are these differences due to a different industrial distribution between foreign and all Korean firms? In order to examine whether any systematic differences in the performance of foreign and domestic firms existed, we examined the statistical significance of the average performance of foreign and domestic firms for each of 27 manufacturing industries.[10]

Table 9.8 sets out the number of industries where the relationship in performance between the foreign and domestic firms was in the same direction as in Table 9.7 and the number of industries where such relationships were statistically significant.

TABLE 9.8   Distribution of the relationship in the performance of foreign and domestic firms

	Total number of industries	With the same sign as in Table V–1	Statistically significant among those with the same sign[a]
Total assets per capita	27	14	3
Wage rate	27	25	19
Value added to net sales	27	23	13
Value added per capita	27	12	3
Net profit to total assets	27	17	4
Total debt to net worth	27	19	14

[a]Significance level used was 5%, and the formula used to check the significance was the same as in Table 9.7.

In the case of capital intensity, although there were some industries where foreign firms had a much higher capital intensity than domestic firms (e.g. beverages, basic chemicals, chemical fertilizers, synthetic rubbers and resins), there were others where the reverse held true.[11] Thus it could not be argued that, in general, foreign affiliates used more capital-intensive methods of production than their domestic counterparts.

In the case of wage rates, foreign firms' remuneration per worker was higher than that of domestic firms in almost all industries, and for most of them the difference was statistically significant. However, this appears to be because of the relatively larger average size of foreign firms, and the fact that foreign affiliates tend to produce the relatively more skill-intensive product lines within an industry.

Turning next to value-added ratios, the ratios were generally higher for foreign affiliates than for domestic firms. However, the differences were significant in only 13 out of 27 industries. In the case of value added per capita and profitability, there were very few statistically significant differences in the performance of foreign and domestic firms. In the case of total debt to net worth too, although in the majority of cases foreign firms had lower debt ratios, there were many industries where the differences were not statistically significant.

Some qualitative observations

Due to a scarcity of good statistical data, our examination of foreign firms' influence on sectoral efficiency had to depend to a great extent on qualitative conjectures, and observation has to limited to a few major sectors.

Let us begin with the textile industry. In the case of chemical fibres, foreign firms have certainly contributed to the growth and prosperity of the industry both through competition among themselves and competition with foreign products in the world market through exporting activities. In consequence the productivity of the industry has improved markedly during the past two decades.

In the basic chemicals, synthetic resins, and rubber sectors, most foreign subsidiaries enjoy monopolistic positions in the domestic market and protection from imports. Therefore the direct contribution to sectoral efficiency is likely to have been small. However, as producers of raw materials for Korea's major export industries (textiles, footwear, tyres, and plastics products), they would appear to have made some contribution to stabilizing the supply of raw materials and thus to the growth of these export industries.

Foreign investments in the petroleum refining and chemical fertilizer industries have made some indirect contribution to the growth of these sectors by providing the engineers and technicians necessary to operate the chemical plants. In addition, they have helped develop the engineering industry in Korea by providing engineers with learning experiences.

In the case of the electronics industry, it is a mixed picture. Most of the export-platform-type foreign investments have had only a marginal effect on sectoral efficiency in Korea. They have helped train some labour but this training has been mostly limited to simple assembly jobs. However, it does appear that they have passed on new knowledge and helped to improve the quality and output of their sub-contractors and hence of the final products. This is particularly noticeable in the case of the Japanese affiliates.

It is too early to determine the effects of the participation of foreign firms on the machinery industry. Major investments in this area began only in the late 1970s. There was some earlier investment in the automobile industry, but, as noted previously, the foreign firm was outcompeted by the local firm.

In general, the effects of foreign firms in improving sectoral efficiency in Korea during the past two decades appear to have been positive, but not significant. Export-platform-type investments did not require much local input other than labour, and import-substituting foreign investments were heavily protected from imports. Also, as would be expected, research and development activities by subsidiaries of foreign firms were almost non-existent in all industries.

The above findings seem to be supported by a World Bank study (Westphal, Rhee, and Pursell, 1981). In discussing how Korea has established an independent base of technological knowhow and marketing expertise in many sectors, the authors concluded that FDI had played a very minor role in enhancing Korea's ability in these areas and that Korea's industrialization had been directed and controlled almost entirely by Korean nationals.

9.7   OUTWARD INVESTMENT BY KOREAN FIRMS

A test of Dunning's hypothesis for Korea

Before we conclude the paper, we will examine Dunning's (1981) hypothesis regarding the relationship between the levels of net outward investment (outward investment minus inward investment) and stages of development, and review the character of outward investment by Korean firms.

Professor Dunning, applying his eclectic theory of international producing, argues that the level of net outward investment in a country is related to its per capita GNP and development pattern in the following way. In Stage I, there is no outward investment by the country, primarily because the country's own enterprises possess few advantages over firms from other countries. At the same time, there is little incoming investment by foreign firms, as there are insufficient location-specific advantages offered by the host country.

In Stage II, inward investment begins to increase as the domestic market grows and infrastructure develops. Import-substituting investments will be attracted first, followed by export-platform-type investments. At this stage, outward investment remains small, except in some neighbouring areas, as indigenous enterprises have not yet generated sufficient ownership advantages of their own.

In Stage III, outward investment by nationals begins to increase, as indigenous firms improve their competitive capacity and develop their own country-specific ownership advantages. On the other hand, as the ownership advantages of foreign firms in the mature or standard technology sectors become eroded, incoming investment begins to stabilize. As a result, per capita inward investment starts to fall, and outward investment begins to rise.

In Stage IV, a country becomes a net outward investor, as the ownership advantages of its firms increase and the propensity to exploit these advanatges in a foreign location grows.

We would like to test this hypothesis against time-series data on Korea for the period from 1962 to 1982. Dunning has designated Korea a newly industrializing country to fall in Stage III. Table 9.9 shows Korea's

TABLE 9.9. Korea's international direct investment position 1962/82 ($ millions)

	Outward direct investment (I_o)	Inward direct Investment (I_i)	Net outward investment $(I_o - I_i)$
1962	—	0.6	−0.6
1963	—	2.1	−2.1
1964	—	3.1	−3.1
1965	—	10.7	−10.7
1966	—	4.8	−4.8
1967	—	12.7	−12.7
1968	—	14.7	−14.7
1969	—	7.0	−7.0
1970	7.5	25.3	−17.8
1971	6.9	36.7	−29.8
1972	5.1	61.2	−56.1
1973	3.9	158.4	−154.5
1974	23.1	162.6	−139.5
1975	9.2	69.2	−60.0
1976	8.2	105.6	−97.4
1977	17.8	102.3	−84.5
1978	43.4	100.5	−57.1
1979	22.8	127.0	−104.2
1980	21.1	96.6	−75.5
1981	40.1	105.4	−65.3
1982	129.4	100.6	28.8

Source: Ministry of Finance. Investment is defined as capital flows plus reinvested profits of existing firms.

inward, outward, and net outward investment position by year over the past two decades. According to the table, there was a tendency in Korea towards growing negative net outgoing investment up until 1973 and towards declining but still negative net outgoing investment after then. In

1982, however, for the first time Korean firms invested more abroad than foreign firms invested in Korea.

In broad terms, Dunning's characterization of the relationship between a country's position of net outward investment and the level of development fits the Korean case quite well. However, there are a couple of important qualifications which should be added to this observation.

As pointed out by Dunning himself, much depends on the nature of the government's FDI and industrialization policies. In Korea, as pointed out earlier, procedures for the entry of foreign firms have become more restrictive since 1973. Therefore, much of the stagnant level of incoming foreign investment since then has been more a result of restrictive foreign investment policy in Korea than of declining investment opportunities in Korea or waning ownership advantages for foreign firms.

At the same time, depending on the character of the industrialization strategy adopted, different countries will show wide differences. For example, if a country runs a surplus in its current account balance, as in Singapore or Taiwan, outward investment will be encouraged. On the other hand, if the country runs consistent deficits in its current account, its ability to invest abroad will be severely limited.

As these differences in environment, system, and policy (ESP) variables will strongly influence the speed and character of changes in investment patterns described by Dunning, we believe that a very strong or precise hypothesis about the form of the development cycle may be difficult to make.

Status of outward direct investment by Korean firms

Outward direct investment (ODI) by Korean firms began as early as 1968, but ODI at the early stages was small in scale and limited mainly to forestry development in Indonesia (to provide logs to the Korean plywood industry) and construction activities in Indonesia and Guam. There were also several investments in high-seas fishing bases and trade agencies.

During the early 1970s, some additional ODIs were made in areas of forestry development, fishing, construction, and trade agencies. The first manufacturing ODI occurred during this period to produce food seasonings in Indonesia.

After 1975, as Korean exports continued to increase, many Korean firms began to set up trade agencies in various countries. The number of trading agents reached 194 and the amount of their investment $36.7 million by the end of 1982. Thus, in terms of the number of investments, these

trade agencies accounted for 56.6% of the stock of Korea's ODI (at the
end of 1982), although in value terms they accounted for only 13.6%.

In the late 1970s, mining began to emerge as another major area[12] of
ODI, while Korean firms also began to invest in overseas transportation
and warehousing activities. In addition, ODI continued in the areas of
forestry, construction, and trade.

Table 9.10 shows the industrial distribution of Korea's ODI by period.
Like Japanese ODI in the early days, Korea's ODI was relatively concentrated in overseas resource development. ODI in agriculture, fisheries,
forestry, and mining all fall into this category, and together they accounted for 56% of all ODI by Korean firms through the end of 1982.

TABLE 9.10   Industrial distribution of outward direct investment ($'000s)

	1968–72	1973–77	1978–82	Total	%
Agriculture			893	893	0.3
Fishery	552	5,493	3,168	9,213	3.5
Forestry	9,032	10,335	17,785	37,152	13.8
Mining			103,007	103,007	38.2
Manufacturing		7,578	25,873	33,451	12.4
Food processing		1,600		1,600	0.6
Other fibre yarns			630	630	0.2
Fabricated textile products			923	923	0.4
Wood and wood products			7,234	7,234	2.7
Paper and paper products		1,348		1,348	0.5
Printing and publishing		60		60	
Synthetic resins, rubber and other chemical products		541	464	1,005	0.4
Rubber products			8,200	8,200	3.0
Non-metallic mineral products		1,761	4,110	5,871	2.2
Basic metal products		1,220	2,401	3,621	1.4
(Steel products)		1,220	2,401	3,621	1.4
Fabricated metal products			100	100	
General machinery			551	551	0.2
Electrical machinery			278	278	0.1
Electronic and communication equipment			819	819	0.3
Other manufacturing		1,048	163	1,211	0.4
Services	4,199	37,202	44,340	85,741	31.8
Construction	2,750	1,697	25,985	30,432	11.3
Transportation and ware-housing		1,700	1,042	2,742	1.0
Trade	1,050	20,562	15,045	36,657	13.6
Other services	399	13,243	2,268	15,910	5.9
Total	13,783	60,608	195,066	269,457	100

Source: Ministry of Finance.

The other two major areas of foreign activity by Korean MNEs were in the fields of construction and trade. To support construction activities, mainly in the Middle East and more recently in South East Asia, many Korean construction firms set up subsidiaries in those countries. By 1982, several of the 50 largest international construction firms in the world were Korean. Clearly Korean firms seem to have established a country-specific ownership advantage in this sector of activity. In addition, as noted earlier, many trade agencies were established in trading-partner countries to promote sales in those countries.

Manufacturing investments by Korean firms have been relatively small, accounting for only 12.4% of total ODI. The major manufacturing investments so far have been in the fields of plywood, tyres, cement, and steel pipes. These are products in which Korea currently enjoys a country-specific advantage but that comparative advantage is eroding. In the future, as Korea's wage rates continue to rise, and as Korean firms search for new ways of entering protected industrial markets, ODI in manufacturing is expected to rise, both in developing and industrial countries. This predicted pattern is certainly consistent with Dunning's investment development cycle.

A review of the characteristics of Korea's ODI tells us that its effects on changes in Korea's industrial structure should have been minimal in the past. Most of the commodities which Korean firms developed abroad were available in the international market, some (in the mining area) have just begun their operation, and fish caught in the high seas were sold directly in the international market. Therefore the foreign activities by Korean firms in resource development do not appear to have made any significant contribution to the development of industries in Korea which use the resources domestically.

Neither is it obvious that the overseas activities of the Korean construction companies directly affected domestic economic structure, although indirectly, by increasing foreign exchange earnings, they have affected growth. The expansion of overseas construction activities may have marginally helped the growth of domestic construction-material-producing industries and the heavy equipment industry, but here again the effect appears to have been minimal, as the proportion of materials or equipment supplied by domestic Korean firms has been small. Furthermore, the expansion of overseas construction activities has not been so much a result of ODI in the field, rather it has been the cause.

ODI in trade activities, although it may have helped the growth of Korean exports in general, has not been related to any changes in the activities of any specific industry. In one or two manufacturing sectors, however, ODI does seem to have had some impact on the restructuring of the Korean economy. Two industries may be noted for special reference.

Hurt by the deep recession in the US construction market, Korea's ply-wood industry began to shrink rapidly in the early 1980s. The industry also began to lose its competitiveness, as Korean wage rates rose and as resource nationalism in forest-rich countries strengthened. The response to these events was for two Korean companies to set up plants in Indonesia to manufacture plywood. These appear to have been the first true cases of relocation of production facilities by Korean firms.

The second case is that of the fabricated metal and machinery industry. There is some suggestion that ODI has enabled Korean machine-makers to export manufacturing plants. In the future, as the foreign manufacturing activities of Korean firms increase, the growth of the fabricated metal and machine industry may be facilitated.

Overall, however, the ODI by Korean firms appears to have exerted very marginal influence on changes in Korea's industrial structure, at least up to the end of the 1970s.

9.8 SUMMARY AND CONCLUSIONS

This chapter has examined the relationship between direct foreign invest-ment, trade, and industrial structure in Korea. We have found that the pattern of foreign direct investment in Korea has been strongly influenced by Korean government policy, which has been as much directed to chang-ing the economic structure as exploiting its current advantages. In addition, we have found that foreign firms' influence on sectoral efficiency in Korea has been positive but marginal. The impact of the foreign activi-ties of Korean firms on Korea's industrialization process also seems to have been very small, although it is expected to become stronger in future.

The Korean case-study confirms that the effects of foreign direct invest-ment depend on the environment, system, and policies (ESP) of the host countries as much as on the strategy and behaviour of foreign investors themselves. If the absorptive capacity of domestic businessmen, techni-cians, engineers, and labourers is underdeveloped, transfers of technology or skills cannot be effectively realized. Similarly, if the economic system of the host country is full of inefficiencies or biases, only those foreign firms who would enjoy special benefits from the biases in the system would come in. The same holds true for irrelevant policies. Thus any examina-tion of the effects of foreign investment must take into consideration the underlying ESP status in the host country.

In the case of Korea, it seems that the absorptive capacity of the nation's labour force has been high due to the relatively high level of edu-cation and the good work ethic. Also, the economic system has not been excessively biased. Therefore industrial policies and foreign investment policies followed by the government have been important factors in determining the effects of foreign investment in Korea.

In general, it can be said that when the government followed an export-oriented industrialization strategy (1962–73), the effects of FDI on allocative and sectoral efficiency were positive. FDI in exporting industries contributed to allocative efficiency in Korea, while most FDI in import-substituting industries provided essential raw materials for exporting industries or for domestic consumption. On the other hand, when the government pursued an overly ambitious import-substituting industrialization strategy (1973–80) with heavy import protection, the positive effects of FDI may well have been much less. Inefficiency was inevitable for many new industries, particularly at their early stage of development, and resource allocation became biased as the government sought to overdevelop some industries into exporting industries with the help from foreign investors.

In conclusion then, changes in Korea's economic structure have been pretty much determined by the Koreans themselves, rather than by the activities of foreign-based MNEs. Foreign investors have had some influence in industries like electronics through their exporting activities, but their effects on both allocative and sectoral efficiency appear to have been marginal in determining the overall pattern of industrial development in Korea.

However, as the Korean government plans to open up the opportunities for both inward and outward investment in the future, its role in determining industrial development of Korea may become more important.

NOTES

1. For a more comprehensive analysis of the role of FDI in Korea's recent economic growth, refer to Koo (1983).
2. For a comprehensive discussion on industrial policies followed by Korea, see Westphal and Kim (1977).
3. The relative growth of transportation activities in 1980 seems to have occurred both because of the second oil shock which sharply increased the cost of transportation services and of the rapid growth of shipping and airline companies.
4. Domestic demand structure is influenced by the changes in income, which in turn are influenced by exports. Therefore, in the case of Korea, total effects of exports on changes in industrial structure should have been much greater, although this cannot be shown statistically.
5. However, coming into the 1980s, a fundamental change also occurred in the policies on foreign investment. With the realization that the restriction of FDI in some key industries like consumer electronics and computers had resulted in underdevelopment

of these industries in Korea, and that the FDI is one of the most effective or indeed the only instrument for efficient technology transfer, particularly for highly advanced industries, the governmemt reversed its position and began to liberalize the inflow of direct foreign investment.

6. As regards the changing form of foreign investment in Korea, refer to the author's study (1982), 'New Forms of Foreign Investment in Korea', KDI Working Paper Series 82-02. In this study, the author showed that in Korea the incidence of less-than-foreign-majority-owned investment increased considerably from about 1973, relative to that of majority-foreign-owned investments.

7. Consumer electronics is another field where the market structure had been differentiated oligopoly. However, most FDI in the field of electronics was either to produce parts and components or, in the case of final consumer goods, to export their entire products.

8. Refer to Koo (1983).

9. The government carried out another survey in 1983 regarding the performance of foreign firms during 1978 to 1982. However, most of the results were not available when the author was writing this chapter.

10. Several industries had to be omitted because either there was no foreign investment, or only a single foreign investment, or no domestic producers.

11. The higher capital intensity of foreign firms in Table 9.7 appears to have been the result of high (in absolute amount) capital intensity of foreign firms in some industries where the general level of capital intensity was very high.

12. This was because of three large investments amounting to a total of $93 million by the semi-state-run steel company in Korea (POSCO) in Australia, Canada, and the Antilles to develop bituminous coal.

REFERENCES

Caves, R. E. (1971). International corporations: the industrial economics of foreign investment, *Economica*, **38**, February

Caves, R. E. (1974). *International Trade, International Investment, and Imperfect Markets*, Special Papers in International Economics, No. 10, November, Princeton University

Dunning, J. H. (1981). *International Production and the Multinational Enterprise*, London: Allen and Unwin

Kim, K. (1980). *Patterns of Industrialization and Their Causes in Korea*, Korea Development Institute (in Korean)

Kojima, K. (1973). *Direct Foreign Investment*, London: Croom Helm

Koo, Bohn-Young, (1982). *New Forms of Foreign Investment in Korea*, Working Paper 82-02, Korea Development Institute

Koo, Bohn-Young, (1983). *Role of Foreign Direct Investment in Korea's Recent Economic Growth*, Working Paper 81-04, Revised Korea Development Institute

Vernon, R. (1966). International investment and international trade in the product cycle, *Quarterly Journal of Economics*, **80**, May

Vernon, R. (1971). *Sovereignty at Bay*, New York: Basic Books

Westphal, L. and Kim, K. (1977). *Industrial Policy and Development in Korea*, World Bank Staff Working Paper No. 263, Washington DC

Westphal, L., Rhee, Y. W., and Pursell, G. (1981). *Korean Industrial Competence: Where It Came From*, World Bank Staff Working Paper No. 469

10

India

SANJAYA LALL

10.1 INTRODUCTION

The case of India holds special interest for the study of inward and outward foreign direct investment (FDI) in a developing country. India now has a fairly large industrial sector, ranking about twentieth in the world and fourth in the developing world (after China, Brazil, and Mexico). This sector has achieved a high degree of depth and diversity. It can produce for itself most of the capital and intermediates it needs, while manufactured consumer goods have been entirely provided within India for the past two to three decades. Indian industry is primarily national in ownership, and displays the greatest degree of self-reliance in technology.

At the same time, India has turned in a generally poor performance in terms of growth of GNP or manufacturing industry. It has steadily lost its share of export markets in most traditional and manufactured products. Most analysts trace this to a constellation of highly interventionist, inward-looking policies directed to non-economic objectives. In the context of the present survey, two features of FDI flows deserve mention. First, there has been practically no new foreign investments in India in the past 15 years, and the net FDI inflow has been largely negative as a result of capital outflows and dilution of foreign equity holdings. Second, India has, at the same time, emerged as a significant Third World exporter of FDI in manufacturing.

The interventionist regime has, in other words, succeeded in restricting MNEs from the developed world during the period which witnessed the most powerful historic expansion of international production, at the same time promoting the development of competitive ownership advantages of its indigenous enterprises. In the context of the ESP paradigm, India started with an extremely favourable economic environment—some natural resources, a potentially large internal market, a great supply of technical manpower and an enormous one of cheap raw labour. In the initial period, it also had one of the Third World's largest stocks of FDI and one of its most developed industrial sectors. Despite the size and diversity of the country, it has enjoyed a fairly stable political framework. Its social environment has bred a long tradition of commercial and industrial entrepreneurship.

With this sort of headstart in industrialization, India might have followed a quite different path, along market economy lines, from that it actually has done. In fact the impact of FDI on Indian economic structure has been overwhelmingly dominated by policy considerations. These considerations are now briefly described.[1]

The framework of Indian industrial and FDI policy 1960–80

As with most industrializing countries in the 1960s, India launched a policy of import-substitution. It moved quickly into local production of the entire range of heavy, capital-intensive and complex producer goods, as did some other large Third World countries. Unlike them, however, India persisted in wholesale import-substitution when others realized the bottlenecks and inefficiencies inherent in this strategy and moved to different degrees of outward orientation and specialization in production. India persisted in pursuing a form of industrial autarky, with trade intended to supply inputs which the country could not physically produce. It then sought to promote exports by giving subsidies to counter the high costs, rigidities and difficulties of producing and selling from a fragmented, technologically obsolescing, managerially slack, and infrastructure-starved production system.

These characteristics are common to most inward-looking regimes (Balassa *et al.,* 1982). India added several peculiar distortionary measures of its own. The 'commanding heights' of the economy were reserved for the public sector, which has turned out over time to be grossly inefficient, overmanned, and mismanaged. The private sector was subjected to a battery of controls which divided capacities into non-economic units, held back competitive forces, forced very expensive degrees of self-sufficiency and arbitrarily inhibited investment and expansion into profitable activites. The most notable regulation was the MRTP (Monopoly and Restrictive Trade Practices) Act, under which any firm of over a certain size (currently about $20 million) or with a dominant share of any market (over 20%) was labelled a 'monopoly' house, and automatically subjected to additional restrictions on growth. Since most MNE affiliates are MRTP firms, this regulation is of particular significance here. The peculiar features of the anti-monopoly regulation were the very low threshold, the automatic nature of resulting controls, the complete absence of considerations of minimum efficient economic size and the presumption that the 'public interest' was always threatened by large size with no further need of proof. Surprisingly, far more dominant public sector enterprises were totally exempt.

Foreign affiliates were subjected to yet more stringent controls. Enterprises with over 40% foreign ownership were classified as FERA (Foreign Exchange Regulation Act) firms, and were basically told to leave the country or dilute their equity. The only exceptions allowed (under which they could retain 51–74% shareholding) were if they met stiff requirements of inducting 'high technology' or being 'export-oriented'. Since the imposition of FERA in 1974, of a total of 800 or so affiliates in the country, 61 left India, 112 were asked to dilute foreign shares to 51–74%, 231 to dilute to 40% or less, 72 diluted on their own, and the rest were already under the 40% limit. Several sectors of industry were closed to foreign firms altogether. In many others, official entry conditions were so difficult, cumbersome and restrictive that new capital inflows were effectively excluded. In terms of the present discussion, therefore, it is vital to remember that *MNEs now have a marginal, highly circumscribed and non-market governed role in India*. Of all the NICs, India has excercised the tightest control on MNE entry.

Next, throughout the 1960s and 1970s India had a clear preference for importing foreign technologies via arm's length licensing arrangements rather than direct investments. However, even licensing was subject to stringent controls (Lall, 1984). The government laid down the sectors where licensing was allowed. Each contract was closely scrutinized to ensure that indigenous technologies were not being excluded, to apply prescribed royalty rates (1.8–3% of sales after tax), to reduce the life of the agreement and to permit horizontal transfer of technology by the licensee. This complex structure of controls, designed to protect local technology and reduce payments for foreign technology, succeeded in keeping down technology inflows: it also led to a lot of second-rate technology being imported and to growing technological lags in Indian industry. More important in the long run, the combination of total protection against imports, substantial protection against MNE entry, and restriction on licensing, in a market charactreized by slow growth (see below), conspired to reduce the *demand* for new technologies within the country, exacerbating the inefficencies and uncompetitiveness of Indian industry.

Finally, there were widespread price controls. Designed to protect the 'common man' from the rapacity of industrialists, this served to hold back investment, modernization and growth in a range of industries, from textiles and cement to paper and pharmaceuticals. On the other hand, articles designated 'luxury goods' (most consumer durables) were subject to punitive excise duties, thus inhibiting the growth of what are normally the high-growth, 'sunrise' industries in other NICs, the future direction of their export thrust.

Much of what has been written still applies today. The contribution of MNEs to the Indian economy, their effects on competitiveness and structure, must be assessed in this unique setting. Similarly, the development of ownership advantages by local enterprises must be weighted against the national economic welfare implications of the policy structure. Not that these can be done properly in this chapter—but the context must be duly emphasized.

10.2   INDIA'S INTERNATIONAL INVOLVEMENT

Overall performance

In 1980, India, with a per capita GNP of $240, ranked the nineteenth lowest in the world (according to the *World Development Report 1982*). The average annual growth in the per capita income in 1960–80 had been 1.4%, compared to 7.0% for South Korea, 5.1% for Brazil, 6.8% for Hong Kong, 7.5% for Singapore, 2.6% for Mexico (and 6.6% for Taiwan in 1960–78). Even trouble-stricken Argentina had managed 2.2%, from a much higher base than India.

India's manufacturing output grew by 4.5% per annum in 1970–80, compared to 16.6% for Korea, 9.3% for Brazil, 9.3% for Hong Kong, 9.6% for Singapore, 5.9% for Mexico (13.2% for Taiwan, 1970–8). The only NIC which performed worse in manufacturing in the 1970s (though it did better in the 1960s) was Argentina, at 1.0%. India's insipid overall performance was also characterized by sharp cyclical fluctuations and a marked deceleration over time in industrial growth. This is not to say that other factors than inefficient, inward-looking strategies have not contributed: certainly a decline in net aid receipts and growing infrastructural problems worsened the situation. But other NICs compensated for declining aid by switching to export-oriented policies, and the bad management of infrastructure was symptomatic of the general inefficiencies which characterized government intervention in the economy.

Trade

The size of the Indian economy perhaps dictates that trade will never figure very largely in total activity. However, the 'self-reliant' nature of

India is certainly exacerbated by its low income levels and the policies assiduously pursued by the government. Thus, in 1980 India's total merchandise exports ($6.7 billion) came to 4.7% of GDP and merchandise imports ($12.9 billion) to 13.8%; manufactured exports by themselves ($3.7 billion) came to 2.6%.

India's import involvement is not very interesting to discuss because it is, as mentioned earlier, so tightly controlled. About 51% consists of food, fuels, and primary materials, and the rest of producer goods (equipment is 19% of total imports, the rest being intermediates[2] and components) not actually manufactured in the country. It is India's involvement in export markets which is of greater relevance here.

It is hardly surprising, in view of the policies pursued, that India's export performance has been markedly poorer than other industrializing countries'.[3] In the early 1950s India was the Third World's largest exporter of manufactures. By 1978, it ranked seventh. Its annual growth rate of manufactured exports was 1.3% in 1953–60 and 6.7% in 1960–6, compared to 9.9% and 27.5% for Brazil, 14.0% and 80.0% for Korea, 29.5% and 36.5% for Taiwan, and 24.5% in the second period for Singapore (Balassa *et al.,* 1982, p. 45). In 1966–78, the annual compound rate of manufactured export growth was 12.7% for India, compared to 43.4% for Korea, 36.7% for Taiwan, 31.1% for Brazil, 26.0% for Argentina, 23.2% for Singapore, 20% for Hong Kong, and 19.7% for Mexico (Wolf, 1982, p. 36). Not only did it fare badly in the new manufactured products into which other NICs diversified rapidly (mainly engineering products), it also lost ground in traditional manufactures like textiles, footwear and clothing, and in primary products like food and raw materials.

It is evident, as a recent study (Wolf, 1982) shows, that the main factor inhibiting India's export growth has been its overall industrial strategy. Exports have largely squeezed out of a slack, high-cost structure by a haphazard set of incentive policies, often in response to large excess capacities generated by slow and cyclical domestic market growth. A few enterprises have managed to generate genuine competitive advantages within this framework, which have enabled them to develop a genuine commitment to exports and to invest overseas. Unfortunately these remain the proverbial exceptions to the rule in Indian industry.

Technology flows

This section deals first with technology imports and then with technology exports by India; inward and outward FDI are reserved for later discussion.

(a) Technology imports

In general terms, India has, over the past 20 years, had the lowest reliance on foreign technologies, in *any* form, of all the NICs.[4] Technology imports by means of foreign turnkey projects and foreign engineering consultants have been effectively banned since 1968; before this, in 1957–67, some 254 agreements for plant construction had been signed with foreign contractors. Since 1981, a few large agreements have been signed overseas, mainly as a result of project-financing arrangements. In the 1970s, however, when most NICs were building large-scale industries employing foreign engineering firms to set up state-of-the-art process plant, India had opted for domestic contractors (who had bought foreign process designs).

Licensing of foreign technology, while the preferred means of technology import, was also inhibited by a variety of measures. The entire sum of foreign 'collaboration agreements' (in Indian terminology this includes both FDI and licensing) approved by the government amounted to 6,959 in 1957–82. While the absolute number appears large, a significant number (63% between 1975–81) of approvals *never materialized*, for unknown reasons. A comparison of total licensing payments (the Indian data are estimates) shows that, as a percentage of manufacturing value added in 1979/80, India paid about 0.7%, Korea 1.1%, Brazil 1.9% and Mexico 2.7%. Given that India was in much heavier, more complex activities than all the NICs except for Brazil, and that it imported little technology in other forms, this low reliance on licensing is even more striking.

The picture is similar when embodied technology import in the form of capital equipment is considered. India has not only the lowest *relative* reliance on imported capital goods, the absolute value of such imports (excluding transport equipment) came to $1.6 billion, compared to $4.4 billion for Brazil, $3.5 billion for Mexico, and $5.3 billion for Korea. Furthermore, the import content of locally manufactured capital goods was also the lowest in India—under 10%, compared to about 20% for Brazil, 45% for Korea and 50% for Mexico.

This low level of technological dependence has, with a simultaneous effort to manufacture the entire range of industrial goods, generated a great deal of indigenous technological effort. The effort has drawn upon the largest pool of technically qualified manpower in the Third World: in 1977–8, India had some 2 million scientists and engineers, compared to 0.6 million in Brazil, 0.8 million in Korea, and 0.4 million each in Mexico and Argentina. The above discussion has stressed that the production and export of products is not efficient in India—however, even high-cost and highly-regulated production requires local technological implementation, assimilation, and adaptation. The technological effort inherent in expanding production has been supported by an active policy of encouraging local industrial R&D, backed by a large network of state laboratories working on all aspects of manufacturing and other technologies (Lall, 1984a).

(b) Technology exports

The substantial technological base India has built up, in concert with high-cost production, has led to its becoming a relatively more important exporter of technology than of products (Lall, 1982a, 1984c). Depending on the nature of the industry, the technologies exported by India have been simplified and adapted to low-income consumers (consumer goods); rendered more rugged, less automated, less specialized (capital goods); or substituted different raw materials, descaled and adapted to tropical conditions (process industries). A major part of the 'adaptation' has been simply the result of using older technologies than developed countries, but the rest has resulted from deliberate technological effort.

India is the largest exporter of industrial turnkey projects among the NICs. By early 1982, it had won over 200 contracts valued at $2–2.5 billion overseas, compared to about $285 million for Brazil, $106 million for Argentina, $43 million for Mexico, and under $800 million for Korea (see Lall, 1984b). In the consultancy field, India has earned some $125 million overseas in the sale of various engineering and managerial (including software) services. In licensing and technical services, Indian enterprises have earned significant sums in royalties and fees abroad, in a large variety of industries (Lall, 1984c). While precisely comparable data are not available for other NICs, what data exist strongly suggest that India is among the leading exporters of industrial technology in the Third World.

The fact that India has achieved this in the markets of less industrialized countries does not necessarily signify that the technology *in use* within the country is efficient or competitive. Indeed, it is officially admitted that it is not. This is one of the manifestations of the curious paradoxes which Indian industrialization presents, and which form a constant refrain in this chapter.

Direct investment flows

The previous section argued that India had simultaneously managed relatively low-technology imports and high-technology exports relative to other NICs, filling the gap, as it were, by indigenous technological effort.

Very much the same applies to direct investment flows.

As far as foreign MNE investment in India is concerned, the data are rather patchy and sometimes conflicting. It is necessary, therefore, selectively to utilize official data which seem best to represent the true Indian position. A fairly comprehensive survey of foreign-majority- and minority-owned firms (but excluding foreign 'branches') in 1963–4 by the Reserve Bank of India (RBI, 1968) showed that total foreign equity in 591 firms stood at Rs 1,960 million ($412 million). Of this, the manufacturing sector accounted for Rs 1,417 million ($296.4 million), with 68% of the equity held by foreign-majority-owned firms. Within the manufacturing sector, the main areas of foreign investment were chemicals (27.9%), and machinery and transport equipment (28.4%); metal products attracted 14.1%, traditional activities like textiles, food, beverages and tobacco 16.2%, and miscellaneous (including the important industry, rubber) 13.3%. The proportion of foreign shareholding, among a sample of 827 firms, was highest in food, beverages and tobacco (79%), followed by chemicals and pharmaceuticals (48%), and electrical machinery (39%).

These data relate to equity actually owned overseas. The total paid-up share capital controlled by the 591 corporations was $852 million (of which manufacturing industry accounted for $652 million). By 1971, the total share capital in 200 branches and 429 foreign firms (all those with 25% foreign equity or over) was placed at $1.270 million (Chaudhuri, 1978, p. 165).

After 1971, there are no comprehensive data available on stocks of foreign capital in India. The best recourse is to work with data on selected foreign-controlled firms which are regularly published in the *Reserve Bank of India Bulletin* as part of their compilation of balance-sheet figures of the large corporate sector.

In 1977–8, for instance, 276 foreign-controlled firms in manufacturing had a total share capital of $804 million, some 30% of the share capital held by the RBI sample of 1,353 large manufacturing firms in India. The value added by these 276 foreign-controlled companies came to about $1.4 billion, which was 7% of total value added in manufacturing in 1979 in India (*World Development Report, 1982*). If it is assumed that this sample accounts for the great bulk of foreign industrial activity in the country,[5] it would be fairly safe to take the overall foreign share of industry at *just under 10% today.*

What about foreign shares in different industries? To calculate these, resort must be had to a convenient but not entirely reliable method: taking dividends paid abroad as a percentage of total dividends paid by Indian firms in a given period as a proxy for foreign ownership. The problems with this measure arise from the fact that inter-industry differences are influenced by differences in profit rates and by pay-out ratios as well as by foreign ownership. Nevertheless, these are the best indicators available and are, at least, suggestive of the broad magnitudes involved. Note that these show only the shares of foreign firms in selected samples of large publicly-quoted companies in the country, *not the shares in total manufacturing*.

TABLE 10.1 Share of total dividends on Indian firms in the large corporate sector accounted for by dividends paid abroad by foreign affiliates

Industry	(No. of firms)	Dividends abroad %
1. Edible oils	(12)	—
2. Sugar	(60)	0.73
3. Other food products	(30)	47.69
4. Tobacco	(7)	38.26
5. Cotton textiles	(241)	6.33
6. Silk and rayon textiles	(14)	2.89
7. Woollen textiles	(9)	3.13
8. Breweries, distilleries	(20)	—
9. Transport equipment (other than motor)	(14)	18.34
10. Motor vehicles and components	(42)	21.56
11. Electrical machinery	(112)	25.99
12. Machinery other than transport, electrical	(149)	15.42
13. Foundries, engineering workshops	(72)	10.23
14. Ferrous, non-ferrous metal products	(71)	25.54
15. Chemical fertilizers	(13)	34.47
16. Dyes and dye stuffs	(10)	16.18
17. Man-made fibres	(13)	12.56
18. Plastics raw materials	(11)	20.44
19. Other basic industrial chemicals	(44)	18.97
20. Medicines and pharmaceuticals	(52)	43.38
21. Paints, varnishes	(15)	20.69
22. Other chemicals	(45)	50.48
23. Cement	(18)	2.43
24. Rubber and products	(19)	42.45
25. Paper and products	(42)	4.59
26. Glass and glassware	(12)	13.24
27. Printing and publishing	(24)	3.80
28. Industrial, medical gases	(11)	28.69

Source: Lall and Mohammad (1983b).

The calculations of foreign ownership, available for 28 industries, are presented in Table 10.1. The highest foreign shares are held in 'other chemicals' (50.5%), 'other food' (47.7%), pharmaceuticals (43.4%), rubber (42.5%), tobacco (38.3%), and chemical fertilizers (34.5%). The lowest are in textiles of various kinds, paper, printing and publishing. Two have no foreign equity. The average level of foreign ownership in the large corporate sector by this measure is around 20% (which seems reasonable compared to the 10% of *total* value added in manufacturing mentioned above).

The industrial distribution of 'foreign presence' in the large corporate sector is more or less in line with what received theory suggests. However, the tight regulations imposed on MNE, and private corporate, activity in India does affect foreign presence. The findings of an econometric analysis of this are reported in the next section.

The stocks and shares of foreign capital in India do not indicate how restrictive towards MNEs the government has been. On this, data on fresh capital investments approved in the past 15 years are more illuminating. Data collected by the Indian Investment Centre show that in 1969–82 new foreign investments of Rs 770 million ($77 million at current exchange rate) were approved. Of this, a substantial proportion never materialized (since over 60% of all collaborations, including direct investments, did not materialize in 1975–81). If it is assumed conservatively that half of the approvals did lead to investments, a figure of *under $40 million for the 14 years to 1982* results (an average of *$2.9 million per annum*). This is, moreover, a gross figure, since it does not take account of repatriations. Compare it to *net* direct investment inflows of $14 billion into Brazil in 1979–80, $7 billion in Mexico in the same period, $648 million in Korea (and presumably about the same in Taiwan) and $1.5 billion in stagnant Argentina. In fact, there is no market economy in the Third World with a substantial industrial sector which has constricted MNE entry to anywhere near the extent of India.

Let us turn now to India's direct investments overseas.[6] Though the first recorded direct investment in modern times took place in 1962, it was not until the 1970s that Indian MNEs really took off. By late 1980, India's overseas commitment was $45 million in 118 ventures in operation and another $17 million in 87 ventures under implementation. Indian regulations require that very little overseas investment be made in cash. The breakdown of existing Indian foreign equity is: cash 6%, capital goods 69%, capitalized knowhow 11%, others 14%. The government regards foreign investment mainly as a method of export promotion. And, indeed, by this criterion, foreign ventures have been quite successful. Up to 1980, the ventures had generated $40 million in dividends, $14 million in royalties, and $108 million in 'additional exports' (products sent for assembly, etc. abroad, excluding the initial capital equipment provided).

The main destination of Indian investments was South and East Asia, which took nearly 60% of the total equity, followed by Africa (29%), W. Asia (5%), and the OECD countries (7%). The main industries in which

Indian MNEs were involved were textiles (25.4% of equity), paper and pulp (18.0%), engineering (16.9%), food and palm oil processing (11.0%), and hotels and restaurants (7.8%). Manufacturing as a whole took 82% of the total.

In the field of manufacturing investments, India is the third largest among the NICs, after Hong Kong and Singapore (Lall *et al.*, 1983). The two island economies are something of a special case in the Third World, and their openness, high wages and small size set them apart from the other NICs. Among the larger economies, Indian industry reveals the highest *net* propensity to export direct investment, whatever measure one uses to define this 'propensity'. A simple application of Dunning's eclectic theory would suggest one or both of two things: India is generating ownership advantages for its industrial enterprises more rapidly than other NICs, or, given similar advantages, location factors are leading Indian enterprises to exploit them overseas to a greater extent. It is argued later that both factors seem to apply, but with important qualifications.

This concludes the description of India's international involvement in manufacturing industry. In brief, this has been extremely limited as far as exports of manufactures and imports of technology and inward direct investment are concerned, and relatively large for technology exports and outward direct investments. This has implications both for the extent and nature of ownership advantages which the Indian regime has generated, and for the locational costs of exploiting them at home and abroad. Section 10.5 below will analyse these intriguing questions.

10.3 FOREIGN MNEs AND INDIAN INDUSTRIAL COMPETITIVENESS

This chapter has dwelt at considerable length on the policy framework to show that foreign enterprises were given very little freedom in India: in consequence, many of the 'normal' effects of MNEs on industrial structure and performance cannot be expected to obtain here. Nevertheless, most of the largest MNEs have been present in India for long periods, and the government has sought to exploit one of their chief advantages: advanced technology. These factors may allow some traces of 'normal' market-determined tendencies to show through. This section reviews the evidence on this under four headings: industrial distribution of FDI; export performance and MNEs; technology and R&D; and local linkages. Market structure is excluded because there are no data available on concentration levels in Indian industry.

Industrial distribution of FDI

Practically all the evidence on the industrial determinants of FDI has concerned the highly industrialized countries with liberal investment and trade regimes. The general findings are that 'foreign presence' would tend to be greater in activities characterized by high levels of innovation and marketing (what Caves terms 'product differentiation'), and those requiring large size of enterprise (which facilitates the launching of multiplant and capital-intensive ventures).[7] There may be exceptions, however, some latecomers like Japan may start by investing more in low-technology small-scale activities (Ozawa, 1979); those entering the most advanced country, the US, may shy away from highly concentrated and 'differentiated' sectors (Lall and Siddharthan, 1982); and, of course, Third World MNEs, of which more below.

As far as developing host countries are concerned, there is practically no econometric analysis of the distribution of FDI. Nevertheless, *a priori* reasoning strongly suggests that, given the weak competitive position of indigenous enterprise, the usual advantages of MNEs would be accentuated: thus, they would tend to dominate in high-technology, high-marketing, high-skill and capital-intensive activities. The counteracting force would be government restrictions on foreign entry. In the case of India, not only did the government rule out several sectors altogether, its stifling regulatory apparatus severely constricted investments even in sectors which were apparently permitted to MNEs. Most of the received wisdom of MNEs is thus perforce inapplicable to India. However, two points need to be noted: first, India had a fair stock of foreign investment by the 1960s, before restrictions were really clamped down. Second, the emphasis on getting FDI mainly as a vehicle for advanced technology sought to exploit at least one of the two main advantages of MNEs. On both grounds, therefore, some elements of the normal MNE characteristics should obtain in India.

Using foreign over total dividends as a proxy for foreign ownership in the Indian corporate sector, a statistical examination has been conducted recently of the industrial distribution of FDI (Lall and Mohammad, 1983b). A log linear function, using multiple regression techniques, was fitted. Here only one result, the essence of the findings, is presented:

$$FS = 0.488 \overset{***}{\text{Royalty}} - 0.300 \, HPE + 0.679 \overset{***}{\text{Profitability}}$$
$$(2.94) \qquad\qquad (0.24) \qquad\quad (2.05)$$

$$+ 2.292 \overset{***}{\text{Fixed Assets}} - 2.630 \overset{***}{\text{Capital Intensity}}$$
$$(3.38) \qquad\qquad\quad (3.34)$$

$R^2 = 0.656 \, n = 28$ (Parentheses show t values
(Significance levels: *** at the 1% level)

The dependent variable is foreign share of ownership in the large corporate sector (as shown in Table 10.1). The independent variables are: royalty – total royalties paid as a percentage of sales, a measure of technological intensity; HPE – ratio of total employee remuneration going to 'highly paid employees', a measure of managerial intensity; profitability – profits before tax on net worth, a measure of general efficiency in the given environment; fixed assets – fixed assets per firm, a proxy for scale economies (possibly also capturing the existence of multiplant economies); and capital intensity – plant and machinery per highly-paid employee (total employment data were not available, but another measure of capital intensity based on US data gave very similar results). Other variables tried but not shown included advertising as a proportion of sales, average wage in similar US industries, and local R&D as a percentage of sales.

The results of the statistical analysis suggest that

> the determinants of foreign direct investment in the large corporate sector of India are somewhat different from those of developed countries. Research and development expenditures and marketing requirements play an insignificant role, though sophisticated technology remains the main reason why India received (and seeks) foreign capital in this form. Foreign firms do not enter industries requiring high levels of general skills, though they concentrate on management-intensive activities and on the more profitable sectors of manufacturing. India shares with the developed countries the propensity to attract MNCs to scale-intensive (or multiplant-intensive) industries, but its peculiar regulatory system seems to keep them out of capital-intensive activities where they may be thought to have special advantages. (Lall and Mohammad, 1983b, p.154.)

The most noteworthy result is the absence of foreign enterprises in marketing-intensive industries, certainly a result of government policy, though perhaps also aided by the low-income characteristics of much of the home market. It must be noted, however, that in the early days of India's industrialization, it was MNEs like Unilever and British American Tobacco which brought modern marketing methods to the country in low-income, mass-consumption goods. The subsequent size of local firms in most consumer industries, based upon the deliberate restriction of MNEs (and derived from a political nexus between the ruling Congress Party and large Indian business houses), led to a general deterioration of marketing in India relative to world standards, a point touched on again below in the context of Indian MNEs.

Export performance of FDI

While a large proportion of world trade in manufactured products is now handled by MNEs, and a handful of NICs have clearly benefited from MNEs using them as bases to serve world markets, the eclectic theory does not predict that MNEs will become important exporters from every host country. Clearly, two factors will crucially influence whether MNEs in a given country (which have been attracted there by a protected local market) will choose to use that location to export: first, the costs of producing in and exporting from that location, and second, the appropriability of benefits arising from export activity in that location. Thus, the lower the production, transport, infrastructural and other costs, the greater the incentive to expand exports, and the lower the degree of appropriability (the higher the tax rate or the extent of local participation) the lesser this incentive (Katrak, 1983).

In the global context, the above discussion should have clarified why India cannot be a major export base for MNEs. Despite low labour costs and large supplies of skilled labour, production in India is difficult and costly; for MNEs, the pressure for dilution of equity is a further handicap. The government does permit higher foreign shareholding in export-oriented enterprises, but this incentive is counterbalanced by high cost and regulations. It is only some MNEs already in India who seek to benefit from this provision; new entrants find the environment comparatively unattractive.

Given the anti-export bias of all Indian industry, however, it is still possible that MNEs perform better than indigenous counterparts, because they have access to a package of advantages that may give them an edge in international markets. Previous researchers in India have resorted to simple comparisons of export/sales ratios of selected samples of local and foreign firms without attempting to correct for industry- or firm-level differences for government incentive policies. There are, however, three sets of statistical attempts to 'explain' export performance of MNEs in India which use several variables.

Katrak (1983) uses RBI data on exports by foreign subsidiaries (foreign ownership of 50% or more) in 1964 and 1969 to test for the effect of foreign ownership shares. While the degrees of freedom are extremely limited ($n = 10$ for each year) Katrak's regression results support his hypothesis that higher degrees of foreign ownership promote export performance (exports as a proportion of sales) for 1964 and for 1964 and 1969 combined. Katrak's other variables, capital intensity and protection rates, both have negative effects, though the latter barely reaches statistical significance.

Katrak's results are suggestive, but they pertain to fairly old data, and the small number of observations and lack of a variable for export incentives reduces their value. Moreover, they do not permit a comparison of foreign with local firms.

The next statistical exercise is by Lall and Mohammad (1983c), using the same data on the large private corporations described in the previous sub-section. The dependent variable is exports over sales, and independent variables are foreign ownership (measured as above), capital intensity (measured by the capital-output ratio), managerial skill intensity (HPE as in the above regression), and export incentives (reported in a World Bank study). The number of industries covered here is 24, containing just over 1,100 enterprises (of both Indian and foreign ownership).

The variables for foreign ownership and export incentives are collinear, so the following result excludes the latter (it may be noted that incentive has the expected positive sign, and, when tried without foreign ownership, almost reaches conventional significance levels).

$$E/S = 0.116 \overset{*}{\text{ FS}} - 0.793 \overset{*}{\text{ HPE}} - 0.862 \overset{**}{\text{ K/O}} \qquad R^2 = 0.382$$
$$(1.961) \qquad (1.834) \qquad (2.688)$$

(Significance levels: * 10%, ** 5%).

Foreign shares thus turn out to have the predicted positive and significant sign. Capital intensity also has the predicted (negative) sign: a labour-surplus country like India has its comparative advantage in labour-intensive activities. HPE turns in the wrong sign: we could have expected higher managerial skills to promote international competitiveness in the large corporate sector. The negative sign may imply that most managerial effort is devoted to serving domestic markets.[8] In the Indian setting, perhaps this sign should have been expected.

The final set of findings concerns some firm-level investigations conducted by the present author on the leading 100 engineering and 45 chemical firms in India. Some earlier results, for the top engineering firms in 1976–8, were published in Lall and Kumar (1981); the later results, for 1978–80, still have to be written up. Unfortunately, none of the efforts to explain export performance yielded very significant results, underlining the perfunctory interest which even the largest Indian firms have in foreign markets. Without going into the detailed findings, it may simply be reported that foreign ownership failed to yield any statistically significant results in both attempts. In Lall and Kumar (1981), a dummy variable was used for foreign ownership, since data on extent of foreign shareholding were not at hand. In the later regressions, foreign share was available, but had no impact on the dependent.

It may be worth remarking, however, that in the later set of regressions, 'foreign association' in general (measured by the *total number of foreign collaborations*, technical and financial, per firm) did have a positive and significant impact. This was true of the groups of engineering and chemical firms separately and in combination. However, it is difficult to deduce from this the impact of MNE investment as such on export performance.

The evidence on MNEs and Indian exports thus leaves much to be desired. In the corporate sector as a whole, foreign ownership seems to be positively associated with exports of manufactures, but in the groups of top 100 engineering and 45 chemical firms there is no such statistically meaningful relationship. Within the group of foreign subsidiaries, there is some evidence that in the 1960s greater foreign ownership promoted export performance. The one clear fact is that the environment has not been conducive to export activity in general, and the country missed out completely on the wave of export-oriented investments that went to several neighbouring countries of South-East Asia.

Technology and R&D

In the absence of recent data on the transfer of technology to India by MNEs,[9] this section is limited to an analysis of the impact of MNEs on local technological activity within the country. There are two ways of assessing this impact: through the participation of MNE affiliates in technology exports by India, an indirect measure of the growth of local technological capability; and through actual R&D activity performed by the affiliates in India.

As far as exports of technology are concerned, nearly all turnkey projects are undertaken by Indian-owned firms. Since major international contractors and consultants are not permitted to have bases in India, this is to be expected in the consultancy or process-contracting sectors. However, a number of major capital-goods manufacturing MNEs are present in India, and may have expected to undertake foreign turnkey work in the engineering goods sector. Their activity in this area has been relatively restricted (Lall, 1984c). A number of possible reasons may be adduced for this. First, their parent companies may prefer to source their international turnkey jobs elsewhere, because of restrictions on Indian operations. Second, Indian capital goods may be too old-fashioned for deployment by MNEs (though this is often the selling edge of Indian firms in less industrialized markets). Third, affiliates of MNCs may have lower or 'shallower' technological capabilities than local firms, because basic design functions are kept centralized in the home countries of the parent firms. This is an important argument, which will be considered more fully in a moment.

As far as the exports of disembodied technology by means of licences, technical assistance and the like are concerned, it appears that foreign enterprises *are* very active in India. In a study of the determinants of disembodied technology exports by large Indian firms, Lall and Mohammad (1983a) entered foreign ownership (as defined earlier) as one of the explanatory variables: while the variable failed to reach conventional levels of significance, its sign was consistently positive. More recently published data (RBI *Bulletin*, July 1981) show that, of the group of 1,353 large industrial corporations surveyed, the 276 foreign-controlled firms earned foreign royalties of Rs 16.4 million (about $2 million) in the 3 years 1975–6 to 1977–8, as compared to Rs 10.5 million ($1.3 million) for 1,077 Indian companies. Thus the average per firm was Rs 59.4 thousand for the foreign and Rs 9.7 thousand for the Indian companies. As a proportion of sales, royalties earned in 1977–8 for the foreign group came to 0.014% and for the Indian group 0.0002%. In the same year, royalties earned as a proportion of royalties paid overseas came to 13.2% for the foreign and 4.2% for the Indian firms.

It is interesting to glean a few further facts about overseas royalty earnings by the foreign-controlled firms from the RBI article. First, all of it arose in the engineering and chemical ('modern') sectors. Second, all of it was earned (in 1977–8) by UK firms, numbering 134 in total. Third, nearly 90% of the royalties earned abroad came from less than 40 UK firms which were in the largest size category employed by RBI, with net assets over Rs 100 million ($12.5 million). In sum, therefore, a handful of long-established, large British firms (probably concentrated in the engineering sector, see below) were making a relatively important contribution to India's technology exports in this form.

Coming now to R&D efforts by foreign and indigenous firms, reference is made to a paper which examines the impact of MNEs on local technological development in host LDCs (Lall, forthcoming). This paper distinguishes between different levels of local technological development, concentrating on the build-up of local 'knowhow' (production engineering and management) and of local 'know-why' (basic product/equipment design and R&D). Using R&D data for the 145 largest engineering and chemical firms mentioned earlier, it concludes as follows:

> the two sectors show different tendencies. Taking a large number of regressions . . . into account, engineering has a positive and consistently significant sign, while chemicals has a negative and only occasionally significant sign. The two sectors also show interesting differences in the impact on R&D of firm size, age, export performance, and the proportion of highly paid employees: clearly, generalizations across different sectors cannot be drawn. Foreign ownership has a positive relationship

with R&D in one major sector. *There is no support for the case that MNCs in general are less R&D intensive than local firms.* (Lall, forthcoming, emphasis in original)

A further comment is necessary here. It has been generally noted that in major developed host countries like Canada (Economic Council of Canada, 1983) and Australia (Parry and Watson, 1979) MNE affiliates perform less R&D locally than indigenous firms. This 'truncation' of R&D by MNE affiliates is neither unexpected nor, *per se*, undesirable. Scale economies in innovative activity and its close linkages with the science infrastructure in the home country call for a centralization of efficient R&D effort. The transfer of the fruits of R&D from parent to affiliate generally ensures that the latter deploys the most advanced and competitive technologies, confining its own technological effort to relatively minor activity. There are notable exceptions, of course, where affiliate R&D assumes independent significance, but, by and large, low R&D does not imply that the host economy suffers from the utilization of backward technologies.

What, then, of the Indian data, which suggest that affiliates perform as much, sometimes more, R&D than large local firms? The nature of technological activity in a developing country like India differs substantially from developed host countries. In developing countries, both foreign affiliates and local firms undertake R&D primarily to implement and adapt imported technologies. Indian policies for technological self-reliance (which also affect formal technology imports by affiliates) and indigenization of components raise the need for local R&D to higher levels than most other NICs. In this setting, competitive production necessitates similar technological efforts among large firms in comparable industries, regardless of ownership. Moreover, in this setting, a high level of local technological effort is *not necessarily a 'good thing'* (Lall, 1984b). The competition which affects technological behaviour is within an insulated, fragmented market, and technologies in use may lag well behind those in advanced, and competing developing, countries. There is a scale of comparative advantage in undertaking technological, as well as production, activity, and pushing firms beyond their appropriate level can create distortions and raise costs. India may, in other words, do far better by having lower levels of R&D at home but importing and efficiently 'productionizing' advanced technologies (as Korea and Brazil are doing).

On the technology front, therefore, MNE affiliates perform quite creditably in India, within the constraints set by its policies. At the same time, these constraints prevent the country from realizing the full benefits of technologies possessed by MNEs. Efforts to develop local technological capabilities further than comparative advantage permits, within an environment which breeds inefficiency, generates a few benefits and many costs.

Linkages

This section can be brief. There are few systematic studies of MNE's local linkages in India. Both foreign and local manufacturers have achieved the maximum possible degree of local sourcing of inputs and components. Given this, both have set up remarkably complex networks of linkages with local suppliers, providing them with technology, designs, advice, and non-financial assistance (Indian rules make financial linkages impossible). Lall (1980, 1983) investigates the linkages set up by local affiliates of a truck manufacturer and a food/toilet products firm, and compares them to local firms. These linkages have greatly assisted the growth of small-scale suppliers and have involved considerable cost and effort on the part of the principals.

There is no reason to believe, on the basis of this admittedly limited evidence, that foreign firms are different from local ones in establishing local linkages. The extent of linkages has been determined by the import-substituting strategy: as with other matters, MNEs have responded as rationally as local firms.

10.4 INDIAN MNEs

What are the ownership advantages of Indian MNEs vis-à-vis MNEs from other NICs, and the reasons for India's relatively high international activity? A recently concluded research project on Third World multinationals (Lall *et al.*, 1983) goes into some detail on the possible sources of monopolistic advantages of Indian MNEs. As far as technology is concerned, it concludes:

> the two main factors which emerge as underlying Indian MNCs' technological advantages are *production experience* and *basic design (R&D) capability*. Capital goods production is significant as an additional advantage in a relatively few cases. The ability to reproduce a given technology, and the ability to modify it (often very slightly) to particular circumstances, are the main technological strengths of Indian MNCs .... It may not appear that the proprietary technology of Indian investors constitutes a particularly powerful asset. The asset is certainly not unique to Third World firms .... Many of the foreign ventures in the sample may equally have been set up by developed country firms .... In these cases, the edge of Indian firms may reside in several factors: partly in the contingent circumstances of *'being first'* ... partly in having *special cost advantages* ... and partly in the *efficiency and uniqueness* of the adaptions which Indian MNCs have made to products and processes. (Lall *et al.*, 1983, pp. 59–60; emphasis in original)

The study goes on to review other sources of ownership advantages, and says:

> The technological advantage that exists may receive an important boost from managerial skills specially developed in difficult home environments. In the case of producer goods, this seems to be supported by an adequate grasp of marketing techniques, if not by well-known brandnames. Conglomerate ownership seems to supplement some firm-specific factors, and ethnic/government connections may have a very minor and occasional edge for our sample firms. (Lall et al., 1983 p. 67)

There is no doubt that there are beneficial aspects to the technological development which underlies India's ownership advantages. The ability to assimilate and reproduce complex technologies can provide a base for autonomous growth and for rapid development of dynamic comparative advantage. A technologically progressive industrial sector can generate widespread linkages with other activities, and so create mutually beneficial externalities.

In India's case, however, the costs of the peculiar strategy followed have probably outweighed the benefits. Apart from the broader macro-economic inefficiencies resulting from the policy package, the development of ownership advantages in particular enterprises has gone hand-in-hand with technological lags even in the Indian MNEs as compared with their competitors in the NICs, and even more so compared to the advanced countries. Thus, the fact that India can provide technologies to less-industrialized countries does not mean that these technologies (in use at home) can produce goods which can compete with, say, Korea and Taiwan in the large, sophisticated markets of the rich countries. The ownership 'advantage' of many of its MNEs is thus an odd one: it is an advantage in certain limited circumstances, and its possession in fact implies obsolescence (and slow growth) at home. Moreover, there has been a lopsided development of capabilities, with technological capabilities growing, to some extent, ahead of managerial, marketing and similar capabilities. The sheltered market has particularly hampered the proper growth of consumer goods industries, and poor marketing, inadequate quality control, bad/outdated design, and so on, are factors which mark India's firms from, say, their Hong Kong counterparts.

Under normal circumstances, the technological prowess of Indian MNEs would be regarded as economically beneficial for the home economy. Under the highly policy-distorted conditions of India, there are reasons to believe that such advantages imply a net cost to the economy. MNE theory must, therefore, be refined further to take account of the case of 'immiserizing ownership advantages', a parellel to immiserizing growth under distorted conditions in the trade literature.

It is possible to argue that the relatively high internationalization of Indian enterprises reflects not so much the possession of greater advantages as the influence of location factors, making overseas production preferable to exporting. The influence of locational factors is undeniable, for reasons amply discussed above. However, locational factors do not explain the phenomenon wholly. The greater technological autonomy of India as compared to other NICs is obvious. Its greater achievements in technology exports by means other than FDI (e.g. turnkey projects) suggests that in certain kinds of (tailor-made, highly skilled, labour-intensive) production, exports from India are quite competitive, and the added disembodied engineering element is a distinct competitive advantage.

What have been the effects of overseas direct investment on the Indian economy? Taking the policy context as given, we may briefly discuss the scanty data at hand under three headings.

TABLE 10.2   Main Indian investors abroad (as of 30 June 1981)

Group/Firm	No. of ventures	Indian equity (*Rs '000*)	Share %
1. Birla Group	18	142,760	15.1
2. Thapar Group	9	126,908	13.4
3. Tata Group	7	99,714	10.6
4. JK Group	4	42,966	4.5
5. Modi Group	2	40,874	4.3
6. HMT[a]	2	37,688	4.0
7. Usha Martin Black	2	33,900	3.6
8. Oberoi Hotels	4	26,750	2.8
9. Shahibag Enterprises	2	21,128	2.2
10. Larsen & Tubro	2	18,700	2.0
11. Godrej Group	4	13,731	1.5
12. Kirloskar Group	8	11,794	1.2
13. Sarabhai Chemicals	2	7,212	0.8
14. Indian Tobacco Company	3	4,585	0.5
15. Chemical Construction Co.	3	3,836	0.4
16. Mahindra & Mahindra Group	2	3,350	0.4
17. ITDC[a]	1	2,926	0.3
18. Mafatlal Group	1	583	0.1
Sub-total	76	639,405	67.7
Others	131	305,607	32.3
Grand total	207	945,012	100.0

[a]Government of India enterprises: HMT stands for Hindustan Machine Tool and ITDC for Indian Tourism Development Corporation (which has invested in hotels abroad).
Source: Lall *et al.* (1983).

(1) *Industrial structure*: The bulk of equity overseas is held by a handful of large Indian business houses (Table 10.2). The top 5 MNEs, accounting for 48% of total Indian equity, are all from the leading 20 business groups in the country, with another 4 numbering among the 18 largest overseas investors. While Indian industry is oligopolistic, government policies have inhibited further concentration, leading some of the large houses to start the process of international diversification. Foreign investments are still a small fraction of investments within the country, but clearly expansion overseas is linked to large size domestically. It cannot, however, be asserted that expansion overseas has a significant effect on firm size or industry structure within India: the phenomenon is too new and marginal for such feedbacks to have taken place.

TABLE 10.3   Foreign exchange earnings generated by Indian foreign ventures (Rs million)

Year	Dividends	Royalties etc.[a]	Additional exports
Up to 1969–70	4.3	4.2	39.3
1970–1	0.5	1.1	4.4
1971–2	1.0	1.3	10.1
1972–3	1.7	1.7	13.3
1973–4	2.5	2.3	42.1
1974–5	3.4	2.9	73.6
1975–6	2.6	13.0	97.8
1976–7	4.0	13.0	104.7
1977–8	5.3	19.6	146.8
1978–9	5.4	21.8	161.4
1979–80	5.5	27.1	163.6
1980–1[b]	na	na	3.7
Total	361.1	108.0	861.7
(a) Units in operation	26.7	68.4	817.4
(b) Abandoned	9.4	20.9	40.5
(c) Under Implementation	—	18.7	3.8

[a]Includes technical fees, royalties, management fees, engineering service fees and selling agency commissions.
[b]Data incomplete.
Source: As Table 10.2.

(2) *Foreign exchange*: Table 10.3 shows data, essentially up to 1979–80, on the foreign exchange earnings generated by Indian foreign investments. It separates dividends from royalties and technical fees, and also shows 'additional exports' generated in the form of materials, spares amd components sent to affiliates (excluding the initial investment in the form of

capital goods). It is apparent that the rate of return by means of dividend repatriation is relatively poor, under 2% per annum. This reflects the poor performance of many affiliates: in 1978–9 only 15 out of 117 ventures in operation declared profits. The poor performance, in turn, reflects teething problems on the part of many new investments, and the survival problems of others suddenly exposed to greater competition than at home. However, larger affiliates tend to fare quite well, and many of them receive substantial protection in their host countries. In the longer term, therefore, dividend remittances should improve.

(3) *Technology*: A few firms have invested abroad deliberately to get access to foreign technologies not readily available within India (Lall *et al.*, 1983). It is likely that these firms have enjoyed beneficial feedbacks to their operations at home. Others have not gone abroad to seek foreign technologies as such, but the force of competition and exposure to new technologies has probably induced them to upgrade their own technologies.

On the whole, the effects of foreign investment seem to have been beneficial, taking the larger policy framework as given. If this framework is *not* taken as given, of course, many serious questions arise about the value of the industrial development which has spawned these investments, and about the merits of exporting capital from a country as poor as India.

10.6 CONCLUSIONS AND POLICY IMPLICATIONS

By adopting its *mélange* of restrictive trade, technology and industrial policies, India has not only had too little MNE entry. It has also failed to exploit the technological, managerial and marketing advantages offered by MNEs. Existing affiliates have been unable or unwilling to bring new techniques, products and methods on a continuous basis to existing, and potentially new, activities. Very few new MNE investments have taken place, and those that have have been minuscule by world standards. This has also held back the competitive process which would spur indigenous firms to new levels of technology and efficiency. It has clearly stifled India's potential comparative advantage in export markets.

By the same reasoning, India may have overpromoted overseas investment by its own enterprises. An over-regulated corporate sector, fostered in an over-protected market and forced to over-extend its technological learning, has developed certain ownership advantages. Some of these advantages are socially beneficial; some clearly find a market in certain less industrialized countries. But by and large they have not led until now to a sustained increase of India's productivity, its efficiency, or its penetration of the world's major export markets.

Given that there *are* ownership advantages, their exploitation abroad is beneficial in the given framework. If the industrial economy of India is really to move forward, however, there is little doubt that the basic rules of the game will have to be changed. These changes must involve more liberal investment and operating conditions for MNEs, but they must also entail a thorough-going revision of policies on industrial licensing, public-private sector ownership, export-import controls an access to foreign technologies. The essential need is to get industrial units which are competitive in world markets and stay abreast of changing technologies. To achieve this, it would be necessary in most cases to have much larger scales of production, better technologies, more efficient management and marketing, adequate infrastructure, improved labour relations, and a vastly superior administrative framework.

MNEs can contribute towards these objectives in several ways. Directly, they can introduce better technologies, set up larger scale facilities, apply advanced managerial and marketing skills, and provide better access to international markets. Indirectly, they can offer increased competition to local counterparts, transfer technologies to vertically linked local firms and create a general environment which is more 'international' for the consumers, government, and industry. However, liberal MNE operations in the *present* protected Indian economy may not benefit the host country: MNEs would enter and grow, but their operations would probably assume various inefficient characteristics dictated by the structure of regulations.[10] It is only liberalization of FDI in the context of a wider liberalization of industrial regulation, firmly rooted in a more trade-oriented regime, which would enable India to extract real economic benefits from MNEs. The first stirrings of economic liberalization which have marked policies in the past two or three years have not, umfortunately, showed signs of moving towards this broader objective.

It is beyond the scope of this analysis to discuss the nature, costs, and consequences of major changes in Indian industrial policy. In the narrower context of FDI policy, some specific suggestions may be made for inward and outward flows separately.

On inward FDI, liberalization will have two aspects. First, existing MNE-linked firms within India should be granted freedom to operate and expand on equal terms with wholly Indian firms (and the latter should be freed from the arbitrary and harmful constraints of the MRTP Act). They should also be freely permitted to increase foreign ownership shares regardless of the technological or export-orientation of their operations: if the macro-economic signals are set correctly, the more efficient firms will out-compete less efficient ones precisely by introducing better technologies and entering export markets. In the interim phase, however, flexible performance requirements may be imposed to ensure that export markets are duly served. This may, in turn, require much freer access to imported inputs and consequently less emphasis on maximizing local content. Second, new MNE entrants must be granted much greater freedom than exists at present to choose sectors for investment and degree of foreign shareholding, and must be relieved of the cumbersome bureaucratic requirements that now deter entry. Given the government's preoccupation to foster national ownership, it is likely that some sectors will remain out of bounds to MNEs, and that some form of joint-venture condition may be retained. Even so, there may be a lot of room for manoeuvre before political limits to liberalization are reached.

On outward FDI it seems reasonable to assume that domestic liberalization, modernization, and growth will attract to local investment some of the capital which is currently being invested overseas. However, this will not affect a part of FDI outflow which supports an export drive overseas; in fact, with greater export orientation and a stronger domestic technological base, such FDI may be expected to increase. The government should support this, by permitting more equity investments in the form of cash, providing better information and infrastructural support to prospective investors, and giving more liberal fiscal concessions than are presently allowed. A development which should be especially favoured (and indeed the government favours it now in principle) is the setting up of joint ventures overseas by Indian and developed country MNEs. This is a logical extension of the application of comparative advantage to the FDI field, with the developed country MNEs providing high technology and brand names, the Indian MNEs production engineering and management. One further measure may be to tie inward DFI by a large MNE with its joint venture in third countries with its Indian partner.

One final comment: this section has deliberately eschewed arguments for promoting indigenous enterprise by keeping out MNEs. India has gone too far in just such policies, and it is time to swing the pendulum the other way and let long-established Indian groups face some competition at home.

NOTES

1. See Bhagwati and Desai (1970), Bhagwati and Srinivasan (1975), Lall (1983a), and Wolf (1982). For a concise comparison of Indian industrial strategies with other NICs, see Chapter 3 of Balassa (1982). An earlier, and still illuminating, analysis is by Little, Scitovsky, and Scott (1970).

2. Intermediates are taken here to include pharmaceuticals, the only manufactured goods imported directly for consumption by India.
3. For a longer discussion see Chapter 7 of Lall (1981).
4. This section draws heavily upon Lall (1984b).
5. It was noted earlier that there were 200 branches and 429 foreign-controlled firms in India in 1971. The justification for taking 276 foreign-controlled firms in 1977–8 as the bulk of foreign MNEs in India is that most branches were wound down after FERA (most of them were not in manufacturing, anyway), and a large number of affiliates diluted their equity. In any case, there is a high level of concentration by size among foreign investors, which would by itself justify the assumption.
6. For more detailed analyses see Lall (1982b) and Lall *et al.* (1983).
7. See Caves (1982) and Dunning (1981).
8. Another possible interpretation may be that HPE indicates skill requirements in which India is poorly endowed. I am grateful to Homi Katrak for this point.
9. An earlier study is by Balasubramanyam (1973).
10. For a theoretical analysis see Bhagwati (1978).

REFERENCES

Balassa, B. and associates (1982). *Development Strategies in Semi-Industrial Economies*, Baltimore: Johns Hopkins Press. A World Bank Research Publication

Balasubramanyam, V. N. (1973). *International Transfer of Technology to India*, New York: Praeger

Bhagwati, J. N. (1978). *Anatomy and Consequences of Exchange Control Regimes*, New York: National Bureau of Economic Research

Bhagwati, J. N. and Desai, P. (1970). *India: Planning for Industrialization*, London: Oxford University Press

Bhagwati, J. N. and Srinivasan, T. N. (1975). *Foreign Exchange Regimes and Economic Development: India*, New York: National Bureau of Economic Research

Caves, R.E. (1982). *Multinational Enterprise and Economic Analysis*, Cambridge: Cambridge University Press

Chaudhuri, P. (1978). *The Indian Economy*, London: Crosby, Lockwood, Staples

Dunning, J. H. (1981). *International Production and the Multinational Enterprise*, London: Allen and Unwin

Economic Council of Canada (1983). *The Bottom Line: Technology: Trade and Income Growth*, Ottawa: Minister of Supply and Services

Katrak, H. (1983). Global profit maximisation and the export performance of foreign subsidiaries in India, *Oxford Bulletin of Economics and Statistics*, **45**, 205–222

Lall, S. (1980). Vertical inter-firm linkages in LDCs: an empirical study, *Oxford Bulletin of Economics and Statistics*, **42**, 203–226

Lall, S. (1981). *Developing Countries in the International Economy*, London: Macmillan

Lall, S. (1982a). *Developing Countries as Exporters of Technology*, London: Macmillan

Lall, S. (1982b). The export of capital from developing countries: The Indian Case, in J. Black and J. H. Dunning (eds), *International Capital Movements*, London: Macmillan

Lall, S. (1983). Technological Change, Employment Generation and Multinationals: A Case Study of a Foreign Firm and a Local Multinational in India, Geneva: International Labour Office, Multinational Enterprises Programme, Working Paper no. 27

Lall, S. (1984a). India's technological capacity: effects of trade, industrial and science and technology policies, in M. Fransman and K. King (eds), *Technological Capability in the Third World*, London: Macmillan

Lall, S. (1984b). Exports of technology by newly industrialising countries: an overview, Editor's Introduction to Special Issue of *World Development* on 'Exports of Technology by Newly Industrialising Countries', **12**, 471–480

Lall, S. (1984c). Exports of technology by India, *World Development*, Special Issue on 'Exports of Technology by Newly Industrialising Countries', **12**, 535–565

Lall, S. (forthcoming). Multinationals and technology development in host LDCs, in International Economic Association, *Structural Change, Economic Interdependence and World Development: Proceedings of the Seventh World Congress*, Madrid, September 1983

Lall, S. and Kumar, R. (1981). Firm-level export performance in an inward-looking economy: the Indian engineering industry, *World Development*, **9**, 453–463

Lall, S. and Mohammad, S. (1983a). Technological effort and disembodied technology exports: an econometric analysis of inter-industry variations in India, *World Development*, **11**, 527–535

Lall, S. and Mohammad, S. (1983b). Multinationals in Indian big business: industrial characteristics of foreign investment in a heavily regulated economy, *Journal of Development Economics*, **13**, 143–157

Lall, S. and Mohammad, S. (1983c). Foreign ownership and export performance in the large corporate sector of India, *Journal of Development Studies*, **20**, 56–67

Lall, S. and Siddharthan, N. S. (1982). The monopolistic advantages of multinationals: lessons from foreign investment in the U.S., *Economic Journal*, **92**, 668–683

Lall, S. in collaboration with E. K. Y. Chen, J. Katz, B. Kosacoff, and A. Villela (1983). *The New Multinationals: The Spread of Third World Enterprises*, Chichester: John Wiley

Little, I. M. D., Scitovsky, T., and Scott, M. F. (1970). *Industry and Trade in Some Developing Countries*, London: Oxford University Press

Ozawa, T. (1979). International investment and industrial structure: new theoretical implications from the Japanese experience, *Oxford Economic Papers*, **31**, 72–92

Parry, T. G. and Watson, J. F. (1979). Technology flows and foreign investment in the Australian manufacturing sector, *Australian Economic Papers*, **18**, 103–118

RBI (1968). *Foreign Collaboration in Indian Industry: Survey Report*, Bombay: Reserve Bank of India

Wolf, M. (1982). *India's Exports*, London: Oxford University Press, for the World Bank

11

Portugal

Vitor Corado Simões*

11.1 INTRODUCTION

Within a Western European context Portugal is a developing country; in consequence the Portuguese socio-economic situation is somewhat peculiar and contradictory. Portugal is about to join the EEC, but in many respects her industrial structure is closer to that of some Third World countries. She has a relatively long established manufacturing tradition, but she remains largely specialized in low-technology sectors. She has a long colonial history, yet unlike her richer Northern neighbours has few large MNEs of her own. Finally, Portugal is a country where the export of manpower has prevailed over the import of capital.

Today, Portugal is a relatively open economy, and highly dependent on international trade and commerce. This dependence is manifold, and embraces both the acquisition of raw materials, intermediate products, and final goods and the acquisition of embodied and disembodied technology. In 1980, Portuguese foreign trade in goods and services was about 70% of GDP, compared with a 60% average for EEC countries. By contrast, the role of foreign direct investment (FDI) in the Portuguese economy is below that of most West European countries.

The combination of these features makes the analysis of the interaction between direct investment flows and the Portuguese economic structure particularly interesting. Since Portugal is a substantial net recipient of FDI, this chapter will be mainly concerned with the effects of foreign-based MNEs on Portuguese economic structure and international competitiveness. From a normative viewpoint, it is predicated that FDI should play a positive role as a complement to local factors of production, increasing labour efficiency and skills and stimulating the development of

*I wish to acknowledge the invaluable help provided by Dr Michael Fuller, who, sadly died during the writing of this book. I am also grateful to Dr Jaime S. Andrez for his comments and computing support. Finally, my thanks are also due to the Management Council of the Foreign Investment Institute and to the Director of Studies Department for comments and for making possible the utilization of relevant statistical information.

domestic capabilities through its spillover and demonstration effects. As foreign affiliates in Portugal are mainly oriented towards manufacturing industry, which is also playing a key role in the international specialization and modernization of the Portuguese economy, we shall concentrate our analysis on that sector.

The very nature of the subject approached in this chapter advises a dynamic and sectoral approach. Section 11.2 will present a brief historical perspective of the trends and main features of FDI inflows and outflows over the past 35 years or so; these flows will be related to changes which have occurred in the Portuguese environment, system and policy, *viz* the ESP characteristics identified by Koopman and Montias (1971). Section 11.3 will provide data on the relative importance of FDI in the Portuguese economy, a typology of its sectoral characteristics, and an analysis of its determinants. The following sections will consider the impact of inward FDI on a variety of indices of economic structure, including revealed comparative advantage (RCA), skill and capital intensities, and the conduct of foreign affiliates. The conclusions drawn from this analysis and some policy implications will be presented in the last section of the chapter.

11.2   HISTORICAL TRENDS OF FOREIGN INVESTMENT FLOWS

Throughout the last two decades, Portugal has been a net importer of direct investment capital, the inflow of FDI being more than five times the outflow. Moreover, as emphasized by several authors (Matos, 1972; Rodrigues, 1977; Donges, 1979), the characteristics of the international involvement of the Portuguese economy in this period have been strongly influenced by internal government policies.

Three phases can be identified in the post-war development of the Portuguese economy: (i) the nationalistic stage, (ii) the 'opening-up' stage, and (iii) the later phase. These stages broadly correspond to different policy attitudes of the Portuguese administration vis-à-vis foreign investment and to changes in the economic system.

Nationalistic phase

This period covering the late 1940s and the 1950s was characterized by a suspicion, and even hostility, of the Portuguese authorities towards foreign capital. International investment transactions were very low, with the annual average of both inflow and outflow in the 1950s approximating only 0.035% of gross domestic product (GDP) in 1958. The characteristics of the Portuguese economy and government policy provide some explanations for this limited international involvement. The level of development of the Portuguese economy was quite low, with an overwhelming predominance of agriculture in the economic structure and of the landowners in social relationships. Foreign affairs were marked by a retrograde nationalism and a concern to protect the country from outside modernizing influences. The economic system was a formal market economy distorted by strong government intervention. Particularly relevant was the system of *condicionamento industrial* (manufacturing investment control), geared to controlling the establishment of new plants and the introduction of new industries.

The main juridical instrument specifically directed towards foreign investors was the Law on the Nationalization of Capital, enacted in 1943. This law decreed that only national firms—defined as those with at least 60% of Portuguese equity—were allowed to provide public services and/or engage in activities deemed of great interest from the military or economic standpoint. In a phase of European reconstruction and strengthening of capital flows—called by Dunning the 'honeymoon phase' (Dunning, 1982)—Portugal adopted an isolationist stance, remaining inward-looking and nationalist.

However, although foreign firms were not encouraged to invest in Portugal in these years, a good number of affiliates were set up and were able to exploit monopolistic or oligopolistic markets fostered by the *condicionamento industrial*. About 40% of foreign firms were set up in the wholesale trading sector, mainly to meet the country's need for intermediate and equipment goods. FDI in manufacturing was directed towards export industries exploiting natural resources (wood and cork, paper pulp) and/or aimed at supplying the domestic market (chemicals). Although reliable data on investment outflow are lacking, one can be sure that it was very small and mainly oriented towards the (then) colonies. These investments were almost exclusively in agriculture and in mining and quarrying.[1]

'Opening-up' phase

This stage, encompassing the 1960s and early 1970s, was marked by a liberalization of government policies, aimed at encouraging FDI inflow. The internationalization of the Portuguese economy was increased and reached its summit in 1973–4 when the average inward and outward investment flows taken together account for 0.64% of GDP.

A more liberal economic, social, and political environment induced significant changes in government policies towards foreign investment in the 1960s.[2] First, came the Stockholm Convention which created the European Free Trade Association (EFTA). Second, was the signing of the OECD Code of Liberalization of Capital Movements,[3] this was followed by the easing of foreign exchange controls. The last step was the promulgation of a decree liberalizing to a substantial degree the inflow of foreign investment (Decree Law 46312, issued in 1965).

TABLE 11.1   Direct investment flows into and out of Portugal[a]
(Annual averages) (10^3 US$)

	Inflows	Outflows	Balance	Coverage index (%)[b]	Cross-invest. index[c]
1964–5	11,994	818	11,176	6.82	−0.872
1966–8	13,534	441	13,093	3.26	−0.937
1969–71	18,094	3,061	15,033	16.92	−0.711
1972–4	50,950	20,659	30,291	40.55	−0.423
1975–7	23,517	3,688	19,829	15.68	−0.729
1978–80	64,008	8,443	55,565	13.19	−0.767
1981–2	98,989	14,389	84,600	14.54	−0.746

[a]Direct investment flows in the capital of enterprises. Reinvestments and real estate transactions are not included (the amount of real estate transactions for the period 1964–8 was obtained by estimate).

[b]Coverage index $= \dfrac{\text{Exports}}{\text{Imports}} \times 100$

[c]Cross-investment index $= \dfrac{\text{Exports} - \text{Imports of FDI}}{\text{Exports} + \text{Imports of FDI}}$

Sources: Bank of Portugal, reports of the Boards of Directors, various years.
Bank of Portugal, *Boletim Trimestral*, **4**, no. 4, December 1982.

This improvement of the image of Portugal as a possible location for investment resulted in a continuous growth in FDI inflow. Details are set out in Table 11.1. The sharp rise observed in 1972–4 (corresponding to three times the annual average inflow in 1969–71), can also be related to policy measures taken at the beginning of the decade. These included the promulgation of the Law on Industrial Development, which reduced the importance of the *condicionamento industrial*; the trade convention with the EEC; tax and tariff incentives to exports; and the signing of several tax treaties with industrial countries. A large share of the foreign firms established in this period went to labour-intensive industries (e.g. clothing, footwear, electronics, instruments) to take advantage of low wage costs in Portugal; most of their output was exported.

The beginning of the 1970s marks the emergence of Portuguese investment abroad. Table 11.1 shows that the cross-investment index rose from −0.94 in 1966–8 to −0.42 in 1972–4. It is perhaps worth noting that, in several instances, Portuguese firms investing abroad were simultaneously establishing joint ventures with foreign partners in Portugal.

Investments abroad were highly concentrated, involving few companies, industries, and countries. Most outward investors were large firms, usually linked with dominant economic groups in Portugal. The largest share of capital exports was accounted for by the banking sector and went to serve the needs of Portuguese emigrants in France, Germany, Venezuela, Brazil, Canada, and South Africa (Remédio, 1982). Investments in manufacturing were mainly oriented towards the former colonies: traditional light industries and primary manufacture of colonial raw materials, not uncommonly associated with agricultural or livestock production.

The investment by Portuguese firms abroad was strongly determined by country-specific advantages (colonial rule, migrant communities, accumulation of technology and skills due to the building of domestic infrastructures during the 1950s and early 1960s). However, only large firms with technological capacity were fully able to exploit the above advantages. It may therefore be presumed, according to the eclectic theory of international production, that these were the only firms that had the requisite ownership advantages to enter the arena of international production.

The later phase

The fall of the Salazar/Caetano regime marked the dawn of a new phase in the international involvement of the Portuguese economy. Both the inflow and the outflow of investment experienced sharp decreases in 1975. The first declined from $61 to $17 million and the figure remained below the 1973–4 level until 1979; the latter decreased some $20 million and has not yet recovered to its old value.[4] The cross investment index fell to −0.73 in 1975–7 from −0.42 in 1972–4.

These changes reflected both domestic and international phenomena. Following the first increase in oil prices, the international investment climate worsened and industrial countries were embroiled in a major economic crisis. Within Portugal, the change of the political regime led to significant modifications in the economic environment, such as the independence of the former colonies and the emergence of free trade unions.

The economic system itself underwent a major upheaval. Although the nationalizations of 1975 were directed at the leading Portuguese economic groups and not at foreign affiliates, they discouraged potential foreign investors and some existing affiliates were closed. Direct and indirect nationalizations strongly increased state intervention in the economy, despite the abolition of the *condicionamento industrial*. This deterioration in the investment climate forced a reappraisal of government policy, and since 1976 intensive efforts have been made to woo back the foreign investor. The first Foreign Investment Code, which was issued in 1976, aimed at establishing the 'rules of the game', balancing the safeguard of Portugal's own interests and the promotion of FDI, although 'in more strict terms than those laid down in 1975'.[5] However, the practical effects of the law were insignificant, and it remained in force for only 17 months. In 1977 a new Foreign Investment Code was promulgated which—together with its regulatory decrees—sets out the current attitude of the Portuguese administration towards FDI. The most relevant features of this code, markedly more liberal than its predecessor, include: (i) case-by-case authorization of new foreign investments;[6] (ii) readiness to authorize small increases in the capital of existing companies and for investments in priority sectors;[7] (iii) the introduction of two authorization regimes (general and contractual), the latter being available to investments characterized by their size or long-term social profitability; (iv) the granting of rights and conditions to foreign investors similar to those enjoyed by Portuguese companies; (v) the liberalization of the transfer abroad of dividends, profits, and the proceeds of liquidation or sale of foreign affiliates; and (vi) the provision for technology transfer contracts to be scrutinized, evaluated, and registered.[8] As part of the code, a Foreign Investment Institute was set up to evaluate the likely consequences of FDI and technology transfer, for receiving and guiding foreign investors, and acting with regard to them as the sole representative of public administration.

These legislative actions, together with the changes occurring in political and labour areas and in economic policy, have made a significant contribution to an improvement in the foreign investment climate since 1978. The figures shown in Table 11.1 confirm a steady growth in FDI inflows since that year, with the annual average in 1981–2 being four times that of 1975–7.

It is remarkable that the worsening in domestic investment conditions in 1974–5 led to a relatively higher decrease in outward than inward FDI. The coverage index declined from 40% to only 16%. This index contracted again in 1978–80, suggesting a stronger recovery in investment inflows. Such a phenomenon is a consequence of the characteristics of Portuguese investment abroad, with country-specific factors prevailing over firm-specific ones (Dunning, 1981). More specifically we might mention three factors leading to a fall in FDI outflow: (i) the difficulties of Portuguese firms in adapting to new economic and labour conditions compelled them to concentrate on their domestic activities and discouraged capital involvement in foreign business; (ii) the independence of the former colonies and the policy of the new States towards FDI; and (iii) the nationalization of the dominant economic groups which were linked to the biggest firms investing abroad. [9]

More than 40% of authorized investment abroad in 1979–82 was in the banking sector. The motives for investment changed, however, with the desire to gain access to Euromarkets and of obtaining credit lines abroad becoming an important determinant (Remédio, 1982). In 1975–7 investments in industrial sectors were oriented towards Brazil (cement and metalomecanics) and Venezuela (construction industry); after 1978, the former colonies and North Africa were the main destination.

11.3 FOREIGN-RELATED PRODUCTION IN PORTUGAL: AN OVERVIEW

The relevance of foreign-related production

Usually analysed separately, FDI and licensing should be approached in an integrated manner. Indeed, the setting up of a manufacturing plant abroad, the granting of a licence to an independent firm, and exports constitute three alternative ways of exploiting the ownership advantages of a company in the supply of a given market.[10] The choice between licensing and investing abroad depends on various factors.[11] Generally, licensing will be preferred when investment conditions are adverse, when technologies are mature, codifiable, and easily transferable, and where the MNE practises an 'every tub on its own bottom' policy towards its affiliates. From the host country standpoint, FDI and licensing constitute alternative channels for the acquisition of foreign technology and other intangible assets. Some countries, such as Japan, have favoured non-equity arrangements for importing intermediate products; in others, for example Singapore, FDI has been the preferred modality.

Taken together, FDI and licensing may be considered as the external vector of a country's production, in the sense that the production both of foreign affiliates and of domestic firms under licence utilizes production, marketing and/or management know-how obtained from abroad. It is in this sense we define foreign-related production in a country as that which is based on foreign factors of production (including technology) and lends an outflow of revenues, namely through profits and royalties. Although this concept could be extended to include other kinds of production linked to foreign firms (such as subcontracting and turnkey plants), here we will restrict it in the way defined.

Table 11.2 gives an estimate of the magnitude of foreign-related sales in Portuguese manufacturing. By comparing the value of these with that of the foreign penetration[12] it can be concluded that the overwhelming majority of foreign-related sales in Portugal are undertaken by foreign affiliates; indeed production by domestic companies under licence to foreign companies is only 9% of the former. However, in some industries, such as beverages, pottery and chinaware, non-electrical machinery and (since 1980), glass products, manufacturing under licence is relatively more important than the production of foreign affiliates.

Although reliable quantitative data on the export propensity of licensed production are lacking, it is believed that it is appreciably below that of foreign affiliates, which is estimated at 27% in 1981. Indeed, even in sectors where FDI is export-oriented, the major part, if not the whole, of production under licence is sold in the domestic market. It seems that only in clothing, chinaware and glass is licensing aimed at servicing foreign markets, and in some instances (e.g. glass products) this appears to be directly linked with international sub-contracting. This finding is consistent with those of several international studies on the determinants of licensing and on the strategy of technology suppliers, who, in order to avoid competition from licensees through the segmentation of licensed territories, may impose a variety of restrictions, including export restrictions, on their licensees (UNCTAD, 1973; Vaitsos, 1971; Madeuf, 1981).[13]

We conclude then that if licensing can be considered as an alternative to FDI when the latter is oriented towards the domestic market, the same does not hold when FDI is export-oriented and integrated in a worldwide system of product or process specialization.

Typology of FDI in Portugal

The findings presented above indicate that the appraisal of the effects of foreign-related production on the economic structure and international competitiveness of the Portuguese economy needs to identify both the sectoral orientation of such production and the characteristics and conduct of foreign affiliates. To accomplish this task we shall set out a sectoral typology of FDI in Portugal, capable of providing a general picture of the reasons for such investment.

TABLE 11.2   Foreign-related sales in Portuguese manufacturing industry (1978)

Industry[a]		Foreign-related sales[b]	Foreign penetration[c]	Weight of licensing in intern. sales[d]
Food products	{	0.172	0.172	1.00
	{	0.232	0.228	1.02
Beverages		0.217	0.112	1.94
Textiles		0.068	0.067	1.01
Wearing apparel		0.261	0.243	1.07
Leather		..	..	..
Footwear		0.056	0.056	1.00
Wood and Cork products		0.045	0.045	1.00
Furniture		0.029	0.024	1.21
Pulp and paper		0.264	0.264	1.00
Printing and publishing		0.239	0.239	1.00
Industrial chemicals		0.367	0.308	1.19
Other chemical products		0.503	0.424	1.19
Rubber products		0.461	0.461	1.00
Plastic products		0.091	0.080	1.14
Pottery, chinaware		0.007	0.004	1.75
Glass and products		0.251	0.245	1.02
Non-metal products n.e.c.		0.108	0.098	1.10
Ferrous metals		0.189	0.175	1.08
Non-ferrous metals		0.452	0.400	1.13
Metal products		0.130	0.120	1.08
Non-electrical machinery		0.207	0.140	1.48
Electrical engineering		0.683	0.673	1.01
Transport equipment		0.541	0.513	1.05
Professional goods		0.467	0.465	1.00
Other industries		0.219	0.196	1.12
All manufacturing		0.213	0.196	1.09

[a]See Table 11.3

[b]Foreign-related sales $= \dfrac{S_F + S_L}{S_T}$, where S_F are the sales of foreign affiliates; S_L, the sales of goods manufactured under licence by domestic firms, assuming a royalty rate of 5% and a gap of one year between sales and royalty payments, and S_T, the sales of all companies, for each industry.

[c]Foreign penetration $= \dfrac{\text{Sales of foreign affiliates}}{\text{Total sales of companies established in Portugal}}$.

[d](3) = (2)/(1).

.. Not computed.

Source: Own computations, from Foreign Investment Institute, various publications and Inquiry to FDI; Simões, Afonso, and Pires (1982): and Simões (1981).

Market orientation will be taken as the starting point for constructing such a typology. Indeed, in contrast to that in other Southern European countries, manufacturing FDI in Portugal has been to a large extent directed to the export sector. Available data indicate that exports of foreign manufacturing affiliates in Portugal amounted to 27% of sales in 1981, while 90 to 195% of the production of foreign firms in Greece in 1977 and 90% of the production of the biggest foreign affiliates in Spain in 1974 was geared towards local markets (Vaitsos and Saussay, 1980).

The differences in these export propensities of foreign affiliates are partly a reflection of historical forces, including the attitude of the Portuguese authorities towards FDI referred to in Section 11.2: for example, while firms established before 1960 exported only 12% of their sales, in 1981 the corresponding percentage for those set up since that year was 38%. But of no less relevance are industry differences, although in several instances the sectoral breakdown utilized is not detailed enough to provide a clear distinction between exporting and non-exporting activities.

TABLE 11.3   General features of FDI in Portugal

	Export intensity[a] (1981)	Foreign penetration[b] (1978) %	FDI increase 1970–9[c]	FDI increase 1979–82[d]	Length of establishment[e] (1981)
Traditional labour-intensive					
Textiles	0.298	6.69	2.22	0.58	1.15
Wearing apparel	0.688	24.31	0.63	2.44	0.13
Leather	0.645	..	5.43	6.50	0.00
Footwear	0.960	5.56	3.69	2.80	0.89
Other industries	0.409	19.64	0.37	2.45	0.34
Modern labour-intensive					
Non-electrical machinery	0.277	14.05	3.35	0.68	0.26
Electrical engineering	0.399	67.33	1.12	1.12	0.92
Transport equipment	0.355	51.28	0.07	2.32	0.49
Professional goods	0.384	46.50	1.82	0.12	0.00
Resource-based					
Beverages	0.518	11.20	0.73	0.00	2.68
Wood and cork products	0.558	4.51	1.13	3.87	0.77
Pulp and paper	0.706	26.41	0.85	0.00	1.79
Ferrous metals	0.289	17.46	2.19	1.21	0.89
Inward-oriented H-M technol.					
Industrial chemicals	0.109	30.78	1.01	0.35	1.48
Other chemical products	0.065	42.38	1.14	0.91	1.69
Rubber products	0.055	46.18	0.11	0.10	2.68
Plastic products	0.088	8.03	4.28	2.52	0.00
Non-ferrous metals	0.029	40.02	2.68	0.00	1.79
Metal products	0.137	12.04	1.23	0.32	0.47

TABLE 11.3 (*continued*)

	Export intensity[a] (1981)	Foreign penetration[b] (1978) %	FDI increase 1970–9[c]	FDI increase 1979–82[d]	Length of establishment[e] (1981)
Inward-oriented, market-intensive					
⎧ Food products	0.160	17.18	0.35	0.06	1.53
⎩	0.008	22.77	0.96	0.89	1.46
Printing and publishing	0.046	23.93	1.90	0.10	0.95
Inward-oriented low technology					
Pottery, chinaware	0.015	0.39	5.50	0.00	0.00
Glass and products	0.127	24.50	0.00	0.33	0.00
Non-metal products n.e.c.	0.031	9.84	0.60	0.38	1.24
Furniture	0.204	2.37	0.00	0.18	0.00
Manufacturing	0.270	19.56	—	—	—

[a]Share of exports in the sales of foreign affiliates (1981).
[b]See Table 11.2.
[c] $\dfrac{\text{Sales of foreign affiliates established in the sector in 1970–9}}{\text{Total sales of foreign affiliates established in 1970–9 in manufact.}}$:

$\dfrac{\text{Sales of foreign affiliates in the sector}}{\text{Total sales of foreign affiliates in manufacturing}}$.

[d] $\dfrac{\text{Capital of foreign affiliates establ. in the sector in 1979–82}}{\text{Total capital of manufacturing foreign affiliates establ. in 1979–82}}$:

$\dfrac{\text{Capital of foreign affiliates in the sector}}{\text{Total capital of foreign affiliates in manufacturing}}$.

[e]Proportion of foreign affiliated established before 1960 in the sector divided by the proportion of foreign affiliates established before 1960 in manufacturing.
Source: Own computations based on data provided by the Foreign Investment Institute, namely Inquiries to FDI in Portugal, 1977–8 and 1981.

In some industries, however, foreign firms were established with the purpose of supplying the local market. These were usually in replacement of imports and in sectors where they had ownership advantages over their domestic counterparts. By contrast, in others, the location in Portugal was essentially aimed at profiting from local natural resources and labour, the bulk of the production being exported. This distinction leads to consideration of two main groups of industries (see Table 11.3):

(i) exporting industries, i.e. those with an above-average export propensity; and
(ii) industries oriented towards the domestic market, where the export share of sales is below average.

Both groups include sectors with different characteristics, making a further breakdown advisable. Exporting industries may be classified into three types:

(1) *Resource-based industries* where FDI seeks to benefit from the availability of natural resources and similar inputs. These include beverages, pulp and paper, wood products and metallurgy of ferrous metals (where energy prices, geographical location, and infrastructure would have been the determinants of the main investment).

(2) *Traditional labour-intensive industries* mainly established since 1960 to benefit from cheap and plentiful supplies of labour: textiles, wearing apparel and footwear and a residual class of miscellaneous industries fall into this category.

(3) *Modern labour-intensive industries* usually undertaken by high-technology sectors with the goal of integrating the output of the Portuguese affiliates into their worldwide (or European) strategies. Here it is usual to locate assembling activities and the manufacture of more standardized and relatively unskilled labour-intensive products in Portugal to take advantage of one of the country's main comparative advantages. This group encompasses the bulk of mechanical and electrical industries as well as electronics, transport equipment, and professional goods. However, it is worth noting that foreign affiliates in the automotive industry are mainly geared to supplying the domestic market.

With respect to the domestic-market-oriented sectors, we might classify these according to their technological intensity and characteristics of end products.[14] Again we consider three groups:

(4) *Inward-oriented, high-medium-technology industries*, including chemicals,[15] non-ferrous metals, and metal products. These industries, although relatively R&D intensive, can be characterized by the development of worldwide standardized products and processes (Vernon, 1979).

(5) *Inward-oriented, marketing-intensive industries*, corresponding to sectors of low technology but requiring strong interrelationships between producers and consumers and high advertising expenditure. Two industries were of this type, the packaged food industry and printing and publishing. In the first, notwithstanding the existence of some exporting firms linked to agriculture (especially tomato paste), Affiliates of large MNEs account for about 70% of local foreign-related sales. Regarding the second, it seems that marketing techniques have been the main ownership advantages of foreign firms vis-à-vis their domestic competitors.

(6) *Inward-oriented, low-technology industries*, comprising furniture, pottery, chinaware, glass, and non-metal products.

TABLE 11.4 Typology of FDI in Portugal (1981)

	Sales (%)	Exports (%)	Capital (%)	Foreign penetration (%)
Traditional labour-intensive exporting industries	7.51	16.95	6.56	9.86
Modern labour-intensive exporting industries	38.32	51.46	34.34	49.62
Resource-based exporting industries	8.86	18.29	15.95	14.38
Inward-oriented, high-medium-technology industries	27.93	8.41	31.23	27.73
Inward-oriented, marketing-intensive industries	12.64	3.89	7.26	19.08
Inward-oriented, low-technology industries	4.74	1.00	4.66	9.58
Manufacturing	100.00	100.00	100.00	19.56

Source: Author's computations based on data provided by the Foreign Investment Institute.

Table 11.4 provides an insight into the relevance of FDI in each type. This table reveals that both the foreign penetration ratios and the share of sales to the total foreign-affiliate manufacturing sales is highest in the modern labour-intensive export industries and inward-oriented, high-medium-technology industries, and lowest in the inward-oriented, low-technology sectors. This suggests that FDI in Portuguese manufacturing has been mainly directed towards the sectors in which (i) the technology and/or managerial gap between foreign and domestic firms is likely to be greatest; (ii) the incentives to internalizing these advantages are strongest; and (iii) where the advantages of the Portuguese economy are strongest.

Another relevant feature is that sales of exporting industries account for a higher proportion of total sales than those of inward-oriented sectors: 55% against 44%. This suggests that any study of the international competitiveness of the Portuguese economy needs to take account of the influence of foreign affiliates on the structure of Portuguese exports.

11.4   FDI AND EFFICIENCY

The effect of FDI on host-country welfare and resource-allocative efficiency is a controversial subject and its appraisal is commonly influenced by explicit or implicit ideological premises (Lall and Streeten, 1977).

From a host-country viewpoint, higher productivity or profitability by foreign affiliates does not necessarily correspond to a more appropriate resource allocation. International investment is often associated with oligopolistic markets and the establishment of foreign affiliates may be determined by international rivalry and fostered by tariff protection. Therefore the superior performance of foreign firms, rather than being evidence of higher efficiency, may simply reflect their ability to appropriate oligopoly or monopoly rents. Even when market distortions do not exist, it cannot be assumed that the value added generated by foreign affiliate activity will *ipso facto* benefit the host country. This depends on the share of that value added (including taxation) which accrues to residents in the host country.

On the other hand, one should not forget the spillover effects that the activity of foreign subsidiaries may have on domestic enterprises, for example competitors, suppliers, or consumers. Technologies and new management methods introduced into the country by foreign MNEs may have a dynamizing effect on indigenous firms and contribute to increasing their efficiency.

Profitability

A preliminary remark should be made concerning the comparison of the profitability of foreign- and domestic-owned firms in Portugal. Since withholding taxes on royalties are lower in Portugal than taxes on profits, foreign affiliates have an additional motivation for concluding technology transfer agreements: but in effect these can be used as a channel for transferring profits abroad. Therefore foreign firms show a high propensity for technology payments, which usually take place inside multinational groups; in 1981, 90% of technology payments made to foreign manufacturing companies were made by affiliate entities. These payments exceeded by 61% the amount transferred abroad as profits and dividends.

Notwithstanding this evidence, in the research undertaken on the behaviour and performance of the 200 biggest Portuguese manufacturing enterprises in 1979, it was found that foreign affiliates had a higher profitability, defined as the profits/turnover ratio, than their domestic counterparts (Simões and Cristóvão, 1982); the profitability differential was significant at 2.5%.

The gap was more marked when majority-owned foreign firms were compared with minority-owned and domestic firms taken together and was significant at a 5% level. According to the same study, these findings could not be explained by differences of sectoral distribution and/or the technological intensity between foreign and domestic enterprises.

However, considering the gross value/added turnover the performance gap decreases. This means that foreign firms privilege the remuneration of capital over the remuneration of the other factors of production, when compared with domestic companies. Provided that the differences are more significant for foreign-majority-owned firms, it might be concluded that the net effect of the higher productivity of foreign companies is appropriated mainly by the owners of the capital.

In the absence of additional official statistics on profitability, the present study utilized data on 5,000 domestic and foreign firms for 1978–80 (Banco Português do Atlântico, 1981), to examine whether or not sectoral profit was correlated with higher foreign penetration. The result indicates that there is no significant relationship between the two variables.[16]

To sum up, there is reason to suggest that foreign affiliates in Portugal are more profitable than their indigenous counterparts. However, this difference is chiefly appropriated by the parent companies of the affiliates. Indeed, our estimates reveal that the proportion of profits repatriated by foreign affiliates in 1979–80 was about 62%.

Productivity

Profitability refers to the remuneration of a single factor of production and is often subject to several manipulations, due to tax evasion; its usefulness is thereby undermined. Thus productivity may be considered as a more accurate indicator for appraising the contribution of foreign affiliates to the efficiency of resource allocation.

Comparative data for 1977 on the productivity of both domestic and foreign companies are presented in Table 11.5. Although they should be viewed with some caution, due to statistical problems and limited reduced coverage, it is clear that the labour productivity of foreign affiliates is higher than that of their domestic counterparts.[17]

Productivity differences are especially marked in high-medium technology-intensive and/or marketing-intensive sectors where foreign affiliates are mainly set up to the supply of Portuguese market. Examples include light chemicals, rubber, plastics, food industry, publishing and printing. To some extent, this productivity gap is the result of a preference, within each sector, of foreign affiliates for more sophisticated and capital-intensive activities, while domestic firms undertake the bulk of standard and low-technology productions. Another possible explanation might be the greater size of foreign firms, since Portuguese industrial structure is characterized by the existence of a myriad of small-sized, inefficient firms. However, this last hypothesis has only limited validity, for even if the comparison is restricted to the biggest enterprises, foreign affiliates perform better, the difference being significant at a 5% level (Simões and Cristóvâo, 1982).

Therefore, it might be said that FDI, according to the data available, has made a positive contribution to the improvement to the technical efficiency of Portuguese manufacturing industry. But how far has it been directed towards the highest productivity sectors? Table 11.7 reveals that industries with above average productivity show higher foreign penetration levels than the remainder (32% against 13%), and attract about 73% of the sales of foreign affiliates. The rank coefficient of correlation between foreign penetration levels and productivity is $+0.41$, significant at 5%. However, it does not appear that foreign affiliates (measured by their share in overall sales in the sector), are more strongly represented in sectors where productivity differences *most* favour foreign companies.[18]

TABLE 11.5 Profitability and productivity of foreign and domestic firms in Portuguese industry

	Profitability on sales (%) (1978–80)	Labour productivity[a] (1980)	Productivity[b] increase (1972–80)	Relative[c] productivity (1977)
Traditional labour-intensive				
Textiles	3.72	72	5.532	1.744
Wearing apparel	3.67	54	5.571	1.309
Leather	2.50	95	5.452	..
Footwear	3.75	56	6.119	..
Other industries	4.49	83	6.016	..
Modern labour-intensive				
Non-electrical machinery	4.70	94	3.065	0.646
Electrical engineering	5.32	146	6.052	2.483
Transport equipment	2.69	146	3.749	1.593
Professional goods	4.86	63	3.513	1.551
Resource-based				
Beverages	3.92	179	3.370	..
Wood and cork products	4.13	55	4.189	2.025
Pulp and paper	3.27	188	5.362	2.847
Ferrous metals	3.87	155	5.175	1.007
Inward-oriented H-M technol.				
Industrial Chemicals	3.67	141	2.302	0.955
Other chemical products	2.77	175	2.794	3.832
Rubber products	2.85	106	3.006	3.144
Plastic products	2.88	102	4.238	3.236
Non-ferrous metals	3.13	91	5.419	1.160
Metal products	4.40	100	5.168	1.302
Inward-oriented, market-intensive				
Food products	1.84	88	4.410	4.583
Printing and publishing	5.85	105	4.493	3.493
Inward-oriented low technology				
Pottery, chinaware	5.21	69	3.657	1.202
Glass and products	3.56	90	3.647	..
Non-metal products n.e.c.	3.91	100	4.557	1.920
Furniture	−0.21	82	6.258	0.985
Manufacturing	—	100	4.661	2.217

[a]Value added/Hours worked by operatives (Manufacturing = 100).

[b]$\dfrac{\text{Productivity in 1980 – Productivity in 1972}}{\text{Productivity in 1972}}$.

[c]$\dfrac{\text{Gross output – (Energy + Consumed materials) (Foreign affiliates)}}{\text{Hours worked by operatives}}$

$\dfrac{\text{Gross output – (Energy + Consumed materials)}}{\text{Hours worked by operatives}}$ (Domestic firms).

.. Not computed due to lack of data.

Sources: Profitability: Banco Português do Atlântico (1981)

Productivity: Own calculations based on Estatísticas Industriais (INE), various issues and on data provided by the Gabinete de Estudos Básicos de Economia Industrial (GEBEI).

Next, where has the increase in foreign investment occurred since 1970? First, in the period up to 1978, the increase in FDI was marked by a relative preference for sectors with lower labour productivity levels, a phenomenon which is to be associated with the stronger orientation of FDI in this period towards traditional labour-intensive export industries. Second, in the four subsequent years,*viz* 1979–82, the growth of FDI was higher in the industries with productivity above average (81% of FDI in this period went to these industries). However, this positive association is almost exclusively explained by investment inflow in the automotive industry, since all the remaining sectors with sharp increases recorded below average productivities.[19] Empirical evidence suggests the existence of a negative (but not significant) association between foreign penetration and productivity growth in 1972–80. Phrasing it differently, it does not seem that a higher sectoral distribution of new foreign investment has induced greater allocative efficiency.

Finally we attempted to estimate the contribution of foreign direct investment to gross domestic product. We assumed that, in the absence of FDI, all the resources released would be used by Portuguese firms and that the level of employment would remain unchanged. It was further hypothesized that the relationship between value added and its proxy used in the computation of compared productivities (i.e. value added less consumption of materials and energy) was similar for domestic and foreign-owned enterprises. The results obtained indicate that in 1977 FDI contributed to a net increase in the Portuguese GDP of about 16.7 million contos (i.e. $436.3 million), equal to almost 14% of total value added in manufacturing. However, only one sixth of this increase accrued to Portuguese workers, through higher wages.

Notwithstanding the simplistic assumptions involved in such an estimate, and ignoring its spillover effects, it may be inferred that foreign investment has had a positive effect on resource allocation. The strong propensity to export profits, the use of royalties as a privileged channel for transferring funds abroad, and the slight advantage that accrued to labour from the increase in value added, suggests, however, that the major beneficiaries of this investment may well have been the MNEs themselves.

After this short analysis of the performance of foreign firms, we now turn to an appraisal of their contribution to international competitiveness. Has FDI strengthened the ability of Portugal to compete in the world economy?

11.5   FDI AND COMPARATIVE ADVANTAGE

Previous chapters in this volume have set out some of the difficulties in identifying the comparative advantages of countries. These difficulties are compounded in the case of countries in intermediate development stages, like Portugal (Vellas, 1981). Moreover, specialization is to be balanced with the need for adequate linkages in the productive structure. However, with these reservations in mind, the analysis that follows is based on the identification of Portuguese comparative advantages as 'revealed' by international trade flows.[20]

Static approach

A first question to be answered when assessing the effects of FDI on the international competitiveness of Portugal is the following: Does FDI show any preference for those industries where the country enjoys RCAs?

Analysis of Tables 11.3 and 11.6 taken together shows that all sectors with foreign penetration levels above 30% (which account for 61% of total foreign affiliate sales) had values for the RCA index below zero. Conversely, all industries with foreign penetration levels below 10% recorded positive RCA indices. The strong negative correlation between the two variables is confirmed by a Spearman rank coefficient of -0.613 and is significant at a 5% level.

TABLE 11.6   RCAs and factor intensities in Portuguese industry

	RCA^a 1980	RCA^b Δ 1969–80	Capital/ labour ratio	Skill intensity^c (1980)	Relative skill intensity^d (1977)
Traditional labour-intensive					
Textiles	1.294	−0.064	77	55	0.738
Wearing apparel	4.473	+1.189	26	58	1.108
Leather	−0.708	−1.371	73	66	..
Footwear	4.785	+2.174	31	55	1.310
Other industries	1.544	−0.447	59	113	0.505
Modern labour-intensive					
Non-electrical machinery	−1.756	+0.127	145	136	0.280
Electrical engineering	−0.253	+0.505	69	129	1.890
Transport equipment	−0.899	+1.904	79	103	1.033
Professional goods	−1.007	+1.199	55	78	0.632
Resource-based					
Beverages	3.402	−0.704	269	139	..
Wood and cork products	2.957	−0.119	54	74	0.737
Pulp and paper	1.434	+0.407	217	110	0.878
Ferrous metals	−1.434	+0.057	223	83	1.159

TABLE 11.6 (*continued*)

	RCA^a 1980	RCA^b Δ 1969–80	Capital/ labour ratio	Skill intensity^c (1980)	Relative skill intensity^d (1977)
Inward-oriented H-M technol.					
Industrial chemicals	−1.091	−0.146	365	157	1.556
Other chemical products	−0.971	−0.183	75	260	1.299
Rubber products	−1.599	−1.209	117	103	1.027
Plastic products	0.368	+0.098	71	113	1.219
Non-ferrous metals	−2.011	+0.332	105	94	1.103
Metal products	0.332	+0.270	67	112	1.715
Inward-oriented, market-intensive					
{ Food products	−0.128	−0.618			
	−1.071	−0.032	96	121	1.640
Printing and publishing	−0.001	+0.660	72	199	1.441
Inward-oriented low-technology					
Pottery, chinaware	1.883	+0.882	56	71	1.114
Glass and products	0.856	−0.081	94	141	..
Non-metal products n.e.c.	0.514	−0.345	134	128	1.242
Furniture	2.829	+1.381	54	78	1.113
Manufacturing	—	—	100	100	—

^{a}RCA $= \log \dfrac{1 + \dfrac{X_i}{M_i}}{\dfrac{EX_i}{EM_i}}$, where X_i are the exports and M_i the imports of products of each industry.

$^b\Delta$KCA 1969–80 $=$ RCA$_{1980}$ − RCA$_{1969}$.

^{c}Skill Intensity $= 1 - \dfrac{\text{Operatives}}{\text{Total personnel}}$ (Manufacturing $= 100$).

^{d}Relative skill intensity $= \dfrac{\text{Skill intensity (foreign affiliates)}}{\text{Skill intensity (domestic firms)}}$

.. Not computed due to lack of data.

Source: Revealed Comparative Advantages: Own computations based on Instituto Nacional de Estatística, Estatísticas do Comércio Externo, 1969 and 1980.
Capital/Labour Ratio: own computations based on data provided by the Gabinete de Estudos e Planeamento do Ministério da Indústria and on Estatísticas Industriais.
Skill Intensities: own computations based on data provided by the Gabinete de Estudos Básicos de Economia Industrial (GEBEI) and on Estatísticas Industriais.

Comparison between sectoral patterns in RCAs and FDI clearly points to diverse orientations. Indeed, about 79% of sales and 65% of exports by foreign manufacturing affiliates in 1981 were within industries where Portugal had a negative RCA index in 1980; moreover, foreign penetration in sectors with a positive RCA index was 11%, while for those with a negative RCA index it was about 32%.

This marked divergence in sectoral patterns calls for closer examination. Almost all sectors with positive RCA indices are characterized by low technology levels and broadly correspond to those which, in the suggested typology of FDI in Portugal, we identify as resource-based, traditional labour-intensive and inward-oriented low-technology industries. We have seen that, with a few exceptions (wearing apparel, pulp and paper, glass products), foreign penetration is appreciably below average in these sectors. On the other hand, the two groups of industries with strong foreign penetration are both characterized by technological intensity. It may be suggested therefore that the contradiction between sectoral patterns in FDI and RCAs is, to a large extent, the result of FDI preference for sectors in which foreign firms enjoy substantial overseas advantages rather than in those in which the Portuguese economy enjoys strong local advantages. Portuguese comparative advantages lie mainly in traditional industries with relatively small technological sophistication which, as a rule, require low-skilled labour. All in all, this corresponds to a productive and export structure dominated by traditional sectors, especially textiles. Leaving aside the sectors whose RCAs are resource-based (pulp and paper, beverages, non-metal products n.e.c.), all industries enjoying RCAs also display below average capital/labour indices; the Spearman rank correlation coefficient between these variables is -0.50, and declines to -0.87 if the sectors referred to above were not considered.

These findings should not be understood as inferring an undesirable sectoral choice by foreign affiliates. Indeed, a specialization following in the wake of current RCAs is, in the author's opinion, very far from being the most appropriate for Portugal. This argument is based on five main reasons. First, an increasing specialization in traditional light industries requiring low-skilled labour would place Portugal in more acute competition with those countries which are now starting their industrialization and whose main advantage is the availability of unskilled labour. Second, those industries are increasingly exposed to protectionist measures from developed countries and to agreements on self-limitation of exports. Furthermore, such a specialization would imply 'freezing' an industrial structure already suffering from serious distortions and disequilibria. A fourth reason lies in the need to promote the development of industries with a positive contribution to the modernization of the industrial structure and with spillover effects on other sectors. Finally, it should be stressed that labour skills constitute a basic factor in the development process, the international specialization of economies being determined to a large extent by their relative labour skill levels (Vellas, 1981).[21]

The identification of desirable areas for specialization therefore requires us to go beyond static RCAs and to engage in a dynamic analysis.

Dynamic approach

An examination of RCA trends over time is helpful and provides more acceptable information on the evolution of Portuguese specialization. Accordingly, the change in RCA values between 1969 and 1980 for each sector has been calculated as an index of dynamic comparative advantage.

If the sectoral structure of FDI is negatively correlated with that of static RCAs in 1980, it appears to be positively correlated with changes in RCAs between 1969 and 1980. In fact, Table 11.7 shows that about 60% of total foreign affiliate sales and 80% of their exports in 1981 were concentrated in branches with increasing RCA indices; simultaneously, foreign penetration in these sectors was above average, reaching 29%. Statistical tests, however, do not indicate any significant relationship between dynamic RCAs and foreign penetration.[22] It should be noted that, as a rule, industries with growing RCAs show recent foreign establishments; the relationship between the trend in RCAs and the sectoral index of the length of establishment of foreign affiliates leads us to reject the null hypothesis at a significant level of 1%.

These findings, taken together with the higher export intensity of foreign firms established after 1960, suggest that the trend in comparative advantages for Portugal in the 1970s cannot be separated from the influence of exporting sectors penetrated by foreign firms. To some extent this fact illustrates the integration of Portugal into the international division of labour sponsored by MNEs. Indeed, almost all the sectors which, in the second half of the 1960s and the first of the 1970s, were most affected by the worldwide reallocation of production, were characterized by a strengthening of the RCA indices. Especially remarkable is the growth in RCAs for all modern labour-intensive export industries, where foreign penetration is high. FDI in these sectors, aimed at exploring the advantages of availability and low wages, has considerably aided the restructuring of the Portuguese economy in this respect.

An examination of the relationships between the growth in RCAs and that in FDI inflow shows that in the 1970s FDI preferred sectors with increasing RCAs, notwithstanding the sign of the static RCA index. This finding is corroborated by the positive, although not significant, value of the Spearman rank coefficient ($+0.149$). We accept, of course, that the causal relationship between both variables is difficult to establish; in fact if FDI was primarily oriented towards industries with growing RCAs, it should be underlined that, in several cases, such a trend was itself fostered by the inflow of FDI.

The pattern is different for the period 1979–82. Foreign investment now seems to be mainly attracted to industries with decreasing comparative disadvantages. This result is to a large extent due to the important investments undertaken in the automotive sector. Indeed, isolating the effect of these investments, our conclusions would be different, with a relative preference of FDI for industries with positive but declining RCAs.

To sum up, the channelling of FDI towards sectors with negative static RCAs should not be considered an undesirable phenomenon, bearing in mind the imbalance in the Portuguese productive structure, strongly marked by the relative prevalence of traditional sectors in comparison with the situation in EEC countries (Lopo, 1981). The available evidence suggests that foreign affiliates have had a positive effect on the dynamization of Portuguese comparative advantages through their establishment in sectors where domestic firms are not capable of obtaining full benefit from their resource endowments; that is where 'X' inefficiency exists the example of modern labour-intensive export industries, despite some serious shortcomings to be pointed out later, clearly indicates that foreign firms can play, and have played, a positive role in fostering Portuguese competitiveness.

11.6 FDI AND FACTOR ENDOWMENT

The examination of comparative advantages as 'revealed' by international trade data, even from a dynamic viewpoint, is not in itself sufficient to suggest the appropriate economic structure for a given country. The availability of factor endowments and their possible upgrading also needs to be taken into account.

Consideration of the possible effects of international investment on this process further complicates the question, since FDI can play a complementary role vis-à-vis local factor endowments. The specific contribution of FDI to the specialization of countries is found exactly in the possibility of putting together foreign mobile factors, some of them firm specific, with indigenous immobile factors. However, to be really helpful to the country, this combination needs to be viewed from a dynamic perspective. The complementarity of FDI vis-à-vis domestic investment should not be envisaged as the mere utilization of host country immobile resources, but also their upgrading. More specifically, FDI should stimulate domestic entrepreneurship and the improvement of local labour skills.[23]

In view of the intermediate stage of Portuguese development it will be assumed that Portugal should specialize in labour-intensive industries requiring skilled personnel. Indeed, the option for this kind of sector is necessary so as to benefit from the country's labour availability and to combat competition, actual or potential, from the newly industrializing countries. This strengthening of skilled-labour intensiveness has strong dynamic effects stemming from the so-called 'learning advantage' and is simultaneously compatible with higher intra-industry and intra-firm specialization.

Most of the authors who have studied the international competitiveness of Portuguese industry have pointed to the shortage of indigenous capital and accordingly have advocated the allocation of resources to industries with low capital requirements and where scale economies are not relevant.[24]

However, we might contend that since FDI is a means of providing capital, it should be directed towards capital-intensive sectors. Past experience shows that foreign investors have usually tried to avoid high risks, preferring instead to utilize domestic credit facilities rather than increasing the equity capital of their affiliates (Oliveira, 1982). Although foreign ownership levels have also been influenced by other considerations, it is perhaps surprising that the major part of foreign-minority-owned affiliates is to be found in capital-intensive industries.[25] Therefore it seems not advisable to suggest a specialization of FDI in industries with strong capital requirements.

A short analysis of the characteristics of inward investment with respect to the relative use of different factor inputs can be based on data set out in Table 11.5. This shows that about 60% of the sales of foreign affiliates are within sectors with low capital requirements and above average skill intensity: these sectors are also characterized by an above average foreign penetration level. The industries with such features broadly correspond to light chemicals and to the groups identified as modern labour-intensive export industries and inward-oriented marketing-intensive industries. It should be stressed that foreign penetration is positively correlated with both skill intensity and capital intensity, but mainly with the former: the rank correlation being $+0.375$ and significant at a 5% level. This preference of FDI for skill-intensive sectors probably reflects the predominance of FDI in industries with more sophisticated technology and/or with stronger product differentiation. However, a sectoral comparison of skill indices for domestic and foreign firms does not indicate statistically significant differences.

If this overall sectoral orientation of FDI can be deemed positive, the same is not true for the characteristics of the inflow in the 1970s. In fact, available evidence suggests that in this decade (especially in the first half) FDI preferred less skill-intensive industries. In the period 1979–82, the sectoral structure of FDI shows a move towards low capital-intensive sectors.[26] This contention is supported by the finding that, with the exception of the ferrous metals sector, all capital-intensive sectors experienced below average FDI increases and a shrinking in their growth rates vis-à-vis those of the previous decade.

TABLE 11.7 Summary of the characteristics of the FDI in Portugal

| | | | Stock | | FDI increase | |
| | | | | Foreign | | |
			Sales (%)	penetration	1970–9[a]	1979–82[a]
RCAs		> 0	21.25	11.03	1.073	0.715
		< 0	78.75	32.03	0.980	1.098
		Increasing	59.06	29.07	1.075	1.343
		Decreasing	40.94	17.02	0.891	0.553
		> 0 Increasing	11.42	15.03	1.200	0.587
		> 0 Decreasing	9.81	8.55	0.956	0.885
		< 0 Increasing	47.52	40.05	1.038	1.582
		< 0 Decreasing	31.25	25.87	0.882	0.432
Capital/Labour (K/L Ratio)		High[b]	29.92	21.38	1.332	0.369
		Low	70.08	22.13	0.858	1.489
Skill Intensity (SI)		High	82.36	28.52	0.871	1.001
		Low	17.64	10.75	1.603	0.997
SI High	K/L	High	21.49	24.60	1.178	0.282
SI Low	K/L	High	8.42	11.24	1.709	0.734
SI High	K/L	Low	60.87	29.80	0.764	1.521
SI Low	K/L	Low	9.22	7.86	1.497	1.286
Productivity		High	73.08	32.43	0.852	1.069
		Low	26.92	13.45	1.402	0.784
Export Intensity		High	54.69	22.78	0.947	1.401
		Low	45.31	21.05	1.346	0.463
Research Intensity[c]		High	35.58	45.20	1.041	0.609
		Medium	32.94	27.88	0.967	1.727
		Low	31.48	13.55	0.988	0.529

[a]As explained in Table 11.3.
[b]High means above average and low means below average.
[c]The breakdown of industries according to research intensity was based on Bergsten, Horst, and Moran (1978) and on Dunning and Pearce (1981).
Source: Own computations based on other tables and on data provided by the Foreign Investment Institute.

However, these results need to be interpreted with some caution, and it cannot necessarily be inferred from them that foreign affiliates do not contribute with new technologies and/or promote the training and skill upgrading of their personnel. They simply indicate that in the later period FDI has shown a clear preference for industries requiring relatively less skilled labour; in other words, FDI is mainly seeking Portuguese labour availability instead of the utilization of skilled personnel.

To conclude, the sectors in which FDI has been directed towards the supply of the domestic market, although more capital-intensive, show a higher recourse to skilled labour than export-oriented ones. The difference was sharp in the 1970s: 72% of the sales of all foreign affiliates established in that period were within above average skill-intensive sectors, while the corresponding figure for exports slightly exceeded 50%. These results confirm that export-oriented FDI in the 1970s was mainly determined by unskilled labour availability, and somewhat accentuated the bias of the Portuguese industrial structure towards low skill-intensive sectors.

11.7   FDI AND FOREIGN TRADE

Export intensity and factor requirements

When presenting our FDI typology in Section 11.3, emphasis was placed on the export-propensity of a good number of foreign manufacturing affiliates: indeed, about 25% of Portuguese exports of manufactured goods in 1981 were undertaken by foreign firms.

A joint examination of data presented in Tables 11.6 and 11.8 reveals the existence of a strong negative relationship between the export propensity of their affiliates and the sectoral capital/labour coefficients. Excluding industries where export-oriented foreign affiliates have been established to utilize natural resources, the Spearman rank coefficient was −0.54 and significant at a 1% level. Furthermore, the 1970s were characterized by the strengthening of foreign affiliates' export intensity in both traditional and modern labour-intensive exporting industries, while all the sectors with above average capital requirements, except non-ferrous metallurgy, experienced a decrease in their exporting propensities.

Additionally, and confirming the conclusion of the last section, empirical evidence suggests the existence of a negative, although not significant, association between the export intensity of foreign affiliates and their utilization of skilled personnel. Therefore, while recognizing that export-oriented FDI increased the degree of utilization of Portuguese immobile factors of production, it should not be forgotten that its chief purpose in the more recent past has been to benefit from low wages.

TABLE 11.8   Foreign trade by foreign affiliates in Portugal

	Export intensity (1981)	Relative[a] Export intensity (1978)	Sectoral[b] Export concentration (1978)	Coverage Ratio (1981)	Imports/ purchases (1981)
Traditional labour-intensive		1.264	0.502		
Textiles	0.298	0.942	0.274	1.182	0.467
Wearing apparel	0.688	1.144	0.980	3.759	0.329
Leather	0.645	..	..	12.171	0.089
Footwear	0.960	1.778	0.473	2.156	0.689
Other industries	0.409	2.109	1.984	1.564	0.641
Modern labour-intensive		0.828	1.927		
Non-electrical machinery	0.277	1.136	0.096	0.653	0.726
Electrical engineering	0.399	1.187	3.149	1.057	0.660
Transport equipment	0.355	0.616	0.854	0.754	0.716
Professional goods	0.384	1.610	3.583	0.865	0.768
Resource-based		1.927	1.246		
Beverages	0.518	2.113	1.134	27.367	0.036
Wood and cork products	0.558	1.451	0.262	9.626	0.096
Pulp and paper	0.706	2.046	2.560	3.157	0.289
Ferrous metals	0.289	5.509	3.933	1.541	0.595
Inward-oriented H-M technol.		0.946	1.076		
Industrial chemicals	0.109	0.641	0.881	0.346	0.480
Other chemical products	0.065	1.238	2.058	0.196	0.576
Rubber products	0.055	1.786	3.953	0.123	0.821
Plastic products	0.088	4.133	1.597	0.231	0.655
Non-ferrous metals	0.029	0.419	0.800	0.053	0.688
Metal products	0.137	1.411	0.553	0.740	0.278
Inward-oriented market-intensive		0.771	0.603		
⎧ Food products	0.160	0.862	0.611	1.990	0.133
⎩	0.008	0.186	0.196	0.111	0.101
Printing and publishing	0.046	0.732	0.658	0.409	0.297
Inward-oriented low-technology		0.400	0.124		
Pottery, chinaware	0.015	3.012	0.056	0.428	0.131
Glass and products	0.127	0.365	0.270	1.205	0.150
Non-metal products n.e.c.	0.031	0.040	0.020	0.857	0.066
Furniture	0.204	0.406	0.028	0.763	0.496
Manufacturing	0.270	1.201	—	0.890	0.506

[a]Relative export intensity

$$= \frac{\text{Estimated foreign affiliates exports of products of the industry}}{\text{Total exports of products of the industry}}$$

: Foreign Penetration Index for the industry.

*b*Sectoral export concentration

$$= \frac{\text{Estimated foreign affiliates exports of products of the industry}}{\text{Total exports of products of the industry}}$$

$$: \frac{\text{Estimated total exports of manufact. by foreign affiliates}}{\text{Total Portuguese exports of manufactures}}.$$

.. Not computed due to lack of data.

Sources: Export Intensity, Coverage ratio and imports/purchases: Foreign Investment Institute (Inquiries to DFI in Portugal, 1977–8 and 1981).

Relative export intensity and sectoral export concentration: own computations based on Foreign Investment Institute (Inquiry to DFI in Portugal, 1977–8) and on INE, 'Estatísticas do Comércio Externo', 1978.

Historical trends in export intensity of foreign firms

Data on the exports of foreign affiliates in 1981 indicate clear differences in their behaviour according to the period of establishment in the country. Older firms, set up before 1960, have a generally low export propensity, the average being 12% of total sales. After 1960, the characteristics began to change, with a significant increase in export intensity. For firms set up between 1960 and 1964, the export propensity in 1981 was 39%. For those established between 1965 and 1969 the figure is even higher, *viz* 49%; these firms are mainly concentrated on traditional labour-intensive export industries and on resource-based export industries, and also on modern labour-intensive export industries, with the exception of transport equipment.

The average export intensity of foreign-owned firms set up in the 1970s decreased to 31%. Leaving aside transport equipment (where new FDI in this period was almost nil), one finds that the most dynamic groups were both modern and traditional labour-intensive and export-oriented. In the latest period (1979–82) the importance of these two groups further increased, and particularly that of the modern industries, due to significant investments in the automotive sector. At the same time, all inward-oriented groups, particularly those characterized by low technology, experienced below average growth rates.

Trade balance of FDI

Up to now the conduct of foreign affiliates has been examined from the export side. However, when one takes into account their imports, foreign manufacturing affiliates recorded a negative trade balance: in 1981, with their exports equalled only by 89% of the imports.[27] Two points are worth mentioning in this respect. First, in spite of their smaller export propensity, foreign-minority-owned affiliates have a positive trade balance, in contrast to their majority-owned counterparts. This fact seems to suggest that the former have stronger links with the domestic productive system and a higher propensity for the acquisition of locally manufactured inputs. For example, their import/purchases ratio was 42% in 1981 compared with 54% in the case of majority-owned firms.

Second, and somewhat strangely, according to Table 11.8 there does not seem to be any association between trade deficits and inward-looking industries or between export-oriented groups and trade surpluses. It can be suggested that the trade deficit of foreign affiliates in Portugal is concentrated mainly in the technology-intensive sectors, the more so as these sectors, independently of their export-orientation, show the highest import/purchases ratios.

The fact that foreign affiliates record a net trade deficit does not mean that their effect on such balance is a negative one. In some cases, for example, the only alternative to local production by foreign affiliates is to import manufactured goods, with a worse impact on the balance of payments. Unfortunately the data available only enable us to make a comparative analysis of export behaviour of foreign and domestic firms and not of their imports.

Compared export intensities of domestic and foreign-owned firms

Comparative analysis of export propensities will be based on two indices presented in Table 11.8. The first—relative export intensity—aims at comparing the exports/sales ratios for foreign affiliates, and for the whole of manufacturing firms established in Portugal. The second—foreign affiliates' sectoral export concentration—relates the weight of foreign affiliate exports in the total exports of each sector with the corresponding weight for manufacturing.[28] The first feature to underline is that foreign affiliates show an export intensity about 20% higher than that of domestic firms. They also display a marked specialization in their market orientation, producing either to export or to supply the domestic market, while for domestic firms this distinction is not clear (Rodrigues, Ribeiro, and Fernandes, 1977).

The complementarity between the two indexes advises their joint analysis for the various groups of industries. Foreign affiliates in traditional labour-intensive export sectors have a relative export intensity close to average as well as a low export concentration index; this means that although they exhibit high export propensity in these industries, the bulk of exports is accounted for by national enterprises. The opposite happens with modern labour-intensive export industries, where (somewhat surprisingly) foreign affiliates display an export performance below that of domestic firms. This finding derives from (i) the very definition of the index, since foreign penetration of these sectors is generally high, and (ii) the influence of the automotive sector, clearly inward-oriented.[29] Conversely, sectoral export concentration is high, especially in the electrical engineering, electronics and professional goods industries, where foreign affiliates accounted for about 75% of total Portuguese exports in 1978. This fact gives additional support to the contention that FDI has utilized Portugal as a supplier of low-wage labour.

Resource-based export industries have both indices significantly above average, suggesting that foreign affiliates present a higher capacity for exporting manufactured goods involving local resources than do domestic firms. However, the validity of this assumption should not be extended to all sectors with significant utilization of natural resources, as is confirmed by the low relative export propensity indices for glass products, other non-metallic minerals, and even for the food industry.

Turning now to those sectors in which foreign affiliates have been set up mainly to supply the local market, the results obtained for marketing-intensive and for low-technology industries are consistent with a *priori* expectations. Perhaps more interesting are the findings for inward-oriented medium/high-technology industries, whose global indices are very close to unity, although they are markedly higher for some sectors such as light chemicals, rubber and plastics. It can, therefore, be concluded that, given the low exporting capacity of Portuguese firms in these sectors and their small importance in total Portuguese exports, foreign firms, although mainly concerned with the supply of the domestic market, have made a slight positive contribution to exports.

Local content of foreign affiliates' exports

In connection with the study of foreign affiliates' export propensity (and with the characterization of their foreign trade in general), two additional questions may be raised: (i) to what extent do the goods exported by them incorporate an acceptable share of local value added, and (ii) to what extent is foreign trade by foreign enterprises undertaken inside the groups to which they belong?

In 1981, the average import/purchases ratio for foreign affiliates was very high, slightly over 50%. Although this value may be somewhat inflated as a result of simultaneous commercial activity by several firms importing goods for sale from other affiliates, it suggests that the contribution of foreign enterprises to the development of domestic supply industries has been a limited one. It is true that there are good grounds for some complaints by foreign firms about the inadequate capacity and quality of their potential domestic suppliers. On the other hand, it seems undeniable that the behaviour of at least some foreign affiliates is a reflection of the reasons for their establishment in Portugal. One of these is most certainly the integration of Portuguese affiliates worldwide into the strategies of product and/or process specialization of the parent company. Indeed, about 34% of foreign affiliates' imports (and 31% of their total foreign trade) take place on an intra-firm basis. It is remarkable that intra-firm trade has been especially important for the group of modern labour-intensive export industries and particularly in those sectors where the setting up of foreign affiliates was prompted by the low wage costs of the Portuguese economy.

To what extent have foreign affiliates increased their utilization of locally produced inputs in recent years? To answer this question, an analysis of the import/domestic purchases ratio in 1978 and 1981 was conducted for a sample of 167 firms. The results suggest that the average ratios did not change between those years.

We conclude, therefore, that not only has the link between foreign affiliates and their domestic suppliers been weak, but that, more importantly, it has not been developed in the last few years. Particularly striking is the decrease in the relative utilization of domestic inputs in labour-intensive industries whose export propensity is greater, and whose international location is strongly influenced by wage differentials (clothing, footwear, electronics, electrical machinery, optics, and instruments).

These findings suggest that international corporate integration may not always be consistent with host-country policies geared towards the strengthening of the links between domestic and foreign-owned affiliates, a point already made by several other authors in this book.

11.8 CONCLUDING COMMENTS AND POLICY ISSUES

Data presented in the previous sections indicate that, by and large, the contribution of FDI to the restructuring of the Portuguese industrial system has been a positive one, as foreign affiliates show higher productivity levels and display a greater orientation towards high-technology and skill-demanding industries than their domestic counterparts. Indeed, in the absence of FDI inflow—and even allowing the possibility of obtaining the intermediate products supplied by other means—the Portuguese industrial structure would certainly be more biased towards traditional sectors.

With respect to international competitiveness, a number of positive aspects stemming from FDI can also be identified. These include: (i) a general dynamization of Portuguese exports, particularly in the sectors where Portugal previously did not present exporting capacity (paper pulp, ship repair, electrical engineering, electronics, professional goods); (ii) a diversification of the export structure raising the contribution of higher productivity sectors;[30] (iii) an amelioration of the Portuguese comparative *dis*advantage in high-research or technology-intensive sectors; and (iv) demonstration effects on Portuguese entrepreneurs encouraging them to enter international markets.

Set against these positive features of FDI may be others which may be less conducive to the kind of economy structure desired by the Portuguese authorities. According to the estimates presented, a relatively large share of the value added generated by foreign firms is appropriated by them and transferred abroad, both through the export of profits and through the strong utilization of intra-firm technology contracts. Sketchy evidence also suggests a wide use of transfer-pricing manipulation. Further, vertical linkages with indigenous companies seem to have been small. It is true that in several industries (food, metalomechanics, ship repair, some branches of chemicals, and in mechanical and electrical engineering), foreign firms gave rise to significant backward linkages and have helped to promote the development of the domestic productive system. In others their contribution to an integrated development of Portuguese manufacturing has been rather weak; in such cases foreign affiliates assume an 'enclave' character, with great dependence from abroad for the purchase of inputs and with high levels of intra-firm trade (footwear, electronics, professional goods). Available evidence also suggests that backward linkages have not increased in the last few years, since the degree of utilization of domestically purchased inputs remained unchanged between 1978 and 1981.

The integration of Portugal in the system of international division of labour, led by MNEs, had two main and interrelated types of consequences. On the one hand, it promoted exports and enabled the setting up of new manufacturing activities with positive employment effects. On the other, it brought about an excessive concentration of FDI in branches requiring low-skilled labour (clothing, assembly of electronic components), some of them with scarce links with the local productive system. Our research has shown that FDI inflow in the last 15 to 20 years—especially between 1965 and 1974—has been mainly geared towards profiting from Portugal's labour availability and low wages, the utilization of indigenous skilled labour being usually of secondary importance. But if recent investment in the automotive industry is anything to go by, this feature may be about to change.

In inward-oriented sectors the strong market power and the aggressive advertising of foreign affiliates have been used to inhibit the development of local competitors, particularly where the domestic market is rather small; moreover, the growth of foreign affiliates also led to the elimination of small-sized domestic firms or implied their take-over, as in the case of pharmaceuticals. Neither do foreign affiliates undertake much research and development, or other high value activities, in Portugal.

It should not necessarily be concluded that the shortcomings identified in the characteristics and conduct of foreign affiliates should be exclusively envisaged as a consequence of their 'foreign' nature; a share of responsibility should also be attributed to the policies pursued by the Portuguese government. The high trade protection and the regime of *condicionamento industrial* helped to promote the creation and sustenance of monopolistic and oligopolistic situations, which protected low efficiency and enabled foreign affiliates to gain extra rent through the high barriers to entry facing potential competitors. The import-substitution experience in the automotive sector, for instance, led to a proliferation of inefficent, small-sized assembly plants. Another example is the incentives granted to foreign firms investing in high energy-demanding industries, which turned into a loss for the Portuguese economy after the sharp increases in oil prices.

The interests of MNEs investing in Portugal do not correpond *ipso facto* to national economic goals. Phrasing it differently, the inflow of capital, technology, and management skills through FDI does not necessarily guarantee a benefit to the host economy in the long run, since corporate policies may be in conflict with the host country's objectives. On the other hand, policy-makers should be aware of the distinctive nature of MNEs and of several differences in the conduct and goals of foreign affiliates vis-à-vis their domestic firms. Therefore, for countries to benefit fully from FDI, a conscious recognition of the need to operate the appropriate policies is required. These should take into account the Portuguese economic goals, the main characteristics of international investment and the grounds where the potential positive contribution of FDI is more likely to become effective.

It has already been argued that FDI should play a complementary and dynamizing role vis-à-vis domestic investment. In particular, it should be mainly directed to activities demanding relatively skilled labour, since, in the medium term, Portuguese comparative advantages are unlikely to lie in the low-wage sector. This contention is supported by the proposed entry of Portugal into the EEC. Indeed, this accession will imply an increase in Portuguese nominal wages that—without corresponding to the equalizing of wages with the other EEC countries—would suggest a decline in the Portuguese relative attractiveness for low-skilled, low-wage-cost industries. On the other hand, the small size of the Portuguese market does not advise the encouragement of import-substitution FDI. This is not to say that import substitution is not in itself desirable. Rather it means that for industries benefiting from economies of scale, import-substituting firms must simultaneously export a significant share of their output. This view is strengthened by tariff dismantling which will most probably stimulate intra-industry trade (Pontes, 1982; Feitor, 1982), as well as intra-firm trade, since regional integration will favour the development of 'corporate integration'.

Since 1978, Portugal has adopted a system of previous evaluation of FDI projects. It is based on the assumption that the regulation of the conditions of establishment of foreign-owned firms would better accomplish the goals of Portuguese industrial and economic policies, and simultaneously promote the balancing between the interests of both foreign investor and host country. The purposes of the evaluation process are: (i) to make the foreign investor aware of the Portuguese economic objectives, and (ii) to share as equitably as possible between the investor and the host country the costs, benefits, and risks of the projects (Carvalho and Valverde, 1981). As far as one can judge, the most important effects of such a system have been to increase the financial involvement of foreign partners in some projects, through higher contributions of equity capital, and the definition of terms and conditions for the conclusion of technology transfer agreements stemming from investment projects.[31, 32]

At the same time, the policy has suffered from two main shortcomings, along with some degree of bureaucracy. First, the interaction between FDI and industrial policies has been insufficiently considered, mainly because, until recently, there had been no identification of industrial priorities. Second, the usefulness of *a priori* controls on the setting up of foreign affiliates was severely limited by the lack of instruments for further follow-up of the authorizations granted; in consequence, many of the conditions imposed at the time of the authorization of foreign investments did not have any practical effect. Therefore, notwithstanding a number of positive aspects of current FDI policy mentioned above, it has been inadequate both to encourage the orientation of foreign firms towards the right industries, and to guarantee that they behave in the desired way.

Portugal's entry into the EEC will entail the withdrawal of the present system after a short transitional period. This will not mean, however, that Portugal should renounce the definition and implementation of a policy towards FDI.[33] In fact, a good number of EEC member countries have implicit or explicit policies aimed at influencing the terms and conditions of FDI inflow and the behaviour of foreign affiliates. Therefore, taking into account the remarks outlined above, some suggestions on policy issues may be put forward.

First, we would recommend that a stronger connection between FDI and industrial policies is promoted, both to maximize allocative efficiency and to stimulate the desired conduct and strategy of foreign affiliates. A reappraisal of the definition of priority sectors for FDI might be undertaken in accordance with the objectives of industrial policy; to identify the industries where investment is most likely to play a complementary and dynamizing role vis-à-vis domestic investment.[34] In turn, industrial policies should take account of the sectoral penetration of FDI and the distinctive characteristics and behaviour of foreign affiliates. Industrial policy should also allow for and encourage the positive spillover effects of foreign affiliates on the domestic system, namely through training of Portuguese personnel, sub-contracting arrangements with local enterprises, and technological support both to their suppliers and to their customers.

Second, competition policy should be more actively pursued to safeguard the consumer against the anti-competitive practices of foreign affiliates, to prevent the misuse of monopolistic or oligopolistic market power, and to forestall predatory take-overs.[35] The recently enacted and long-awaited competition law, despite its various shortcomings, is a helpful step for promoting a more positive conduct of FDI.

Third, as pointed out above, there are sound suspicions about the utilization of transfer-pricing mechanism as well as of intra-firm licensing and service agreements for the remittance of profits abroad. These findings lead to the suggestion that it would be appropriate to envisage measures to reduce the gap between the taxes on profits and on royalties (and other technology payments); such measures should, however, have in mind the legitimate needs of both domestic and foreign-owned firms for importing technology from independent suppliers. Additionally, other steps towards the control of tax evasion could be taken in the wake of the recent Italian legislation on that subject.

However, at the same time, we would stress that the benefits that Portugal may obtain from FDI also depend on the ability of the Portuguese authorities to create the right investment climate. This means that actions aimed at enabling a more efficient utilization of the available resources, as well as their upgrading, might be undertaken. Moreover, this kind of action concerns both domestic and foreign investment. Three aspects deserve special mention. First, the development of the infrastructures (transport, power supply, communications, industrial estates), which could probably be articulated with regional policies; second, the strengthening of technical education and professional orientation; and third, a re-examination of the costs and benefits of all tariff and non-tariff barriers to trade in goods and services.

A last remark concerns the suitability of promotion channels other than wholly or majority-foreign-owned affiliates for obtaining the foreign assets needed. In fact, the figures presented on foreign-related production in Portugal suggest that the possibilities of using licensing as an alternative to FDI (and also as a stimulus for domestic firms to increase their efficiency and quality standards) have not been fully exploited. Similarly the development of joint ventures could be encouraged, as they may foster a better integration of foreign assets with the domestic productive system. It is further recalled that foreign-minority-owned firms are more prone than other foreign affiliates to engage in investment abroad from Portugal. This point seems to be an important one; indeed, despite the balance of payments deficits, outward investment should be encouraged, as far as it contributes to the development and upgrading of domestic manufacturing and has positive feedback effects.

To conclude this bird's-eye-view on policy issues, it might be said that the effects of international investment on host countries need to be envisaged from a pragmatic perspective, and not on the basis of ideological creeds. There is no invisible hand to ensure that the interests of MNEs and host countries are automatically reconciled. But there is room for making them as compatible as possible so that the former may contribute in the best way possible to the latter's goals and aspirations.

NOTES

1. In the latter, association with foreign partners was frequent.
2. See, on this subject, Matos (1972), Rodrigues (1977), Rodrigues, Ribeiro, and Fernandes (1977) and Romão (1983).
3. The signing of the Code was, however, accompanied by strong reservations.
4. The existence of illegal capital flows (confirmed by the Report of the Board of Directors of the Bank of Portugal for 1982) must also be recognized.
5. See the preamble to Decree Law 236/76.
6. Evaluation procedures have been developed in a very liberal manner, as the low percentage of rejections of FDI applications (2–3%) confirms.
7. The listing of priority sectors is provided for in Resolution 382/80. Priority sectors were defined as those where FDI could more positively play a complementary role vis à vis national investment, with strong spillover effects and calling for technology, capital, or marketing relations which are beyond the reach of national firms. It is interesting to note certain similarities between these criteria and Kojima's thesis on the tutorial role of FDI (Kojima, 1978).
8. Several aspects of the Code were modified in 1982, but the main framework was kept unchanged.
9. Again, one should not forget the existence of illegal capital outflows which are obviously not considered in the statistics available.
10. It should be borne in mind that they are alternatives concerning the manufacturing of a good and not in absolute terms. That is, both FDI and licensing often originate trade in raw materials, intermediate products, and equipment goods.
11. See, for instance, Caves (1982), Johnson (1970), Buckley and Casson (1976), Parker (1978), and Teece (1981).
12. The expressions for computation of both indexes are shown in Table 11.2.

13. According to unpublished research undertaken by the Foreign Investment Institute, about 50% of the contracts celebrated between 1973 and 1977 involving trademark and/or patent licensing included export restrictions. Explicit export restrictions were also found in 24% of the licensing contracts registered with the FII in 1981–2.
14. Data on technological and marketing intensities by industries were collected from Bergsten, Horst, and Moran (1978), and further adapted to International Standard Industrial Classification (ISIC). The breakdown of industries according to their technological level used by Dunning and Pearce (1981)—and also based on Bergsten, Horst, and Moran—was equally considered.
15. Petroleum refining is not considered, since the main activity of foreign-owned oil companies domiciled in Portugal is not manufacturing but wholesale trade.
16. The value of Spearman's rank correlation coefficient is -0.131.
17. This confirms the findings of other studies on former periods (Silva *et al.*, 1977; Donges, 1979), or based on a smaller number of firms (Simões and Cristóvâo, 1982).
18. The rank correlation between foreign penetration and relative productivity is also positive ($+0.200$), but is not significant.
19. In fact, the rank correlation between FDI growth in 1979–82 and productivity is negative -0.172, although not significant.
20. For the sake of comparability with other research undertaken in Portugal on this subject, the RCA index is defined as

$$\text{RCA}_i = \log \frac{\dfrac{X_i}{M_i}}{\dfrac{\Sigma X_i}{\Sigma M_i}}$$

where X_i are the exports and M_i the imports of the ith industrial sector.
21. Similar criticisms of RCAs have been made by other authors, mainly Silva Lopes (1979) and Pontes (1982).
22. The Spearman rank correlation coefficient is -0.009.
23. Similarly to what Gilpin argues for American investment abroad (Gilpin, 1975), foreign investment in an industrializing country like Portugal should help the development of domestic industries and promote the rejuvenating of the local economic structure.
24. See, for instance, Donges (1979), Balassa (1979), and Feitor (1982).
25. The rank correlation between the capital/labour index and an index of domestic ownership in foreign firms is $+0.328$, significant at 10%.
26. The rank correlation is -0.33 and is significant at 10%.
27. If all foreign affiliates domiciled in Portugal were considered, the export/import ratio would be significantly smaller (28%) due to the specialization of commercial affiliates in import activities.
28. Data on exports of services by manufacturing firms have obviously not been considered, since general statistics published by the Instituto Nacional de Estatistica refer only to foreign trade on goods.
29. It should be recalled that data are referred to 1978. In more recent years export-propensity of foreign affiliates in the automotive industry experienced a significant increase.
30. Of the Portuguese exports of manufactured goods 35% were, in 1978, from sectors with above average productivity, while the corresponding ratio for domestic firms was only 25%.
31. These comments concern especially investments under the general regime, since the contractual one implies a detailed agreement on the benefits and obligations of the investor and the Portuguese government regarding the launching of the project, the conduct and performance of the foreign affiliate, and the incentives to be granted.
32. The centralized representation of the Portuguese administration before foreign investors, undertaken by the Foreign Investment Institute, has also proved to be a very positive and useful feature.
33. The Foreign Investment Institute could play a key role in the conception and coordination of the implementation of such a policy.
34. Promotional activities should be mainly focused on these sectors.

35. An adequate screening system of FDI inflow through takeovers and of takeover activities of established foreign affiliates, taking into account competition rules, should be envisaged.

REFERENCES

Afonso, Isabel (1983). As empresas com capital estrangeiro e as empresas nacionais—alguns elementos comparativos, *Investimento e Tecnologia*, 2

Agmon, T. and Hirsch, S. (1979). Multinational corporation and the developing economies: potential gains in a world of imperfect markets and uncertainity, *Oxford Bulletin of Economic Statistics*, **41**, no. 4, November

Balassa, Bela (1979). Portugal in face of the Common Market, in Fundação Calouste Gulbenkian and the German Marshall Fund (eds) (1980)

Banco Português do Atlântico (1981). *Indicadores Económicos e Financeiros da Central de Balanços (1978–80)*, Porto, Banco Port. Atlântico

Bergsten, C. F., Horst, T. and Moran, T. H. (1978). *American Multinationals and American Interests*, Washington DC: Brookings Institution

Buckley, P. J. and Casson, M. (1976). *The Future of the Multinational Enterprise*, London: Macmillan

Carvalho, F. Lopo and Valverde, R. (1981). Avaliação de projectos de investiment estrangerio. *Investimento e Tecnologia*, 1

Caves, Richard E. (1974). Industrial organization, in Dunning, J. H. (ed.), *Economic Analysis and the Multinational Enterprise*, London: Allen & Unwin

Caves, Richard E. (1982). *Multinational Enterprises and Economic Analysis*, Cambridge: Cambridge University Press

Chenery, H. B. (1979). *Structural Charge and Development Policy*, Washington DC: World Bank

Contractor, Farok. J. (1981). *International Technology Licensing*, Lexington: D. C. Heath

Contractor, Farok. J. (1983). Licensing in international strategy, *Les Nouvelles*, June

Costa, Carlos A. P. (1976). Participação estrangeira no capital social das sociedades nacionais, *Boletim Mensal de Estatistica*, **IX**, no. 7

Deubner, C. (1981). *Foreign Capital in Portuguese Industrialization: Past Experience, Perspectives After EC-entry and the Option of Luso-Spanish Cooperation*, Paper presented at the Conf. on Underdevelopment, Emigration and Industrialization in Portugal, McGill Univ., Canada (mimeo)

Donges, Juergen B. (1979). Foreign Investment in Portugal in Fundação Calouste Gulbenkian and the German Marshall Fund (eds) (1980)

Donges, Juergen B. (1980). *Industrial Development and Competitiveness in an Enlarged Community*, Paper presented at the Conf. on Portugal and the Enlargement of the European Community, Lisbon 1980 (mimeo)

Dunning, John H. (ed.). 1974, *Economic Analysis and the Multinational Enterprise*, London: Allen & Unwin

Dunning, John H. (1981), *International Production and the Multinational Enterprise*, London: Allen & Unwin

Dunning, John H. (1981). A note on intra-industry foreign direct investment, *Banca Naz. Lavoro Quart. Review*, no. 139, December

Dunning, John H. (1982). International business in a changing world climate, *Banca Naz. Lavoro Quart. Review*, no. 143, December

Dunning, John H. and Pearce, R. D. (1981). *The World's Largest Industrial Enterprises*, Farnborough: Gower

Eckaus, R. S. (1979). Strategies of development and the international division of work, in Fundação Calouste Gulbenkian and the German Marshall Fund (eds) (1980)

Emmanuel, Arghiri (1981). *Technologie Appropriée ou Technologie Sous-Developpée?*, Paris: PUF

Feitor, Renato (1982). *A Indústria Portuguesa Face à Adesão à CEE: Impacto e Perspectivas*, Lisboa: GEPMIE (mimeo)

Freitas, J. Abel (1983). *Lucratividade na Indústria Transformadora com base no Stock de Capital Fixo*, Paper presented at the Confer. on Trends and Perspectives of Change in the Portuguese Economy, Lisboa

Fundação Caloustre Gulbenkian and the German Marshall Fund (eds) (1980). *2ª Conferência sobre a Economia Portuguesa*, Lisboa: F. C. Gulbenkian

Giersch, H. (ed.) (1974). *The International Division of Labour – Problems and Perspectives*, Tübingen: J. C. B. Möhr

Gilpin, Robert, (1975). *U.S. Power and the Multinational Corporation*, New York: Basic Books

Graca, Eduardo, Ribeiro, J. M. Félix, and Ribeiro, Luísa S. (1983). Especialização internacional da economia Portuguesa e investimento estrangeiro, *Investimento e Tecnologia*, 1

Gruber, W. H. and Vernon. R. (1970). The technology factor in a world trade matrix, in R. Vernon (ed.) *The Technology Factor in International Trade*. New York: National Bureau of Economic Research

Helleiner, G. K. and Lavergne, R. (1979). Intra-firm trade and industrial exports to the U.S., *Oxford Bulletin Economic Statistics*, **41**, no. 4, November

Hirsch, Seev (1976). An international trade and investment theory of the firm, *Oxford Economic Papers*, **28**

Hood, Neil and Young, Stephen (1979). *The Economics of Multinational Enterprise*, London: Longman

Hufbauer, G. C. (1970). The impact of national characteristics and technology on the commodity composition of trade in manufactured goods, in R. Vernon (ed.) *The Technology Factor in International Trade*, New York: National Bureau of Economic Research

Hymer, S. (1960). *The International Operations of National Firms: A Study of Direct Foreign Investment*, PhD Dissertation (published by MIT Press, 1976)

Johnson, H. G. (1970). The efficiency and welfare implications of the International Corporation, in Kindleberger, C. P. (ed.), *The International Corporation – A Symposium*, MIT Press

Kojima, K. (1978). *Direct Foreign Investment*, London: Croom Helm

Koopmans, T. C. and Montias, J. M. (1971). On the description and comparison of economic systems, in A. Eckstein (ed.), *Comparison of Economic Systems*, University of California Press

Lall, Sanjaya (1978). TNCs, domestic enterprises and industrial structure in host LDCs: a survey, *Oxford Economic Papers*, no. 30, July

Lall, Sanjaya and Paul Streeten (1977). *Foreign Investment, Transnationals and Developing Countries*, London: Macmillan

Lopo, V. Teixeira (1981). *Portugal and the EEC – Industrial Aspects*, Paper presented to the Special MCE Briefing, London (mimeo)

Madeuf, Bernardette (1981). *L'Ordre Technologique International*, Paris: La Documentation Française, 4641/2

Magee, S. (1981). The appropriability theory of the multinational corporation, *Annals of the American Association of Political Social Science*, no. 458, November

Martins, Maximiano and Guimarães, Rui (1982). *A Política Industrial face ao Futuro*, Paper presented at the First Conference of Portuguese Economists, Lisboa (mimeo)

Matos, L. Salgado (1972). *Investimentos Estrangeiros em Portugal*, Lisboa: Seara Nova

Michalet, Charles-Albert (1976). *Le Capitalisme Mondial*, Vendôme: PUF

Monkiewicz, Jan (1983). Portugal, in UNIDO, *Technology Exports from Developing Countries (I): Argentina and Portugal*, New York: United Nations

Mucchielli, J-L. and Thuilhier, J.-P. (1982). *Multinationales Européennes et Investissements Croisés*, Paris: Economica

Newfarmer, R. S. (1978). *The International Market Power of Transnational Corporation*, UNCTAD/ST/MD/13

OECD (1977). *Pénétration des Entreprises Multinationales dans l'Industrie Manufacturière des Pays Membres*: Paris, OECD (and subsequent revisions) (mimeo)

OECD (1980). Impact of Multinational Enterprises on National Scientific and Technological Capacities – Analytical Report, Paris: OECD, SPT (80) 4 - 1st Rev. (mimeo)

OECD (1981). *Investissement International et Entreprises Multinationales – Tendences Récentes des Investissements Directs Internationaux*, Paris: OECD

Oliveira, Isabel Roque de (1982). *O Investimento Estrangeiro em Portugal*, Paper presented at the First Conference of Portuguese Economists, Lisboa (mimeo)

Parker, J. E. S. (1978). *The Economics of Innovation*, 2nd edn, London: Longman

Pincheson, Edward (1983). The pattern of foreign involvement in Portugal, *Multinational Business*, 1

Pontes, J. Pedro (1982). Tecnologia e especialização industrial na Adesão à CEE, *Análise Social*, XVIII, 70

Remédio, M. A. Boavida (1982). Aspectos institucionais de internacionalização da Banca Portuguesa, *Banco de Portugal – Boletim Trimestral*, no. 1/82

Rendeiro, João O. et al, (1981). *Competitividade e Especialização Perante a CEE*, Lisboa: GEPMIE (namely Vol. IV: A vantagem comparativa revelada do comércio externo)

Rodrigues, António (1977). A penetração e a importância dos capitais estrangeiros na economia Portuguesa, *Economia e Socialismo*, no. 10, January

Rodrigues, E. F., Ribeiro, J. Félix, and Fernandes, Lino (1977). *O sector Exportador Português e a Internacionalização da Produção*, Lisboa: GEBEI

Rodrigues, E. F., Ribeiro, J. Félix, and Fernandes, Lino (1982). Ascensão e crise das exportações Portuguesas (1965–73; 1973–79), *Estudos de Economia*, II, no. 4. July–September

Rodrigues, E. F., Ribeiro, J. Félix, and Fernandes, Lino (1984). *A Especialização de Portugal em Questão*, Lisboa: B. F. N.

Romão, António (1983). *Portugal face à CEE*, Lisboa: Livros Horizonte

Roque, Fátima (1982). *Factors Influencing Comparative Advantage of the Portuguese Economy*, Paper presented at the First Conference of Portuguese Economists, Lisbon (mimeo)

Rugman, Alan M. (1980). A new theory of the multinational enterprise: Internalization versus internalization, *Columbia Journal of World Business*, **XV**, no. 1, Spring

Santos, E. Marques dos (1982). *A Indústria Transformadora Portuguesa no Contexto Internacional*, Lisboa: GEPMIT (mimeo)

Savary, Julien (1981). La France dans la division international du travail – une approche par l'investissement direct international, *Revue Economique*, no. 4, July

Schatz, Sayre P. (1981). Assertive pragmatism and the multinational enterprise, *World Development*, **9**

Silva, Armindo (1981). A indústria transformadora Portuguesa e a Adesão à CEE – um estudo das vantagens comparativas reveladas, *Estudos de Economia*, **II**, no. 1

Silva, Armindo *et al* (1977). *Empresas Multinacionais e Internacionalização do Capital (com uma Aproximação ao Caso Português)*, Lisboa: Iniciativas Editoriais

Silva Lopes, J. (1979). Comment on Bela Balassa's paper, Fundação Calouste Gulbenkian and the German Marshall Fund (eds) (1980)

Simões, Vitor Corado (1981). *Payments on Technology: Portugal*, Paper presented at the workshop on the Technological Balance of Payments, Paris (OECD/DSTI/SPR/81.34/16) (mimeo)

Simões, Vitor Corado (1982). *Importação de Tecnologia e Politica Tecnológica*, Paper presented at the First Conference of Portuguese Economists, Lisboa (mimeo)

Simões, Vitor Corado (1982a). *Importação Contratual de Tecnologia e Desenvolvimento Tecnológico em Portugal*, Paper presented at the IED/IIPE Workshop on Technological Innovation, Training and Employment, Lisboa (mimeo)

Simões, Vitor Corado (1983). *Efeitos dos Contratos de Importação sobre as potencialidades de Exportação de Tecnologia,* paper delivered at the Workshop on Innovation and Technology Transfer – National Perspectives, Ordem dos Engenheiros, Lisboa

Simões, Vitor Corado (1983a). Origem do capital e vocação exportadora do investimento estrangeiro na indústria Portuguesa, *Investimento e Tecnologia*, **2**

Simões, Vitor Corado, Afonso, Isabel, and Pires, Manuela C. (1982). O investimento estrangeiro em Portugal – resultados do inquérito, *Investimento e Tecnologia*, **1** and **2**

Simões, Vitor Corado and Cristóvão, António (1982). *Caracterização e Comportamento das Maiores Empresas Industriais com Capital Estrangeiro: uma análise comparativa*, Lisboa IIE, mimeo (A summary was published in *Investimento e Tecnologia*, 2/1982)

Streeten, Paul (1974). The theory of development policy, in Dunning (ed.) *Economic Analysis and the Multinational Enterprise*, London: Allen & Unwin

Taveira, Elisa (1983). *Impacto da Integração Económica no Investimento Directo Estrangeiro*, Paper presented at the Conference on Trends and Perspectives of Change in the Portuguese Economy, Lisbon

Teece, David J. (1981). The multinational enterprise: market failure and market power considerations, *Sloan Management Review*, Spring

UN (1978). *Transnational Corporations in World Development: A re-examination*, New York: United Nations

UNCTAD (1973). *La Función del Sistema de Patentes en la Transmissión de Technologia hacia las Países en desarrollo*, UNCTAD/TD/B/AC. 11/19

UNCTAD (1978). *Dominant Positions of Market Power of Transnational Corporations: Use of the Transfer Pricing Mechanism*

UNCTC (1983). *Transnational Corporations in World Development: Third Survey*, New York: United Nations

Vaitsos, C. V. (1971). The process of commercialization of technology in the Andean Pact, in H. Radice (ed.), *International Firms and Modern Imperialism*, Harmondsworth: Penguin, 1975

Vaitsos, C. V. (1974). *Intercountry Income Distribution and Transnational Enterprises*, Oxford: Clarendon Press

Vaitsos, C. V. (1982). *Regional Integration cum/versus Corporate Integration*, UNCTC (mimeo)

Vaitsos, C. V. and Saussay, Philippe (1980). Le second élargissement de la CEE et les stratégies des firms transnacionales, *Revue d'Economie Industrielle*, **12**, 2

Vellas, François (1981). *Échange International et Qualification du Travail*, Paris: Economica

Vernon, R. (1979). The product cycle hypothesis in a new international environment, *Oxford Bulletin of Economic Statistics*, **41**, no. 4, November

Vidal, M. José and Redondo, Ana M. (1981). A Competitividade Externa da Indústria Portuguesa, *Banco de Portugal, Boletim Trimestral*, 4/81

12

Singapore

DONALD LECRAW*

12.1 INTRODUCTION

Singapore is a small, open, newly industrializing country (NIC), which has
relied heavily on international trade, finance, and direct investment for its
economic development. The small size of Singapore's domestic market on
the one hand, and its requirements for the technology, capital, management skills and access to export markets on the other have impelled
Singapore towards high levels of trade and inward investment by MNEs.
There has also been a substantial amount of outward foreign direct investment (FDI) by firms based in Singapore.

Trade and inward and outward FDI have played crucial roles in the
growth and structural change of Singapore's economy. From 1960 to 1981
Gross Domestic Product (GDP) grew by 8.6% annually in real terms and
GDP per capita grew by 7.8% annually to reach $5,240. Over the same
period, the share of GDP of the total industrial sector rose from 18 to
41%, and the share of manufacturing rose from 12 to 30%. This growth
and structural change can be largely attributed to inward and outward
FDI and international trade. From 1960 to 1982, the gross fixed assets of
foreign-owned firms expanded by over 20% annually in real terms and
trade expanded by 9% annually.

Singapore is perhaps the most open economy in the world. In 1982, its
gross exports were 150% of GDP and eight times manufacturing value
added. In the same year, gross fixed investment by MNEs was almost $6
billion, equal to one-third of GDP, the highest percentage of any country
in the world. Singapore, an island city state with a population of 2.4 million, received 2.2 million tourists in 1982, and was a major transportation,
communication, finance, and trade centre for South and Southeast Asia.

Singapore's openness to trade and investment is in direct contrast to
India's closed development strategy described by Lall in Chapter 10 in this

* The research for this paper was partially funded by the Centre for International Business
Studies, The University of Western Ontario.

volume. It is tempting to compare Singapore's open development strategy and its phenomenal economic growth (described below) and India's poor record of economic development and its inward-looking development strategy. The causal link, however, is left to the reader.

Before turning to an analysis of the effect of inward and outward investment flows on Singapore's economic growth, structure, and international competitiveness, a brief review of its development history is necessary to serve as a background. This overview will be brief, since the main outline of the development of Singapore's economy is well known (Wong, 1979).

12.2   SINGAPORE'S ECONOMY 1960–80

Over the period 1960 to 1980, Singapore achieved one of the highest average annual growth rates in real GDP per capita of any non-oil-exporting country in the world (7.5% annually), the third highest annual growth rate of real GDP (behind Hong Kong and South Korea), the lowest rate of inflation (5% annually), a falling rate of unemployment (from 13.5% in 1960 to 3% in 1980), rapidly expanding exports (8.6% annually in real terms), a strong currency, low international debt, and large foreign exchange reserves. Over this twenty-year period Singapore's economy performed as well as or better than that of any country over any twenty-year period in world history. The word 'achieved' (instead of 'experienced' or 'had') is used intentionally since Singapore's economic performance has been largely due to the sound formulation and vigorous implementation of government economic policies and to the hard work and diligence of its people rather than to fortuitous circumstances such as improvement in the terms of trade. Singapore has no natural resources beyond its port, its location, and its people. Singapore's strategic location at the centre of the ASEAN region, the area with the fastest economic growth in the world, and at the centre of the oil and natural gas deposits of neighbouring countries, has contributed to its growth, but without the initiative of its government and its people this advantage would not have yielded the benefits it did.

The growth of Singapore's economy was accompanied by substantial changes in its economic structure both at constant factor cost and at current market prices, although as revealed in Table 12.1 real output increased in all its major economic sectors. From 1960 to 1982 the share of trade (and agriculture) in GDP declined continuously while the shares of the other major sectors increased as Singapore restructured from a trade entrepot to a manufacturer-trader and financial centre. By 1982, the

TABLE 12.1   Gross domestic product of Singapore by industry 1960–82

	(At 1968 factor cost)				GDP share (constant 1968 prices)				GDP share (market prices)
	1960	1970	1980	1982ᴾ	1960	1970	1980	1982	1982
Agricultural and fishing	87.7	128.5	159.1	145.6	4.1	2.5	1.3	1.0	1.3
Quarrying	7.5	19.2	43.7	71.7	.4	.4	.4	.5	.5
Manufacturing	279.7	1,007.0	2,909.6	3,013.5	13.2	19.7	23.9	21.2	30.6
Utilities	53.4	144.9	357.0	401.5	2.5	2.8	2.9	2.8	2.3
Construction	79.3	343.0	611.1	978.4	3.7	6.7	5.0	6.9	7.9
Trade	713.4	1,538.1	3,139.3	3,474.8	33.6	30.1	25.8	24.4	23.8
Transport and communication	297.6	593.1	2,334.8	2,942.4	14.0	11.6	19.2	20.7	12.3
Financial and business services	247.5	716.4	2,162.7	2,952.6	11.7	14.0	17.8	20.8	17.6
Other services	391.9	723.6	1,336.8	1,547.3	18.5	14.2	11.0	10.9	10.3
Less: Imputed bank charge	35.7	106.8	893.6	1,309.9	(1.7)	(2.1)	(7.3)	(9.2)	(6.7)
Total	2,122.3	5,107.0	12,160.5	14,217.9	100	100	100	100	100

P = Preliminary.
Source: Department of Statistics.

manufacturing, trade, transport and communication, and financial and business services sectors each accounted for about 20% of GDP (at 1968 factor cost). At current market prices, the structural change was even more dramatic, particularly for the manufacturing sector.

The development pattern is in marked contrast to those in the other ASEAN countries, and low- and middle-income countries generally, in which resources from the agricultural and natural resources sectors were shifted to the modern manufacturing sector. Instead, in Singapore, resources have generally been reallocated from traditional employment with low value added to employment with higher value added within the same broad sector. In the manufacturing sector, employment in low-value-added industries comprised 68.6% of manufacturing employment (68.2% of value added) in 1960, but only 38.3% (25.3%) in 1982. Further details are set out in Table 12.2. The share of entrepot trade in total declined dramatically relative to exports of domestically-produced goods, and the modern trade, transportation and communications sectors increased their shares. Within the service sector, insurance and banking (particularly international banking) grew more rapidly than other services, to double their share of GDP from 1960 to 1980.

TABLE 12.2   Distribution of employment and value added in Singaporean manufacturing industry

	Employment		Value added	
	Low value-added industries	High value-added industries	Low value-added industries	High value-added industries
		(Total manufacturing %)		
1960	68.6	31.4	68.2	31.8
1965	67.5	32.5	58.0	42.0
1970	57.9	42.1	38.5	61.5
1975	44.3	55.7	26.9	73.1
1976	42.7	57.3	28.7	71.3
1977	42.5	57.5	28.7	71.3
1978	42.7	57.3	28.8	71.2
1979	40.8	59.2	27.8	71.2
1980	38.4	61.6	24.2	75.8
1981	37.8	62.2	24.7	75.3
1982	38.3	61.7	25.3	74.7

Government economic policy has had a substantial impact on the pattern and speed of Singapore's growth. In the early 1960s, Singapore faced many difficult and potentially disruptive problems (United Nations, 1961). From 1947 to 1957 the population had grown by 4.3% annually due to a high birth rate and net immigration. By 1960, unemployment had reached 13.5%, up from 5% in 1957. The Singapore-Malaysia

Federation was under severe stress and seemed likely to split apart thereby depriving firms in Singapore of 85% of their potential home market. It was also likely that the British naval base, the largest single employer in Singapore, would be closed within the decade. Entrepot trade, which comprised half of Singapore's total trade, was projected to decline as colonial trade patterns changed with the post-war withdrawal of the colonial powers and as neighbouring countries raised trade barriers to protect their domestic industries and to conserve foreign exchange (Goh, 1969).

At the time of independence, the government had planned to foster industrial development by means of tariff protection and promotion of import-substituting production. For a short period during the mid-1960s, Singapore followed a strategy of mild import substitution. This strategy, however, was based on access to the market of Peninsular Malaysia. Following the dissolution of the Malaysia-Singapore Federation, duty-free access to this market was terminated. By force of events, Singapore had to turn away from import substitution towards export promotion since its small population could not support industrialization oriented towards the domestic market.

In the mid-1960s the government instituted a strategy of growth through labour-intensive industrialization. In order to reduce the high unemployment rate the government reduced tariffs and non-tariff barriers to trade and encouraged labour-intensive manufacturing industries: textiles and garments, and later electrical assembly and parts and shipbuilding (Lee, 1973). This policy faced several problems. Although wages in Singapore were far below those in high-income countries, they were significantly above those in Hong Kong, Korea, and Taiwan, countries which had larger internal markets, yet were engaged in a strategy of export-led growth (Cohen, 1975). In order to attract the substantial FDI that this economic strategy required, Singapore offered generous investment incentives to MNEs in the form of low taxes, few controls over operations, no local ownership requirements, and a substantial investment in infrastructure development (Hughes and Seng, 1969; Lee, 1977). The government also recognized that stability, especially political stability and a motivated yet passive labour force, would increase the attractiveness of Singapore as a site for FDI. To achieve this situation, the government severely limited the rights of workers to strike and bargain for wage increases and the rights of its citizens to engage in radical political dissent (Lim, 1975).

This strategy of export-led growth headed by exports of MNEs and sectoral change led by FDI investment in the manufacturing sector was highly successful in terms of economic growth, if at some cost in terms of worker's rights and civil liberties (Deyo, 1981). The economy boomed even though the Singapore-Malaysia Federation was dissolved, the British naval base was closed, and entrepot trade declined. By the early 1970s, unemployment had been reduced to 4%, real wages were rising rapidly, and labour shortages had developed despite efforts by the government to limit wage increases by wage controls and by encouraging immigration. Wage rates in Singapore's manufacturing sector were higher than those of its major competitors, Hong Kong, Taiwan, and South Korea, by 3, 45, and 49% respectively, but well below those in its major export markets—Japan (150% higher), the UK (225% higher), West Germany (277% higher), and the United States (588% higher). The achievement of full employment by the mid-1970s and a rapid influx of guest workers led the government to modify its strategy of growth via labour-intensive industrialization by instituting policies to encourage higher value added, increased capital and technological intensity in the manufacturing sector, and diversification into service industries (transport and communications and business and financial services).

In the late 1970s and early 1980s, unemployment continued to fall, wages rose, there was increased competition from other industrializing countries with far lower wage rates, and protectionism increased against some labour-intensive products in Singapore's markets abroad. In response to these trends, the government instituted policies to accelerate the shift of the manufacturing sector away from labour-intensive industries with low value added per worker towards capital- and skill-intensive industries with higher value added per worker. Labour was shifted out of textiles, sawn timber, and food processing into electronics, professional and scientific instruments, and into service industries such as ship and aircraft repair, and services for the offshore oil industry.

The government encouraged these shifts by investment and tax incentives, training programmes, tariff reductions, government investment and, from 1979 to 1981, mandatory rapid increases in wages and increased payments by firms and workers into the government-run pension plan, the Central Provident Fund.[1] The emphasis changed from increasing output and employment to increasing value added per worker and value added per unit of output in Singapore. In its efforts to increase the value added per unit of output of goods produced in Singapore, the government also encouraged forward and backward integration by producers and increased use of locally-produced inputs and capital equipment.

In 1979, the Economic Development Board designated eleven industries and supporting industries for these eleven industries as 'primary targets for promotion': automotive components, machine tools and machinery, medical and surgical apparatus and instruments, specialty chemicals and pharmaceuticals, computers, computer peripheral equipment and software development, electronic instrumentation, optical instruments and equipment (including photocopying machines), advanced electronic components, precision engineering products, and hydraulic and pneumatic control systems. The government planned that incentives for these industries would not only increase GDP per capita, but would also allow Singapore to decrease its reliance on exports of products such as textiles and consumer electronics that faced increased protection in the long run in many of Singapore's export markets and increased competition from countries with lower wages. Singapore also has combated increased trade barriers for some of its products in high-income countries by diversifying its exports of manufactured products to non-traditional markets in both high- and middle-income countries and by increasing the range of the products it produces and exports.

This 'Second Industrial Revolution' in Singapore was to rest on five pillars of growth: manufacturing, trade, tourism, transport and communications, and knowledge-intensive services (computer, financial, medical and consultancy services). In the area of finance, the ASEAN Dollar Market (ADM), leasing, insurance, the stock market, the futures market, and funds management were planned to grow especially rapidly. A National Computer Board was established to bring about the complete computerization of the civil service and to encourage the use of computers in the private sector as well.

The balanced nature of Singapore's economy and its past development allowed the government to take what it realized was a calculated risk of decreased growth in the manufacturing sector in the short run in order to shift the economy onto a path it hoped would lead to sustained long-term growth. The sectoral balance and stability that have accompanied Singapore's rapid growth augur well for its growth prospects in the future since Singapore is not dependent on only one sector to drive its growth. As a consequence, Singapore was able to be more daring and innovative in its sectoral development strategies since problems in one sector could (potentially) be offset by successes in others. Moreover, since development will largely come in the future, as it has in the past, from intra- rather then inter-sectoral reallocation of resources, growth can be accomplished with less disruption, fewer adjustment costs, and a lower risk of misallocation of resources.

The development strategy followed by Singapore has made its economy highly dependent on international trade, finance, investment, and tourism, and hence potentially at the mercy of cycles in the world economy. The only down-turns in Singapore's economic expansion have occurred in 1975–6 when the world economy was buffeted by the rapid increase in oil prices and in 1982–3 when the world economy and world trade stagnated. The success of its current economic strategy will depend in large part on the timing, rate, strength, and duration of the recovery of the world economy.

In general, the government of Singapore implemented its overall development strategy through the private-enterprise market system and devoted its efforts to influencing the macro-economic environment- —tariffs and non-tariff barriers to trade, the exchange rate, taxation, savings, the investment climate, finance, labour relations and wages, human resources and infrastructure development—so that private enterprises would be attracted to invest in industries in which Singapore had a comparative advantage and the private sector could successfully fulfil the central role it had been given. The government's share in total national expenditures was only 8% in 1960 compared to 12% in upper-middle-income countries.[2] The government, however, has also invested as a sole owner and joint-venture partner in areas in which private investment was not forthcoming to the desired extent—steel, petrochemicals, shipyards—in industries that were natural monopolies—utilities, water, transportation and port services—and in infrastructure development—the port, roads, and industrial and housing estates.[3]

In1980, total investment in which there was some degree of government participation totalled several billion dollars. Some of these enterprises competed directly with privately-owned firms, but in general they were not seen as a threat to the private sector, although occasionally there were complaints of unfair competition. Once a government-owned enterprise has become economically viable, often part of its equity has been sold to the public. Despite this direct involvement at the micro-economic level, the government has remained firmly committed to fostering private enterprise and to the competitive market system as the means to achieve economic growth and resource allocation.

12.3   FOREIGN DIRECT INVESTMENT—AN OVERVIEW

Government policies towards domestic savings and investment and foreign direct investment have played a crucial role in Singapore's development. In the early 1960s, in order to foster the industrialization and development of the economy, the government implemented policies to increase gross domestic investment (GDI) and gross domestic savings (GDS). In 1960, GDS was negative (-3% of GDP). From this dismal base, GDS rose to 20% of GDP in 1970 and 33% in 1981. GDI rose from 11% of GDP in 1960 to 42% in 1981. The gap between domestic savings and investment has been financed by borrowing from abroad and, most importantly, by foreign direct investment.

Singapore's policies to increase GDS and GDI have included low corporate and personal taxation; investment incentives for foreign and locally-owned private firms; government investment; forced savings via the government-run pension plan to which both employers and employees must contribute; and creation of an attractive investment climate through infrastructure and human resource development and tight control of labour costs and practices. These policies have been very successful. No country came close to matching Singapore's increase in investment and savings over this period. In 1981, Singapore's investment share of GDP, 42%, was the highest in the world.

Foreign direct investment has played a central role in Singapore's economic development strategy. Over the twenty-year period from 1960 to 1980, foreign capital financed about a third of total investment and foreign direct investment comprised about 90% of investment in the manufacturing sector and 20% of investment in the service sectors. The foreign owned share of the economy was high and rose over the period from 1960 to 1980. In 1981, the foreign share of GDP was more than 25%.[4] In the late 1970s there was a trend towards increased reliance on foreign sources to finance investment. This trend may continue in the future as Singapore moves from labour-intensive to capital and knowledge-intensive industries.

TABLE 12.3 Contribution of foreign firms in manufacturing sector[a] in Singapore 1975–81 (% of total)

	1975	1976	1977	1978	1979	1980	1981
No of establishments	22.0	22.0	22.8	21.7	23.9	24.9	25.1
No of workers	52.0	53.9	54.5	52.5	57.5	58.4	58.5
Output	72.3	73.1	73.4	71.5	73.8	73.7	76.0
Value added	62.7	64.1	65.2	63.4	67.3	67.4	67.7
Total sales	71.8	73.4	73.0	71.8	73.9	73.9	75.9
Direct exports	84.1	84.7	84.5	83.7	85.2	84.7	86.8
Capital expenditure	64.6	66.6	67.4	69.8	63.1	64.6	61.8

[a]Includes establishments with more than 50% of foreign equity.
Source: Department of Statistics.

FDI has been concentrated in manufacturing and in some service industries. For the manufacturing sector in 1981, Table 12.3 shows that wholly-foreign-owned and majority-foreign-owned, joint-venture firms accounted for 76% of manufacturing output (up from 50% in 1963), 67.7% of value added (52% in 1963), 58.5% of employment (29%), 86.8% of exports (54.4%), and 71.8% of capital expenditure (62%). Over the period from 1975 to 1981 FDI increased its share relative to local investment in manufacturing: almost 90% of net investment commitments in manufacturing were by foreign firms. FDI has played a less dominant role in the service and trade sectors. In 1980, about one fifth of total paid-in capital in these sectors was from foreign-owned firms (see Table 12.4).

TABLE 12.4   Foreign and local paid-up capital of limited companies in trade and services sectors, Singapore

Sector	No. of companies	Paid-up capital Total (S$mill.)	Paid-up capital Local (S$mill.)	Paid-up capital Foreign (S$mill.)	Foreign share (%)
Wholesale trade (1975)	2,880	1,182.3	855.8	326.5	27.6
Retail trade (1975)	765	224.4	193.5	31.0	13.8
Restaurants and hotels (1975)	189	299.5	274.8	24.6	8.2
Real estate and business services (1974)	944	1,054.4	866.0	188.4	17.9
Social, community, and related services (1974)	56	5.7	5.1	0.6	10.0
Recreational and cultural services (1974)	74	57.1	42.5	14.5	25.5
Personal and household services (1974)	43	6.6	5.9	0.7	10.6
Transport, storage, and communication services (1974)	572	346.9	311.9	35.0	10.1
Financial services (1974)	668	1,236.9	1,052.5	184.4	14.9
commercial banks	180	491.3	432.2	59.1	12.0
merchant banks	19	81.1	38.7	42.5	52.4
discount houses	4	16.0	11.2	4.7	29.1
finance companies	83	207.2	164.3	42.8	20.7
investment companies	136	319.8	299.5	20.3	6.3
Insurance services (1974)	123	69.2	65.4	3.8	5.5

Sources: Singapore, Department of Statistics, *Report on the Census of Wholesale and Retail Trades, Restaurants and Hotels, 1975;* Singapore, Department of Statistics, *Report on the Census of Services, 1974.*

Table 12.5 sets out the geographical origin of FDI in Singapore. Since 1970 the US has remained the dominant investor. The share of FDI from the US rose rapidly from 1960 to 1970 (to a third of all foreign-owned, gross fixed assets) and declined marginally during the 1970s. In the early 1980s, investment commitments by US-based MNEs in Singapore's manufacturing sector represented 46% of total foreign investment commitments. Although FDI from the United Kingdom continued to rise in real terms, its share of FDI declined continuously over the twenty-year period from over 60% in 1960 to 20% of foreign-owned gross fixed assets in 1970 and 16% in 1982. The share of FDI from the Netherlands was 14.7% in 1982, largely represented by one large petroleum refinery. FDI from Japan increased eightfold from 1970 to 1982 from 7% to 16.4% of the stock of FDI. FDI from Sweden, Switzerland, Germany, France, Italy, and Australia has also been substantial.

Although Japanese FDI in the manufacturing sector increased rapidly in the 1970s, it did not play as dominant a role in Singapore as it did in the

TABLE 12.5 Foreign investment in manufacturing by country of origin as at December 1970–1982
(In terms of gross fixed assets) (S$ million)

	1970	1971	1972	1973	1974	1975	1976	1977	1978	1979	1980	1981	1982ᵃ
USA	343	501	840	992	1,082	1,118	1,233	1,366	1,601	1,817	2,215	2,645	3,282
Japan	68	108	137	237	354	454	525	633	801	1,049	1,185	1,372	1,584
Europe of which:	423	641	900	954	1,034	1,170	1,306	1,407	2,005	2,434	2,952	3,356	3,781
EEC	406	616	863	912	996	1,110	1,238	1,324	1,907	2,290	2,763	3,044	3,449
Sweden	3	5	4	6	3	22	26	30	30	35	40	105	124
Switzerland	12	17	27	31	27	29	30	38	54	94	120	176	177
Other European countries	2	3	6	5	8	9	12	15	14	15	29	31	31
Others	161	325	406	476	584	638	675	739	835	1,049	1,168	1,266	1,006
Total	995	1,575	2,283	2,659	3,054	3,380	3,739	4,145	5,242	6,349	7,520	8,639	9,653
EEC	406	616	863	912	996	1,110	1,238	1,324	1,907	2,290	2,763	3,044	3,449
UK	199	294	375	390	424	481	555	566	791	1,030	1,227	1,412	1,581
Netherlands	183	275	356	381	420	473	525	571	904	1,011	1,216	1,310	1,423
Germany	3	21	96	102	106	105	112	130	144	166	223	181	221
France	8	10	15	17	21	22	18	21	23	36	41	74	91
Italy	10	12	15	15	15	15	16	21	28	28	29	41	100
Other EEC countries	3	4	6	7	10	14	12	15	16	19	27	26	33

ᵃReclassification of sources of foreign investment from 1982.

ASEAN countries, despite the Japanese view that 'Singapore has been the most attractive country for Japan as an investment market among [the] five ASEAN nations; and the 'exceptionally magnanimous' attitude towards Japanese FDI by the government.[5] One possible explanation for this seeming paradox lies in differences in the motivation for FDI between Japanese and American MNEs in the ASEAN region. During the 1960s and early 1970s, Singapore's relatively cheap, skilled, and disciplined labour force and low import tariffs were very attractive to export-oriented US-based MNEs. Conversely, Singapore's small internal market and general absence of tariff barriers made Singapore relatively less attractive to Japanese MNEs since they could supply the market by exports. Prior to 1970, the largest Japanese investments in Singapore were in the assembly of motor vehicles, printing, tyres, and cement, all industries that had some protection by tariff and non-tariff barriers to trade. In 1980, when the government reduced the level of protection, some Japanese MNEs withdrew their investments. Japanese MNEs, however, have also invested heavily in export-oriented industries such as textiles and electronics.

Singapore has one of the most liberal policies towards FDI of any country in the world. Essentially the government makes no distinction between foreign-owned and locally-owned firms. Controls are minimal or non-existent on foreign exchange and licensing, the extent of foreign equity positions, industry (except for public utilities and telecommunications services that are reserved for the government), imports of machinery and raw materials, local content requirements, employment of foreign personnel, ownership of real estate, and acquisitions or takeovers. The government, however, has encouraged (but has not required) local equity participation and the use of locally-produced inputs. There are no anti-trust or other laws regulating competition and no laws on monopolies or market dominance. The government believes that free trade and the market system minimize possible anti-competitive practices by MNEs and their harmful effects. Statistics are not available on the profitability of FDI, but for 1980–1 the top 50 firms on the Singapore Stock Exchange earned an average of almost 30% on capital. If anything, Singapore's policies towards FDI have become more liberal over time as it has implemented the second phase of its industrialization strategy.[6]

This policy of encouraging FDI has caused mild protests from some local businessmen who have charged that the government has discriminated against them in its incentive programmes. The programmes as such essentially did not discriminate between foreign- and locally-owned firms, but often only foreign-owned firms have had the necessary capital, technology, and access to export markets necessary to qualify for the incentives. This situation offered scant consolation to local entrepreneurs. MNEs have also sometimes been charged with being isolated with few linkages to the economy (importing most of their raw material and component inputs, machinery and equipment and exporting their output), pre-empting local entrepreneurs and stunting their growth, absorbing the highest-skilled workers and managers, employing foreign managers (20% of all managers, engineers and technicians in Singapore are foreign), and increasing Singapore's reliance on unstable export markets and on decisions made at corporate headquarters abroad.

In light of these problems, in the late 1970s, the government began to encourage foreign investors, especially those from high-income countries, to form joint ventures with local entrepreneurs, increase the ratio of local value added to output, and de-package their investments. Singaporean businessmen who entered joint ventures with foreign partners had a lower failure rate (6% over the past twenty years) than those who had no foreign partners (38%). Joint ventures between firms from Hong Kong and Taiwan and local businessmen had a 17% failure rate. The prime minister of Singapore, Mr Lee Kuan Yew, stated: 'The bigger and more established an MNE is in his field, the higher his success rate and the bigger his contribution to jobs and GNP. . . . The less experienced the industrialist and the less advanced his technology, the higher the failure rate.'[7] Not surprisingly, government policy in the early 1980s was to attract large, experienced, technology-intensive MNEs as Singapore moved from labour-intensive to capital- and technology-intensive manufacturing. This policy was successful in 1982 in attracting major MNEs from the United States, Europe, and Japan in such industries as microchips, disc drives, software cartridges, electronics, compressors, engineering services, and instruments.

Since foreign-owned and joint-venture firms have accounted for such large shares of total investment in the manufacturing sector and of exports of manufactured products (and will account for similar shares in the future), the patterns of Singapore's past and future development and structural change in the manufacturing sector and its exports have been and will continue to be closely linked to the extent and pattern of FDI in Singapore.

TABLE 12.6 Direct investment by Singapore in selected Asian countries

	Stock FDI 1980 (S$millions)
Thailand	8.7
Malaysia	276.3
Indonesia	217.5
The Philippines	3.2
Hong Kong	19.3

Source: Interviews in Singapore and FDI statistics of the host countries.

Data on *outward* direct investment from Singapore are limited. The government does not publish (or keep?) statistics on outward FDI by locally-owned firms. What data are available come from statistics on the inward FDI several neighbouring countries. Table 12.6 taken from Wells (1983) augmented by more recent data from the UNCTC (1983). These data are of dubious accuracy, difficult to interpret and *not* comparable among sources. Nonetheless, they do support several conclusions: (i) firms in Singapore have made substantial foreign direct investments, possibly totalling on the order of S$1 billion by 1980; (ii) Singapore ranks second, behind Hong Kong, as a source of FDI among low- and middle-income, non-oil-exporting countries; (iii) the amount of Singapore's outward FDI has increased over time; (iv) almost all of Singapore's FDI has been concentrated in neighbouring countries. Three factors have influenced this investment pattern. Singapore has invested in countries with lower income per capita levels. Among these countries there is a strong relationship between the level of Singapore's trade and the level of FDI. Ethnic ties have also been important channels of FDI. These characteristics of Singapore's outward FDI will be analysed at the end of the next section.

12.4   ANALYSIS OF THE DETERMINANTS AND THE EFFECTS OF FDI

The statistics on inward FDI in Singapore allow the testing of several hypotheses on the determinants and effects of FDI in Singapore. Dunning in Chapter 1 of this volume advanced several 'propositions' concerning inward and outward FDI in the United Kingdom. He has already described the theory behind these propositions in his paper so this theory will not be repeated here. The description of the development of Singapore's economy and its development strategy provides the background against which these propositions concerning determinants and effects of inward and outward FDI in Singapore can be evaluated. The openness of Singapore's economy to trade and investment should lead to stronger support for these propositions than found by Dunning in his analysis of the United Kingdom.

Singapore has had location-specific advantages to attract FDI based on its highly motivated, productive, but relatively low-paid workforce, its geographic location, its infrastructure of transportation, communication and finance, and, to a lesser extent, its internal market. MNEs have invested in Singapore to utilize their ownership-specific advantages in technology, capital, management, and access to foreign markets for inputs and outputs. These location- and ownership-specific advantages are broadly the same as those of other low- and middle-income countries and of the MNEs that have invested in them. The relative importance of these advantages for Singapore and for MNEs as determinants of FDI, however, has been quite different from most other countries.

Singapore's small domestic market (population 2 million, augmented by 2 million tourists), combined with zero tariffs on most imports and low tariffs on the remainder, has reduced the importance of Singapore's market as a location-specific advantage for import-substituting FDI. Some import-substituting FDI was attracted to Singapore prior to the late 1960s first by the prospect of access to the Singapore-Malaysia market and then by Singapore's mild import substitution strategy. The inflows of this type of investment had largely ceased by the early 1970s and the remaining stock was severely reduced as these firms relocated when faced by rising wages and tariff reductions in the late 1970s.

Singapore's location at the centre of the resource-abundant countries of Southeast Asia, its history as a trade entrepot, and its port facilities led to location-specific advantages which attracted FDI in petroleum refining and rubber, timber, vegetable oil, and food processing. Starting in the mid-1970s, the governments in Indonesia, Malaysia, Thailand, and the Philippines instituted policies to encourage the upgrading of their natural resource and agricultural products prior to export. This trend has decreased the location-specific advantage of Singapore in these industries and pushed MNEs to locate new investment outside Singapore as well as to pull investments out of Singapore, and it has fostered outward FDI by Singapore-based firms.

A first impression for the level of FDI in Singapore's manufacturing sector can be obtained from the aggregate statistics. In 1982 wholly- and majority-owned foreign establishments accounted for a quarter of total establishments in the manufacturing sector, almost 60% of employment, over three-quarters of output, almost 70% value added, 70% of domestic, and almost 90% of export sales, and over 70% of capital expenditure and net fixed assets. These are among the highest foreign-owned or controlled shares of manufacturing of any country in the world. Estimates of *outward* FDI from Singapore also place it near the top of the list of foreign investors among low- and middle-income countries, a remarkable record for a country with a population of only 2 million and a high degree of foreign ownership of its manufacturing sector.

Some estimates of the value of foreign investment in the main sectors of manufacturing industry are set out in Table 12.7. Table 12.8 gives details of the participation ratios of foreign investment at a three-digit SIC level. In 1975 the share of book value of fixed assets (value added) of foreign-owned and joint-venture firms ranged from 6.1% (4.9%) for beverages and 9.6% (10.4%) for leather products to 99.5% (98.8%) for precision

TABLE 12.7   Foreign investment in manufacturing industry by industry group—gross fixed assets as at end 1970–1982 (S$ million)

	1970	1971	1972	1973	1974	1975	1976	1977	1978	1979	1980	1981	1982 [a]
Food and beverage and tobacco	31	54	70	93	113	123	130	143	176	211	241	301	363
Textile				132	159	154	141	152	150	205	215	194	101
Wearing apparel, made-up textile and footwear	45	116	156	43	61	81	89	103	106	137	151	147	72
Leather and rubber, processing of natural gums except rubber processing	26	41	43	34	27	30	35	38	46	53	62	47	37
Wood and cork products	17	70	90	137	162	160	153	162	163	220	249	254	135
Paper and paper products	18	27	34	35	44	41	42	47	59	89	102	131	132
Industrial chemicals		70	63	64	73	90	100	63	73	96	122	176	187
Other chemical products except plastics	61	37	61	62	68	81	102	113	115	154	173	267	400
Petroleum and petroleum products	555	752	1,158	1,267	1,336	1,426	1,520	1,617	2,304	2,627	3,160	3,490	3,903
Plastic products	8	22	30	32	43	41	46	64	75	98	98	180	157
Non-metallic mineral products	31	34	41	43	52	57	71	83	82	93	125	131	129
Basic metal industries	19	25	38	27	28	39	42	54	75	49	60	74	88
Fabricated metal products except machinery and equipment	34	56	89	176	258	77	99	124	130	213	261	310	355
Machinery except electrical						250	336	385	487	448	562	702	923
Electrical/electronic machinery, apparatus, appliances and supplies	82	149	215	249	316	354	412	505	620	938	1,212	1,498	1,868
Transport equipment	51	80	91	125	168	209	247	287	326	387	339	421	492
Precision equipment and photographic and optical goods		26	97	109	116	142	150	172	212	272	314	240	239
Other manufacturing industries	17	16	7	31	30	25	24	33	43	59	74	76	72
Total	995	1,575	2,283	2,659	3,054	3,380	3,739	4,145	5,242	6,349	7,520	8,639	9,653

Data for 1974 to 1978 are not comparable with those of previous years on account of reclassification of companies according to the Singapore Industrial Classification 1969. Data for 1979–1982 are not comparable with those of previous years on account of reclassification of companies according to the SSIC (revised 1978).

[a] Reclassification of sources of foreign investments from 1982.

Source: Economic Development Board.

TABLE 12.8 Relative shares of wholly-foreign-owned and joint-venture firms in industry value, employment, and fixed assets Singapore, 1975

ISIC industries	Percentage share in industry's:			Relative capital-labour ratio	Relative value added per worker	Relative value added per fixed asset
	Value added	Employment	Book value fixed assets			
311–12 Food	64.8	48.9	67.3	2.15	1.93	0.89
313 Beverages	4.9	9.1	6.1	0.66	0.55	0.81
314 Cigarettes	99.0	88.9	99.5	24.87	12.37	0.50
321 Textiles	93.1	92.3	98.0	4.07	1.13	0.28
322 Garments	64.6	65.6	81.6	2.33	0.96	0.40
323 Leather products	10.4	12.9	9.6	0.72	0.78	1.09
324 Footwear	32.0	33.8	29.9	0.84	0.92	1.11
331 Wood products	72.1	57.4	90.8	7.32	1.92	0.26
332 Furniture	54.6	51.4	72.5	2.49	1.13	0.46
341 Paper products	61.2	45.4	75.5	3.70	1.90	0.51
342 Printing, publishing	54.2	36.6	53.8	2.02	2.05	1.02
351 Industrial chemicals	88.0	88.6	97.2	4.46	0.94	0.21
352 Other chemical products	87.0	61.6	82.9	2.24	3.08	1.38
353–4 Petroleum products	100.0	100.0	100.0	—	—	—
355 Gums processing	62.1	46.8	74.6	3.34	2.72	0.76
356 Rubber products	80.9	71.0	70.5	0.99	1.73	1.77
357 Plastic products	56.2	56.8	75.0	2.28	0.98	0.43
361–2 China, earthen, glass products	93.2	81.0	98.0	11.52	3.22	0.27
363 Bricks, tiles, clay products	27.5	42.8	68.5	2.90	0.51	0.17
364 Cement	49.6	59.7	36.6	0.39	0.67	1.70
365 Cement, concrete products	19.9	24.5	29.6	1.30	0.77	0.59
369 Asbestos, stone products	43.8	36.1	96.1	43.64	1.43	0.03
371 Iron and steel	90.5	73.3	96.7	10.72	3.47	0.33

TABLE 12.8 (*continued*)

ISIC industries	Percentage share in industry's:			Relative capital-labour ratio	Relative value added per worker	Relative value added per fixed asset
	Value added	Employment	Book value fixed assets			
372 Non-ferrous metals	97.0	94.6	99.5	11.29	1.82	0.16
381 Fabricated metal products	61.7	53.1	64.8	1.62	1.42	0.88
382 Calculators, refrigerators, air conditioners, industrial machinery	76.0	63.5	76.4	1.85	1.82	0.98
383 Radios, TVs, semiconductors, other electrical machinery	93.1	90.4	88.7	0.83	1.39	1.72
384 Transport equipment, oil rigs	57.1	59.6	73.7	1.92	0.90	0.48
385 Precision equipment, optical goods	98.8	96.2	99.3	5.61	3.29	0.58
390 Miscellaneous manufactures	61.8	59.2	78.2	2.47	0.86	0.44
Total manufacturing	75.7	67.2	85.3	2.83	1.52	0.54

Source: Department of Statistics, Singapore, based on Chia (1979).

equipment and optical goods, 99.5% (97%) for non-ferrous metals, 99.5% (99%) for cigarettes, and 100% for petroleum products.

There are several factors which might account for the size of the foreign share of the thirty industries.

(1) The higher the revealed comparative advantage, RCA, as measured by the ratio of Singapore's share of exports of all low- and middle-income countries of a particular industry divided by Singapore's share of total manufactured exports of all low- and middle-income countries and the higher the ratio of exports of a given industry to imports, the higher the level and share of FDI. The rank correlation between FDI level (share) and the export/import ratio was 0.73 (0.67), significant at the 1% level, and the rank correlation between the RCA and FDI level (share) was 0.85 (0.72), also significant at the 1% level. This suggests that Dunning's proposition 1 in Chapter 1 was supported for inward FDI in Singapore.

(2) Part of Dunning's proposition 8 was also supported for Singapore. For the 1963–75 period, the industries in which FDI increased fastest had a higher increase of export/import ratio and RCA than did industries in which the FDI did not increase as quickly. The rank correlations between change in FDI and change in the export-/import and RCA ratios were 0.57 and 0.62 respectively.

There is of course a problem of causality here. Does the observed relationship run from the export/import ratio and RCA of an industry in Singapore to FDI, or vice versa: that is, did foreign firms invest in naturally export-oriented industries or did the foreign investment cause these industries to be export-oriented with an RCS? As described in the previous section, the Singapore government has believed that the causality works in both directions. It has formulated policies to attract FDI to industries in which it has identified an export potential based on a potential comparative advantage for Singapore in order to realize this potential. The rank correlation of exports/imports and the RCA of *Hong Kong* (with a population, wage level, and export orientation similar to that of Singapore, but with a lower level of FDI) with the FDI in *Singapore* was lower, but still significant at the 5% level (Geiger, 1973).

(3) Another part of proposition 8 was also supported. Productivity (as measured by value added per worker) increased faster in industries in which the FDI increased most quickly (1963–76) and in which the FDI share was high. The rank correlation coefficients between increases in value added per worker and increases in FDI share and FDI level were 0.62 and 0.45.

Value added per worker is not always a good measure of productivity, however. Total factor productivity is the correct measure, but it cannot be calculated as data are not available to estimate the production functions of each industry. This is a particularly important problem for the analysis of FDI in Singapore since the unweighted average capital/labour ratio of foreign firms relative to locally-owned firms was 5.76 (the weighted average was 2.83). The unweighted average value added/capital ratio of foreign-owned firms relative to locally-owned firms was 3.37 and the weighted average ratio was 1.86. Given these large differences in the ratios of value added/labour and value added/capital between foreign- and locally-owned firms, entry by foreign firms would increase the value added per worker ratios of an industry *even if* foreign-owned and locally-owned firms had the same total factor productivity. The previous conclusions about the relative efficiency of foreign- and locally-owned firms based on labour productivity must therefore be viewed with caution.

(4) Proposition 5 was also supported. In 1976, the FDI share was positively related to the relative efficiency of foreign firms (including joint ventures) and locally-owned firms as measured by value added per worker (see Table 12.8). For the six industries in which value added per worker for foreign-owned firms was at least 20% below locally-owned firms (50% below the *average* relative value added per worker ratio of 1.5 for all manufacturing) the FDI share was 30%. For the seven industries in which value added per worker was 100% higher in foreign-owned firms, the foreign share was 86%. (For the six industries in which the relative value added per worker for foreign-owned firms was 50% higher than the average, the FDI share was 91%.) The rank correlation between the relative value added per worker of foreign-compared to locally-owned firms and FDI share was 0.69.

(5) Proposition 3, relating skill ratios to inward and outward FDI, cannot be tested directly with the available data. If the thirty, three-digit industries of the manufacturing sector are ranked by their R&D intensity or the ratio of non-operative/operative workers *in the United States*, the rank correlations with FDI share are 0.52 and 0.63. For all manufacturing, the remuneration per worker was 17% higher for wholly-owned foreign firms than for locally-owned firms. This difference may reflect both a greater proportion of skilled workers in foreign-owned firms as well as generally higher wages for each job category.[8]

(6) Proposition 6 was also supported. The FDI was positively related to industry growth within the manufacturing sector. The rank correlation was 0.84. Moreover *increases* in the FDI stake were positively correlated (0.58) with industry growth. As with exports, however,

there is a causality problem here since FDI comprised such a large percentage of total manufacturing investment. There were also positive rank correlations between industry growth in *Hong Kong* and FDI share and increases in the FDI stake in Singapore (0.48 and 0.37). Although these correlations were lower, they support the proposition that inward FDI was directed at the sectors in which Singapore had a comparative advantage.

The analysis to this point has only examined part of some of Dunning's propositions, that is concerning the impact of *inward* FDI on to Singapore's economic structure. Data on Singapore's *outward* FDI are sparse to say the least. Singapore's government does not publish (or collect?) this data. The only 'hard' data available are from host countries. Unfortunately these data are incomplete, inaccurate, biased, and non-comparable among countries. Thailand, for example, reports FDI data from the Board of Investment for 'promoted firms'. There are no published data for other foreign firms, yet these are thought to represent from a third to a half of all FDI in Thailand. Whether firms based in Singapore are under- or over-represented among promoted firms or whether there is an industry bias in the reported data is not known. Data on Indonesia's government *approvals*, of Singaporean direct investment are available, but not on that implemented or on the growth of investment. And so it goes on.

Although data on Singapore's outward FDI do not lend themselves to statistical analysis, they can give impressionistic support to several of Dunning's propositions. Outward FDI by Singapore-owned firms in the manufacturing sector has been largely concentrated in industries in which the FDI share in Singapore was relatively low: textiles and garments, food and beverages, leather products, wood products, rubber products, gum processing, and bricks, tiles, and clay products. This is hardly surprising. If virtually no locally-owned firms operate in an industry, the amount of outward FDI by these few locally-owned firms would not be expected to be significant. Quite the opposite: given the very high FDI share in the manufacturing sector, it is surprising that Singapore's outward FDI was so large relative to that from other low- and middle-income countries. (An unknown, but possibly significant amount of Singapore's recorded outward FDI may have been foreign-owned firms in Singapore, however.) These outward investors have developed firm-specific advantages in product and process technology, management, and access inputs and output markets that have allowed them to invest abroad in competition with other MNEs and locally-owned firms in the host country.

Locally-owned firms in Singapore have developed ownership-specific advantages in several areas. Their production has been more oriented towards the domestic market than has that of foreign firms in their industries. In 1976 wholly-locally-owned firms accounted for 22.9% of value added, but over 30% of domestic sales and only 8.6% of exports. Locally-owned firms (and to a lesser extent joint ventures) have developed products which are appropriate both to the income level and to the consumer demand segments in Singapore. These product characteristics have often been overlooked by MNEs producing in Singapore for both the local and the international market. Such products from Singapore's firms have often been exported to neighbouring countries whose demand patterns are more similar to those in Singapore than to those in the home countries of other MNEs. Rising wages in Singapore and trade protection and other government industrial policies in neighbouring countries have given these locally-owned firms in Singapore the incentive to invest abroad. Singapore's relatively well-developed capital market has facilitated raising capital for the investments. As noted above, the capital intensity of locally-owned firms was far lower than that of foreign-owned firms. This labour-intensive technology is often more appropriate for the wage levels and capital costs of neighbouring countries than was the production technology of other MNEs. As rising wages and rising foreign investment put pressure on locally-owned firms, they were able to use their advantage in product and process technology to produce abroad in such industries as textiles and garments, machinery, fabricated metal products, earthenware, glass and non-metallic mineral products, plastics, and paper and printing.

Locally-owned firms in Singapore have also acquired ownership-specific advantages in upgrading, processing and packaging agricultural and forest and natural resource products as traders and processors of the raw material, both from neighbouring countries for sale in high-income markets and from the United States, Canada, and Australia for sale in neighbouring countries. Government policies in neighbouring countries to upgrade natural resources prior to export and to process imported natural resources prior to domestic sale have pushed firms in Singapore to invest abroad in these countries. These firms have been able to utilize their firm-specific advantages in product and process technology and their sourcing and marketing systems to compete in these markets.

There has also been considerable disinvestment by some foreign-owned firms in Singapore, especially since the late 1970s. Two factors can be identified to account for this outflow. First, in the early stages of Singapore's industrialization some firms were attracted to Singapore by its relatively low wages compared to industrialized countries and, in the case of textiles and garments, to avoid quotas placed on these exports from Hong Kong and Taiwan. Rising wages in Singapore and the formation of export-processing zones in neighbouring countries with lower wages have led some of these firms to pull up stakes and move to countries with lower wages. These forces have also led some locally-owned, export-oriented firms to invest abroad. Second, Singapore went through a mild import-substitution phase in the 1960s during which some FDI was attracted to Singapore to serve its domestic market. Tariff reductions in the late 1970s and early 1980s largely removed this tariff protection and some of these import-substituters have withdrawn their investments.

There has also been substantial inward and outward FDI in Singapore's trade and services sectors. Approximately 20% of all paid-up capital in these sectors was from foreign-owned firms in 1980. The FDI share in trade and services was low compared to its share in manufacturing, but high when compared to all the other countries in the world. Prior to independence, Singapore had well-developed trade and finance sectors based on its position as an entrepot for Southeast Asia. Locally-owned firms had well-developed, firm-specific advantages in trade and finance. Chia (1971) concluded that capital was not the binding constraint on development during the early phases of Singapore's development. Locally-owned firms in the trade and services sector could expand in competition with MNEs. Only in merchant banking did foreign firms have firm-specific advantages in servicing new industrial investors, especially MNEs, which allowed them to have a share of more than 50% of the industry. FDI shares were also above average in discount houses (an organization unique to Britain), wholesale trade (based on past British trading houses), and recreational services (tour operations for foreign tourists). FDI shares were low in restaurants and hotels, social services, personal and household services, transport, storage and communication, investment companies, and insurance.

As in the manufacturing sectors, FDI in the service sector was concentrated in those sectors in which MNEs had firm-specific advantages and Singapore had location-specific advantages. (No data are available on outward FDI from Singapore in the trade and services sectors to support any analysis of its determinants or effects on the economy.) In general the trade and services sectors expanded rapidly from 1960 to 1982, led by transport and communications (13.7% annual real growth 1970–81) and financial and business services (10.8% annual real growth) with construction and trade and commerce lagging (5.5% annual real growth). These growth rates should be compared with the growth of the manufacturing sector of 11.3%.

The relative growth rates of Singapore's broad economic sectors do not seem to have been related to FDI share. FDI share was high in the manufacturing sector and its growth was high; FDI share was low in transportation and communications and financial services, but their growth was high. FDI share was low in trade and commerce and utilities and their growth rates were relatively low. Within these broad sectors, however, FDI share and inflows of FDI tended to be concentrated in fast-growing industries or industry segments.

12.5   CONCLUSION AND POLICY IMPLICATIONS

This analysis of the determinants and effects of inward and outward FDI in Singapore shows a clear pattern. Inward FDI has been in response to the location-specific advantages arising from Singapore's wage levels (and capital costs), location, government incentives and infrastructure development, and the firm-specific advantages of MNEs in capital, management, technology, and access to export markets. Outward FDI has responded to similar factors as Singapore's location-specific advantages (often in industries in which Singapore was losing its comparative advantage) declined relative to those in neighbouring countries and locally-owned firms developed firm-specific advantages of their own which they could utilize through production abroad in countries which had developed location-specific advantages for Singapore-based MNEs.

Inward and outward FDI has played a major role in restructuring Singapore's manufacturing sector and its overall rapid development. The high stake of FDI in Singapore's economy and its importance in future development, however, have imposed certain costs. Singapore has been highly dependent on continuing inflows of FDI for its growth in the past and this dependence will continue in the future. One of Singapore's most attractive locational advantages is the stability of its government and its labour force. This stability has come at a cost of a certain degree of political authoritarianism and government control over wages, working conditions, and labour-management relations. Singapore is no longer a low-income, low-wage country; its GNP per capita exceeds that of Hong Kong, Israel, Ireland, Greece, Portugal, and Spain. Other countries with far lower wages have embarked on export-led industrial policies so that Singapore's labour-intensive exports have come under increasing competitive pressure. In order to compete with exports from these countries Singapore can either restrain wages or increase the human and physical capital intensity of its manufacturing sector. Yet its past reliance on MNEs to provide a package of technology, capital, management, and access to markets may have stunted the development of both its own R&D capabilities and its ability to acquire technology at arm's length. In 1982, R&D expenditures in Singapore totalled only S$40 million. Despite these impediments, some locally-owned firms in Singapore have developed the capability to transfer, adopt, adapt, and innovate in product and process technology, but compared to their competitors in Taiwan, Korea, and Hong Kong their capabilities are still limited (Ting, 1980). The level of general education, of scientific, engineering, technical, and management education in Singapore is quite low when compared to other countries with similar levels of income. Through the late 1970s, an essential part of the investment package supplied by MNEs operating in Singapore was the trained, skilled, and experienced management and technical personnel. The demand for local workers from these more human-capital-intensive jobs was relatively low. During the 1960s and 1970s, Singapore's workers could easily acquire the skills necessary for production-line assembly operations. The skills necessary to achieve Singapore's planned restructuring towards human-capital-intensive industrialization are more difficult, expensive, and time-consuming to acquire. Singapore is now undertaking massive investment in human capital, but this effort will only pay off in the long term.

Singapore's export orientation and its open economy have also left it at the mercy of the world economy and led it to specialize in relatively few products. In 1982 Singapore's non-oil exports fell in current US dollars by 3.5%. (This decline, however, was less than the 7.5% decline in total world exports.) For a highly trade-dependent economy such as Singapore's the effect of an export decline was severe. The balanced nature of Singapore's economy partially cushioned this shock as the financial services and construction sectors continued to expand when manufacturing output contracted. The government responded to this slow-down in the economy in 1982–3 by further investment in infrastructure development—port facilities, telecommunications, transportation—and a further reduction in tariffs to increase the efficiency of the economy. This response to adversity in its external environment followed naturally from Singapore's belief in the benefit of free trade and an open investment policy. It is in direct contrast to the reactions of most other countries, which have tried to ameliorate the effects of adverse external events by protectionist policies.

The government of Singapore has recognized that inward and outward FDI by MNEs has had an important and distinctive role to play in Singapore's economic development. Singapore's industrial policy has been to attract investment by MNEs on the one hand and to influence their behaviour so that Singapore receives the greatest possible benefits from their investment on the other. Singapore has implemented this policy not by overt regulation of the operations of MNEs, but rather by regulating the macro-economic environment in which they operated: exchange rates, savings rates, wage rates, and infrastructure development. This policy and the way it was implemented have been successful. Singapore's economy has grown and restructured rapidly and it is well placed to achieve rapid growth and further structural change in the future.

NOTES

1. The government also had a policy of depressing the value of the Singapore dollar on foreign exchange markets. This reduced wages in Singapore when expressed in US dollars.
2. By 1981, government expenditures as a percentage of GDP had risen to 10%, compared to 17% in high-income countries and 15% in upper-middle-income countries.
3. See *Business International* (1980), p. 4 for a list of fourteen wholly government-owned and joint-venture firms.
4. The share of GDP due to resident foreigners and resident foreign companies, that is, the sum of foreign expatriate wages and salaries and operating surpluses of foreign-owned firms.
5. Quoted in the *Oriental Economist* (March 1979), p. 51.
6. This is somewhat of an overstatement since the government is currently discouraging investment (from any source) in 'busy finger' industries such as low-quality garment manufacture and has removed or reduced tariffs in most of the few industries that had previously been protected in order to attract FDI.
7. Quoted in *Asia Research Bulletin*, January 1980, p. 528.
8. Hughes and Seng (1969) also found significant differences in the ratios of skilled to unskilled workers and administration to production workers between foreign- and locally-owned firms.

REFERENCES

Asia Research Bulletin (January 1980). Lee Kuan Yue, 528

Business International (1980). *Singapore*, Geneva: Business International

Chia, S. Y. (1971). Growth and pattern of industrialization, in Yon Poh Seng and Lim Chiong Yah (eds), *The Singapore Economy*, Singapore: Eastern University Press

Chia, Siow Yue (1979). Foreign Investment in Singapore, Department of Economics and Statistics, University of Singapore

Cohen, Benjamin (1975). *Multinational Firms and Asia Exports*, New Haven, Conn.: Yale University Press

Deyo, Frederick C. (1981). *Department Development and Industrial Order*, New York: Praeger

Geiger, Theodore (1973). *Tales of Two Cities – States: The Development Progress of Hong Kong and Singapore*, Washington, DC: National Planning Association

Goh, Chok Tong (1969). Industrial growth: 1959–66, in Ooi Jin-Bee and Chiang Hai Ding (eds), *Modern Singapore*, Singapore: University of Singapore

Hughes, Helen and Yon Poh Seng (eds) (1969). *Foreign Investment and Industrialization in Singapore*, Madison, Wisconsin: The University of Wisconsin Press

Lee, Soo Ann (1973). *Industrialization in Singapore*, Victoria, Australia: Longman

Lee, Soo Ann (1977). *Singapore Goes Transnatioual*, Singapore: Eastern University Press

Oriental Economist (March 1979). Japanese Investment in Singapore, Singapore: Asia Research Bulletin

Ting, Wen Lee (1980). A comparative analysis of the management technology and performance of firms in newly industrializing countries, *Columbia Journal of World Business,*

United Nations (1961). *Proposed Industrialization Programme for the State of Singapore,* UN Commission for Technical Assistance Department of Economics and Social Affairs.

UNCTC (1983). *Transnational Corporations in World Development: Third Survey,* New York: United Nations

Wells, Louis T., Jr. (1983). *Third World Multinationals,* Cambridge, Mass.: MIT Press

Wong, J. (1979). *ASEAN Economies in Perspective,* London: Macmillan

13

Some Conclusions and Policy Implications

JOHN H. DUNNING

13.1 INTRODUCTION

The task of drawing some general conclusions from the studies set out in previous Chapters is not an easy one; that of suggesting clear cut and universal policy guidelines on the basis of the conclusions nigh impossible. Yet it is not unreasonable to expect an Editor who sets his contributors a fairly specific task to, at least, attempt to identify common ground in the concepts, ideas and findings they present, and to pinpoint and evaluate any differences revealed; and then to set out some of the policy options open to governments, be they positive or negative to MNEs, or be they general or specific to particular countries and/or sectors.

13.2 HOW DIFFERENT ARE MNEs FROM UNINATIONAL COMPANIES?

It is abundantly clear from all the studies, that MNEs or their affiliates, possess a number of distinctive features *qua* their uninational counterparts. Their range and structure of output is different, they generally record a higher productivity and/or profitability, they are prone to engage in more international transactions and they are likely to be more vertically or horizontally integrated. There is nothing very original in these findings, but for the first time, and within a single volume, the evidence is assembled across countries and sectors. Understandably, the contributors have chosen to concentrate on varying aspects of these differences, the relevance of which will clearly depend on the extent of MNE participation in the economy. The Singapore, Belgian, UK, Canadian, and Swedish studies all emphasize that, in the absence of MNEs, the structure of dom estic activity would be very different from what it is. The French, German, US, Korean, and Portuguese studies take a midway position. Only in India do MNEs assume a relatively insignificant role.

What then are the distinguishing characteristics of MNEs? The first is that MNEs possess certain so-called ownership advantages vis à vis their non-MNE competitors. While some of these advantages are country of origin specific, others arise from their ability to capture the economies of integration of producing or marketing activities, undertaken in more than one, and usually several, countries.

The second reason is that MNEs judge resource usage and allocation in any one of their affiliates from what is good for the enterprise as a whole rather than from the viewpoint of an individual production unit. It follows that whenever there are benefits or costs resulting from operation of the affiliate which are external to it, but internal to the MNE of which it is part, then the interests of the two will diverge. In such cases, their conduct and behaviour will be different from what would happen if the separate affiliates were under independent ownership, as will their response to changes in exogenous variables.

The studies also show that the extent and pattern of these differences are likely to vary between industries, the strategy of firms, and their degree of multinationality, but mainly perhaps according to the type of FDI and the ESP variables of the country in which they operate. Thus in India, where almost all inward investment is import-substituting and very strongly government-influenced, the foreign impact is minimized. Taken together with the efforts of Indian companies to escape the strait-jacket of domestic regulation, ESP variables, according to Lall, have worked against allocative efficiency in the Indian economy. By contrast, in Singapore where economic signals are especially favourable to foreign MNEs, inward investment has helped upgrade the quality of indigenous resources. But since most of these subsidiaries are export-oriented and closely integrated into the global or regional strategy of their parent companies, their impact is likely to be very different from that of their indigenous competitors. The writers of the Portuguese and Korean studies suggest there is a mixture of the two kinds of foreign affiliates in their economies; but in Korea, Dr Koo makes a special point in distinguishing both their characteristics and their effects on economic structure.

The size of the recipient economy may also be an important environmental variable. Canada, Sweden, and Belgium are economies in which MNEs dominate many industrial sectors; hence their distinguishing characteristics stand out. By contrast, as Pugel shows, there are various distinctive features about US MNEs vis à vis those of other nationalities. It is also clear that the fastest growth in MNE activity—at least within the manufacturing sector—is occurring in sectors in which rationalized investment is taking place and where MNEs seek to take advantage of the different ESP characteristics of the countries in which they produce. There is also evidence of a growing amount of intra-industry trade between the affiliates. This form of dependence on the division of labour fashioned by MNEs has a number of special characteristics which are particularly felt by small economies which are part of custom unions or free trade areas. Canada, for example, has long been sensitive to being part of the US economic environment. Portugal anticipates more of rationalized investment (of the kind earlier attracted to Belgium) when she joins the EEC. Of all European countries, Sweden has become the least involved in international corporate integration; indeed of the *developed* country studies in this volume, her pattern of inward investment in recent years most resembles that of India—although since 1979 the French policy also has an Indian flavour to it.

As it happens, and perhaps a little unfortunately, none of the countries considered in this book is primarily reliant on its natural resources for its prosperity, so the type of rent-sharing MNE activity prompted by the availability of these resources and related activities is not given much attention. Yet in countries ranging from those heavily dependent on a particular mineral, such as copper in New Guinea or bauxite in Jamaica, or on agricultural products such as forest products in Swaziland, bananas in Costa Rica, or on tourism as, for example in the Seychelles and Fiji, MNEs may and do have distinctive effects on economic structure. Here the issues again are the type of corporate integration pursued and its location. Do MNEs for example, decentralize the secondary-processing and higher-value activities which host countries are seeking, or simply treat their affiliates as resource-exploiting enclaves?

In seven of the twelve countries studied, foreign MNEs clearly have a more important effect on domestic economic structure than do their own MNEs. The US, where the stock of outward investment still exceeds that of inward investment by three times, is clearly an exception, but Japan, the UK, Sweden, France, and Germany are also important outward investors, and, in 1982, both Korea and Canada recorded a net direct investment outflow. As can be seen from Table 13.1, there is clearly a move towards a symmetrical cross-hauling of direct investment flows of most of the economies represented in the book.

With respect to outward investment, as Pugel suggests, the impact on structure arises from the effects of foreign production rather than from being part of a foreign parent. In principle, it might be assumed there are fewer distinctive characteristics since the parent company has similar goals to indigenous firms.[1] Nevertheless, conflicts of interest clearly do arise between the perceived good of domestic operations and that of the MNE as a whole; witness, particularly, the relocation of labour-intensive activities from high-wage industrialized economies to Mexico, Southern Europe, and the Far East.

TABLE 13.1 An index of the significance of inward compared with outward foreign direct investment flows, of countries considered in this volume

	Inward direct investment flows as a percentage of outward direct investment flows, average between:						
	1963–65	1966–68	1969–71	1972–74	1975–77	1978–80	1981–82
Developed Countries							
United Kingdom	64.4	65.8	63.2	50.7	52.4	64.4	26.1
United States	7.9	12.4	14.8	29.7	28.3	55.1	528.0
France	178.5	95.8	149.8	63.5	111.1	119.6	54.6
West Germany	281.3	200.5	85.8	118.7	38.6	28.2	26.5
Japan	100.0	33.6	40.8	7.6	7.0	6.9	6.8
Canada	305.6	580.9	278.5	116.5	46.8	36.4	95.2
Sweden	82.7	126.4	55.2	22.0	9.3	26.1	20.6
Belgium and Luxembourg	895.0	553.6	296.8	242.4	294.7	196.4	6,013.64
Developing Countries							
South Korea	—	—	339.5	1,586.7	757.7	223.4	87.6
India	—	—	—	—	—	—	—
Portugal	1,466.3	3,068.9	591.1	317.6	1,523.1	2,350.0	720.0
Singapore	—	—	—	—	—	—	—

Source: Authors' papers and *IMF Balance of Payments Year Book*.

13.3   THE IMPACT OF MNEs ON ECONOMIC STRUCTURE

The differences described in section 13.2 clearly impinge upon domestic economic structure. All the chapters agree there are four main determinants of how much:

(i)   the nature and extent of the foreign investment;
(ii) the value and configuration of the ESP variables (and especially the P variable);
(iii) the type of *market* structure already existing in the industry (which, in turn, is related partly to *industry* and partly to *country*-specific characteristics); and
(iv) firm-specific considerations influencing the strategy of the MNEs themselves.

The importance of these determinants varies between countries: some of the characteristics identified by the authors are summarized in Table 13.2. In some countries, for example Canada, Singapore, and Belgium, foreign affiliates of MNEs are a dominant force; in others, such as France, Japan, and India, they play a less significant or minor role. The economies differ from one another not only in income and development levels but also in the composition of factor endowments and involvement in trade. The economic systems and government attitudes towards FDI vary considerably; in Korea, India, France, Canada, and Japan, government policy appears to be a crucial variable. In others, and especially in countries which are both outward and inward investors, notably the US, Germany, and the UK the government takes a fairly liberal attitude towards MNE involvement. Both Japan and Korea are moving in this direction. We have already emphasized that, in some countries, for example India, Japan, Sweden and the US, the investment by MNEs is mostly local-market-oriented; in Korea and Portugal, as with most of the EEC countries, and Canada (in a North American context) it is a combination of import-substituting and export-oriented. In Singapore it is almost exclusively export-oriented and part of a global strategy of the investing MNEs.

The nature of the investment and strategy pursued by MNEs is also partly home-country specific, though this is becoming less so over time. The UK has been less involved in rationalized FDI than has the US; while Japan has only recently begun to make a major outward thrust in import--substituting manufacturing investment. Government policy is no less relevant. Dr Lall believes that the stifling domestic policies of the Indian government have pushed Indian firms overseas, while Professor Ozawa

TABLE 13.2   Some economic characteristics of countries considered in this volume

	Population mid 1982 (millions)	GNP per capita 1982 ($)	Index of industrialization 1982	Index of Trade 1982	Significance of NME activity	
					Inward	Outward
Developed Economies						
United Kingdom	55.8	9,660	33	41.6	15.6	21.9
United States	231.5	13,160	33	15.6	4.6	28.2
France	54.4	11,680	34	38.7	19.0	nk
Federal Republic Germany	61.6	12,460	46	50.0		
Japan	118.4	10,080	42	25.5	1.6	14.1
Canada	24.6	11,320	29	42.6	44.3	
Belgium	9.9	10,760	35	129.5	38.0	15.0
Sweden	8.3	14,040	31	54.9	5.7	26.1
Developing Economies						
Korea	39.3	1,910	39	67.4	9.5	nk
India	717.0	260	26	14.9	< 10.0	< 5.0
Portugal	10.1	2,450	44	63.1	19.6	nk
Singapore	2.5	5,910	37	333.8	58.5	nk

Notes: Index of Industrialization = Share of industry in GDP.
Index of Trade = Value of merchandise exports plus imports as percentage of GNP.
Significance of MNE activity. Except where otherwise stated, the share of domestic employment accounted for by foreign affiliates and of MNE subsidiaries abroad in the manufacturing sector. In cases denoted by * the measure of significance is share of sales and in those denoted by + share of assets. The dates of the data vary between the mid 1970s and early 1980s.
nk = not known.
Source: *World Development Report* (of World Bank) 1984 and authors' estimates.

emphasizes the complementarity of interests between the Japanese government and its own firms in the design of foreign investment policy. Changing government economic philosophies and priorities may also have quite dramatic affects on FDI—witness the case of Portugal in the 1970s and France since the socialists came to power in 1980. No less important have been shifts in the values of currencies, especially the revaluation of the yen and mark and the fluctuating value of the $ and the £ which have influenced the balance of outward and inward direct investment, via their effects on the locational attractiveness of a country; most of the contributors to this volume conclude that insufficient attention has been paid to the interaction between MNEs and the levels and stability of exchange rates.

In our introductory chapter, we suggested that the impact of MNEs on economic structure essentially rested on the way in which the configuration of OLI advantages, by influencing the level and pattern of foreign production of MNEs, interacted with the SCP paradigm of industrial-organization theory. Multinationals will invest outside their boundaries when they have ownership (O) advantages over the indigenous firms in the country in which they operate, which they find it beneficial to internalize rather than lease to local firms, and which they use in combination with immobile resource endowments located in foreign countries. *Which* MNEs invest in *which* countries will clearly depend on the ability of firms of different nationality, size and so on to generate O advantages, the relative locational pulls and pushes of possible location bases, and the structure of international *intermediate* product markets. They will also depend on the product and marketing strategy of MNEs and potential MNEs, which is closely related to the structure of the international final product market in which they compete. As MNEs increase their spread of foreign production, the evidence strongly suggests that characteristics specific to the strategy of individual firms, rather than those reflecting their country of origin, tend to dominate MNE behaviour. There is now less to choose between the powerful multinational drug, colour TV, motor car, tyre, and oil companies, according to their countries of origin, than there used to be; international oligopolists tend to shed their country of origin. At the same time, new entrants are continually emerging, and they may well reflect the characteristics of their country of origin: for example, Korean construction companies, Indian engineering contractors, Canadian public utility concerns and so on.

MNEs impinge on the economic structure of countries both by their choice of economic activity, and by their conduct and performance in the sectors in which they produce. While the former impact may be related to OLI characteristics of the sectors and the existing market structure, once established, the conduct and performance of MNE affiliates affects their share of industry output, and with it, of market structure; in turn changes in market structure may cause MNEs to reappraise strategy and hence lead to a further reallocation of resources.

In examining economic structure, the contributors to this volume have identified a variety of criteria. In particular, two types of questions were tackled. The first dealt with matters relating to the kind of products produced and how efficiently they were produced by MNEs (vis à vis their indigenous competitors). Reinforcing (or indeed affecting) these are no less fundamental questions to do with the extent to which MNEs affect, both within and between countries, vertical integration, product specialization or diversification, research and development, high value-added cf. low value-added activities, the extent of international specialization and so on. Data limitations often restrict the answers to this group of questions, though most chapters, and particularly the UK, US, Portuguese, Canadian and Swedish studies, offer some incisive insights. The following paragraphs attempt to summarize the conclusions of the authors.

Group 1 questions

(a) Allocative efficiency

Using data derived mainly from Censuses of Production, most authors assert that, in the absence of government or other artificial barriers to trade or investment, MNEs have had a beneficial effect on resource allocation—at least in the static sense. But many studies, notably the Indian, Canadian, Korean, French, and Swedish emphasize that the beneficial effects might have been greater had their own government's policies been different, although the authors accept that such policies might have been successful in promoting other goals, such as matters of income distribution or economic sovereignty. Given such policies, Globerman considers the effects to be ambivalent and mildly beneficial in Canada, and Michalet and Juhl take a similar view about inward investment in France and Germany respectively. In the case of Belgium, Singapore, the UK, the US, and Japan, the impact has been more decisive. In India Lall notes that the restrictionist policies of the government towards inward investment have held back restructuring. Several writers, notably Swedenborg, Pugel, and Ozawa, argue that the effects of outward investment on domestic structuring have been indirectly made through the impact of MNE activity on trade. In the cases of Japan and Korea, government policy has guided

MNEs to the sectors in which the governments believed they had an advantage over domestic firms. Koo thinks they have worked in the case of investment in export-promoting activities but not with import-substituting activities. In the case of Singapore, by a variety of pro-motional measures, foreign MNEs have been encouraged to invest in higher than average value-added activities and to upgrade the quality of labour.

Several authors try to relate the impact of MNEs to various measures of competitiveness. The most widespread measure used is (one variant or another of) Bela Balassa's revealed comparative advantage (RCA). Except in the French and Canadian cases, all country studies agree that foreign affiliates, relative to indigenous firms, tend to concentrate their activities in sectors in which the RCA ratio[2] is positive or greater than 1,[3] or—and this particularly applies in Portugal—is increasing over time. However, there is some divergence of opinion about the interaction of outward direct investment and RCA. The Japanese and UK studies take the view that the foreign production of home-based MNEs is likely to be in sectors in which the RCA is negative (or less than 1), or is declining, but the US, Swedish, German, French, and Canadian studies all strongly sug-gest that exports and foreign investment are more likely to be complemen-tary to each other and tend to be in the same sector. However, these and other studies also argue that one of the main structural effects of outward investment is to enlarge the market of the investing firm and hence better enable it to spread research and development (R&D) overheads and advance (or protect) its international competitive position. Pugel, for example, quotes a US study by Mansfield that asserts that foreign produc-tion, by helping to raise the returns on domestic R&D has increased it by one-seventh. While acknowledging that, in some cases, FDI might dissipate technology quicker than would otherwise be the case, he argues that the possible losses are more than outweighed by the actual gains. Swedenborg supports this argument and asserts that as a result of the strengthening of home-based R&D activities Swedish exports have been raised.

Some studies, notably those of Belgium, the UK, Japan, and Singapore, examine the extent to which MNE activity concentrates in high-value sec-tors. Although the evidence is by no means conclusive, it is highly sugges-tive, and especially so in the four countries just mentioned. Much, how-ever, seems to depend on the type of FDI undertaken. The Korean and Portuguese studies, for example, report a higher value-added context in the import-substituting affiliates than in the export-promoting ones. The Canadian study emphasizes concern over the branch-plant syndrome and the danger that a host country might become an offshore satellite for the main activities of the MNE located in the home countries. Several authors—most notably Dr Simões—emphasize that even where MNEs allocate their investment to high-value sectors the host community does not always benefit as much as it might, since the rent earned on these activities is appropriated by the parent company.

(b) Technical efficiency

MNEs may help to raise technical or sectoral efficiency in two ways: by themselves being more efficient than their indigenous competitors, and through linkages, example, and competitive stimulus, upgrading the productivity of their suppliers, customers, and competitors. Various studies, as well as those contained in this volume, have shown this to be among the most beneficial effects of inward direct investment. Foreign affiliates generally record higher productivity ratios than their indigenous competitors—the French case seems to be an exception—though they do not necessarily concentrate in sectors in which the differential is most in their favour. The US, the UK, Portuguese, Belgian, and Canadian studies pay especial attention to this issue. The spillover effects, through example and competition, partly depend on the existing market structure; in the economies and sectors where there has been a strong indigenous presence it has generally been beneficial. In Singapore—and to some extent in Canada, Belgium, and Sweden—the local markets are often too small to allow economies of plant size to be fully exploited and for there to be other than a monopolistic or oligopolistic market situation; indeed, in some sectors, such as pharmaceutical chemicals, there is evidence that MNEs have squeezed out local firms. In the case of India, and to some extent in Japan, Korea, and France, government policy has not allowed this to happen; and in most other countries, monopoly or restrictive practices legislation has curtailed the extent of participation by foreign affiliates—at least in sensitive sectors—or has insisted on certain performance requirements. Several countries, notably Sweden, Korea, Canada, and France, tend to view takeovers as a form of foreign involvement less favourably than green-field investments.

The UK, US, German, and Swedish studies reveal that outward direct investment has assisted the productivity of the investing firms mainly by enabling them to spread their overheads over a large sales volume and to capture the benefits of a diversified geographical portfolio, and in some cases, to take advantage of international market imperfections. Even where foreign production substitutes for trade there is some suggestion that this has enabled them to improve or maintain their market share in the domestic market. In the late 1970s, there was particular concern in the

US about the growing economic power of some of the conglomerates, for example in the oil sectors, part of which was put down to their multinationality.

On the other hand, the Portuguese and French studies suggest that foreign affiliates import a higher proportion of their sales than their indigenous competitors and/or do not engage in as much local production or sub-contracting as they might. We shall return to this point later.

(c) Adjustment efficiency

Only the UK, Japanese, and Canadian case-studies look directly at the extent to which MNEs have aided the restructuring of resource allocation. Ozawa argues very strongly that Japanese MNEs have been an important handtool of government policy in this respect. Lecraw describes the efforts of the Singapore government to stimulate inward direct investment into the more technology-intensive sectors, while in both Korea and Portugal, MNEs are welcomed for their contribution to export-led growth. In the developed countries, it is clear that home-based MNEs, by relocating their more labour-intensive activities to low-wage-cost countries, have affected domestic economic structure; indeed, they are often criticized for doing just this. Along with Ozawa, Juhl and Pugel believe this can be a major contribution of MNEs to the restructuring of the world economy, although Juhl and Michalet both argue that in relation to other variables, the role of FDI in initiating such change (as opposed to adjusting to it) is fairly insignificant. The studies make it perfectly clear, however, that if MNEs are to play a positive and helpful role, governments must create the right economic climate—including the removal of obstacles to redeployment. A related role of home-based MNEs, and one stressed by the US, Swedish, Japanese, and Belgian studies, is to help create a sustained foreign involvement in those sectors which impact favourably on the structure or efficiency of domestic resource allocation.

Group 2 questions

MNEs may affect economic structure indirectly by impinging upon other firms in the economy, and also by the type of activity they engage in *within* particular sectors.

(a) Spillover effects

The overall impression gained from the studies that deal with the issue, is that the contribution of MNEs depends on:

    (i) government policy (including that specifically directed to MNEs);

    (ii) the existing absorptive capabilities of supplying and competitor firms and their reactions to an MNE presence;

    (iii) the environment for disseminating new technology, management skills, etc.;

    (iv) domestic and international market structure;

    (v) the type of foreign investment;

    (vi) the strategy of MNEs.

In larger advanced industrial economies such as the UK, the US, France, Germany, and Japan, the authors conclude that MNE contributions have been positive and, in certain sectors, substantial. For example, by the additional knowledge of markets and higher quality standards passed on by their suppliers (this is best exemplified by the current impact of Japanese investment on the European colour TV industry), through backward linkages[4] and by entrepreneurial and competitive stimuli to competitors, technical and allocative efficiency has been raised. In the small developed and less developed countries, the spillover effects have been mixed. Globerman argues that in Canada the competitive effects are positive, but in several cases—as in Belgium—foreign firms have swamped domestic producers and increased concentration ratios. In Japan, India, and Korea we have seen that this has not been permitted to happen as limits have been placed on inward investment; but even in these countries and in some not covered by this volume, such as Brazil and Mexico, backward linkages have not been as pronounced as countries would have liked. Most developed countries are aware of the export-enclave syndrome, and attempt to ensure that foreign affiliates produce or sub-contract a proportion of their sales locally. MNEs respond by asserting that the technological and educational infrastructure or quality of local suppliers is not sufficient to enable them to meet the targets required. Here, however, as shown by Korean, Indian, and Portuguese experience, much depends on the type of investment and whether the international or the domestic market is served with the final product. Moreover, in some cases, the ability of affiliates to use local suppliers rests mainly on the design requirements of the final product, which the parent company controls; thus Japanese colour TV affiliates are not able to buy some electronic components from UK sources, simply because the chassis design which determines the nature of integrated circuitry is in the parent company's control, and this design is primarily related to local, that is Japanese, needs. The result is that at varying levels, many countries are worried lest the affiliates of foreign-based MNEs do not bring with them the spillover effects which are hoped for; indeed, in some cases they could be negative effects.[5]

The activities of outward MNEs also have effects on integration and competition in their home countries. In the developed economies, it is argued that multinationalism gives an advantage over indigenous firms, which may act as either a stimulant or a depressant to competition depending on the ability of local firms to respond to it.

(b) Upgrading of human capital; R&D activities

There is a widespread belief that the high-value activities of MNEs tend to be concentrated in the home countries while their overseas satellites engage in low-value activities. It is further asserted that any policy which attempts to sustain the established pattern of the international division of labour may inhibit industrializing latecomers from reaching their full potential. Let us examine these arguments. The case-studies in this volume confirm that a very high proportion of R&D of MNEs is centralized in home countries. The figure for the US is 90% (in 1977), for Sweden 86% (in 1978); other data suggest it to be 85% in the case of the UK and 90% for Germany. It would seem that as firms become more multinational and less ethnocentric in their outlook they direct a higher proportion of their R&D to their affiliates; but, except in a very few cases, the great bulk of fundamental research continues to be undertaken in the home country, while the control of what type of R&D is done and where it is located is still very much a centralized decision and viewed from the perspective of the long-term goals of the MNE as a whole, rather than those of its individual affiliates. Again, a conflict of interest may arise between the international division of labour of R&D activities from a corporate objective compared with that of a particular home or host country.

The evidence of the extent to which affiliates of foreign MNEs engage in more high-value activities than their indigenous counterparts is mixed. In Singapore, Japan, the UK, Portugal, and Germany this seems to be the case; in Canada, Korea, and Belgium it is less likely to be. What are the implications of these data? History records that, almost without exception since the mid nineteenth century, industrializing nations have resorted to some kind of protectionism to assist their infant industries. Usually the measures have been taken against imports from foreign-based companies, but these barriers can be overcome by setting up production units in the country. But unless the foreign-owned production unit is as self-sufficient as, and/or more efficient than, a local firm, it will not create the same local value added. As regards the former, there are some activities it will not undertake, simply because it is a branch plant of a parent company.

In other areas, being part of an international network of activities might enable the foreign firm to create more linkages with local firms than an indigenous competitor would do. However, where the R&D is done by the parent company, the host economy may be deprived of an important part of its opportunities for 'growing up'; this is particularly likely to be the case where the market structure and technology of the industry cannot economically support more than one or two domestic products. Yet even where some local R&D is undertaken by the foreign affiliate, its parent company still retains control over its type and usage, and there is no guarantee that it will be profitable to use such technological capacity in a way consistent with the long-term industrial or development goals of host countries. It is for this reason that some host countries regard the *net* social benefits of the division of (high-value) labour prompted by MNEs lower than the private benefits, and why economies like France, Japan, and Korea have attempted to build up a strong domestic technological base (acquiring technology through the non-equity route) rather than allow foreign MNEs to dominate their sensitive technology sectors.

From the viewpoint of outward investment, there seems little doubt that MNEs tend to employ a higher proportion of high-grade labour than do uninational firms and that their foreign activities enable them to do so. This is the opposite situation to the one just described, with internationalization of activities aiding the upgrading of domestic workers; Ozawa, Pugel, and Swedenborg illustrate these gains and argue they more than offset any possible loss of jobs resulting from outward FDI. Other studies are rather more critical of the actions of MNEs, but often their criticisms would be better directed to governments, for failing to provide the necessary resource reallocative mechanisms to allow displaced labour to be re-employed.[6] More often than not, however, it is the speed of restructuring made necessary by the response of MNEs to international forces (which in itself may well be commendable) which is the crux of the matter, and reveals itself in the divergence between private and social costs.

(c) Linking domestic to international structure

Just as trade links an economy to an international division of labour, so does international production. Indeed, one of the main conclusions of the studies in this volume is that MNEs promote different patterns of the international allocation of economic activity than would otherwise exist. The question of interest and concern to both host and home countries is the extent to which the resulting disposition of output accords with their own interests. Partly, of course, this relates to political values and goals though these are not independent of likely economic outcomes. These outcomes relate to the extent to which there is adequate control mechanism (including that imposed by the market) on the actions of MNEs, ensuring they have to be efficient and that the economic rent they earn is minimized. In industries dominated by MNEs this is not easy to see. Not only may oligopolistic behaviour result in sub-optimal efficiency, excessive discretionary expenditure, wasteful advertising, and so on; policies towards the redeployment of their activities to help sponsor changes in international resource allocation are likely to be cautionary. In countries in which they are faced with no effective competition, this may slow down or stifle the development of an indigenous technological capacity.

The chapters in this book suggest that the evidence on these claims is somewhat mixed. That MNEs do introduce an element of openness, and hence vulnerability, into national economies there can be little question. Their activities in any one country reflect response to changes in the world economic environment in the other countries in which they operate. For good or bad, they are conduits of change, and countries which wish to insulate themselves against such change may well be concerned about their structural impact. At the same time, there is little evidence that the adverse consequences of change can be laid at their door. Their recent record on employment in both developed and developing countries, compared with that of uninational firms, is a creditable one, even though their reactions to economic signals may be a rather speedier and more unevenly distributed than host countries would like.

MNEs are also an integrating force in the world economy. Again, whether the kind of integration they promote, the way they bring it about, and the distribution of the resulting benefits is acceptable to participating nations is another matter. But inevitably, increasing corporate internalization and the growth of cross-border, intra-industry, intra-firm trade leads to a change in the structure and location of economic activity. Potentially this is the greatest contribution MNEs *qua* MNAs can make to advanced industrial economies, and especially large free-trade areas. But how far corporate integration is consistent with regional integration again rests on the policies of governments, the international market structure in which MNEs operate, and their individual strategies, But, as several authors assert, without the common ownership of separate production activities undertaken by MNEs, these benefits could not be achieved at all. MNEs overcome market failure in intermediate product markets by internalizing transactions. Where there is effective competition between MNEs in end-product markets, the benefits of this internalization will be shared by the contributing agents and consumers. However, without appropriate safeguards, there is a possibility that MNEs might use regional integration to promote their own ends at the expense of the countries in which they operate. This view was forcibly expressed by Constantine Vaitsos in a paper prepared for UNCTC (1982). Earlier, two economists of radically different schools of thought (Hymer, 1971; Johnson, 1970), argued that whatever the contributions of MNEs might be 'even' development and the promotion of many social goals and aspirations were unlikely to be among them. Such thinking has clearly influenced policies by governments to MNEs in some countries, notably Latin America and India. All too frequently, however, this has led to the type of restrictionist policies which have reduced rather than enhanced the contribution of MNEs to long-term structural goals. The consensus of the authors of this volume is that the market-replacing activities by MNEs have generally led to an economic structure which is more, rather than less, consistent with the goals of countries which wish to exploit their dynamic comparative advantages. In other words, the benefits of their arbitrage function has probably counteracted any adverse affects arising from their abuse of monopoly power. We accept, of course, that this is a very generalized statement, and that, in almost all the countries surveyed, there are some specific areas of concern about the impact of both inward and outward FDI.

13.4   POLICY TOWARDS MNEs

Having summarized some of the ways in which MNEs impinge on domestic and international resource allocation, what policy conclusions can be drawn? First, and perhaps most important, we would reiterate the point that government policies, both general and specific to MNEs, themselves affect the contribution MNEs can make to economic structure and restructuring. The contrast between the policies pursued by India and Singapore among developing countries, and the US and France among developed countries, and the response of MNEs could not be plainer. But in all the countries surveyed, the role of policy in affecting the behaviour and performance of MNEs was emphasized. Globerman believes that Canadian tariff and other policies led to an inefficient distribution of the activities in which foreign-based companies were involved. Swedenborg criticizes the Swedish government's imposition of 'artificial barriers to trade'; while Koo notes that the import-substitution policies in Korea have led to an inappropriate restructuring of Korean industry. Generally, it might be expected that since the purpose of import controls is to use indigenous resources to produce the goods previously imported, then the firms supplying the imports should respond more quickly (since they already have the market) than local firms; if the policy is inappropriate then clearly foreign firms will not make an ideal contribution.

A rather different approach to government policy is taken by Ozawa. He argues that where governments intervene to reduce market imperfections rather than countering these imperfections by creating others, the result can be beneficial to resource allocation. Taking the Japanese case as an example, Ozawa asserts that domestic economic structure has been improved by the Japanese government's following a trade, technology and industrial policy consistent with its perception of Japan's dynamic advantage. Positive interventionism to reduce market distortions should be distinguished from negative interventionism to counteract one set of market distortions by another, or even counteracting the effects of the market for non-economic reasons.

Similarly, policy towards outward investment may affect the way in which domestic investment is oriented. Ozawa shows how the Japanese government has tried to encourage its own multinationals to relocate activities abroad in sectors in which it is perceived Japan is losing its comparative production advantage. This is in stark contrast to the more negative attitude of European countries and the US, whose fears about the impact of MNEs on domestic jobs more than outweigh any long-term structural benefits perceived.[7] However, this fear, in turn, must relate to government policy and the attitudes of labour unions and industry to restructuring and adjustment assistance, and indeed to industrial policy and inward investment. Pugel, Dunning, and Juhl all agree that many of the anxieties about the export of technology through outward investment from the US and UK are misguided or unfounded, but they accept that for the benefits to be fully realized, the exporting economies must continue to upgrade or restructure their own technological capacity to replace that which is exported. Again, several authors emphasize the inappropriateness of *micro*-economic policies of governments towards multinationals as a means of solving macro-economic problems; this is particularly seen in the debate about the impact of MNE activity on employment and the balance of payments, where there is not only a temptation to wrongly attribute to the MNEs the causes for something which is not of their making, but also to argue that the eradication of the perceived cause is necessarily the best means of eliminating its effects.

Accepting that policy does affect MNE behaviour, what should that policy be? We have emphasized that policy has multifaceted objectives and that these are not always consistent with each other; moreover, even where objectives do not compete, their priorities may differ. Economic structure and restructuring is only one—albeit an important—policy goal; but at times this may be overridden or constrained by more pressing or expedient political and strategic objectives. We believe that one of the most decisive strategic decisions in which countries may differ is the extent to which and the way in which they wish to participate in the international division of labour, and particularly that fashioned by MNEs. Globerman sets out the arguments of the two schools of thought—the *continentalist* and the *nationalist*—very well, and a lot of the debate on policy towards MNEs rests on which particular perspective one wishes to take.

The studies show that, in all but the Indian case, the benefits of international production are well acknowledged, but that no country operates a completely *laissez faire* policy towards either inward or outward direct investment: and, while all countries recognize the gains to be had from importing technology and other intermediate products, via the market or contractual route, others, noticeably India in this volume, still regard this as a means towards achieving technological autonomy, at least in the basic sectors. Of the advanced economies, Japan and France are perhaps the most nationalistic in approach and, in consequence, they place the most widespread constraints on inward and outward direct investment. As in India, it is accepted that the overriding objective of sovereignty may have to be sacrificed to achieve economic efficiency, simply because local firms are unable or unwilling to allocate resources as productively as foreign firms can. At the same time, it is strongly held that only by developing a strong indigenous technological capability can industrializing countries maintain their competitive strength; in consequence, most national governments are not prepared to let this particular goal be dictated by market forces or by MNE hierarchies.

However, while interventionist policies are the rule rather than the exception, the nature and degree of interventionism varies a great deal. We have already referred to the role of trade barriers in inducing import-substituting investment; certainly over the last five years a lot of Japanese investment in Europe has been of this kind. Then there may be a range of entry restrictions over the type or extent of foreign investment allowed, and/or performance requirements expected of foreign affiliates, dealing, for example, with sourcing of inputs, employment of foreign personnel, exports, dividend policy and so on. At the same time, there may be a whole range of incentive 'distortions' which, whatever their justification on other grounds, do not necessarily make for the best pattern of resource allocation. These include tax holidays, regional subsidies, capital allowances, export rebates and so on. Previous evidence would suggest that MNEs tend to respond to these incentives at least as positively as indigenous companies (Dunning, 1981); this is confirmed by the case-studies, notably those of Singapore, Portugal, Korea, Belgium, and Canada, and particularly so when the production planned is for external markets and can be sited in various countries.

Few of the studies go so far as to assess the effectiveness of government policies but most are critical of micro-economic attempts to discriminate either in favour of or against inward investment. There appears to be more support for incorporating international investment into macro-economic policy in the way in which the Japanese and Singapore governments have done; though even here the examples of France and India together show that such policies are not entirely successful. This is not to say that such positive interventionist policies of the kind described by Ozawa necessarily accept the signals of the international market as they are; there is a good deal of discriminatory interventionism, as European and US exporters are all too ready to claim. But at least Japan does have an overall industrial and technological policy of which trade and foreign investment and transfer of technology are integral parts. The UK, Portuguese, Korean, and Belgian chapters argue for Japanese-type policies to be introduced in their economies, but the authors of the US, Canadian, German, and Swedish studies would clearly prefer governments to take a neutral stance.

It would seem that several of the countries studied in this book are moving towards a coherent and integrated strategy of international production. This is especially so in the case of Portugal, with her accession to the EEC in mind. Simões, perhaps more than most authors, accepts that the presence of foreign affiliates in a country may require modification to existing economic policies; he cites competition and restrictive practices legislation as an example. Like Dunning, Michalet, Van Den Bulcke, and Koo, he also recognizes that there may be social costs and benefits specific to MNE activity which governments need to take account of, adapting their policies so that private costs and benefits may be brought into line with their social goals. In his chapter, Koo is somewhat sceptical of the ability of governments to know what is the best economic structure; indeed, from the Korean experience, he believes that many government policies are irrelevant to the restructuring process. Juhl agrees and argues that, since firm-specific factors are crucial to MNEs' resource allocative decisions, governments cannot have the necessary knowledge to intervene usefully. He, like Pugel and Swedenborg, recommends a neutral stance towards MNEs.

Yet, to be realistic, governments cannot be expected to adopt such a stance. First *any* interventionist policy, be it directed to MNEs or to all firms, is likely to have a different effect on the structure of resource allocation by its own firms, as it will on the domestic and foreign activities of its own MNEs. Moreover, many neo-classical economists accept that only governments can help overcome some kinds of market distortions. Indeed, they frequently urge governments to create the right economic climate for change and for adjustment to change; to provide the right technological and educational infrastructure to enable the market to operate properly, to engage or subsidize certain types of R&D. And certainly, whenever one country's government breaks its neutral stance and artifically stimulates changes in its own economic structure to the cost of another country's structure—not least via trade and international production—then retaliatory interventionist policy is likely to follow. If Korea subsidizes its shipbuilders, why shouldn't the UK? If Singapore gives generous investment incentives to foreign firms to invest why shouldn't Hong Kong and Korea? If Japan places non-tariff barriers on French imports, why shouldn't France place such barriers on Japanese imports? If India adopts a restrictionist dividend policy, why shouldn't home countries react to protect their own balance of payments which may be adversely affected by such a move? If the US imposes unacceptable extra-territorial requirements on the conduct of its UK affiliates which do not accord with the interests of the UK, why shouldn't the UK goverment take steps to counteract or negate these requirements?

As one looks into these kinds of issues more deeply, one soon realizes that some form of international harmonization of policies is the only way to reconcile the conflicts of interest which arise. Yet, in practice, instead of getting together to remove distortions, countries attempt to mitigate the harmful affects by imposing their own distortions. Sooner or later it becomes clear that this is a negative sum gain; and sooner or later it is recognized that the real conflicts exist not between governments and MNEs but between governments! Add to these different goal conflicts, differences in taxation, imperfections in the foreign exchange and capital markets and potential risk, and one is in a world far removed from that of the perfect market so revered in economics textbooks.

13.5 POLICY RECOMMENDATIONS

Do any specific policy guidelines or recommendations come out of these studies? If there is one general message it is this. If governments—of whatever political persuasion—are to get the most economic benefits out of the MNEs, and assuming for the moment that this is their overriding objective, they must operate their economies efficiently, and intervene only in the flow of goods and resources across the exchanges, to counteract any market distortions arising from the monopoly power of MNEs or the policies of other governments.

This message is much less innocuous and *laissez faire* than it may appear at first sight. Let us discuss each of its three parts in turn. First, for a government to put its own house in order may itself require deliberate interventionist policies, such as improving infrastructure and management capability, devoting more resources to investment, education and training, taking steps to remove X inefficiency in its own firms, eliminating institutional rigidities and so on. Second, to counteract any adverse effects of monopoly power on the part of foreign firms, anti-trust/restrictive practice policies may need to be introduced and/or strengthened, and/or encouragement and/or financial support given to indigenous firms to offer effective competition. Third, to ensure that the pursuit of global policies by MNEs to minimize international transaction costs can be reconciled to the needs of home and host countries may require certain performance guarantees and constraints on behaviour of their affiliates. This is perhaps the most difficult of policies to pursue effectively as there may be considerable uncertainty as to the right course, and lack of information about the policies of MNEs; it also involves some kind of assessment of the alternative ways of obtaining, at least, some of the resources offered by MNEs.

On this third issue aspect of policy, very little progress has been made. Very few governments seem to be aware of the implications of the internationalization of industries, as it affects not only their domestic economic structure but also their ability to control the activity of MNEs. In the past, host countries have often welcomed FDI but not the foreign investor; the resources have been wanted but not the control over the resources. In the case of import-substituting investment supplying goods for the local market, the debundling of the package of resources provided by FDI so as to ensure that the control over their use remains in indigenous hands has had some success—though nowhere near as much as many countries, particularly developing countries, had originally supposed; this was mainly because the power of control did not *de facto* rest in the *ownership* of the package. In the case of rationalized investment designed to meet the needs of international markets and taking advantage of differences in costs and markets throughout the world, debundling may be a completely inappropriate strategy. This is because the very benefits of multinationalism (unlike that of a single act of FDI) arise not from the individual, or even the package of, resources supplied to affiliates, but from the externalities associated with the operations of geographically dispersed production units, which the MNE is able to recoup, but from which, via its improved international competitive strength, each of the affiliates ultimately benefits. The dilemma is that without some kind of centralized and extra-territorial control, this benefit would not arise, and that, bearing in mind that policy is affected by the behaviour of competitors and the gamut of policies throughout the world, it cannot always be designed to meet the interests of each country of operation. In a sense then, individual governments bargaining with the affiliates of MNEs are attempting to counteract what they see to be distorting or potentially distorting elements in the scenario affecting the disposition of resources by the parent company. It is these elements which cause the international division of labour as practised or encouraged by MNEs to be unacceptable to individual home or host countries.

Sometimes, as we have already suggested, these distortions are exacerbated by countries themselves. A particularly blatant example of extraterritoriality exerted by governments was demonstrated in the recent Siberian pipeline disputes; others relate to constraints on the part of home countries of export of technology, and on the part of host countries of dividend restriction on local purchasing content. More generally, policies towards big business, conglomerates, and geographical diversification all affect the scenario in which international competition is conducted. Governments have a right and a duty to take all these considerations into account when designing the framework in which MNEs operate and the policies to be specifically directed towards them.

Most chapters in this volume address themselves to general government policies, but a few—notably those on Portugal, Korea, Canada, India, and Belgium—are devoted to policies towards MNEs in particular. As we have said, where the effects of MNEs are nothing to do with their multinationality *per se*, then general policies—though they may need to be modified because of the presence of MNEs—are sufficient to take care of the divergence of social and private interests. Where the divergence occurs because of the multinationality, then specific policies may be justified. Many of these can be contained in entry or performance requirements of MNEs; others to do with transfer price manipulation, speculation over exchange rate changes—devices which reflect imperfections in international markets—may need to be controlled by home or host countries.

A third group of issues concerns negotiation directly between home and host governments, or between host governments to achieve harmonization on questions related to investment guarantees, extra-territoriality and so on. Indeed, one suspects this kind of agreement will become more important as the degree of multinationality increases. Codes of conduct and guidelines are one thing, but they are usually addressed to the behaviour of individual affiliates. As yet no code has been proposed for the behaviour of MNEs *qua* MNEs; indeed this may be an impossible task. Yet for a host or home country to formulate policies towards MNEs or their affiliates, so that they may promote the desired economic structure, may require a lot more knowledge and information about MNEs than they are prepared to give. At the point of entry, this bargaining weapon is in the host-country hands; once they are established the power (not least the power of withdrawal) passes to the MNEs. To achieve a reconciliation between the structural goals of individual countries and those of MNEs in an imperfect world may require more information than is presently available. In this respect at least, the Vdreling proposals had some merit.

Some contributors are dubious about a case-by-case approach towards MNEs, and in the light of the mixed evidence about the effects of international production, they argue for neutrality. If imperfections are to be put right, then action should be taken at an international level with respect to taxation, transfer pricing, international monopolies, tax havens and so on. Quite apart from the difficulty of reconciling different goals and priorities, all this takes time; in the meantime it may be asked what are individual states supposed to do? It is natural that they should turn to righting market distortions imposed by MNEs or impediments imposed by other governments. It is natural too, that they should wish to counteract market failure, but to capture the benefit of externalities for themselves, rather than have them internalized by foreign affiliates and then transferred to their parent companies.

At the end of the day the most important first step any government can take is to understand and monitor the role of its own companies operating outside their national boundaries, and of MNEs to whose foreign affiliates it is host. The extent, determinants, and consequences of such MNE activity should then be related to policy objectives, and where conflicts arise, action should be taken to bring private costs and benefits in line with social costs and benefits. But in doing so, governments need to recognize both the trade-offs which might be involved and the fact that their own policies may have to be modified if international production is to play its most useful role. In particular, the chapters in this book have emphasized the need for governments to be aware both of the role MNEs may play in restructuring their economies, and of their own responsibilites in ensuring that MNEs, in achieving their corporate objectives, do not drive out indigenous firms (suppliers as well as competitors) and force host countries to relinquish more economic autonomy than they may wish. All this implies that governments should at least have some broad idea of the kind of industrial structure they are aiming for, so as to provide the appropriate infrastructure to allow enterprise (be it private or public) to help fulfil this objective. It is in this light, that detailed and often country-specific regulations and policies towards inward and outward direct investment should be evaluated; while differing on the nature and extent of the intervention and the institutions set up to control and/or monitor MNEs or their affiliates, the almost unanimous opinion of the contributors to this volume is that *ad hoc*, partial, piecemeal, and discriminatory regulations against MNEs, however expedient they may be in the short run, fail to get to grips with many of the basic issues facing countries.

Finally, we would emphasize that many policy issues surrounding the activities of MNEs cannot be satisfactorily resolved at a national level, any more than can many policy issues surrounding trade. The history of bilateral regulations and policies towards trade suggests that these result only in reducing the level of economic activity: that is they are a negative sum gain. Yet it is recognized that some overall 'rules of the game ' for trade are necessary; hence the establishment of institutions such as GATT. In the case of international production, no such institutional arrangement has emerged; only a poor substitute of guidelines and codes of conduct. But since the major problems arising from the activities of MNEs are not those which arise out of a conflict between MNEs and countries, but between countries in which the MNE operates, it follows these can only be solved at an international level. So far, there is very little sign of the need for such a framework being taken seriously, possibly because the implications of MNEs on international (as opposed to domestic) economic structure have not been properly understood. It is the hope of the contributors of this volume that their thoughts and findings are a small step towards this new appreciation.

NOTES

1. However, the flexibility they have in reaching these goals is much greater and the implications on domestic resources may reflect this.
2. Depending on the ratio used—either $1 + \dfrac{X - M}{X + M}$ or $\dfrac{X - M}{X + M}$.
3. In the Canadian case non-US investment is positively correlated with RCA but US investment is not.
4. The literature on vertical linkages is extensive. For a summary of some of the more recent studies see Lall (1980).
5. As, for example, where a foreign MNE buys out a domestic firm which purchases a large proportion of its components from other indigenous firms, and then proceeds to import these components from its parent company. Whether the final effect of this is beneficial rests on the use made of the displaced resources.
6. But given government ineptitude, which may increase the social cost of outward investment, it is understandable why constraints on MNE activities may be urged.
7. To be fair too, it is easier to accept the costs of restructuring in a growth and full-employment situation. And Japan's recent record on both counts is considerably better than that of Europe or the US.

REFERENCES

Dunning, J. H. (1981). *International Production and the Multinational Enterprise*, London: Allen & Unwin

Hymer, S. (1971). The multinational corporation and the law of uneven development, in Bhagwati, J. N. (ed.), *Economics and World Order*, New York: World Law Fund

Johnson, H. G. (1970). The multinational corporation as an agency of economic development, in Ward, B, d'Anjou, L., and Runnals, J. D. (eds), *The widening Gap, Development in the 1970s*, New York: Columbia University Press

Lall, S. (1980). Vertical inter firm linkages in LDCs: an empirical study *Oxford Bulletin of Economics and Statistics*, **42**, 203–26

UNCTC (1982). *Regional Integration Cum/Versus Corporate Integration*, New York United Nations E.82.II A.6

Index

94

D.